T. Flynn

D1213116

SOCIALIST HUMANISM

an international symposium
edited by ERICH FROMM

Allen Lane The Penguin Press London 1967

Copyright © Doubleday & Co. Inc. 1965
First published by Doubleday & Co. Inc. 1965
Published in Great Britain 1967

Allen Lane The Penguin Press Vigo Street London W1

Grateful acknowledgement is made to the following:
Suderkamp Verlag for 'Man and Citizen According to Marx', Ernst Bloch
in *Naturrecht und menschliche Wurde*
Frederick Praeger for 'Socialism Is a Humanism', Léopold Sédar Senghor
in *On African Socialism*
Allen & Unwin for 'In Praise of Idleness', Bertrand Russell in *In Praise of
Idleness and Other Essays*
The editor of *Diogène* for 'Socialism and Humanism', Lucien Goldmann
in *Diogène*, No. 46

Made and Printed in England by
Latimer Trend & Co Ltd Plymouth

Contents

CONTENTS

V. ON PRACTICE

○ ○

Introduction

One of the most remarkable phenomena of the past decade has been the renaissance of humanism in various ideological systems. Humanism – in simplest terms, the belief in the unity of the human race and man's potential to perfect himself by his own efforts – has had a long and varied history stretching back to the Hebrew prophets and the Greek philosophers. Terentius's statement, 'I believe that nothing human is alien to me', was an expression of the humanist spirit, echoed centuries later by Goethe's, 'Man carries within himself not only his individuality but all of humanity, with all its potentialities, although he can realize these potentialities in only a limited way because of the external limitations of his individual existence.'

Over the ages some humanists have believed in the innate goodness of man or the existence of God, while others have not. Some humanist thinkers – among them Leibniz, Goethe, Kierkegaard and Marx – particularly stressed the need to develop individuality to the greatest possible extent in order to achieve the highest harmony and universality. But all humanists have shared a belief in the possibility of man's perfectibility, which, whether they believed in the need for God's grace or not, they saw as dependent upon man's own efforts (which is why Luther was not a humanist). Non-religious humanists like Gianbattista Vico and Karl Marx carried this further to say that man makes his own history and is his own creator.

Because humanists believe in the unity of humanity and have faith in the future of man, they have never been fanatics. After the Reformation they saw the limitations of both the Catholic and the Protestant positions, because they judged, not from the narrow angle of one particular organization or power group, but from the vantage point of humanity. Humanism has always emerged as a reaction to the threat to mankind: in the Renaissance, to the threat of religious fanaticism; in the Enlightenment, to extreme nationalism and the enslavement of man by the machine and economic interests. The revival of humanism today is a new reaction to this latter threat in a more intensified form – the fear that man may become the slave of things, the prisoner of circumstances he himself has created – and the wholly new threat to mankind's physical existence posed by nuclear weapons.

This reaction is being felt in all camps – Catholic, Protestant, Marxist, liberal. This does not mean, however, that contemporary humanists are willing to forgo their specific philosophical or religious convictions for the sake of 'better understanding', but rather that, as humanists, they believe they can reach the clearest understanding of different points of view from the most precise expression of each, always bearing in mind that what matters most is the human reality behind the concepts.

This volume is an attempt to present the ideas of one branch of contemporary humanism. Socialist humanism differs in an important respect from other branches. Renaissance and Enlightenment humanism believed that the task of transforming man into a fully human being could be achieved exclusively or largely by education. Although Renaissance Utopians touched upon the need for social changes, the socialist humanism of Karl Marx was the first to declare that theory cannot be separated from practice, knowledge from action, spiritual aims from the social system. Marx held that free and independent man could exist only in a social and economic system that, by its rationality and abundance, brought to an end the epoch of 'pre-history' and opened the epoch of 'human history', which would make the full development of the individual the condition for the full development of society, and vice versa. Hence he devoted the greater part of his life to the study of capitalist economics and the organization of the working class in the hopes of instituting a socialist society that would be the basis for the development of a new humanism.

Marx believed that the working class would lead in the transformation of society because it was at once the most dehumanized and alienated class, and potentially the most powerful, since the functioning of society depended upon it. He did not foresee the development of capitalism to the point where the working class would prosper materially and share in the capitalist spirit while all of society would become alienated to an extreme degree. He never became aware of that *affluent alienation* which can be as dehumanizing as *impoverished alienation*.

Stressing the need for a change in the economic organization and for transferring control of the means of production from private (or corporate) hands into the hands of organized producers, Marx was misinterpreted both by those who felt threatened by his programme, and by many socialists. The former accused him of caring only for the physical, not the spiritual, needs of man. The latter believed that his goal was exclusively material affluence for all, and that Marxism differed from capitalism only in its methods, which were economically more efficient and could be initiated by the working class. In actuality, Marx's ideal was a man productively related to other men and to nature, who would respond to the world in an alive manner, and who would be rich not because he *had* much but because he *was* much.

Marx was seeking an answer to the meaning of life, but could not accept the traditional religious answer that this can be found only through belief in the existence of God. In this he belongs to the same tradition as the Enlightenment thinkers, from Spinoza to Goethe, who rejected the old theological concepts and were searching for a new spiritual frame of orientation. But, unlike such socialists as Jean Jaurès, Lunacharsky, Gorky and Rosa Luxemburg, who permitted themselves to deal more explicitly with the question of the spiritual, Marx shied away from a direct discussion of the problem because he wanted to avoid any compromise with religious or idealistic ideologies, which he considered harmful.

Authentic Marxism was perhaps the strongest spiritual movement of a broad, non-theistic nature in nineteenth-century Europe. But after 1914 – or even before – most of this spirit disappeared. Many different factors were involved, but the most important were the new affluence and ethics of consumption that began to dominate capitalist societies in the period between the wars and immediately following the second and the seesawing pattern of destructiveness and suffering caused by two world wars. Today, the questions of the meaning of life and man's goal in living have emerged again as questions of primary importance.

One must realize that, by necessity, the spiritual problem has been camouflaged to a large extent until our present moment in history. As long as productive forces were not highly developed, the necessity to work, and to keep alive, gave sufficient meaning to life. This still holds true for the vast majority of the human race, even those living in industrially developed countries where the mixture of work and leisure, and the dream of ever-increasing consumption, keeps man from realizing his true human potential, of being what he could be. But we are moving rapidly towards a fully industrialized, automated world in which the ten- or twenty-hour work week will be standard, and where the many material satisfactions provided for everyone will be taken for granted. In this totally affluent society (which will be a planned if not a socialist one), man's spiritual problem will become much more acute and urgent than it has ever been in the past.

This volume has a dual purpose. It seeks to clarify the problems of humanist socialism in its various theoretical aspects, and to demonstrate that socialist humanism is no longer the concern of a few dispersed intellectuals, but a movement to be found throughout the world, developing independently in different countries. In this volume many humanist socialists from the East and the West meet for the first time. Reading the volume, contributors as well as readers may become fully aware for the first time of the common response of many socialists to what the history of the past decades and the present threat to the physical and spiritual survival of mankind has taught them.

With five exceptions, all of the contributions were written

specifically for this volume, but in no case did I suggest the topic of a specific essay to the author. I preferred to ask each of them to write on any topic that appeared most important to him within the general frame of reference of socialist humanism. I hoped that in this way the volume would represent the main interests of humanist socialists. It did not seem to me a disadvantage if some topics were dealt with several times by different authors. On the contrary, I thought it would be an interesting and even impressive phenomenon to see the fundamental agreement among most authors represented in this volume and the extent to which a new school of thinking has arisen in various parts of the world, in particular among the scholars of Yugoslavia and Czechoslovakia, whose writings have so far been little known in the English-speaking world.

Despite the authors' common bond, there are important disagreements among them and with the editor. The authors belong to different political parties. Most of them are socialists, but some are not. Most of them are Marxists, but some – including Catholics, independent liberals, and non-Marxist labour party members – are not. No one whose contribution is published here can be held responsible for the views expressed by any other author or by the editor.

As humanists, all of the contributors have a common concern with man and the full unfolding of his potentialities, and a critical attitude towards political reality, especially towards ideologies. This latter is of the utmost importance. Today, more than ever, we find concepts like freedom, socialism, humanism and God used in an alienated, purely ideological way, regardless of who uses them. What is real in them is the word, the sound, not a genuine experience of what the word is supposed to indicate. The contributors are concerned with the *reality* of human existence, and hence are critical of ideology; they constantly question whether an idea expresses the reality or hides it.

There is one other factor common to all the contributors: their conviction that the most urgent task for mankind today is the establishment of peace. No one represented in this volume in any way supports the cold war.

Inevitably there are omissions, which the editor regrets. Most of the authors are either European or North American, even though Asia, Africa and Australia are represented. There is also a rather one-sided emphasis on the philosophical aspect of socialist humanism as compared to the practical and empirical problems of humanist socialist organization, which are dealt with only in the last chapter, on the practice of socialist humanism. Indeed, a great number of important problems of socialist organization are not only not represented here, but have been little discussed in socialist literature in general. (Such problems are, for instance, the distinction between real human needs and artificially produced needs, the possibility of a revival of handicrafts as a luxury industry, new forms of democratic participation based on small face-to-face groups, etc.)

To sum up: it is perhaps no exaggeration to say that never in the past hundred years have there been such widespread and intensive studies of the problem of humanist socialism as today. To demonstrate this phenomenon and to show some of the results of these studies are the purposes of this volume. In this concern for man and opposition to dehumanization we feel a deep sense of solidarity with all humanists, many of whom do not share all of our views, but all of whom share our concern for the full development of man.

I wish to thank all those who have helped me in my editorial task. I have often turned to Thomas B. Bottomore of the London School of Economics and Gajo Petrović of the University of Zagreb for advice, and they have always been most generous in their response. I am grateful to the contributors for responding so cooperatively to my suggestions about space and organization, and to the translators for taking on the difficult job of putting complicated manuscripts in French, German, Italian, Polish and Serbo-Croat into English. Finally my sincere thanks to Anne Freedgood of Doubleday for her ever-present interest in this book and for her extraordinary effort in preparing the manuscript.

Erich Fromm

I. ON HUMANISM

VELJKO KORAĆ

⊚ ⊚

In Search of Human Society

VELJKO KORAĆ is professor of philosophy at the University of Belgrade, where he received his Ph.D. after studying
in Zagreb and Prague from 1933 to 1938. During the
Second World War he fought with Yugoslav partisans. He
did research in the United States during 1962–3 under the
auspices of the Ford Foundation. Primarily interested in
the history of modern philosophy, philosophical anthropology and sociology, he is the author of *Kant's Critique of
Pure Reason, Hegel's Foundation of the History of Philosophy, Personality in Socialism, Marx and Contemporary
Sociology*, and many other books.

One of the most often repeated objections to Marx's socialism is the allegation that it is untenable from the humanist
standpoint, reducing man and society to strictly material factors
and degrading spiritual values, which are the essence of
humanity, to a mere epiphenomenon of material life. Marx's
socialism is said to lack human content, to have as its ideal not
homo sapiens but *homo faber*. These supposed shortcomings of
Marx's socialism are attributed to Marx's materialism, the ultimate aim being to devalue and discredit both.

One of the most characteristic examples of such criticism is
that of the German philosopher Max Scheler. In *Man's Place in
the Cosmos* he goes so far as to identify Marx's conception of
man and society with that of the vulgar materialist Karl Vogt.
Scheler represents Marx as maintaining that 'man does not
create history but is instead himself formed by history under
differing conditions, particularly by economic history and economic structure'. According to Scheler, Marx considers man the
product of economic conditions and believes that spiritual creativity – as expressed through art, science, philosophy, law, etc. –

B

3

is without its own immanent logic and continuity, since any such continuity or true causality is completely supplanted by economic forms.

Being neither new nor original, Scheler's criticisms of Marx's concepts would not merit attention were Scheler not considered the founder of contemporary philosophical anthropology, i.e. that philosophical science which investigates the fundamental explanation of human beings as a special dimension of reality. When such a philosopher makes no distinction between Marx's materialism and that of Karl Vogt, it becomes worth while to ascertain just what it was in Marx's works that Scheler failed to grasp.

In Marx's *Theses on Feuerbach*, the third thesis reads as follows:

> The materialistic doctrine that men are the products of circumstances and education, and that changed men are therefore the products of other circumstances and a changed education, forgets that circumstances are changed by men, and that the educator must himself be educated. Consequently materialism necessarily leads to a division of society into two parts, of which one is elevated above society (e.g. in Robert Owen). The coincidence of the transformation of circumstances and of human activity can be conceived and rationally understood only as revolutionizing practice (Praxis).

It is difficult to believe that Scheler was unacquainted with this text, although experience does show that the heaviest and most reckless criticism of Marx was levelled by those of his opponents who were totally unfamiliar with his writings. But if one assumes that Scheler had in fact read Marx, including the *Theses on Feuerbach*, one must conclude that he, like many others, failed entirely to grasp the critical exception which Marx as a materialist took to the one-sidedness and narrowness of traditional materialism. Contrary to the image Scheler and many others wish to project, Marx's writings clearly indicated the degree to which he emphasized that human history is in fact man's own creation. Does not Marx refer in the first volume of *Capital* to Gianbattista Vico, who wrote that the essential difference between the history of humanity and natural history consists in the fact that the former is the work of man and the latter not? But Marx does not put man above and beyond history in the role of an all-powerful creator with divine qualities, rather he examines man in history itself and asserts that 'the whole of what is called world history is nothing but the creation of man by human labour'. Thus, man is not the work of 'higher' powers (no matter how such powers might be conceived), nor is his being determined once and for all. Creating history he creates himself, creating himself he creates history. The secret of this creation is human labour, which is human only in so far as it purposefully directs natural forces to act in man's interest. In this way man elevates himself above natural necessity as a particular dimension of reality.

Those who suggest that Marx comprehended and explained man simply as the result of material circumstances either do not, or will not, understand the meaning of Marx's fundamental attitude: *the root of man is man himself*. This attitude, which is basic to Marx's conception of man, shows clearly wherein Marx's materialism differs from traditional materialism. It is this view that entitles Marx to assume the most prominent place among the founders of contemporary philosophical anthropology and sociology, and that is the refutation of Scheler's attempt to represent Marx's definition of man as the simple and accidental product of material conditions and circumstances. Marx seeks the root of man neither in nature abstractly conceived, nor in the abstractly-conceived totality of society; he seeks the root of man in human praxis, which is human only to the extent that human labour differs from the labour of every other living creature (that is, to the extent that the worst of human architects is superior to the best of bees, even though in the construction of its honeycomb the bee puts many an architect to shame).

There is no mystery in the assertion that man's nature or essence differs from the nature and essence of other living creatures and that the root of man is man. This only points out the need to regard the purposefulness of human activity as the point of departure for any investigation of man and all kinds of human activity. Purposefulness is that essential feature of the human spirit which enables man to appropriate nature, or, as Marx put it, to humanize nature. While all other creatures, however intelligent, can act only within the limitations of their species, always remaining more or less subject to direct natural necessity, man is capable of freeing himself from that necessity and of assuming

5

the characteristics of other species. Thus only man can universally appropriate nature's scattered potential for his own purposes and so become a universal species reproducing the whole of nature while other creatures reproduce only themselves. While other creatures are always bound by direct necessity, man can be freed of it. There, and only there, does man labour as man.

Thus, when Max Scheler says that man's peculiarity lies in the fact that he can say 'no' even to his own vital needs, that he can be a 'principled ascetic of life', he is actually repeating, in a much narrower context and unwittingly, what Marx had already stated much earlier and more profoundly. Whether man's origin is explained by God's grace or as an accidental result of natural forces, history shows that he structures his own existence by the rational mastery of 'higher' powers, the rational overcoming of immediate natural necessity. Of course, in investigating man, we must clarify all the factors and components of his human existence, and explain everything he creates while creating himself as man; but the fact of his being human remains problematic until we explain the purposefulness of his praxis or the root of what is specifically human 'nature'.

Many interpreters of Marx's ideas, whether they considered themselves his followers or his opponents, made no attempt to grasp the theoretical possibilities of his explanation of man's generic essence for sociology, the social sciences in general, and for socialism. Moreover, some who wished to represent themselves as the most consistent, or even as the only true followers of Marx's thought, declared that one cannot, in the spirit of Marx's philosophy, speak of man as man, of man in general, or of human nature or human essence, but only of man as belonging to a particular social–economic formation, a particular class, etc. The proportions such one-sidedness has assumed are demonstrated by a fair share of contemporary Marxist literature.

However, familiarity with Marx's thought gained from his own works, and not via Stalin's writings or Stalinistic ideas, makes it a simple matter to establish beyond dispute that from his youth to the very end of his life Marx thought and wrote about man as man, and laboured to give the fullest possible definition to human essence. He could not have done otherwise, because to him the question of man was essential, the more so since he was not satisfied with existing definitions. He was the

6

first to realize that, in order to explain society, man as the starting point must first be clearly defined. Those who have not seriously studied Marx's writings believe that after his earlier work he abandoned the discussion of man as man. But this is not true of Marx's work taken as a whole.

In the first volume of *Capital* he expressly points out that in capitalistic society 'the general and the banker have a large role but *man* as man has only a very wretched role'. The human element in man is thus foreign to capitalism. In criticizing Bentham and calling him to account for spiritlessly repeating what Helvétius and other French philosophers of the eighteenth century had said with wit, especially in describing their concept of man, he writes:

> To know what is useful for a dog, one must study dog nature. This nature is not to be deduced from the 'principle of utility'. When the same principle is applied to man, i.e. when we wish to evaluate all human activity, relationships, etc., the first thing in question is human nature in general, and second that which changes with each historical epoch. Bentham is not at all concerned with this. Naïvely and coldly he is content to take the modern English philistine as representative of the type of *normal man*.

Far from neglecting the question of human nature in general, Marx criticized those who did not consider it. He also took exception to the definition of man as a being for ever the same as he appears at one point in history or in a given system. The objection of *mutatis mutandis* has a bearing on those socialistic theories Marx discussed critically because, presupposing man for ever fixed and isolated, these theories proposed an ideal society that would, in the opinion of their expounders, best correspond to man so determined. Marx, however, considered that man had the potential to achieve self-realization through the process of self-creation. Where other socialistic theories failed to examine the causes underlying man's alienation from man and from human society, Marx's theory, based on a new concept of man, proposed to investigate the phenomenon of contemporary class society as the basic condition of praxis.

Establishing through critical analysis man's alienation from man, from the product of his labour, even from his own human activity, Marx raised the question of abolishing all these forms of

7

dehumanization, and the possibility of restoring *human* society. This is his basic problem. As critics of the existing society, other socialists also knew that the society of private property was nothing more than a society of merciless exploitation, dehumanization, and the deformation of man, but they never analysed deeply the reasons for such a state of affairs. They believed that society could be transformed by an ideal plan of a more perfect form of social relationships which would be realized by the triumph of reason as soon as people comprehended what such a plan held out to them. The real liberating forces within society remained unknown to them, as did the real methods for overcoming existing dehumanization and inhumanity. For this reason all attempts to realize such projects very soon came to nothing.

Nevertheless, the idea of socialism was not compromised. Marx was completely aware of this when he confronted various communistic and socialistic doctrines. He criticized them from first to last, even rejecting some for their egalitarian dogmatism, illusionism, and other biases. Every notion of egalitarianism projected in advance he regarded as dogmatism. In place of this he chose consistent criticism of the inhumanity in existing society. Searching for the root of the basic contradictions in that society, he came to the phenomenon of the irreconcilable opposition of capital and labour. Faced with this, he began to seek the explanation of man's generic essence, which he found in the purposefulness of human labour. 'In speaking of labour one deals directly with man himself,' he observed, adding that 'this new formulation of the problem already contains its solution'. He wanted to discover why work wrought marvels for the wealthy but brought poverty and wretchedness to the labourer. What was the contradiction in work itself? If by his own labour man creates himself, why then is his own work something foreign, a hardship instead of a satisfaction? Why is man alienated from man and from his own humanity?

That all these questions necessarily followed from Marx's concept of man is more than obvious, and the answers he gave had a decisive meaning for his entire theory and the practice of it – for it was from these answers that he derived his socialist theory. Their essential content is that man creating himself through the social–historical process becomes only potentially more human because his way of life under the prevailing conditions of division

8

of labour and class antagonism permits his humanity to manifest and confirm itself only partially. Increasing his power over nature, man develops the dimension of his species-being, but remains powerless to direct his social existence because his own being remains alien and unknown. In the society of private property and exploitation, universal alienation manifests itself as the alienation of those potentialities that raise man above all other living creatures. Even the advances of science and technology become instruments of inhumanity. That is why the problem of abolishing alienation and insuring free development presents itself as the problem of social freedom.

Ascertaining that all forms of alienation are a consequence of the alienation of man's working activity, and that private property as 'the sensuous material expression of estranged man's life gave rise to the stupid habit of regarding an object one's own only upon physical possession of it', Marx concluded that, without complete and true emancipation of labour, people could not become human and society could not become human society. The abolition of private property and exploitation are only the first steps in that direction; the humanization of labour is the first immediate task of socialist practice. But to accomplish this it is necessary to know just which social forces can accomplish it. Starting with the fact of alienation, Marx showed that total estrangement and dehumanization (in his words 'the complete loss of man') has become universal in modern society, causing universal suffering. Marx's aim was true *man* – living under emancipated conditions of labour and not disintegrated by the division of labour. His vision of humanity's future was founded on the assumption that such a man was not only possible, but the necessary result of social development and essential to the existence of a truly human society. It was in this spirit that he wrote that 'the standpoint of the old materialism is "bourgeois society"; the standpoint of the new materialism is *human* or socialized humanity'.

Socialism is therefore not Marx's ultimate aim but an approximation. His ultimate aim is *human* society; society in which dehumanization ceases, human labour is truly emancipated, and man has all the conditions necessary to his development and self-affirmation. Marx does not propose an ideal society in which the freedom of the individual is automatically achieved. This he knows to be a delusion, for free society remains an abstraction if every member of that society is not free as an individual. Therefore he makes explicit that a new, *human* society can be only an association of men where *the freedom of each individual becomes the condition for the freedom of all.*

Freedom of human personality, for Marx, is not an empty abstraction, nor is it merely a youthful dream as his conservative detractors would like to maintain. In *Capital* he says clearly that freedom in social relations lies with freely associated men, associated producers, rationally regulating their exchange of matter with nature, bringing it under social control so as to effect the exchange with as little expenditure of energy as possible and under conditions most worthy of their human nature. Only thus can alienated labour, which impoverishes, deforms and robs the worker of his humanity, come to an end. Hence when Marx speaks of the absolute impoverishment of the worker in capitalism and declares that the accumulation of capital is equalled by the accumulation of misery, he is thinking of the worker's inhuman life in all its aspects, not just of his economic poverty. This is what he has in mind when he writes that the accumulation of 'drudgery, slavery, savagery and moral decline are the lot of the very class which creates its own product in the form of capital'.

Truly emancipated labour will provide the conditions for free social life because only then will work become *production*, i.e. a creative activity which transforms the individual into a personality. Marx saw the development of society as the development of each individual, hence the ultimate aim of society's development became the complete and true freedom of the personality, which is the essential condition of freedom for all.

The socialist and humanist theories with which Marx has occasion to deal gave very little attention to this problem; moreover, the majority of them postulated ideal socialism or communism in such a way as to eliminate freedom of the personality.

Marx was an energetic opponent and critic of all such forms of socialism and communism, as his attitude towards Cabet and Weitling well illustrates. Describing their system of ideal society as 'primitive' or 'crude' communism, Marx noted:

This communism, which negates the *personality* of man in every sphere, is only the logical expression of private property, which is this negation. Universal *envy* setting itself up as a power is only a camouflaged form of cupidity which re-establishes itself and satisfies itself in a different way. The thoughts of every individual with private property are *at least* directed against any *wealthier* private property, in the form of envy and the desire to reduce everything to a common level; so that this envy and levelling in fact constitute the essence of competition. Crude communism is only the culmination of such envy and levelling-down on the basis of a *preconceived* minimum. How little this abolition of private property represents a genuine appropriation is shown by the abstract negation of the whole world of culture and civilization, and the regression to the *unnatural* simplicity of the poor and wantless individual who has not only not surpassed private property but has not yet even attained it.[1]

Marx's socialism was thoroughly opposed to every form of unnatural simplicity, and to the levelling and complete loss of the individual in the impersonal and nameless collective. Instead he proposed the free and universal development of the individual as the underlying *condition* of freedom for all. Such an association of people calls first of all for the abolition of classes, but not in the sense of primitive egalitarianism as in Campanella's *Civitas Solis*; rather, as Friedrich Engels stresses, 'the abolition of social classes presupposes a level of production at which the appropriation of the products and means of production, and with them political power, monopoly of education and spiritual guidance, by a special social class will be not only superfluous but a hindrance to economic, political and intellectual progress'. This is why Marx expected that the socialist revolution would begin in the most developed countries of the capitalist world.

However, contemporary history shows that socialist revolutions have not taken place in industrially developed countries but in those barely on the verge of industrial revolution; also that contemporary socialist practice often contains obvious digressions from some of Marx's basic principles of socialist theory. Furthermore, certain socialist developments that have occurred would be extremely difficult to reconcile with any, let alone Marx's, socialism. This, of course, is seized upon as an argument against socialism in general, and especially against Marx's socialism.

1. *Economic and Philosophical Manuscripts*, trans. T. B. Bottomore, in Erich Fromm, *Marx's Concept of Man* (New York: Frederick Ungar, 1961), p. 125.

The dialectical philosophy on which Marx based his socialist theory cannot ignore these divergences, just as objections to his socialism cannot remain ignored. Critical and revolutionary, Marx's philosophy states that a theory comes to life in a people only to the extent to which it is a realization of that people's needs.

The question thus arises as to what and how great is the need for socialism in an underdeveloped country which finds itself on the threshold of industrial revolution. What are the primary needs of such countries? Whether they call themselves socialist or capitalist, there is no doubt that their primary needs are bound up with the development of material production. For this reason the problems of industrialization outweigh all others, even human relationships. Belief in a better life, which has arisen in all parts of the world after victorious socialist revolutions, is a powerful stimulus to action and becomes a potent element in social practice, accelerating social development. But with limited possibilities of realization that belief must of necessity remain restricted to ideologies of human happiness. So it has been in the past and so it is today. For a poor society, as for a poor man, the primary consideration is the satisfaction of elementary needs and the experience of elementary material enjoyment. Since the contemporary socialist and communist ideal of social order (as formulated by Marx and Engels on the basis of their critical analysis of existing society) presupposes a high level of development of productive forces, the potential danger of considering socialism in a purely economic sense as the only and ultimate aim of social progress is constantly present.

The often observed tendency in socialist countries to take technical advance and growth in productive forces (in themselves not an earmark of socialism, because they are just as important a feature of capitalism) as the index for the degree of socialism and social progress attained bears ample witness to this danger, especially as, at the same time, the progress of humanity and personal rights remains secondary. The less developed a country is, the greater its tendency towards primitive egalitarianism and the suppression of personal freedom. It has even come to the point where, in some countries, the ideal of socialism has taken shape in precisely the aspect that Marx most energetically criticized as the 'regression' to the *unnatural* simplicity of the poor and

wantless individual' and as 'universal envy' (China). The wish
to accelerate material technical achievement results in deliberate
human sacrifice, and the attempt to justify such sacrifice by historical necessity. To make the justification convincing, fictitious
history is substituted for the real. The present is sacrificed in the
name of a bright future; living people are the victims to pos-
terity's happiness – just as Christian ideologists promised the
kingdom of heaven in reward for wordly suffering. Remote fictitious goals, which are favoured over immediate objectives, are
presented as absolute ideals for which it is necessary to sacrifice
everything. Thus historical optimism, which motivated and still
motivates people to strive for a better future, is reduced to a
common instrument of current politics and loses all connexion
with socialist ideals.

There are more than enough examples to show how man becomes, in the name of socialism, a mere instrument for certain
fixed aims without regard for objective reality. Man's and
humanity's advancement become an adjunct of the advancement
of an entity which stands above man, and which can be 'society',
'the state', 'technology', etc. In any case, individual man is increasingly deprived of his personality while mankind as a
'greater' goal of history is increasingly emphasized.

All this finds its expression in various sorts of ideological instrumentalism and conformism, in philosophy, science, art,
literature – every variety of spiritual activity. Spiritual creativity
is converted into an instrument of ideology and politics to become submerged by those elements of contemporary behaviour
that have come to be one of the essential marks of present-day
bureaucratism, institutionalism and totalitarianism. The high
ethical standards of socialism are misapplied for entirely profane
purposes, most often for those purposes that correspond to the
interests of the bureaucracy, which thinks only of itself and
identifies that self with society and socialism, speaking of an
ideal future while enjoying *today's* pleasures and considering
itself the single interpreter of historical laws.

The proportions reached by this tendency were demonstrated
by Stalinist practice, which, of course, did not cease at the
moment when Stalin's embalmed body was removed from
Lenin's mausoleum on Red Square. The situation in contemporary China is the best evidence of the tendency towards the

13

revival of Stalinist statism and its transformation into a specific model of primitive and poor egalitarianism. It is this model that wants to impose itself ruthlessly on contemporary mankind as the ideal of socialism – which means that Stalinistic practice wants to impose itself from an even lower level than it used to occupy, a level that really has nothing in common with Marx's ideas of *human* society. In Stalinist practice, faith in socialism was transformed into one of the main levers of despotic arbitrariness which, in the name of certain 'greater' future goals, and the 'future happiness of humanity', became anti-human and anti-critical in the highest degree, until it finally turned into ruthless state idolatry.

Ideologists of bureaucratic-state tendencies have illustrated their departure from Marx's socialist theory on numerous occasions. An outstanding example of this is the following explanation of freedom of the personality in socialism:

> The personality in socialism is free by virtue of the fact that all the people are free. Under the conditions of socialistic collectivism and socialistic democracy the freedom of one member of the society does not and cannot threaten the freedom of another.[1]

Thus, the relationship between the personality and society is posed in such a way as absolutely to submerge the personality in the society, or in 'the people', and this is brought about in the name of 'higher' interests which are also termed collective interests. The fact that this 'collective' interest ceases to be collective as soon as the individual or personal interest is excluded from it is forgotten. But this is the method whereby bureaucracy represents its own interests. It is more than apparent that, with a personality so described, nothing is left of Marx's association of men in which the freedom of each individual is the *condition* of the freedom for all. It is obvious then that practice has indeed become far separated from Marx's socialist theory, because his case is clear enough: where there is no freedom of the personality, there is not and cannot be any freedom for 'the people'.

Critics and opponents of Marx's socialism would like to use just such practice as an argument against Marx's socialism, precisely as they would utilize the materialism of Karl Vogt as argument against Marx's materialism. They forget that this practice

1. The Soviet review *Voprosi Filosofii*, No. 9, 1958.

has abandoned Marx and set up its own ideology, which has nothing in common with Marx's ideas, regardless of what is attributed to him. If, in the countries that experienced socialist revolutions before they had had industrial revolutions, all kinds of distortions of socialist ideas appeared, this still does not speak against either the principles of Marx's socialism, or the possibility of realizing these principles under more developed or different conditions, and with different methods. The contradictions in contemporary trends to socialism appear mostly because some socialist practice wants to impose itself as the only possible model of socialism.

Tendencies to ignore or to conceal these contradictions are contrary to Marx's dialectic principles, which attempt to expose and resolve them – their creative strength lies in *precisely* this attempt. Therefore Marx's philosophy cannot be reconciled with bureaucratic decrees which announce that socialism or communism in a certain country is already an accomplished fact. On the contrary, what is necessary, according to Marx, is unconditional and uncompromising criticism of 'everything existing'. Only to the extent that such criticism exists can the principles of Marx's socialism be verified and affirmed. That is why such criticism increasingly assumes the characteristics of a humanistic revolt against bureaucratic–technocratic pragmatism and against all forms of dehumanization and alienation – whatever the society to which it is applied.

Returning to Marx in the original and to the search for the anthropological and humanist principles of his socialism is not, therefore, an escape into the outlived past. Rather, it is the affirmation of the concept that, in socialism bearing Marx's name, man as man can never be sacrificed to the alleged 'higher' interests of the future, but always remains the ultimate aim of *today's* tendencies towards *human* society, both theoretically and in practice. That is why interest in Marx's ideas is more alive today than it has been at any previous time.

Translated by Jan Dekker

IVAN SVITÁK

◉ ◉

The Sources of Socialist Humanism

IVAN SVITÁK was born in 1925 in Hranice, Czechoslovakia. He graduated from secondary school in Prague and was put on a forced labour squad in an iron foundry. After the war, he was politically active in the Social Democratic student movement while he was earning his Doctor of Law degree at Charles University in Prague and his Doctor of Political Science degree at the University of Political Sciences. After graduation he lectured in the history of philosophy at the University (1950–54), wrote a textbook on the history of philosophy and compiled a philosophical reader. He also wrote three books aimed at popularizing atheism, *Contemporary Problems of Atheism, The Marxist Classics on Problems of Religion* and *How to Overcome Religion*. He was a member of the staff of the Philosophical Institute of the Czechoslovak Academy of Sciences in Prague, has worked in radio and television and with various experimental drama companies, done translations of such authors as Marx, Scheler, Diderot and Camus, and written many articles.

'Where have we come from? Who are we? Where are we going?' These three simple questions were the title of a painting by an artist who, at the close of the last century, left Europe – not because he preferred the empty idyll of the Tahitian islands, but because he wanted to seek the attitudes of life that, by the primitiveness of the questions they posed, could give rise to endless paraphrases of the key problem of the meaning of life. Thus the artist Paul Gauguin, with no philosophical, religious or scientific ambitions, expressed the very questions that may be considered the main problem of all the religions of the world and the basic concept of all past philosophies of man, as well as the central content of every humanism.

Who is man? The answer to Gauguin's simple question is very

difficult and at the same time very important. The most general instruments of human thinking, i.e. categories, cannot really be scientifically defined, precisely because they are categories, or very general notions. They are so basic and fundamental that they are subordinate only to the concept of being, so that a true definition could state only that categories exist. That in itself would have no meaning, and as a definition it would be absurd. The same can be said of man, not only because he is the category of all categories, but because he himself is their creator. He is on both ends of the definition at the same time: he is both *definiens* and *definiendum*. If we nevertheless wish to define man, the best way to do so is by his history. *Man is a history of his own definitions, the determination of himself.* So far, the number of definitions that have been put forward throughout the history and the development of man's understanding of himself are, to a certain extent, in accord with the history of social formations. The image man has created of himself has varied, because man has reflected the world and himself in the world in various ways, depending upon the social relationships he has had. Although biologically *homo sapiens* has remained the same, his consciousness of himself and his self-understanding have changed with his changing social organization. Man's monumental self-portraits, and his understanding of the historical process of his own development of thinking, are still, to a certain extent, the live nucleus of mass ideologies and the basic concept which animates both such ideologies and the arts, religion and philosophy. *Homo peccator*, the essential concept of Christianity; *homo faber*, the centre of liberal doctrine; and the socialist vision of non-alienated, total man – these are various answers to the ancient question of human meaning.

A knowledge of the various answers to the question of man – those currently given by the East and the West, as well as the traditional Christian, liberal and socialist answers – is a prerequisite of mutual understanding. In the dialogue of ideologies, where reproaches for the absence of humanism are often heard, it is important to remember that Marxism stems from the same classical sources of eighteenth- and nineteenth-century European humanism as non-Marxist and non-socialist traditions. An understanding of this *common* source and link between different humanist ideologies – an understanding of man as the central value of history – has become more important today than the study of the differences among the various types of humanism.

Socialist humanism did not develop by the blind mechanism of economic history, but by solving the 'eternal' questions of man and his significance in the universe. In spite of the fact that man's development may seem preordained by the solution of the social problems of industrial society, this is in fact an illusion. Reducing the socialist movement and its concept of man to the realization of social reform and revolution means passing over an important dimension of socialism – its humanistic aim. The birth of socialist thought was the result of the development of European humanism, a tradition that has its deepest roots in ancient Greece, the Renaissance and the Enlightenment.

The Prologue to Marxist Humanism

For many centuries of the Christian era the concept of man was dominated by the idea of the dualism of body and soul. Anthropology was a theological discipline primarily concerned with the relationship of man to God, although the amount of knowledge about the soul was far less than the available knowledge about the human body. Then, in the nineteenth century, came Ludwig Feuerbach. Preserving the secular concept of the Renaissance and the Enlightenment, Feuerbach reversed the theological point of view and proclaimed that man was God, thus becoming one of the discoverers of modern man.

Feuerbach's anthropology, a universal science of man, was the peak of pre-Marxist humanism. It represents a historical development where philosophical knowledge arrived at a formulation of the scope and aim of the study of the human race – a theory of man. Feuerbach's materialistic concept was in sharp contradiction to the spiritualistic Christian concept, because its point of departure was not an abstract *notion* of man, but *concrete man*. Speculative philosophy put the essence of man outside himself; Hegel's system even placed thinking outside man, and made it a special non-human substance. Against this philosophy, which alienates man from his essence, Feuerbach saw man as a sensual being and sketched a grandiose concept of a dialectical triad in which primitive man, living in harmony with his natural essence, goes through religious alienation and becomes a victim of his own projection until the necessity to return to himself brings his reintegration.

In Feuerbach's case, philosophical humanism did not make speculation its basis – as it had during most of its history – but rather a union with the knowledge acquired by the natural sciences. Man, said Feuerbach, should be understood as an entity, not as a thinking ego; he should become a personalized, practical, active agent. Where previous systems had always fused the ego with some act of intellectual consciousness, Feuerbach liberated concrete man in all his reality, not only in his thinking. And in this 'real humanism' lay the basic theoretical position of later Marxism and socialism.

In Feuerbach's system elements of 'vulgar' materialism blend with a deep philosophical understanding of man; a vague anticipation of socialism as human solidarity is joined with the utopian solution of the renaissance of man through love; a mystic relationship between the man–God and his fellow men is linked with an objective, realistic understanding of the importance of concrete human relationships. The indistinct vision of love and the communion of human hearts is the starting point of a road leading to a scientific understanding of man. The conclusion of Feuerbach's *Principles of the Philosophy of the Future* proclaims the necessity of abandoning speculation completely, and this is the beginning of the future humanism of Karl Marx. The whole of man – the total thinking, feeling, loving man – becomes the subject of the new philosophy and of atheistic, humanistic anthropology.

Feuerbach's concept broke through not only Hegelian but all other abstractions, and its importance is multiplied when we realize that in Feuerbach love is a transformed Christian love of one's neighbour. For Feuerbach love is not only sensual bliss but also the very definition of man's social belonging, an expression of his substance, of his unity with other men. Love is human naturalness, an affirmation of man's humanness. Feuerbach's man always exists in a dialectical unity of 'I and Thou', or, to be more exact, man himself *is* 'I and Thou'. *Man is defined as a relationship*. For the first time in the history of philosophical anthropology man is recognized as a constantly *changing relationship*. *I* is firmly anchored in *Thou*. The concrete human relations that Feuerbach's philosophy introduced to us are not as fruitful as

Marx's later concept of man as the whole sum of social relations. But they nevertheless lay the foundation for this concept.

Feuerbach transformed love into a concrete human category, and made it an important aspect of his total man. But, despite his efforts towards a concrete concept, he remained the prisoner of an abstract cult of man, unable to explain him in *all* his social aspects. In the narrow concept of I and Thou, he understood man quite concretely in the field of sexual and family relations. However, this was the only truly concrete aspect he was able to capture. Man as a whole remained a kind of vague, deified man-God. And when the historical process, striving towards a socialist society, replaced the utopian way of achieving love among people, Feuerbach's theories gave way to the revolutionary practice of the people themselves. The theoretical expression of this further phase of humanism was an historical, materialistic and dialectical understanding of man and his role in the transformation of the world.

Fundamentals of Marxist Humanism

This new kind of humanism was formulated for the first time in Paris, in the spring of 1844, by a twenty-six-year-old immigrant from Germany named Karl Marx. His unfinished manuscript had one of the most dramatic fates of any book. Even today any reference to Marx's *Economic and Philosophic Manuscripts of 1844* arouses the interest of both orthodox and unorthodox Marxists. The gist of this work can be expressed as follows: *Communism without humanism is no communism and humanism without communism cannot be humanism.* From the maze of the Hegelian and Feuerbachian prose in which Marx then wrote, at least three important concepts of man emerge, which form the basis of Marxian humanism. Together they comprise an historical triad of the human race's dramatic process of development, from the state of a natural entity through its social development to its own freedom; from the alienation of its humane basis through the overcoming of alienation to the goal of history – communism; from nature through inhumaneness to humaneness. The grand contours of the picture Marx painted of man's self-understanding and self-realization rise above anything that the theories of the Enlightenment created, either in its French mechanistic–materialistic branch, or in its German, Hegelian idealistic branch. Marx transcends the limits of bourgeois society within which even the most radical bourgeois democratic ideology had until then remained. The concept of man as a separate individual was surpassed.

To give a complete picture of Marx's understanding of anthropology, one must refer to his later works. Limiting the Marxist philosophy of man to the works of the *young* Marx would misrepresent Marx's humanism. Since Landshut has tried to introduce ethics into anthropology, anti-Marxist critics have 'theologized' Marx's concept of man. They have misinterpreted the meaning of man's path from primeval freedom through alienation to future freedom as the fall of man, his penitence and salvation. But any interpretation of Marx which is not in accord with the spirit of contemporary science is not correct, whether it be an ideological concept of ethical socialism, theology, revisionism or orthodox dogmatism. And, at the same time, any concept that would exclude from communism the humanistic basis of the young Marx, be it in favour of the mechanics of economic forces, the class struggle, the interest of the ruling class or power of the contemporary state, is an anti-humanist and anti-Marxist concept, regardless of the phraseology used.

Marx's picture of man, compared to earlier philosophical ideas, differs qualitatively, especially in the concept of man as an active subject, his own creator, who struggles with forms of alienation, and consummates himself. This radical change must be stressed, without denying that the existentialist branch of philosophical thinking has formed yet another concept of man. Marx's dialectical anthropology is not final, because knowledge, which becomes part of science, is subject to the criticism of time, and because the further development of science transcends it. The works of Marx are thus not the end of the history of anthropology and humanism, but a turning point, after which anthropological typology continues. The most important mark of dialectical anthropology is the constant broadening of the concept of man, as the model becomes more and more complicated. The cycle of change in the concept of man that has taken place in philosophy during the last six thousand years continues as an exponential curve beyond Marx himself. One can picture the growth of scientific knowledge about man as a quickly rising curve, climbing to the open future, like man himself.

Marx's concept of humanism brought a basic change into the history of humanism, since it was more than the mere metaphysical speculation of the German philosophy of the time. It transcended older philosophies and formed an anti-illusionist, anti-ideological social and historical basis for scientific anthropology. Among other things, it *brought to a close the philosophy of man by laying the basis for a science of man.*

Marx formulated the prerequisites of humanism, founded on a *scientific* anthropology. One hundred years after Marx, there are, of course, a number of specific branches of science which either did not exist in the second half of the last century or were of negligible importance. Scientific anthropology and humanism have a new empirical basis, although the ideas and concepts of Marx's theory have not lost their validity. As the discoverer of the real mechanism of human alienation, Marx is basically in accord with contemporary science – with the understanding of man as a process, an open system, a flowing equilibrium. Modern science is filling in the contours of man sketched by the young and versatile genius with dialectical concreteness during a Paris spring. Marxist philosophy is an organic product of European culture and of a European, that is to say, classical and humanist, concept of man. If Marxist philosophy is now to begin to formulate the socialist humanist concept of man and to expound the ideas contained in Marx's manuscripts, it must do this in accordance not only with the classical heritage of the pre-Marxist concept of man, but with that of contemporary science. Marxist philosophers are aware of the fact that they have yet to formulate a more detailed answer to the question, 'Who is man?' than the broad contours formulated one hundred and twenty years ago by a young German philosopher.

Scientific Anthropology as the Basis of Socialist Humanism

In recent years, problems of theoretical humanism have been neglected and deformed in Marxist philosophy by the personality cult. The achievements of contemporary social science have not been sufficiently absorbed by the philosophy of dialectical materialism. The work of Roger Garaudy, Adam Schaff and Karel Kosík in evaluating contemporary philosophical anthropology and existentialism is an important step forward in the whole approach to the problem, but these authors themselves do not consider their conclusions definite. Marxist historiography has not yet come to grips with the works of Kierkegaard, Husserl and Scheler.

With the enormous specialization that has taken place in the natural sciences during the last hundred years, the amassed knowledge concerning man has come to form several separate branches of science. Besides philosophical anthropologies, of which there are a number, at least eight special branches of anthropology have come into existence that deal with the realities of man by *scientific* methods as well as by philosophical reflection. If there is a point of departure in humanism that follows Karl Marx, it is the attempt to draw conclusions about man on a firmer basis than philosophical reasonings offer; in short, on the basis of science. Marx's contribution was to show how barren were the pretensions of any metaphysics aspiring to capture the world in its totality and express its entirety; he proved that from a scientific point of view man cannot be described effectively by any *philosophical* anthropology; he must be subjected to the analytical scalpel of the scientific method, which can disclose the biological, psychological, historical and social tissues of human existence, and give philosophy the material for forming a synthesis. In the twentieth century, humanism must be supplemented by the scientific analysis of man.

In so far as the main branches of science have produced a great amount of knowledge about man, we may speak of physical, biological, psychological, sociological, cultural, prehistoric, economic and ethnographic anthropology, each of which answers the question of who man is through specialized methods. Without trespassing beyond their own methodology, these sciences treat the origin of man, his specifications in comparison to animals, his personality as the creator of culture, his history, social relationships, ecology, economic possibilities, etc. Single problems have been worked out to various degrees; some remain long-range tasks for a future anthropological synthesis, while for others there is already elaborate and to some extent generalized material. Biological, historical, sociological and psychological data make it possible to issue the most important results of contemporary knowledge about man as a *synthetic science* – anthropology – and to form a sufficiently large fund of knowledge for modern humanism and philosophical theory to draw upon.

In the field of contemporary biology, entirely new knowledge has come to light: man has been shown to be an open, unspecialized entity, the product of a specific rhythm of growth (as described by A. Portmann), which is unique in the development of life and achieves a very special standing in the animal world. Biology has proved that man's first year of life is an extremely important phase of his growth, similar to what in other mammals takes place during the development of the embryo inside the womb, and that the period of acquiring knowledge, which is exceptionally long in man, produces a peculiar rhythm of life in regard to sexual maturity and the cycle of reproduction – all of which suggests that man's distinction from animals has biological foundations.

Similarly, revolutionary information on man has been contributed by modern psychology, which in both its branches, the Pavlovian and the Freudian, has substantially changed the previously held image of man as a reasoning individual by showing that many forces besides consciousness govern him. Whatever the terminology, the psychologists' image of man is always of an entity of many layers, of which reason is not the most important. Man is seen as constantly changing, and all the manifold roles through which the individual passes in his development are taken into account. The psychology of the personality, together with social psychology, delves into the structure of human nature and at the same time provides a great many empirical facts.

After biology and psychology, sociology has achieved the most important new understanding of man. Aristotle's words about the society of man were given a new content when Marx approached man as a set of not only personal but social relations. At the same time, the concept of man as a member of a collective class – a nation, family, or larger or smaller social group – has made it possible to understand the social aspect of human existence and the growing importance of groups in the life of modern man. Whole social classes have accepted the revolutionary idea that a change in man requires a change in the given social relationships; that a programme of changing the world is in accord with the evolution of society. Man is discovering himself as the conscious creator of social relationships and, thanks to Marx and Freud, now knows that, because of alienation, he has been a mere plaything in the hands of forces which he did not understand.

This fuller knowledge of man has not remained the privilege of a few, but has become the theory of living, human, transforming practice. Man knows now that to 'think means to change', as Bertolt Brecht so aptly put it.

Scientific anthropology is beginning to formulate its first answers to the problem of human existence, with due acknowledgement to past thinkers. Man is an open entity, a personality, and the sum of his relationships. He originated in nature, in history, in the development of societies and cultures; he is going forth to a humane world, towards the mastery of technology, the creation and the metamorphosis of man in time. 'Where have we come from? Who are we? Where are we going?' We come from history; we are people; we are going forth to meet ourselves. These are the prolegomena of scientific anthropology to socialist humanism, to the philosophy of man, to the philosophy of man's freedom.

The Future of Humanism

It is of course impossible to reduce socialist humanism to the empirical data of the sciences, because it is also concerned with the problem of values and a vision of the future of mankind, which goes beyond science.

Pierre Leconte du Noüy tells us that the future of man is the only transcendentalism left to materialists who deny God. We agree that the question of the future of mankind is indeed one of the most important. Religious thinkers have been convinced that the history of personalities, nations, and the whole of mankind was in some manner predestined. The question of the goal of history or the future of man was thus senseless, because history was a revelation of God's aims. In the later years of the Enlightenment an uncritical belief in the progress of mankind was prevalent, but the people of the twentieth century have reached beyond this belief, only to strive the harder for their own rational futures as the sole alternative to total destruction. The world of tomorrow is a modern world without war, a world of mutual enrichment of cultures. The future of mankind will be conditioned by the mastery of technology, economic growth, automation of production, and an invasion of the sciences into the everyday life of man, which will perhaps free man for creation and thus change his way of life. This perspective of economic affluence and a society without classes presents a vision whose contours are lost to the scientist in the space of the cosmos and the depth of time, where science remains silent and the philosopher and poet have their say.

This is where true philosophy begins, because here begins an area of reasoning that empirical science cannot encompass. Here scientific anthropology is transformed into active and concrete humanism, into practical human activity, which is leading the world in the direction of socialism. But the essence of socialism is not the growth of material wealth; it is the full development of man and his liberation. The older utopians as well as modern scientists have envisioned a socialist society where man can freely develop his talents and reasoning; where he can cultivate his feelings and grasp the richness and beauty of the world. Socialism has always been a concept of broader freedom for man. Marx saw future society as a realization of the humanist ideas of the past, as real communism, which frees man. Unless socialism brings to life the ideas from which it was born, it cannot bring to life Marx's programme. Marxism is a programme of human freedom, and if it is not this it is not Marxism.

The guarantee of the humanist future of socialism lies only in the people themselves, in their actions. Unlike past centuries, when man was dragged through history as a sacrifice to his own needs, when he was a passive thing in the hands of blind social forces, constantly plagued by war, hunger and oppression, the twentieth century offers man a chance to direct history. Only in our century have people realized that it is possible to change the world. If they go about it with full consciousness, they will not go against their own interests, will not transform themselves into a society of mechanized robots and prefabricated automatons, but will strive for the human content of future society. The actions of the people today, their knowledge that socialism does not exist without humanism, are of the utmost importance. Socialism is concerned not only with the development of productive forces and technology, but also with the content of social relationships, the problems of people, and the character of man. Increased technology without a change in human relations can bring only the dark future of George Orwell's *1984*, not socialism. The inhuman technocracy of Orwell's pessimistic utopia represents a world that has lost its humanist tradition.

Socialism cannot relinquish this tradition without giving up the rationale of its existence and its roots. The people themselves are responsible for socialist humanism, and nobody can take that responsibility away from them – not a strong personality, or weapons, or institutions, or technical perfection. The people alone, in their actions, must answer for the socialist content of humanism.

BOGDAN SUCHODOLSKI

⊚ ⊚

Renaissance Humanism and Marxian Humanism

BOGDAN SUCHODOLSKI was born in 1903 in Sosnowiec,
Poland. He is head of the Institute of Educational Sciences
at the University of Warsaw and a member of the Polish
Academy of Arts and the Polish Academy of Science. He
has published numerous books on educational philosophy
and methods; some of them are *Socialized Culture, Polish
Educational Thought During the Renaissance, Foundations
of a Materialist Theory of Education* and *Programme for
Secular Moral Education*. During the Second World War,
he taught at the underground University of Warsaw, was
pursued by the Gestapo, and forced into hiding.

Whenever we talk about humanism, we see the conflict of
two different attitudes. One of them holds that the term 'humanism' refers to a complex of enduring values formulated centuries
ago in antiquity which was complemented by certain ideas of the
Renaissance – values which are said to have the same significance
for all men, irrespective of where and when they live. The other
attitude is that the term 'humanism' refers to an historically
variable phenomenon, developing and transforming itself in a
determined way in the course of centuries.

There is no denying that the concept of man – and consequently of humanism as well – contains certain permanent elements. But these elements always exist concretely in the specific
conditions of time and space, and are thus enriched both by the
introduction of new elements, and by keeping old elements alive.
Man always exists 'here and now'; his present existence is at
least as important for determining his *essence* as the conviction
that this essence is determined by historical determinants.

From this point of view, the problems of humanism ought not

to be confined to the problem of what men have always been and what they have always valued, but must also deal with what men are becoming in the course of historical development, what – under changing conditions – they desire and are working towards.

The Renaissance first began to comprehend that man's genuine autonomy consisted not only in freedom *vis-à-vis* religious and philosophical authorities, but also in liberation from the slavery of the social world, which was in contradiction to humanity. The 'true man' the Renaissance sought for and discovered was to be free from both the 'outer and inner priest', from the anti-humanistic forms of life shaped either by old feudal privileges or by the new power of money. In perceiving the anti-humanism of these forms of life, the thinkers and artists of the Renaissance were posing the dramatic question, 'How can the true man be found, buried under conditions which show the real, existing man to be his negation?'

From Petrarch and Boccaccio to such diarists as Cellini and Cardanus, from the painters of the Italian *quattrocento* through the portraits and self-portraits of Dürer down to Titian, multifarious knowledge about empirical human variety grew.

Macchiavelli was the first to state his philosophical conclusions. As historian and observer of contemporary life, politician and statesman, Macchiavelli saw how men fought for power, how they succeeded, and how they succumbed to their adversaries. The question, 'Who is man?' was being interpreted as 'What is man like in his social and political life?'

But from the very moment that the empirical conception of man's cognition started to take shape, other questions arose.

One question was whether the true man is really identical with the person who leads a certain life. The new empiricism took for granted all the manifestations of human life and credulously recorded them as authentic. But some thinkers asked whether the way man lives is the result of his nature or of the conditions and circumstances that oblige him to behave in one way and not another, to put on a certain costume and mask without revealing his true identity. This question was posed by Macchiavelli's contemporary and adversary, Thomas More. More pointed out that the English peasants lived as thieves and criminals because the lords had removed their land from them and taken away their means of livelihood. More unmasked the social hypocrisy which punishes culprits compelled by forces beyond their control to commit a misdeed.

In his *Praise of Folly*, More's friend, Erasmus of Rotterdam, took up the idea that man's way of life reveals the social structure and not man's nature. Picturing the world as a realm of stupidity, Erasmus showed how bishops and princes, leaders and judges, scholars and writers yielded to stupidity, until the 'true' man seemed to be mad and had either to perish or to follow their example; that is, to wear the mask which his life and position required. Thus, the king becomes king only by virtue of his crown and purple; the bishop, by his mitre and crosier; the scientist, by his robe and beret. However, this occurs merely in the world's eyes; the truth lies elsewhere.

The criticism of the empirical theory of man's cognition posed the basic problem of modern anthropology: i.e. the reciprocal relationship between the 'real' man and the 'true' man. Towards the end of the Renaissance this question was posed most dramatically by Cervantes and Shakespeare, who demonstrated how true men, not fitting into the social conditions of life, had to perish or betray themselves.

Renaissance humanism, which had started with the idea of liberating men from the trammels of the superhuman world of church metaphysics, thus posed a central problem of the philosophy of man, the problem of liberating him from the secular bonds laid upon all.

Must real empirical man always be a negation of the true man? Will the true man never be able to be a real man? Will there always be a conflict between man and the world created by men? These were questions to which only Utopian answers were being given when the Renaissance came to its close.

One answer was given by Bacon, who believed that social progress could be achieved through the victories of science and technology over the brute forces of nature and over men's delusions; another was given by Campanella, who believed in a social revolution that would liquidate private ownership and open a door to the development of science, technology and art.

Succeeding centuries continued to face these problems. If man was neither to appeal to religious authorities nor to accept with docility the whole social reality as it existed, then he had to rely on his own intellect as the only force capable of understanding and guiding his life. Consequently, believers in the empirical concept of man began to value reason more and more highly as a factor to liberate man from conservatism and opportunism.

Thus a new and almost paradoxical type of rationalism arose. Man's lot was to be improved rationally in terms of reality, or the situation as it existed. Acceptance of such reality was easy; so was criticism from a religious or metaphysical position; but evaluation of the situation within the limits of reality was a fundamental difficulty.

Man from this point of view was a particularly complex being; he lived in a world created by himself which he, however, criticized. If he was not to resort to metaphysical criteria in his criticism, he had at his disposal only the historical and social experience of mankind. But he was obliged, at the same time, to evaluate this criterion.

Under these circumstances, the relationship between human reason and human reality emerged with particular sharpness as the problem of the meaning of human history. Faced with a conflict between reason and history, to choose reason would be tantamount to renouncing history, that is, the only force at the disposal of man, who is a solitary being left on his own in the universe.

Closely bound up with the conflict between reason and history was the conflict between reason and social reality, which was in essence the same conflict, revealed in contemporary life. Philosophers of the seventeenth century were alarmed by the question, 'Which is better, the choice of social institutions and universally observed customs, or reason, particularly in its critical attitude towards society?' As long as the social world could resort to a metaphysical or historical authority, the problem posed no difficulty. Wherever man was left alone to face his social reality, it became essential.

In choosing the social reality despite his own reason, man departed from what was most valuable in him: his critical consciousness, his ability to evaluate, his will to act. But, in choosing the ideals of reason despite social reality, he ran another risk. Who could be certain whether ideals not yet tested in social practice were correct? The conservatives were always of the opinion that it was better to do a stupid thing which had hitherto been done by other men than to do a wise thing which had never yet been done by anybody. If the ideals of reason were not to be guaranteed metaphysically, the testimony of social reality was their only confirmation. Under those conditions, was the social criterion of truth and falsehood to be rejected?

The conflict between human reason and human reality, both in history and in contemporary society, was the principal subject of the deliberations concerning civilization, the social system, and man among the philosophers of the Enlightenment. The Enlightenment stressed the idea that the reality within which people lived, their institutions and views, ought to be transformed according to the requirements of reason. In perpetuating this concept, the Enlightenment saw the stages of its implementation and conceived of history as an avenue of progress leading towards the future.

Thanks to this, the philosophy of man acquired, for the first time in history, a new dimension. True, the genealogy of the theory of progress goes back to earlier times, but it was only in the eighteenth century that the concept became a universally recognized and fruitful philosophy of history and of man. Man was seen as a being who not only created the conditions of his life, but also, in their historical transformations, progressed from one form of existence to another.

It was then that philosophers for the first time ceased to answer the question, 'Who is man?' by indicating what men are like. They recognized that the differentiation within the human race, as recorded by historians and ethnographers, could be understood only when it was taken for granted that man is a being that evolves. One cannot define man's nature by summing up all the data; one can define it only by tracing its development and characterizing its stages of evolution. Thus the Enlightenment could once again take up the problem of human reason in relation to human reality.

It was possible to solve that problem only through a new analysis, far more profound than any hitherto applied.

The Renaissance discovered the role of the activity of man but failed to recognize the difficult problems inherent in it. Only Bacon saw them – and in one aspect only: that of human intellectual activity. He noticed that man in his activities devised false and illusory ideas to which he afterwards succumbed.

Bacon's criticism was the first attempt to inquire into the mechanism of human activities and to show that man's creative achievements nurtured a peculiar kind of parasite that hampered his own development. Not only alien and menacing nature, but also man's own products were his enemy. The defeat of those products was very difficult, if only because they were a human creation.

This first version of the theory of alienation did not find any followers. In the eighteenth century, however, conditions arose which again brought the problem to the fore.

It seemed probable that such parasites might appear not only in intellectual activities, but in others as well, particularly social activities. The attack launched by the ideology of the Enlightenment on the prevailing social system induced philosophers, especially Rousseau, to interpret it as a struggle against the degeneration of social reality at a certain stage of historical development.

The new concept made it possible to pass judgement on the fruits of human activities in all fields. It became possible to evaluate history by distinguishing the authentic and valuable products of human activity from the parasites on such activity; to evaluate social life by distinguishing the expression of valuable human activities from their degeneration. The philosophy of man could point both to the ways in which man develops under the influence of history, and to those in which he degenerates; to the manner in which society creates man and the manner in which it destroys his humanity. The former contradictions between the empirical and the metaphysical cognitions of man were gone. Scholars seeking to define man according to his 'existence' justly criticized those who looked above all for his 'essence', since the concepts of 'essence' have always been of a metaphysical nature. Man was, in fact, richer.

Nevertheless, those who considered man on the basis of his existence erred as well; his existence had hitherto restricted man and prevented his full development. Now that he was potentially richer, it followed that to understand man was not to determine what he is or should be like, but to recognize him as an active being creating his own world and, by overcoming what has been created, changing and developing his own creation. Man develops himself and his own existence, and – consequently – his own essence.

33

This concept of man as determined by both his activities and his ability to overcome their results was simultaneously formulated by J. Salaville in France and Wilhelm Humboldt in Germany. The former expressed it from the point of view of a politician of the French Enlightenment and Revolution, while the latter did it in terms of a scholar engaged in the study of culture and in education. Both of them, however, made the same basic discovery – the vision of man as both creator and slave of his own creations.

The social consequences of this new philosophy of man were perceived by Pestalozzi. Pestalozzi realized the greatness – and also the narrow-mindedness – of the Enlightenment, and the narrow-mindedness of the French bourgeois revolution. Therefore he felt that the ideals of bourgeois individualism and bourgeois collectivism were to be equally opposed; in either case the 'true man' perishes: bourgeois individualism is, after all, a kind of egoism, and the bourgeois slogans of patriotism, nationality and state are merely the same egoism, in a collective version. Pestalozzi saw that it was necessary to get beyond the contradiction of the two poles of anti-humanism (individualism and collectivism) that existed in feudal and bourgeois society. Only on the ruins of bourgeois society, when a new social reality suited to the vital needs of all people arises, would it be possible to create the 'true man', said Pestalozzi, referring back to the great Renaissance discussion of the true man and the real man.

By courageously pointing out that the essential cause of the conflict lay with the social class system that entailed the negation of humanity, Pestalozzi raised the kind of considerations Marx referred to in his criticism of the bourgeois ideal of man and that of 'citizen' (*citoyen*) hailed by the French Enlightenment.

Marx based his theory on the philosophy of man of which he laid the foundations during the course of his famous polemics with Hegel and Hegel's disciples. That philosophy, broaching and solving the problems advanced by the philosophy of the Renaissance and the Enlightenment, provided a scientific interpretation of man as an active being, the starting point for contemporary concepts of man.

Analysing the manifold kinds of human activity, Marx showed how they create a specific environment of human life based on the natural environment and biological needs of the human being, but rising above these preliminary conditions and creating a separate reality that evolves with the development of the material and social activities of man. Man in every period of that historical development is moulded by this reality and is, at the same time, its creator; 'man is man's world'.

Going deeper into the definition, Marx revealed the conflicts of that 'human world' and the corresponding inner conflicts of man. Man's world develops through contradictions arising principally from the resistance of the consolidated system of social relations and their corresponding ideology to the development of productive forces. The world of social institutions and social ideals, created by man, becomes a reality independent of him, a world alien to him, a world that imposes its requirements upon him.

Labour and social life, inexhaustible sources of man's development, change under these circumstances into factors leading to dehumanization. Thus, everything that determines the historical development of man – his rise over and above the level of animal vegetation, his increasing wealth of human needs and aspirations – simultaneously becomes a factor depriving him of his humanity and subordinating him to the requirements of capitalist economy. Man's historical development has hitherto been determined by the fact that man is – in his very essence – menaced by the degeneration of those same activities by which he defines himself.

The Renaissance writers saw this and pointed out that man's world was 'topsy-turvy', but they did not understand the social mechanism of the conflict. That is why their only hope was Utopia. Marx explained how, under the conditions of capitalist economy and the class system, the 'true' man has to succumb to the 'dehumanization' process, and the 'true' society must become an 'apparent' one; the resources of man and the human community must be destroyed under such conditions. Then the real life of man becomes inhuman, and his human aspirations and desires become unreal; that is to say – they degenerate.

Marx analysed the world philosophically in order to change it; his understanding of it increased as he turned to revolutionary activity, which, being directed against the capitalist system, was to overcome the alienation of labour and social life and the dehumanization of man. What Marx called 'revolutionary practice' was to be, under the historical conditions that existed, the main factor of social transformation and the principal force liberating man from the slavery of those forms of social and intellectual life to which he had succumbed.

Marxist anthropology brought to an end all forms of metaphysical speculation on the 'essence' of man. Marx pointed out that such concepts always involved the unwarranted acceptance as absolute truth of experiences acquired by certain social classes in certain historical periods; in other words, they promoted experiences to the rank of objective and invariable principles.

Concepts concerning the 'essence' of man were not – as Marx pointed out – discoveries of his true nature to serve as a basis for social, political and educational activity, but rather expressions of certain socio-political situations, made with a view towards their perpetuation.

Marx also criticized all attempts to determine man empirically. For they, like the metaphysical theories, took the historical state of affairs for granted and considered it immutable. They wrongly presupposed that people are determined by the way in which they live; they did not perceive any internal contradiction within the human world at different stages of its historical development, or the transformations taking place in man against the background of those contradictions.

Marxian anthropology, which determines man by referring to 'the world of man', and which points to the internal mechanism of the transformation process in that world, showed the mutability of the so-called essence of man. It put emphasis on the fact that man was the only being that developed through his commitment to the creation of the objective human world, by succumbing to its requirements and, at the same time, conquering its decaying forms. The development of man is not a spontaneous and purely spiritual projection of his dreams and wishes, nor is it an expression of the subjective desires of an individual or of a group. The development of man is realized through his activities, which must pass the test of objective criteria of various kinds: the criterion of truth for scientific activity, of efficiency for technical activity, of form for artistic activity, and of productive forces and social relations for economic activity. Nothing may be facultative, nothing may be human licence. Only by observing the laws of the objective world can man succeed in his aims, and human creations be perpetuated. At the same time, however, courage and creative ability are necessary. Man must not submit to his own creations. Scientists have the right, and the duty, to reject scientific theories, just as technicians ought to reject solutions already obsolescent. The same applies to organizers of social activities.

This duality in the development of man – his acceptance of the requirements of objective reality and his courage in rejecting previous achievements and forms – is a fundamental tenet of Marx's philosophy of man. This dual development is based upon man's social activities. Such activities, being related to the changes in productive forces and the aspirations of the masses, revolutionize stable social institutions and forms, as well as the corresponding social consequences.

In the complex processes of destroying the old, creating the new, and preserving the enduring, certain elements complement and, at the same time, contradict one another. These are the requirements of productive forces, the manifold trends within the economic 'base', the various currents in the ideological 'superstructure', and general social consciousness. They all create material, social and spiritual situations replete with internal tensions and contradictions for man.

LUCIEN GOLDMANN

⊚ ⊚

Socialism and Humanism

LUCIEN GOLDMANN is director of studies at the École
Pratique des Hautes Études, VI Section, in Paris, where he
is in charge of teaching sociology of literature and philosophy, and also directs the Centre of Studies of Literary
Sociology at the Institute of Sociology at the University of
Brussels. Born in Bucharest, Rumania, in 1913, he studied
in Vienna under Max Adler, read law in Bucharest and
Paris and philosophy in Vienna, Zürich and Paris, and
subsequently worked with Jean Piaget in Geneva. His
books include *Human Community and the Universe According to Kant, Human Sciences and Philosophy, The Hidden
God, Dialectical Research* and *Three Studies on the Sociology of the Novel.*

I

In the minds of the leading Marxist theorists before 1917, the
triumph of the proletarian revolution, the socialization of the
means of production, and the setting up of centralized planning
would inevitably lead to a society organized in such a manner
that, after a preliminary phase of democratic dictatorship of the
proletariat,[1] the social body would then cease to be divided according to classes and the exploitation of man by man would be
abolished. This would subsequently lead to an integration of the
major values inherited from middle-class humanism (universality, individual freedom, equality, the dignity of the human person, freedom of expression) so as to endow them, for the first
time in the history of humanity, with a quality of authenticity,

---

1. *Dictatorship*, in so far as it implies the existence of a proletarian
state which applies measures of constraint to the middle class. *Democratic
dictatorship*, in so far as this state represents the vast majority of the
population and, for the first time in history, applies measures of constraint
only to a small and reactionary minority.

instead of the purely *formal* status that they had previously been granted in a capitalist society.

True, democratic capitalist societies give legal recognition to the equality and freedom of all citizens before the law and to the right of each individual to express his ideas freely. Economic inequality, however, reduces this equality and the individual's freedom to a purely *formal* status since the citizens of such a democracy are divided into a minority of the wealthy and a mass of relatively poor workers, and since this poverty deprives the mass of workers of the possibility of really enjoying the freedoms recognized by law,[1] and of using effectively the right of expressing their ideas publicly.

A socialist society, on the other hand, was expected to re-establish real equality and, in its earliest stage, even to suppress all noticeable differences in wealth, so as to give freedom, equality and human dignity their full meaning. In such a society, exploitation would be abolished, production would be rationally planned, and the suppression of production for the market would reaffirm the qualitative nature of the relationship between human beings and goods or other human beings, all of which would make it possible for this society to achieve a synthesis, at a higher level, of the positive elements of the three great forms of society which had preceded it:

(*a*) the *classlessness* of primitive societies;

(*b*) the *qualitative relationships* of men with other men and with nature which had characterized pre-capitalistic societies;

(*c*) the *rationality* that capitalist society had introduced in privately owned plants and the values of universality, equality and freedom which are closely bound to this rationality.

For all these reasons, the socialist revolution was expected, in the minds of Marx, Engels and the Marxist thinkers who followed them, to mark the end of 'pre-history' and the transition from the realm of necessity to that of freedom.

This scheme of things, worked out in the nineteenth century, continues to dominate most socialist thought in our own age. However, since 1917, the existence, first of a single state, then of

---

1. Anatole France once made a famous remark: The law recognizes the same right for millionaires and *clochards* (or tramps) to sleep beneath the bridges of Paris.

several others (all endowed with a socialist character, which they boast of at the ideological level, though, at the political and social level, they actually function within the framework of a very complex reality), has brought out clearly a more or less striking discordance between, on the one hand, the social, economic and political reality of these societies or states and, on the other hand, the above-mentioned ideological superstructure. Resolving such a discordance should, moreover, be one of the primary tasks of a living socialist philosophy which seeks to operate in those areas of thought where the understanding of reality and the demystification of all ideologies are most advanced.

The discordance between reality and ideology is in itself neither new nor surprising. Great social and political movements have nearly always developed somewhat simplified conceptions of the future and of the possibilities of achieving the values which inspired them. Nearly always, once victory has been achieved and the social reality discovered to be more tangled and complex than had been foreseen, leaders have come forward to take advantage of the situation and to claim that it corresponded exactly to what the revolutionaries had wished and foreseen.

But progressive thinkers have always tried to point out the distances that separated such affirmations from reality, to dismantle the machinery that has made it possible for a revolutionary ideology to become an apologetic 'ideology', and to re-establish the harmony between thought and reality that alone can endow the former with a truly progressive character. Among others, such is the function that Marx and Engels performed in their relationship to the ideologists of the triumphant middle class, and such is certainly the function that all thinkers who wish to keep the legacy of the great founders of Marxism effective and alive should now fulfil in their relationship to:

(*a*) the apologists of the new socialist states which were born of anti-capitalist revolutions;

(*b*) the apologists of the Western capitalist societies which are undergoing an evolution; and

(*c*) the apologists of the societies of the 'Third World'.

This is why we now face an urgent task – that of liberating ourselves from all the slogans that clutter the political life and the thought and theory of the socialist movement, so as to be able to return to the kind of analysis of the world's social and political evolution, since 1917, that would be both positive and accurate. Within the framework of this task, I would like to raise here, if only in a somewhat schematic manner, a problem which seems to me of particular importance.

If we compare the analyses that Marx has left us with the real evolution of both capitalist and socialist societies since, respectively, the end of the nineteenth century and 1917 until today, we find that such a comparison calls for two very important *corrections* which, though they may appear, at the level of *theory*, to be the kind that could easily be integrated within the general body of Marxist philosophy, would in *practice* require considerable changes in the aims and perspectives of socialist action.

Each of these two corrections concerns the problem of relationships between social reality and humanist values, in the Western capitalist societies as well as in those societies that have a socialist character.

Let us therefore begin by referring back to the first of the two major analyses of capitalist societies that Marx has left us:

(*a*) the theory of the fetishism of goods or, to use a terminological correction later introduced by Lukács, of their reification, and

(*b*) the theory of the progressive pauperization of the proletariat and its necessary evolution towards an awareness of its own revolutionary role.

The first of these two theories has proved to be not only valid, but also much more important in any understanding of the evolution of the capitalist world in the twentieth century than Marxist theorists before 1917 would have expected. The second, however, has been rendered obsolete, and indeed has even been contradicted, by the real evolution of a society whose essential structural aspects have been modified.

In spite of his orthodoxy, Lenin was quite characteristically obliged, in order to take into account the social and political reality of his age, to add two very important notions to Marx's analyses:

(*a*) that the spontaneous evolution of the proletariat leads to the creation not of a revolutionary class, but of labour unions, and

41

(*b*) that there exists, throughout the West, a category of the proletariat which varies in its numerical importance but constitutes a 'working-class aristocracy' which is integrated in capitalist society and provides the social foundations for the reformist movement.

To these observations of Lenin, which must be elucidated and developed before we can understand the evolution that has occurred in the first half of the twentieth century,[1] some remarks must be added on the changes Western capitalism has undergone since the end of the Second World War.

There is no room here to develop these ideas at greater length, so I must limit myself to observing that, as the revolution which orthodox Marxists have expected, and, thanks to the experience gained in the great economic slump of 1929–33, and to the pressure of the expansion of the economic and, consequently, the military power of the U.S.S.R. and the whole socialist bloc, the capitalist world has now developed more or less satisfactory devices for economic self-regulation which allow it to avoid, to a great extent, structural crises of overproduction. There has resulted, in the industrialized nations of the West, not only a great expansion of productive forces but also a constantly rising standard of living for the great majority of the population, including the working class.

It may, of course, be possible for a socialist economy to expand production and increase the well-being of the population even faster, but this has not yet been proved unequivocally, and, in any case, socialist action in the industrial societies of the West can no longer be founded on the premise of the increasing pauperization of the proletariat and its *necessary* transformation into a revolutionary force.

In these circumstances, such societies are now beginning to follow a social, economic and political evolution different from the one predicted by Marx, with other perspectives and other dangers.

In these societies, the workers are no longer *necessarily* driven

1. The proletariat of the Western world has some *essentially reformist social layers*, a phenomenon which seems due to the fact that the fraction of the Western working class that has escaped, thanks to the existence of colonial markets and to union action, from the process of pauperization Marx predicted and expected, has been much larger than Lenin thought.

by increasing pauperization to choose the path of socialism. A true socialist world might, and indeed probably would, offer them certain economic advantages and increased well-being. However, they cannot be expected to acquire an awareness of this as inevitably as the Marxist theorists of the nineteenth century believed. The struggle between capitalism and socialism in these societies thus becomes a struggle for domination over the class-consciousness of the workers and the population as a whole. It is particularly important, moreover, that the infrastructure, far from being of assistance to the forces of socialism in this struggle, as Marx and the traditional Marxists believed, operates on the contrary in favour of integration in the existing social order, since the economic changes just mentioned have determined a very profound social and psychological evolution.

However, at a certain level, the evolution of Western capitalist society has confirmed Marx's analysis to a far greater extent than envisioned by nineteenth-century Marxist thinkers, i.e. in terms of Marx's theories of the fetishism of goods.

Marx demonstrated to what extent the appearance of the market reduces all trans-individual values to something merely implicit by eliminating them from awareness and reducing them progressively to the phenomenological and quantitative aspect of two new properties of inert objects: value and price, which transform goods into wares. Marx, and especially Lukács after him, have insisted strongly on the passive character that this development of reification imposes on life and on the behaviour of individuals subjected to those economic laws of a market that acquire the characteristics of a quasi-natural power.

On the other hand, the development of production for the market has now created, for the first time in history, the foundations for the insertion of new values within social life and for their subsequent development, values including those of equality, freedom and tolerance,[1] which contribute greatly to the constitution of Western humanism.

1. I feel that the opposition between *tolerance* and *freedom of thought and expression* constitutes one of the main differences between middle-class humanism and socialist humanism.

The very term *tolerance* indeed implies some degree of indifference to error. Born in the realm of religious belief and faith, it corresponds to the inevitably atheistic and rationalist character of the rising middle class and thus to a social and economic order which has suppressed trans-individual

LUCIEN GOLDMANN

Later, however, the shift from a craft society producing for the market to an industrial capitalist society, which involves so many economic inequalities and the organization of production on a hierarchical basis within the plant, weakened values of humanistic individualism, in both their application and their intrinsic nature. In their application, they have been eliminated from production and limited to the realm of the actual market and the abstract and peripheral fields of law and politics. In their nature, they have purely formal character, which has replaced the real content which they once possessed.

However difficult it may be to contest the validity of these analyses, one must nevertheless admit today that neither Marx nor Lukács was able to see, in the societies they were analysing, to what extent an area of individual activity and values that could still supply a structure for individual awareness was maintained, as a result of the mere existence of the liberal market (and, later, of a monopolistic market subject to very limited state intervention). The development of monopolist imperialism, especially after the Second World War, and the massive interventions of the state, were closely related to the appearance of self-regulating devices, that in actuality eliminated every function of responsibility of the individual in production and in the market, thereby emptying the individual's awareness of all its autonomous or immanent content, and achieving a degree of passivity which even the most pessimistic theorist of the early years of our century would have imagined only with great difficulty.[1]

values. The classical rationalist or empirical middle class becomes tolerant in religious matters because in its eyes faith has lost its importance and effective reality.

A socialist humanism which implies, on the other hand, the *right for each man to express freely his convictions* precludes any such indifference to the opinions of others and presupposes a common and permanent effort to find truth and achieve agreement through free, frank and open discussion.

1. These are realities expressed both by the most important writers of our time, from Kafka to Beckett, Ionesco, Robbe-Grillet, Adamov, and even Sartre (in *La Nausée*) and Camus (in *L'Étranger*), and also by sociologists to whom Marxism is as alien as it is to David Riesman, when he observes, for instance, the shift from a society which is regulated from within to one which is regulated from without. One might, of course, point out the same phenomenon by studying the evolution of modern art.

Of course, this increasing passivity of the population creates a very dangerous situation for culture, especially humanistic culture. It reveals itself in a constant weakening of interest in anything that lies beyond the scope of the consumer needs of the individual or his family unit; at the same time, his standard of living progressively improves, all of which contributes substantially to the integration of the workers within the existing society and counters their evolution towards socialism.

In such a situation the socialists must formulate a programme directed towards acquiring the power to influence the awareness of individuals at the level of superstructures and in their political, social and cultural thinking. There are two possible alternatives which the workers in the contemporary Western world must choose between, consciously or implicitly. They may choose a technocratic society which bestows the powers of decision on a very restricted minority of technocrats who are capable of ensuring a constantly rising standard of living for a great majority of the population, but who will at the same time lead them, if not necessarily, at least probably, into a dehumanized world in which cultural possibilities are reduced to a bare minimum. Or they may choose a socialist, democratic society which is likewise capable of ensuring an equal and perhaps even high degree of well-being, and which would also and above all ensure the development of a sense of individual responsibility within the total population, so as to create the social and economic foundations for a development of its spiritual and cultural life.

The whole problem can be reduced to one of making wage-earners understand that the path of convenience and selfishness may well lead towards integration, but that their own interests and those of their families should inspire them to swim against this stream in order to save both their own dignity and the great cultural values inherited from the past.

In conclusion, I can mention only briefly the very important change that such a novel situation implies at the level of political

---

In a brilliant remark, Erich Fromm pointed out the same phenomenon in his contribution to the debates of the Dubrovnik Congress when he declared that there had at first been people who travelled to learn and thus expand their knowledge, then tourists who took cameras with them, whereas now we have only cameras that travel accompanied by tourists to service them.

aims and perspectives. It appears obvious that the suppression of absolute pauperization, the creation of devices for economic self-regulation, and the progressive indifference, passivity and integration of the population as a whole have all contributed towards depriving the traditional programme of a socialist or proletarian revolution of its practical value and its political chances of success.

This is why, in the capitalist societies of the Western world, the only realistic socialist programme today is one of structural reforms[1] that would analyse the situation, clearly and without hesitation or scruple, in such a way as to make the workers understand that it is entirely in their interest to demand, first, the right to control, and later also to manage, their plants. These rights alone could assure them, in addition to economic advantages, which may vary in importance, an effective participation and responsibility in the major decisions of economic, social and political life, and an opportunity to play an active part in the development of a truly humanist culture.

We thus reach the concept of a path leading to socialism and analogous to that followed by the middle class in feudal society.

1. I first wrote 'reformist', but discussions with several socialists, especially Italian socialists, led me to see that this term might prove confusing. The meaning of words depends on the context in which they are used. In socialist thought of the first half of the twentieth century, there were discussions concerning the two concepts of *reform* and *revolution*, the former meaning mainly an adjustment of more or less important details within the capitalist régime into a socialist one through civil war, the seizure of power by the proletarian parties, and the setting up of the dictatorship of the proletariat which would, among other things, socialize the means of production. But I am now concerned with a third concept which can be identified with neither of these.

This new concept is the idea of a transition to worker management, which can be achieved progressively in one sector after another. It implies the possibility of more or less acute conflicts, although not necessarily of a civil war, or a synchronic transformation of society as a whole preceding such economic changes. Such a transition might, of course, involve a particular nation in civil war, but might in other nations be achieved without such expenditure.

Actually, such a process is in its general lines analogous to the transformation of feudal society into capitalist society, a gradual economic transformation sometimes accompanied by civil war (in England and France), but achieved in other nations without any violent revolution. Such a transformation may therefore be called a *reform* or a *revolution*, but the term in neither case will have the meaning it possessed in Marxist literature of the latter part of the nineteenth century and the first half of the twentieth.

Along such a path, economic transformations, though born of conflict, would be gradual and peaceful and would precede a potential political revolution – which is no longer inevitable in all cases, as the rise to power of the middle class in nineteenth-century Germany demonstrates.

2

If we now proceed to the other side of our analysis, we are obliged to observe that the evolution of societies with a socialist character has also proved to be extremely complex and, above all, different from what had been foreseen or predicted in a necessarily schematic and summary manner by the creators of Marxism.

The differences between these predictions and reality are numerous, but this should not be at all surprising since no theorist, however great, can arrive at anything but a very summary and general scheme of reality, without the aid of empirical, concrete experience. However, this poses no major problem so long as such a scheme of reality, however general, corresponds to the essential structure of reality.

As stated earlier, the philosophy of Marx, Engels and the Marxists who followed them predicted a socialist and, above all, communist society of the future which, thanks to the socialization of the means of production and the setting up of planned production, would bring together the positive qualities of the three great forms of social organization that are characteristic of what Marxists have sometimes called the 'pre-history of humanity', that is to say:

(*a*) *the suppression of social classes and of man's exploitation by man*, which humanity had already known in primitive societies, though at a level of *extreme poverty*;

(*b*) *the qualitative and not yet reified character of interhuman relations between man and nature* which had characterized, in a *barbaric and unjust* manner, pre-capitalist and essentially traditional forms of the organization of production and distribution;

(*c*) the two great contributions of production for the market and especially of capitalist production:

1. *the rational organization of production* and the rapid development of productivity that it brings about and ensures;

capitalist society had introduced this rationalization in its own plants, but not in relationships between them or in production as a whole, whereas the socialist society of the future was destined to extend the application of rationalization to the whole field of the production of goods; and

2. *the humanist values*, born and developed in Western society parallel to the appearance and development of production for the market, especially the values of universality, equality, individual freedom, and, as part of the latter, freedom of expression.

It is obvious that a society founded on true community and real freedom would then be achieved for the first time in history as a result of the simultaneous application of the following principles: the abolition of exploitation, the suppression of class distinctions, the establishment of qualitative relationships between men and nature, the rational organization of production, and, together with a great expansion of productivity, the establishment of real universality, equality and freedom.

Socialist society was expected to restore and further develop the values of Western humanism, since it would not only strip them of their merely formal character by suppressing all exploitation and class distinctions, but also bind them organically to a community both truly human and fully conscious of those transindividual values which would be liberated at last from the heavy handicaps that poverty and exploitation had imposed in the precapitalist periods of history.

In concluding this study, I might mention the importance in theory and in doctrine of the Yugoslav experiment, even though it happens to have been undertaken in a relatively small country. Seeking to react against bureaucratic or Stalinistic centralization, Yugoslavia has integrated to socialist thought *the discovery that the socialization of the means of production does not necessarily imply, as Marx and later Marxists had thought, integral centralized planning and the suppression of the market.*

The greatest achievement of Yugoslav Socialist Democracy, *self-management by the workers*, is a means of ensuring an effective democracy. It also ensures a considerable socialization of the ownership of the means of production, making it possible to suppress both the exploitation of man by man and, in any case, a considerable part of the manifestations of reification. At the same time, it ensures the maintenance of production for the market which can constitute the basis for a real and authentic development of 'freedom', especially that of expression.

Self-management by the workers seems to me to be the only possible foundation for a truly socialist programme in the contemporary world. The character of this self-management and the road taken to reach it will, of course, depend on whether one starts from a capitalist society with a formal democracy, from a dictatorial system like that of Spain, from a socialist society with centralized planning or from the society of a developing country. And it must be kept in mind that maintenance of the market, even if accompanied by the suppression of private ownership of the means of production, may cause important difficulties which can be solved only after serious empirical and theoretical studies have been made.

Translated by Édouard Roditi

LÉOPOLD SENGHOR

⊚ ⊚

Socialism Is a Humanism

LÉOPOLD SÉDAR SENGHOR, President of the Republic of Senegal, an architect of Senegalese independence and a leader of the Party of African Federation and the Senegalese Progressive Union, helped to found the Africa and Malagasy Union and the later and larger grouping of pro-Western African nations in the Monrovia bloc. He is the author of five volumes of poetry and of *On African Socialism*, and edited the *Anthologie de la nouvelle poésie nègre et malgache de langue française*.

In the respective programmes of our former parties, all of us used to proclaim our attachment to *socialism*. This was a good thing, but it was not enough. Most of the time, we were satisfied with stereotyped formulas and vague aspirations that we called *scientific socialism*, as if socialism did not mean a return to original sources. Above all, we need to make an effort to rethink the basic texts in the light of Negro-African realities. Let us first consider the main question.

The anti-federalists have accused us of being atheists, 'Marxists', and of outlawing religion. Surely this smacks of propaganda. Can we integrate Negro-African cultural values, especially religious values, into socialism? We must answer that question once and for all with an unequivocal *yes*.

We are not 'Marxists' in the sense given the word today, in so far as Marxism is presented as atheistic metaphysics, a total and totalitarian view of the world, a *Weltanschauung*. Marx himself once said: 'As for me, I am not a Marxist.' We are *socialists*. In other words, we shall exclude neither Marx nor Engels from our sources; we shall start from their works as from those of the 'Utopian socialists', and we shall add to these sources the works of their successors and commentators. But we shall retain only the method and the ideas: the method, to help us to analyse our situation; the ideas, to help us to solve our problems.

We shall start with Marx and Engels. Whatever their limitations, their inadequacies, or their errors, they, more than all others, revolutionized the political and economic thought of the nineteenth century. The consequences of that revolution are still perceptible in the twentieth. Churchmen themselves cannot deny Marx's contributions and they accept his positive values. And, since the liberation, they have perhaps contributed most to an understanding of Marx – in France, at least. As proof of this, I need cite only two French Marxists. 'A final paradox', writes Henri Lefebvre, the 'Master Marxist' in France, is that 'the most important works on Marxism published recently are signed by Jesuits'. And Lucien Goldmann, speaking of these same volumes, notes that they 'constitute at the moment the principal French contribution to the study of Marxism'.[1] I may particularly draw your attention to Father Bigo's book entitled *Marxisme et Humanisme*. It bears the same title that I gave to an earlier article of my own published in *La Revue socialiste*.[2]

We shall take Marx's ideas, theory and theories as a starting point. Marx borrows economic concepts and vocabulary from his predecessors. To be sure, he is interested in statistics, which were then in limbo, but he cites facts and figures without verifying or criticizing them. What interests him more than things themselves is man's relationship with other men and with things. He is the real founder of sociology. According to a famous expression, his goal is 'to penetrate the real and intimate totality of the relationship of production in bourgeois society'. The fact is that Marx came to economics through philosophy, detouring through Hegel, from whom he borrowed the theory of *alienation*, and Feuerbach, who taught him the importance of *praxis*. His sociology is based on the general theory of alienation, which he develops through the particular theories of *value* and *capital*. I shall take the latter as my point of departure.

For Marx, a commodity is the elementary form of wealth in

1. Henri Lefebvre, '*Le Marxisme et la pensée française*', and Lucien Goldmann, '*Propos dialectiques*', in *Les Temps modernes*, Nos. 137–8 (July–August 1957).
2. Pierre Bigo, *Marxisme et Humanisme* (Paris: Presses Universitaires de France, 1953), and Léopold Sédar Senghor, '*Marxisme et Humanisme*', *La Revue socialiste*, March 1948.

capitalist-type societies, and every commodity has two values: a *use-value* and an *exchange-value*. The use-value of an object is based on human needs; it is 'limited by the physical properties of the commodity [and] has no existence apart from that commodity'.[1] It is the material support of the exchange-value. In a capitalist economy – that is, in a money-market economy – the exchange-value is substituted for the use-value and becomes the *value* in itself, and 'the magnitude of the value of any article is the amount of labour socially necessary, or the labour-time socially necessary for its production'.[2] This is the *labour* theory of value. In other words, within a patriarchal, community economy, commodities born of human needs remain in the hands of men. In a market economy, these same commodities escape from the conscious determination of men, are subject to the monetary law of exchange and establish objective relationships among themselves. The world of things is substituted for the world of men and dominates it. Men are cut off from nature and from each other. They have entered the world of *capital*.

Capital could not be identified with the means of production themselves. The latter existed just as well in the patriarchal community. Capital is the means of production monopolized by a minority of men. For Marx, capital is even more than that. It is an idea that takes life and is personified, a conscious and implacable will that becomes incarnate in a monstrous force. It is money whose final objective is to make money. The objective is not to satisfy human needs, not even animal needs – food, clothing, shelter – but rather to grab the surplus-value of the worker's labour. It is here that the theory of *surplus-value* intervenes.

The value of a commodity is here determined by the amount of labour needed to produce it. This value should normally correspond to the number of hours needed to make this commodity; in a human economy, it should correspond to the number of hours necessary to assure the livelihood of the worker and his family – his material and spiritual life. Let us suppose that this number of hours is five. The capitalist ought to pay the worker on the basis of five hours. However, though he pays him on this basis, he makes him work eight hours, but the value of

1. Karl Marx, *Capital:* Vol. I: *Process of Capitalistic Production* (Chicago: Charles H. Kerr, 1906), p. 42.
2. Ibid., p. 46.

the three extra hours goes to the employer and not to the worker. It is this surplus-value that, according to Marx, permits the 'accumulation of capital', *capitalization*. The employer could object that he has taken the risk and provided the means of production. The socialist replies that the investment is amortized after a few years, whereas the surplus-value remains indefinitely. But this is perhaps not the essential argument. Marx's general theory is a *macro-economic* one. What he is considering is the totality of workers and the totality of capitalists, which eliminates the idea of risk.

In the light of these analyses, we can now explain the general theory of *alienation* that underlies them. The theory of alienation is not precisely discussed in *Capital* but rather in the philosophical works of Marx, as well as in a posthumously published manuscript called 'Alienated Labour'. Without these early works of Marx, it would be difficult to understand *Capital*.

For Marx, man is essentially a *producing artist*. This is what distinguishes him from the animal. Both are placed in nature, better still, both are products of nature – geography and history – and realize their potential only in and through nature, which is given to us at the outset as an inorganic, objective world. The animal does not transform nature; he *naturally* extracts from it his 'immediate means of subsistence' in the sense that he is moved by his instinct. He does not aim beyond the satisfaction of his material needs.

If, on the other hand, man realizes himself *in* nature, he does so even more *through* nature. He does not passively submit to the productive forces of nature, he acts on them:

> [Animals] produce only under the compulsion of direct physical needs, while man produces when he is free from physical need and only truly produces in freedom from such need. . . . Animals construct only in accordance with the standards and needs of the species to which they belong, while man knows how to produce in accordance with the standards of every species and knows how to apply the appropriate standard to the object. Thus man constructs also in accordance with the laws of beauty.[1]

Man realizes himself as a man only by realizing nature, by trans-

1. Karl Marx, 'Alienated Labour', in *Karl Marx: Early Writings*, trans. and ed. T. B. Bottomore (London: C. A. Watts, 1963), 1st manuscript, p. 128.

forming it to his measure, and by becoming a *creator* of culture, of civilization.

Man, then, has rights – over his activity as a conscious producer, over his 'expenditure of labour', and over the objects he produces. In the capitalistic system, however, man undergoes a double alienation, a dual frustration, from the fact that he sells to the capitalist his 'labour power', which is the source of all human good. The product of his labour is snatched from the producer, in the form of surplus-value, to increase the capital. 'So much does the performance of work appear as vitiation that the worker is vitiated to the point of starvation.'[1] The alienation is not only in the product; it is in production itself which, by its human character, should be *free* activity. In the capitalist system, production is imposed on the producer from the outside. 'It is forced labour.' It is not the satisfaction of an inner need for creation, 'but a means to satisfy needs external' to man. '[It is] the personal physical and mental energy of the worker, his personal life (for what is life but activity?) as an activity which is directed against himself, independent of him and not belonging to him. This is the *self-alienation* as against the alienation of the thing.'[2]

Alienated from himself, the salaried producer becomes a stranger to other men behind a screen of objective products. Passively, he is dominated by his products; actively, by his employer, to whom the products belong. Man has become a wolf to man. But the alienation in turn affects the employer, who betrays his human nature. He becomes more and more a parasite, leaving to the technician the role of thinker and inspirer that he himself should play. Thus he destroys the natural harmony of persons and things.

How can one prevent this mutual alienation and, *mutatis mutandis*, regain the natural equilibrium of a patriarchal economy? Here we refer especially to Engels, who is often clearer than Marx though less profound. Before the establishment of capitalism, the productive forces – that is to say, the instruments of production – were weak. They belonged either to the individual or to the family in the framework of family cooperation. Little by little, the factory replaced the individual tools. The work, once individual or cooperative, becomes collective, while

1. Ibid., p. 122.   2. Ibid., p. 126.

the productive forces and the products remain individual and private property is maintained.

This is the imbalance that breaks natural laws and alienates at once both worker and employer. The alienation of the bourgeois lulls him to sleep instead of waking him, but the proletariat, on the contrary, more seriously alienated, is conscious of his physical and moral suffering. Whence class antagonism, which the accumulation of capital and periodic depressions exacerbate, and which calls for revolutionary solution. Inevitably, the proletariat will one day seize political power and establish its 'dictatorship'.

'In reality,' Marx writes, 'it is up to the practical materialist to revolutionize the existing world, to attack in a practical manner and to change conditions.' It is a matter of restoring to the productive forces and the products themselves their natural appropriation, which, under a system of collective labour, can only be collective. Thus the natural balance will be restored. Man will stop being dominated by his products and will dominate them. He will institute a planned, rational organization of production. Only thus will he act on nature instead of being acted on by nature. Then the totality of goods produced by men according to each man's capacity will go to the totality of men according to each man's needs. And man will find his place and his role in the universe. The reign of *freedom* will then succeed that of *necessity*.

We have been able to present merely an outline of Marxian thought. This is difficult to condense into a few pages, for it is much richer and contains many more nuances than 'Marxists' usually claim. Sometimes it may even seem contradictory. Let us now examine it with a critical eye.

We may wonder, first of all, whether the socialism and economics of Marx are really 'scientific'. Yes and no. *No*, if one means by scientific the exact knowledge and formulation of economic facts in laws that permit one to foresee and to organize a balanced economy. *Yes*, if science is defined as comprehension of the real, if it consists of deciphering the complexities basic to economic facts, and especially man's relations to these facts, and if its aim is to reveal 'the economic law of motion in modern society'.

So we must not seek in Marx, not even in *Capital*, an exposé of economic laws. Considering them more or less as contingent 'appearances', Marx was not interested in them. Moreover, he went so far as to predict changes that have not occurred.

In *Conflit du siècle*, Fritz Sternberg has analysed almost all the changes in economic, social and political reality that have taken place since the publication of *Capital*. (They have been listed by other writers.) The changes are important, but in our résumé of Marx's theories, we skipped over most of them; we shall now mention only a few, while noting the recent studies made in France by the Autonomous Socialist Party:

(*a*) The 'class struggle' is much more complex than Marx thought. In fact, the working class is not a simple reality. Moreover, it is diminishing, while the several categories of salaried workers with dissimiliar interests are increasing.

(*b*) The peasants, whom Marx considered more or less impervious to revolutionary ferment and dedicated 'to the stupidity of rural life', have, in underdeveloped countries, belied his judgement.

(*c*) The theory of capitalist concentration has not been borne out by the facts. On the contrary, the number of small and medium-sized businesses continues to grow in Western European countries.

(*d*) Though periodic economic crises have not ceased, they are becoming rarer, and we cannot reasonably foresee a general cataclysm ending the capitalist system, which is adjusting to economic and social evolution.

(*e*) 'Socialism' has not triumphed in the industrial nations of Western Europe as Marx predicted it would, but in the underdeveloped nations of Eastern Europe and Asia.

By excessive simplification of the 'class-struggle' theory – a more precise translation of *Klassenkampf* would be 'class war'[1] – Marx overestimated the role of the determinism of things and underestimated man's freedom and the organizing power of the capitalist state. Thanks to trade-union activity and a more enlightened middle class, the capitalist state has been able, by a policy of intervention and rational organization, progressively to reduce the surplus-value. This surplus-value, reduced by more equitable taxation, has permitted the productive investments of

1. See André Vène, *Vie et doctrine de Karl Marx* (Paris: Éditions de la Nouvelle France, 1946), p. 315.

the post-war era and the institution of social security. Marx welcomed social legislation; in his opinion, it would lead to increased unemployment, bitter class antagonism, and finally, to the revolution. However, social reforms have produced quite the opposite effects.

We may also observe in passing that Marx did not pay enough attention to the role of cooperatives as preached by the utopian socialists. We know from the Scandinavian socialist democracies that these have proved their worth. In Western labour unions, a will to reform has replaced a will to revolt. In the Communist countries, the 'dictatorship of the proletariat', contrary to the teachings of Marx, has made the state an omnipotent, soulless monster, stifling the natural freedoms of the human being, and drying up the sources of art, without which life is not worth living.

One final word on this point. In Marx's day, colonialism was just beginning. He could not foresee its universal development during the second half of the nineteenth century. He spoke, of course, of 'the modern theory of colonization',[1] but merely in the etymological sense of the word. He had in mind only the European colonization of the United States. Furthermore, his macro-economic theory and almost blind confidence in proletarian generosity and conscience prevented him from anticipating the opposition that would develop between colonizers from the dominant countries and proletarians in the dominated territories. It is a now commonplace fact that the European masses' standard of living has been able to rise only at the expense of the standard of living of the masses in Asia and Africa. The economy of European nations consists fundamentally in selling manufactured products to underdeveloped countries at high prices and buying raw materials from them at the lowest possible cost. I am not talking about the United States of America. The problem is different with France, but if the prices paid for raw materials in African countries are subsidized, it is no less true that French prices are generally the highest in Europe. One compensates for the other. In a word, the European proletariat has profited from the colonial system; therefore, it has never really – I mean, effectively – opposed it.

1. *Capital*, I.

There we have a series of facts we must think about, we men from underdeveloped countries, men inspired by socialism. We must not consider Marx as an economist like Keynes, but as a sociologist, a philosopher. This would have astonished the founder of 'scientific socialism', since he refrained from 'philosophizing'. Yet his thought remains that of a philosopher. Beyond the economic 'appearances', it plunges into the human reality that causes them. For the *factual* view of things, Marx substitutes a profound insight into human needs. His is a new humanism, new because it is *incarnate*.

Humanism, the *philosophy of humanism*, rather than economics, is the basic character and positive contribution of Marxian thought. As we said earlier, Marx does not formulate laws from economic facts; he defines 'the economic law of motion of modern society', which is a social 'tendency' rather than a law. In his analysis, he advances by *postulates* and theories that explain the facts.

For a better understanding of the philosophy of humanism, we should like to return to the Marxian concept of labour. Here we should add to the extracts from 'Alienated Labour' a passage from *Capital*, one of the most beautiful and profound that Marx ever wrote. If labour defines man, primitive man is still only *homo faber*, scarcely distinguishable from the animal. His labour is an assimilation of nature, a transformation of nature to satisfy his vital needs, just as is animal activity. To the extent that he acts on nature and humanizes it, man acts 'on his own nature' and humanizes it at the same time. *Homo faber* becomes *homo sapiens*; he introduces 'consciousness and liberty' as well as artistic feeling into his labour. In so doing, he distinguishes himself from the animal:

> But what from the very first distinguishes the most incompetent architect from the best of bees is that the architect has built a cell in his head before he constructs it in wax. The labour process ends in the creation of something which, when the process began, already existed in an ideal form. What happens is not merely that the worker brings about a change of form in natural objects; at the same time, in the nature that exists apart from himself, he realizes his own purpose, the purpose which gives the law to his activities, the purpose to which he has to subordinate his own will. Nor is this subordination a momentary act. Apart from the exertion of his bodily organs, his purposive will, manifesting it-

self as attention, must be operative throughout the whole duration of the labour.[1]

Thus, if labour defines man, a certain kind of labour makes
him more than a man. Man realizes his full potential to the extent that there is division and socialization of labour. From
patriarchal cooperation to the factory, man grows gradually in
consciousness and in freedom. From master of a tool, he becomes master of the world. But, at the same time, he is separated
from the world and from himself: grandeur and wretchedness of
man in and because of labour. Marx's originality is that, starting
from purely materialistic postulates, he arrives at a vision of man
that yields, neither in truth nor in depth, to that of the greatest
philosophers. It recalls the vision of Pascal. This is Marx's
positive contribution: an incarnate conception of man based on
the material and social determinations of man.

This conception goes further than is generally recognized. In
this connexion we refer you to an article by Lucien Goldmann,
'La Réification'.[2] Goldmann tells us that he borrowed the term
from Georg Lukács. Reification appears in the Marxian analysis
of value. In capitalist society, mercantile relations gradually replace human relations; consciousness tends in its forms of
thought and feeling to empty itself from the inside. Its manifestations – religion, ethics, art and literature – lose their real,
autonomous character as they are invaded by the 'ghostly
realities' of the economy. *Homo sapiens* becomes *homo oeconomi-
cus* and regresses to the status of the animal:

> The mercantile economy, and especially capitalist economy,
> tends, in the producer's consciousness, to replace use-value with
> exchange-value, and concrete, significant human relations with
> abstract universal relations between sellers and buyers; thus it
> tends to substitute the *quantitative* for the *qualitative* throughout
> human life [my italics].[3]

Although Goldmann's thought is shaded, we cannot fully accept
his statement that, 'In classic capitalist society, only the proletariat is in a situation that allows it to refuse reification and to
restore its true human character to all the spiritual problems [again

1. *Capital*, I.
2. Lucien Goldmann, '*La Réification*', *Les Temps modernes*, Nos. 156–7
(February–March 1959).
3. Ibid., p. 1449.

my italics].'[1] As Marx has shown us, the proletarian is in fact victim of the greatest alienation. That is why he avoids labour and takes refuge in the satisfaction of animal needs. His sole superiority over the bourgeois is that he feels his estrangement. If, historically, he refused this alienation, it was always because of the initiative of less alienated bourgeois intellectuals, who showed him the road to liberation. It is true that every worker who reflects about problems is already an intellectual. So it is with colonized people, who are the victims of a multiple aliena-tion. The intellectuals – often European intellectuals – have awakened them and made them discover their spiritual, human riches. In truth, and this follows from Marxian analysis, all Western civilization, all machine-civilization, all factory-civili-zation, is reified. We shall see what role the colonized peoples must play in the struggle for *de-reification*.

Along with its positive, revolutionary contributions, however, Marx's humanism presents a negative aspect. Its weakness is that it proceeds from a one-sided conception of man and universe, or perhaps, more exactly, from an equivocal conception. Marx's ambition – and his paradox – has always been to express, throughout his entire work, the dignity of man and his spiritual needs without ever resorting to metaphysics or ethics or religion, not even philosophy. He is a philosopher in spite of himself. Moreover, one needs only to re-read Marx carefully to perceive that his vocabulary, in his numerous lyrical passages, is one of indignation because it is based on an ethic.

In the name of whom or of what, after all, does Marx dare to affirm the dignity of man and man's right to appropriate all the products of his labour? In the name of whom, or of what, does he condemn night labour, child labour, and the African slave trade, unless it be in the name of a certain quality or a transcendent something beyond man? Science notes facts and their relations; it explains, it does not demand. It cannot pass from a factual to a value judgement. We do not underestimate the strength of the arguments advanced by Lucien Goldmann in his article '*Propos dialectiques*' (subtitled '*Y a-t-il une sociologie marxiste?*'). Lean-ing on Max Adler and Georg Lukács, Goldmann shows that Marxism is a *sociology*, at once historical knowledge and action, theory and *praxis*, science and ethics:

1. Ibid., p. 1465.

The dialectical position of Lukács is specifically characterized by the refusal to subordinate the means to the end, the end to the means, the group to the individual, or the individual to the group, etc. End, means, group, individual, party, masses, etc., being in dialectical thinking elements constituting a dynamic totality, within which it is a question of combating, in each concrete situation, the ever-present danger of the primacy of one or another of these with relationship to the others and to the ensemble.[1]

We agree with Goldmann that Lukács's position restores the 'true inner coherence' to Marx's work. We do not feel that it eliminates 'the so-called dualities'.

At this point, we must apply to Marx the Marxian method, the historical method. His life and works reveal him to be primarily a philosopher, a pupil of Hegel and Feuerbach; later, in Paris, he studied 'economics, the history of the revolution, and socialism. The great thinker Saint-Simon exerted the most considerable influence on him'.[2] From the French idealistic sociologists, later termed 'Utopian', Marx inherited his concern for ethics. He assimilated, in the etymological sense of the word, German philosophy and French ethics, while transforming them so that they appear only as fine threads in his writing, especially in *Capital*.

As he advanced in his career, Marx gradually placed more and more stress on materialism, means and *praxis*, while the philosophical thought and ethical concerns of his earlier works were toned down. But, although de-emphasized and hidden, they did not disappear entirely. At the risk of becoming repetitious, we may say that they subtend Marx's writings. One can detect in Marx more than a philosophy and an ethic – a metaphysics, a *Weltanschauung*, but brought back from God to man, from the transcendent to the *immanent*. Father Bigo is right to speak of the 'ambivalence of Marx'. And, in a review of *Capital*, published in the Stuttgart *Observer* on 27 December 1867, Engels put it even more clearly: 'In so far as the book itself is concerned, we must carefully distinguish between the solid, positive pre-

1. Lucien Goldmann, *'Propos dialectiques: Y a-t-il une sociologie marxiste?' Les Temps modernes*, No. 140 (October 1957), p. 743.
2. Karl Kautsky, *'Introduction à l'ensemble du marxisme'*, in Karl Marx, *Le Capital* (Paris: Alfred Costes, 1949), I, xxiv.

sentations and the suggestive conclusions that the author draws from them.' Later on, he explained:

> It is quite different with the author's subjective conclusions, the manner in which he imagines and presents to others the ultimate result of the present movement of social evolution. This has nothing to do with what we call the positive part of the book. Moreover, if space permitted us to discuss the point, we could perhaps indicate that those *subjective* whims are refuted by his own objective expositions [Engels's italics].

This comment by Marx's most faithful collaborator – indeed, co-author – is not negligible. We need say no more about it. In Marx's work there is a positive contribution and a subjective tendency that contradicts it and reaches debatable conclusions. We need not reject the same conclusions that Engels rejects. Marx's atheism is, in our opinion, the fruit of this subjective tendency.

And yet atheism is deep in Marx; it impregnates his entire work, above all the *Philosophical Writings*. It is basic to him. For Marx, the most complete alienation of man stems from religion, because religion separates man from nature, from society and from himself in order to enclose him in an abstract world where he cannot realize his potential. In Marx's view, the religious act is the most absolute act of *dehumanization*. To support this contention, we could quote numerous passages; I shall cite only the famous sentence 'Religion is the opium of the masses'. Nevertheless, appearances to the contrary, atheism is not necessary to the 'positive part' of Marx's work. In some of his writings, he even goes so far as to refuse its 'mediation'.

Historically, Marx's atheism can be explained both by his family environment and by reasons of *praxis*. His father was a Jew who had been compelled to embrace Christianity. Thus young Marx never knew anything but the external practices of religion; he never lived it. Another historical fact is that the triumph of capitalism in Christian countries of the West was accompanied by serious religious deviations. Marx's atheism can be considered as a *reaction of Christian origin against the historical deviations of Christianity*, which violated the essence of religion all the less because the idea of alienation was of religious origin.

Translated by Mercer Cook

RAYA DUNAYEVSKAYA

⊚ ⊚

Marx's Humanism Today

RAYA DUNAYEVSKAYA has lectured widely in the United
States, Western Europe and Africa. Her writings include
*Marxism and Freedom from 1776 until Today; Nationalism,
Communism, Marxist Humanism and the Afro-Asian Revo-
lutions;* and *Existentialism: A Critical Appraisal of Jean-
Paul Sartre's Philosophical Works and Developments.*

It was during the decade of the First International (1864–74)
– a decade that saw both the Civil War in America and the Paris
Commune – that Marx restructured[1] the many drafts of *Capital*
and published the first two editions of Volume I.

Capital sets forth a new concept of theory, a new dialectical
relationship between theory and practice, and a shift of emphasis from the idea of history as the history of theory to the idea of
history as the history of production. It signifies Marx's 'return'
to his own philosophic humanism after more than a decade of
concentration on economics and empiric studies of the class
struggles of his day. Not surprisingly, this return is on a more
concrete level, which, rather than diminishing Marx's original
humanist concepts, deepens them. This is obvious in the section
'The Working Day', which Marx first decided to write in 1866
under the impact of the mass movement for the shortening of
the working day following the conclusion of the Civil War in the
United States. It is obvious in 'The Fetishism of Commodities',
which Marx informs us he changed 'in a significant manner'

1. In his Preface to Volume II of Marx's *Capital* (Kerr edn), Friedrich
Engels lists the original manuscripts in such a way that the pagination tells
the story of the restructuring. For my analysis of this, see pp. 87–91 of
Marxism and Freedom (New York: Twayne, 1958, 1964).

after the Paris Commune. It is obvious in the original categories he created for his economic analysis and the creative practice of the Hegelian dialectic. Humanism gives Marx's *magnum opus* its force and direction. Yet more Western scholars of Marxism are content either to leave the relationship between the now-famous *Economic and Philosophic Manuscripts of 1844*[1] and *Capital* implicit, or to make the continuity explicit only in so far as the ethical foundations of Marxism are concerned.[2] This, it seems to me, leaves the door wide open for those who wish to transform Marx's humanism, both as philosophy and as historic fact, into an abstract which would cover up concrete economic exploitation, actual lack of political freedom, and the need to abolish the conditions preventing 'realization' of Marx's philosophy, i.e. the reunification of mental and manual abilities in the individual himself, the 'all-rounded' individual who is the body and soul of Marx's humanism.

The 1844 *Manuscripts* didn't just 'pave the way' for 'scientific socialism'. Humanism wasn't just a stage Marx 'passed through' on his voyage of discovery to 'scientific economics' or 'real revolutionary politics'. Humanist philosophy is the very foundation of the integral unity of Marxian theory, which cannot be fragmented into 'economics', 'politics', 'sociology', much less identified with the Stalinist monolithic creation, held on to so firmly by both Khrushchev and Mao Tse-tung.

Of all the editions of *Capital*, from its first publication in 1867 until the last before Marx died in 1883, the French edition (1872–5) alone contained the changes that had, as Marx put it in the Afterword, 'scientific value independent of the original'. The revolutionary action of the Parisian masses in 'storming the heavens'[3] and taking destiny into their own hands clarified for

1. Marx's 1884 *Manuscripts* are now available in several English translations, including one issued in Moscow, but one of those more readily available is by T. B. Bottomore, and is included in *Marx's Concept of Man* by Erich Fromm (New York: Frederick Ungar, 1961). Outside of the essay on 'Alienated Labor', I am, however, using my own translation and therefore not paginating the references.

2. See especially *The Ethical Foundations of Marxism* by Eugene Kamenka (New York: Frederick A. Praeger, 1962; London: Routledge & Kegan Paul).

3. *The Civil War in France*, by Karl Marx, is widely available in many languages both as a separate pamphlet and in Marx's *Selected Works* and *Collected Works*.

Marx the two most fundamental theoretical problems: the accumulation of capital, and the fetishism of commodities. Just as his analysis of the struggles to shorten the working day became pivotal to the structure of *Capital*, so these additions became crucial for its spirit, i.e. for the future inherent in the present. The changes were of two kinds. One was tantamount to a prediction of what we today call state capitalism – the ultimate development of the law of concentration and centralization of capital 'in the hands of one single capitalist, or those of one single corporation'.[1] The second was the illumination of the fetishism of commodities inherent in the value-form as emanating from 'the form itself'.[2] Marx concluded that only *freely* associated labour can abrogate the law of value; *only* 'freely associated men'[3] can strip the fetishism from commodities.

At this moment in history, when established state powers claim 'to practise' or to base themselves on Marxism, it is essential to re-establish what Marx himself meant by practice. It was freedom. The notion of freedom, always Marx's point of departure and of return, is concretized through a most painstaking and original analysis of the 'inexorable laws' of capitalist development. This discloses *how* the proletariat, as 'substance' (or mere object of an exploitative society) becomes 'subject', i.e. revolts against the conditions of alienated labour, *thereby* achieving 'the negation of the negation', or self-emancipation. In a word, *Capital* is the culmination of the twenty-five years of labour that began when Marx, in 1843, first broke with bourgeois society and melded what he considered its highest achievements in thought – English political economy, French revolutionary doctrine, Hegelian philosophy – into a theory of liberation, a new philosophy of human activity which he called 'a thoroughgoing Naturalism or Humanism'.

The Hungarian Revolution of 1956 transformed Marx's humanism from an academic debate to a question of life and death. Interest in it intensified the following year when the 'Hundred Flowers' blossomed briefly in China before the totalitarian state caused them to wither abruptly.[4] From 1958 to 1961

1. *Capital* (Chicago: Charles H. Kerr, 1906), Vol. I, p. 688.
2. Ibid., p. 82.
3. Ibid., p. 92.
4. The indispensable book for the English reader is *The Hundred*

65

the African revolutions gave proof of a new, third world whose underlying philosophy, again, was humanism.[1]

The Cold War and McCarthyism helped keep the United States isolated from the West European rediscovery of Marx's 1844 Humanist Essays in the mid 1940s and early 1950s. Now, however, Americans have an opportunity to make up in comprehensiveness of discussion what was lost in the belated start.[2]

Flowers Campaign and the Chinese Intellectuals by Roderick MacFarquhar (New York: Frederick A. Praeger, 1960; London: Stevens). The voices of revolt in China should then be compared with those in Eastern Europe. By now the books, not to mention pamphlets and articles, on the Hungarian Revolution are legion. A few which I consider important for tracing the role that Marx's humanism played are the following: *Imre Nagy on Communism* (New York: Frederick A. Praeger, 1957); François Fejtö, *Behind the Rape of Hungary* (New York: David McKay, 1957); *The Hungarian Revolution*, A White Book edited by Melvin J. Lasky (New York: Frederick A. Praeger, 1957); *Bitter Harvest*, edited by Edmund O. Stillman with Introduction by François Bondy (New York: Frederick A. Praeger, 1959; London: Thames & Hudson). For eye-witness reports, and especially those relating to the Workers' Councils, the issues of *The Review* (periodical published by the Imre Nagy Institute, Brussels) is quintessential. Some reports also appeared in the magazine *East Europe*, which did a competent job on Poland, especially in the publication of the debate on Marx's humanism between the leading philosophers in Poland, Adam Schaff and Leszek Kolakowski. Both of these philosophers are also translated in the collection entitled *Revisionism*, edited by Leopold Labedz (New York: Frederick A. Praeger, 1962; London: Allen & Unwin).

1. *On African Socialism* by Léopold Sédar Senghor (New York: American society of African Culture, 1959); Sekou Touré's 'Africa's Path in History' was excerpted for the English reader in *Africa South*, April-June 1960, Capetown; now available only abroad. See also my *Nationalism, Communism, Marxist-Humanism and the Afro-Asian Revolutions* (American, 1958, and English, 1961, editions available at *News & Letters*, Detroit, Michigan).

2. I do not mean to say that I accept the West European intellectual's attitude on either the question of the degree of belatedness, or the low level of discussion in the United States. Four or five years before Europe's first rediscovery of Marx's early essays, when Europe was under the heel of fascism, Herbert Marcuse dealt with them in his *Reason and Revolution*. It is true that this was based on the German text of the essays, that no English translation was available and that the discussion of Professor Marcuse's seminal work was limited to small groups. It is also true that I had great difficulty in convincing either commercial publishers or university presses that they ought to publish Marx's humanist essays or Lenin's *Philosophic Notebooks*. I succeeded in getting both these writings published only by including them as appendices to my *Marxism and Freedom* (New York: Twayne, 1958). Even then they did not become available

The Freedom Now movements of the Negroes, on the one hand, and, on the other hand, the 1962 missile crisis over Cuba, which made real the nuclear threat, have helped rekindle the debate. In his own way, the scholar too must grapple with the inner identity of the Marxian economic, political, sociological, scientific and philosophic categories. It was the late, non-Marxist, anti-Hegelian economist, Joseph Schumpeter, who pinpointed Marx's genius as 'the *idea* of theory', the transformation of 'historic narrative into historic *raisonné*'.[1]

Elsewhere[2] I have made a detailed analysis of all four volumes of *Capital* and their relationship to the 1844 *Manuscripts*. Here space considerations limit me to the two basic theories – the Marxian analysis of value and the fetishism of commodities – which are, in reality, the single, decisive, unified theory of alienation, or historical materialism, dialectically understood.

Marx's discovery that 'it is not the consciousness of men that determines their existence, but, on the contrary, their social existence that determines their consciousness'[3] was no departure from either his own theory of alienated labour or the theory of alienation as the central core of the Hegelian dialectic. But Marx's precise analysis of the actual labour process under capitalism is more concrete, alive, shattering – and, of course, revolutionary – than any stage of alienation in Hegel's *Phenomenology of Mind*. In true Hegelian fashion Marx focuses on creativity, but, unlike Hegel, he bases it on the actual process of production.

---

to a mass audience. It was not until 1961, when Erich Fromm included a translation of the 1844 *Manuscripts* in *Marx's Concept of Man*, that Marx's humanism reached a mass audience in the United States, and received widespread attention in American journals. Nevertheless, I see no substantive reason for the intellectual arrogance of the European Marxologists since, in Europe as in the United States, it was only after the Hungarian Revolution that the discussion of humanism reached the level of either concreteness or urgency. When I refer to the belatedness of the discussion, I have in mind the long period between the time the 1844 *Manuscripts* were first published by the Marx–Engels Institute in Russia, in 1927, under the editorship of Ryazanov, and the time they received general attention.

1. *A History of Economic Analysis* by Joseph Schumpeter (Oxford: O.U.P., 1954).
2. *Marxism and Freedom*. See especially Chs. V–VIII.
3. *A Contribution to the Critique of Political Economy* (Chicago: Charles H. Kerr), p. 11.

F

There, facing not just an idea but a *human being* who has ideas, Marx develops his earlier concept of the worker's 'quest for universality'.[1] The 'new passions and new forces' he now sees are born not only to overthrow the old order, but to construct a new one, 'a society in which the full and free development of every individual is the ruling principle'.[2]

So organically related are the economic, political and philosophic concepts in *Capital* that, when, in 1943,[3] the Russian theoreticians first openly broke with the Marxian analysis of value, they had to deny the dialectic structure of *Capital* and ask that, in 'teaching' it, Chapter I be omitted. It does not speak highly of 'Western' philosophy that it never saw the philosophic implications in this economic debate, and therefore also failed to discern the reason why the theoretical magazine of Soviet Marxism (*Under the Banner of Marxism*), which had carried on the tradition of Marx's dialectic philosophy, ceased its publication. Thereafter, without further ado or any reference to any previous interpretation of Marxian economics, the revision of the Marxian analysis of value became the standard Communist analysis. The wholeness of Marxian theory has always been the *bête noire* of established Marxism. It took the collapse of the Second International and a break with his own philosophic past to make Lenin, at the end of 1914, fully grasp the organic connexion of Marxian economics with Hegelian philosophy. And from then on he became uncompromising in his criticism of all Marxists, himself included. In one of his 'aphorisms' he wrote, 'It is impossible fully to grasp Marx's *Capital*, and especially the first chapter, if you have not studied and understood the *whole* of Hegel's *Logic*. Consequently, none of the Marxists for the past half century has understood Marx!'

There is no more remarkable piece of analysis in the annals of

1. *Poverty of Philosophy* (Chicago: Charles H. Kerr), p. 157.
2. *Capital* (Kerr edn), Vol. I, p. 649.
3. *Pod Znamenem Marxisma* (*Under the Banner of Marxism*), Nos. 7–8/1943. The crucial article on the law of value from this issue was translated by me under the title, 'Teaching of Economics in the Soviet Union'. Along with my commentary, 'A New Revision of Marxian Economics', the article was published in *The American Economic Review* (September 1944). The controversy around it, in which Professors Oscar Lange, Leon Rogin and Paul A. Baran participated in the pages of that journal, lasted for a year, at the end of which (September 1945) my rejoinder, 'Revision or Reaffirmation of Marxism?' was published.

political economy – and no more Hegelian kind of writing in Marx's 'early Hegelian period' – than the final section of Chapter I of *Capital*, entitled 'The Fetishism of Commodities'. There philosphy and economics are connected with history as integrally as content and form are welded together in a great work of literature. By the time Marx introduced further changes into the French edition, after the Paris Commune, those fifteen pages were as tightly drawn as the strings of a violin. We must remember that Marx considered the greatest achievement of the Commune to be 'its own working existence'. The *totality* of the reorganization of society by the Communards gave Marx a new insight into the whole question of the *form* of value, not only as it was historically determined, but also as it conditioned bourgeois thought in turn. Under capitalistic conditions of production, philosophy had been reduced to an ideology, i.e. false consciousness. The categories of thought proper to capitalistic production were uncritically accepted by all, including even Adam Smith and David Ricardo, the authors of the epoch-making discovery that labour was the source of all value. This is why despite their discovery, they could not dissolve the fetishism of commodities. Classical political economy, concludes Marx, met its historic barrier here.

The commodity form of the products of labour became a fetish because of the perverse relationship of subject to object – of living labour to dead capital. Relations between men appear as the relation between things because in our alienated society that is all 'they really are'.[1] Dead capital is the master of living labour. The fetishism of commodities is the opiate that, to use a Hegelian expression, passes itself off as 'the very *nature* of the mind'[2] to all *except* the proletariat who daily suffer from the domination of dead labour, the stranglehold of the machine. Therefore, concludes Marx, no one can strip the fetishism from the commodities *except freely associated labour*. Obviously the Russian theoreticians, in 1943, were determined that no one should.

The necessary ideology to cover up the exploitation of the

1. *Capital*, Vol. I, p. 84.
2. See Hegel on 'The Third Attitude to Objectivity': 'What I discover in my consciousness is thus exaggerated into a fact of the consciousness of all and even passed off for the very *nature* of the mind' (Hegel's *Logic*, first Wallace translation, Oxford: O.U.P., 1892).

labourer did not change its essence when it changed its form from the private to the state capitalism that calls itself Communism. Nor has the ideological rift between China and Russia undermined the exploitative relationship in either land. Were Marx to return to earth, he would have no difficulty whatever in recognizing in its new form – the State Plan and its fetishism – the state capitalist development he predicted as the ultimate effect of the inexorable laws of capitalist development. Our generation should understand better than any previous generation that it is not a question of nationalized *v.* private property. It is a question of freedom. Wherever and whenever freedom was limited, Marx struck out against the barrier, in practice and in theory. Thus, when classical political economists spoke of 'free labour', by which they meant wage labour, Marx wrote caustically: 'For them there was history, but history is no more.'

It should be obvious that Marx's primary theory of value or 'abstract', 'value-producing' labour, is a theory of alienated labour. In the humanist essays Marx explained why he analysed economic facts

> in conceptual terms as *alienated labour*. . . . How does it happen, we may ask, that man *alienates his labour?* How is this alienation founded in the nature of human development? We have already done much to solve the problem in so far as we have *transformed* the question concerning the *origin of private property* into a question about the relation between *alienated labour* and the process of development of mankind. For in speaking of private property one believes oneself to be dealing with something external to mankind. But in speaking of labour one deals directly with mankind itself. This new formulation of the problem already contains its solution.[1]

By the time he completed *Capital*, however, Marx felt the need to create economic categories to analyse the alien character of labour under capitalism both as an activity in the factory and as a commodity in the market where 'alone rule Freedom, Equality, Property and Bentham'.[2]

Marx created special economic categories not only to expound his theory of value and surplus-value, but also to show how

1. See 'Alienated Labour', in *Marx's Concept of Man* by Erich Fromm, pp. 103, 108.
2. *Capital*, Vol. I, p. 195.

degraded human relations were at the point of production itself. By splitting the category of labour into labour as activity and labour power as a commodity – as if the labourer could indeed disjoint his hands from his body and have them retain their function – Marx was able to show that, since labour power cannot be so disembodied, it is the labourer himself who enters the factory. And in the factory, continues Marx, the labourer's ability becomes a mere appendage to a machine and his concrete labour is reduced to a mass of congealed, abstract labour.

Now there is, of course, no such creature as an 'abstract labourer'; one is a miner or a tailor or a steelworker or a baker. Nevertheless, the *perverse* nature of capitalist production is such that man is not master of the machine; the machine is master of the man. By the instrumentality of the machine, which 'expresses' itself in the ticking of a factory clock, a man's skill becomes unimportant so long as he produces a given quantity of products in a given time. Labour time is the handmaiden of the machine which accomplishes the fantastic transformation of all concrete labours into one abstract mass.

Marx considered his analysis of concrete and abstract labour his original contribution to political economy, 'the pivot on which a clear comprehension of political economy turns'.[1] In the process of his analysis of the capitalist's 'werewolf hunger for surplus labour' as 'a live monster that is fruitful and multiplies',[2] Marx creates two other new categories: constant *capital* (machines) and variable *capital* (wage labour). All labour, paid or unpaid, he insists, is *forced* labour. And this labour is so alien an activity that it has itself become a *form of capital*.

The precision, as well as originality, of this description of alienated labour is not, of course, merely a category of the 'deductive Hegelian dialectic'. It is a category of the dialectic *empiricism* of Marx re-creating an altogether new level of truth. Only politically motivated, self-induced blindness can, when reading Marx's pages upon pages on the labour process under capitalism, conclude either that the mature Marx departed from his theory of alienated labour, or that alienated labour is a 'leftover' from Marx's 'left Hegelian days' before he worked his way out of 'Hegelian gibberish' into 'scientific materialism'. At the

1. Ibid., p. 48. 2. Ibid., p. 217.

same time, because Marx's economic categories have so incontrovertible a class character, it is impossible to denude them of their class content. Although some of today's near-Marxists loudly proclaim the 'neutralization' of these categories, they apply them *to capitalism and to capitalism only*. Because the Marxian law of value is the supreme manifestation of capitalism, not even Stalin – at least not for very nearly two decades after he already had total power, the State Plan and the monolithic party – dared admit its operation in Russia since he claimed the land was 'socialist'. It was only in the midst of a world war that the Russian theoreticians openly broke with the Marxian concept; in practice, of course, the ruling bureaucracy had long since followed an exploitative course.

In 1947 Andrei Zhdanov dramatically (or at least loudly) demanded that 'the philosophical workers' replace the Hegelian dialectic with 'a new dialectical law': criticism and self-criticism. By 1955 the critique of Marxian concepts concerned his humanism. V. A. Karpushin wrote in 'Marx's Working Out of the Materialist Dialectics in the Economic-Philosophic Manuscripts in the Year 1844':

> Marx was the first philosopher who went beyond the confines of philosophy and from the point of view of practical life and practical needs of the proletariat analysed the basic question of philosophy as a truly scientific method of revolutionary change and knowledge of the actual world.[1]

The Russian Communists were not, however, about to favour 'revolutionary change' where revolutionary change meant *their* downfall. Therefore, when the Hungarian Revolution tried the following year to transform reality by *realizing* philosophy, that is to say, by making freedom from Russian Communism a reality, the debate ended in machine-gun fire. Thus the violation of the *logos* of Marxian theory was followed by the destruction of liberty itself.

Soon after, the Russian theoreticians unloosed an unbridled, vitriolic attack on all opponents of *established* Communism, whom they gratuitously labelled 'revisionists'. Unfortunately, too many Western scholars accepted the term and referred to the ruling Communists as the 'dogmatists', despite such wild

---

1. *Voprosy Filosofii (Questions of Philosophy)*, No. 3/1955.

gyrations and 'flexibility' as, on the eve of the Second World War, the Hitler–Stalin Pact and the united front between Mao Tse-tung and Chiang Kai-shek; and, more recently, the rift between Russia and China. At the same time, the single grain of truth in the duality of Lenin's philosophic legacy – between the vulgarly materialistic *Materialism and Empirio-Criticism* and the creative dialectics of his *Philosophic Notebooks* – has provided a field day for the innate anti-Leninism of 'the West'. Elsewhere[1] I have analysed 'Mao's Thought', which is supposed to have made 'original contributions to Marxism', especially his *On Practice*, and *On Contradiction*, as they relate to his rise in power. Here I must limit myself to the fact that the humanist debate was in danger both of becoming a purely academic question, and of being separated from the 'political' debates on 'revisionism'. Fortunately Marxism does not exist only in books, nor is it the possession only of state powers. It is in the daily lives of working people trying to reconstruct society on new beginnings.

The liberation from Western imperialism, not only in Africa but in Latin America (Fidel Castro too first called his revolution 'humanist'), unfurled a humanist banner. Thereupon the Russian Communist line changed. Where, at first, it was claimed that Leninism needed no sort of humanization, nor any of the reforms proposed by the proponents of 'humanist socialism', the claim now became that the Soviets were the rightful inheritors of 'militant humanism'. Thus M. B. Mitin, who has the august title of Chairman of the Board of the All-Union Society for the Dissemination of Political and Scientific Knowledge, stated that Khrushchev's Report to the Twenty-first Congress of the Russian Communist Party was 'the magnificent and noble conception of Marxist–Leninist socialist humanism'.[2] And in 1963, at the thirteenth International Congress of Philosophy, held in Mexico, it was the Soviet delegation that entitled one of its

1. See the new chapter, 'The Challenge of Mao Tse-tung' in the paperback edition of *Marxism and Freedom* (New York: Twayne, 1964). For an analysis of a similar perversion of Lenin's partisanship in philosophy into Stalin's monolithic 'party-ness in philosophy', see the well-documented and perceptive analysis *Soviet Marxism and Natural Science, 1917–1932* by David Joravsky (New York: Columbia University Press, 1961; London: Routledge & Kegan Paul).

2. *Pravda*, 6 February 1959. The English translation used here appears in *The Current Digest of the Soviet Press*, 3 June 1959.

reports 'humanism in the Contemporary World'.[1] Thus, curiously, Western intellectuals can thank the Russian Communists for throwing the ball back to them; once again, we are on the track of discussing humanism.

Let us not debase freedom of thought to the point where it is no more than the other side of the coin of thought control. One look at our institutionalized studies on 'Marxist Leninism' as the 'know your enemy' type of course will show that, in methodology, these are no different from what is being taught under established Communism, although they are supposed to teach 'opposite principles'. The point is this: unless freedom of thought means an underlying philosophy for the realization of the forward movement of humanity, thought, at least in the Hegelian sense, cannot be called 'an Idea'. Precisely because, to Hegel, 'only that which is an object of freedom can be called an Idea', even his Absolutes breathed the earthy air of freedom. Our age can do no less. It is true that the Marxian dialectic is not only political or historical, but also cognitive. However, to claim that Marx's concept of the class struggle is a 'myth' and his 'glorification' of the proletariat only 'the end product of his philosophy of alienation'[2] flies in the face of theory and of fact. In this respect, George Lichtheim's criticism that such an American analysis is 'a sort of intellectual counterpart to the late Mr Dulles's weekly sermon on the evils of communism'[3] has validity.

Marx's humanism was neither a rejection of idealism nor an acceptance of materialism, but the truth of both, and therefore a new unity. Marx's 'collectivism' has, as its very soul, the individualistic element. That is why the young Marx felt compelled to separate himself from the 'quite vulgar and unthinking communism which completely negates the personality of man'. Because alienated labour was the essence of all that was perverse in capitalism, private or state, 'organized' or 'anarchic', Marx concluded his 1844 attack on capitalism with the statement that

1. The report of this conference by M. B. Mitin appears in *Voprosy Filosofii*, No. 11/1953. For a different report of the same conference see *Studies in Soviet Thought*, No. 4/1963 (Fribourg, Switzerland).

2. *Philosophy and Myth in Karl Marx* by Robert Tucker (Cambridge: C.U.P., 1961).

3. George Lichtheim's 'Western Marxist Literature 1953–1963' appears in *Survey*, No. 50, January 1964.

'communism, as such, is not the goal of human development, the form of human society'. Freedom meant more, a great deal more, than the abolition of private property. Marx considered the abolition of private property to be only 'the first transcendence'. Full freedom demanded a second transcendence. Four years after these humanist essays were written Marx published the historic *Communist Manifesto*. His basic philosophy was not changed by the new terminology. On the contrary. On the eve of the 1848 revolutions, the Manifesto proclaimed: 'The freedom of the individual is the basis of the freedom of all.' At the end of his life the concept remained unchanged. His *magnum opus*, like his life's activity, never deviated from the concept that only 'the development of human power, which is its own end' is the true 'realm of freedom'.[1] Again, our age should understand better than any other the reasons for the young Marx's insistence that the abolition of private property is only the first transcendence. 'Not until the transcendence of this mediation, which is nevertheless a necessary presupposition, does there arise positive Humanism, beginning from itself.'

'Positive Humanism' begins 'from itself' when mental and manual labour are reunited in what Marx calls the 'all-rounded' individual. Surely our nuclear age should be oppressively aware that the division between mental and manual labour, which has been the underlying principle of all class societies, has reached such monstrous proportions under capitalism that live antagonisms characterize not only production, but science itself. Marx anticipated the impasse of modern science when he wrote in 1844: 'To have one basis for life and another for science is *a priori* a lie.' We have been living this lie for one hundred and twenty years. The result is that the very survival of civilization as we have known it as at stake.

The task that confronts our age, it appears to this writer, is, first, to recognize that there is a movement from practice – from the actual struggles of the day – to theory; and, second, to work out the method whereby the movement *from theory* can meet it. A new relationship of theory to practice, a new appreciation of 'Subject', of live human beings struggling to reconstruct society, is essential. The challenge of our times is not to science or machines, but to men. The totality of the world crisis demands

1. *Capital*, Vol. III, pp. 954–5.

a new unity of theory and practice, a new relationship of workers and intellectuals. The search for a total philosophy has been disclosed dramatically by the new, third world of underdeveloped countries. But there are also evidences of this search in the struggles for freedom from totalitarian régimes, and in the West. To discern this mass search for a total philosophy it is necessary only to shed the stubbornest of all philosophies – the concept of 'the backwardness of the masses' – and *listen* to *their* thoughts, as they battle automation, fight for the end of discrimination or demand freedom *now*. Far from being intellectual abdication, this is the beginning of a new stage of cognition. This new stage in the self-liberation of the intellectual from dogmatism can begin only when, as Hegel put it, the intellectual feels the 'compulsion of thought to proceed to . . . concrete truths'.

The espousal of *partiynost* (party principle) as a philosophic principle is another manifestation of the dogma of 'the backwardness of the masses', by which intellectuals in state-capitalist societies rationalize their contention that the masses must be ordered about, managed, 'led'. Like the ideologists in the West, they forget all too easily that revolutions do not arise in the fullness of time to establish a party machine, but to reconstruct society on a human foundation. Just as *partiynost*, or monolithism, in politics throttles revolution instead of releasing the creative energy of new millions, so *partiynost* in philosophy stifles thought instead of giving it a new dimension. This is not an academic question for either the East or the West. Marxism is either a theory of liberation or it is nothing. In thought, as in life, it lays the basis for achieving a new *human* dimension, without which no society is truly viable. As a Marxist humanist, this appears to me the whole truth of Marx's humanism, both as philosophy and as reality.

MIHAILO MARKOVIĆ

⊚ ⊚

Humanism and Dialectic

MIHAILO MARKOVIĆ took part in the Yugoslav war of
liberation, 1941–5, before starting his studies at the University of Belgrade, Yugoslavia. He took his Ph.D. in
philosophy first at the University of Belgrade and then in
London at University College, where he studied under
A. J. Ayer and wrote a thesis on *The Concept of Logic.*
Since 1955 he has taught at the Serbian Academy of
Sciences and Arts. He is currently the head of the department of philosophy and sociology and, along with numerous other posts, edits the list of contemporary philosophy
for Nolit, a publishing house in Belgrade. Among his
several books are *Formalism in Contemporary Logic, The
Dialectical Theory of Meaning* and *Logic.*

I

One of the most fundamental problems in contemporary
philosophy, in my opinion, is how to make humanism a dialectical philosophy and dialectic a humanist method.

By *humanism* I mean a philosophy that tries to solve all philosophical problems in the perspective of Man, that embraces not
only anthropological problems, like human nature, alienation,
freedom, etc., but also all other ontological, epistemological and
axiological problems. A humanist *ontology* is a philosophical
theory of the objects of the *human* world, whose boundaries are
constituted by all kinds of human activity, including sense-per-
ception, the construction of theories, mathematical operation
with symbols, etc., as well as the physical operations of the
human body. A humanist *epistemology* is a theory of human knowledge. Logic should not be reduced to the investigation of exact,
purely formalized schemata of thinking, which presuppose a
much more precise language than the one actually used in the

empirical sciences and in ordinary life. A humanistic logic would investigate, besides formal logic, the general conditions of validity of a way of thinking which is expressed in real human language and which operates with vague concepts and incomplete statements. A humanist *axiology* is a theory of concrete, historically given and variable values – not of certain absolute, transcendental ideals and norms.

Such a humanist approach to philosophy demands a philosophical method which accepts the unity of subject and object, and of theory and practice; which is historical without falling into historicism; synthetic in that it takes into account the results of previous analysis; critical rather than ideological; and objective, without positivist blindness for human values and practical interests. The philosophical method that meets these requirements is the dialectical method developed and applied by Marx.

Many followers of Marx have misinterpreted his method and construed it as a more or less closed *methodology*, a *teaching*, supported by a number of *examples* from special sciences, mainly the natural sciences. But for Marx dialectic was primarily a weapon of social criticism, a means of explaining existing social reality that would immediately point the way to revolutionary action. This activist and revolutionary nature of dialectic needs to be revived and applied to the human problems of our time.

Contemporary humanist philosophy is, in most cases, methodologically below the level of Marx. It suffers from methodological eclecticism, from an abstract and unhistorical approach to the problems of man, and sometimes from the deliberate underestimation of the methodological questions. This situation is partly the result of a widespread revolt against Stalinist dogmatism, including the dogmatic form of dialectic found in the textbooks in *Diamat* (dialectical materialism) in the Stalinist era, with their muddled categories, arbitrarily selected examples and obvious propagandistic function.

Such a caricature of dialectic must be replaced by a methodological re-examination of contemporary progressive humanist thought.

2

Marx's dialectic is inseparable from his humanism. In his *Economic and Philosophical Manuscripts* Marx noted that Hegel's dialectic, as expounded in *Phenomenology of Mind*, is essentially a criticism of society, albeit a 'concealed, unclear and mystifying criticism'. The mystification lies in the concept of all forms of human alienation – religion, wealth, state power, politics, law, civil life – as alienation from pure abstract thought, which implies that the supersession of alienation is only a supersession in thought. This is the negative moment of Hegel's dialectic. The positive moment is 'the insight, expressed within alienation, into the *appropriation* of the objective being through the supersession of its alienation'. And Marx adds:

> It is the alienated insight into the *real objectification* of man, into the real appropriation of his objective being by the destruction of the *alienated* character of the objective world, by the annulment of its alienated mode of existence. In the same way, atheism as the annulment of God is the emergence of theoretical humanism, and communism as the annulment of private property is the vindication of real human life as man's property – the emergence of practical humanism.[1]

What Marx discovered in Hegel's *Phenomenology of Mind* remained the essential feature of his method. Dialectic is primarily a method of criticism – not, however, a criticism of concepts, but a criticism of real social relationships; not a fictitious and mystifying, but a real and truly revolutionary, criticism.

Marx's main critique of previous forms of materialism was their lack of dialectic, and of an initial humanist position. According to *Theses on Feuerbach*, materialism has considered reality an object of contemplation, and has thus neglected the importance of 'revolutionary practical and critical activity' (First Thesis). By such activity man proves the truth of the results of his thinking (Second Thesis), and changes the circumstances whose product he is (Third Thesis). The essence of this change is that man is able to grasp the world in all its contradictions, to criticize it theoretically, and to supersede it practically by removing its essential contradictions (Fourth Thesis). Philosophical criticism should not take as its object the human essence conceived as an abstract property of each individual. In order to be concrete, it

1. Marx, *Economic and Philosophical Manuscripts*, trans. T. B. Bottomore, ed. Erich Fromm in *Marx's Concept of Man* (New York: Frederick Ungar, 1961), pp. 188–9.

must aim at the real human essence – which is the totality of social relationships (Sixth Thesis).

This is a pregnant sketch of both a method and a humanist programme. *Das Kapital* is the realization of both. In the well-known postscript to the second edition of that work Marx stated explicitly what he considered dialectic to be:

> In its mystifying form dialectic has become a German fashion because it appears to be able to glorify reality. In its rational form it provokes the anger and horror of the bourgeoisie and its doctrinaire representatives because it is not satisfied with the positive understanding of the existing state of affairs – it also introduces an understanding of its negation, its necessary destruction, because it conceives every form in its movement and therefore in its transition, because it cannot bear to have anybody as a tutor, and because it is essentially critical and revolutionary.

3

After Marx, dialectic was interpreted mainly as an abstract doctrine of method, a set of ready-made formulae, which could be illustrated by an ever-increasing number of scientific results, and which were a sacrosanct and invariable part of ideology. Thus, Marxist dialectic started its alienated, ideological life.

This was inevitable. Once the labour movement became a vast organization, it had to secure a certain minimum ideological unity; it had to fix a *Weltanschauung* (which, under given conditions, might have been solely that of Marx); it had to give to Marx's theoretical and methodological principles a complete and rigid form which Marx himself would certainly not have subscribed to.

Even if it had not been made one of the fundamental elements of ideology, Marx's dialectic, like every great theory, would sooner or later have become a subject of scientific investigation.

Besides the transformation of dialectic into a methodology – which was conditioned both politically and scientifically – it was reasonable to expect the further development of dialectic as a concrete, alive method of looking critically at human reality. Such an expectation would have been in accordance with Marx's original conception; on the other hand, both reality and our knowledge of it have changed during the eight decades since Marx's death. Marx knew well that a method and a theory of a subject to which it is applicable are mutually dependent; therefore the application of a method is its self-development.

This further development of dialectic has not been realized for several reasons:

(a) Dialectic has always been a favourite target for the attacks of bourgeois ideologues who have called it unscientific, speculative, mystifying, etc. In *Anti-Dühring* Engels was already facing the central problem of whether scientific facts verify or falsify the laws of the dialectical process which were discovered by Hegel and 'interpreted by Marx in a materialistic way'. Thus, the question of the character of dialectic was posed one-sidedly, from the point of view of its defence and not of its self-development.

(b) Right-wing social democrats headed by Bernstein rejected 'the dialectical scaffolding' of Marx's theory for the same reasons that they dismissed his theory of revolution and the ultimate goals of socialism as a 'residue of utopianism'. An opportunistic attitude towards capitalist reality was irreconcilable with a method directed towards a radical transformation of that reality. The opportunists also found a way to make use of science – not, however, in order to defend dialectic, but to refute it. The theory of evolution was used to prove that there are no jumps in history, that the concept of revolution is unscientific, and that progress in society comes only from small modifications and legislative reform. How did the orthodox Marxists react to this? Instead of developing Marxist theory and method in new specific conditions, they called for loyalty to Marx.

(c) The first successful socialist revolutions were accomplished in relatively backward countries. Instead of bringing the question of human relationships into focus, these revolutions had to emphasize technology and rapid industrialization. Problems of coal and steel pushed back problems of man. Communism was conceived of more as a wealthy society, and less as a humane and democratic one in which 'free development of each individual is the condition of the free development of all' (*Communist Manifesto*).

(d) For Marx and Engels, capturing political power was only 'the first step in the worker's revolution' (*Communist Manifesto*). Stalinism reduced the concept of revolution to the overthrow of the bourgeoisie and the creation of a socialist state. What should follow is the *building* of a new society. What role would a method 'which into the understanding of the existing state of affairs introduces an understanding of its negation, of its necessary destruction' play in the building-up process?

If revolution is the whole social epoch in which not only the institutions of the old society but also the provisional forms of the newborn social order (for example, the class rule of the proletariat) will be successively superseded, then such a concrete and critical method is needed to constantly direct revolutionary thought towards identifying the essential shortcomings of the given society, i.e. those whose annulment is necessary for further progressive movement. But in a society in which public criticism was not tolerated, a philosophical method implying such criticism could not have been tolerated either. In a society in which there are sacrosanct authorities, a method 'which does not bear anybody's tutorship' could not possibly survive. Bureaucracy needs apologies, not criticism. It requires its philosophers to direct all their critical and revolutionary zeal towards the external, capitalist enemy. In socialism it is desirable to see growth in all its aspects: growth of material goods, of culture, growth of the unity of all social strata. But when everything negative is construed as only 'a remnant of bourgeois and petty-bourgeois consciousness in the heads of people', it is impossible for any *new* contradictions to arise in the process of socialist development. To be sure, it has been customary to talk of dialectic as a guide to action. But this has meant little more than a *subsequent rationalization* of various *past* political conceptions and decisions. This is why Stalinism did not reject dialectic as a whole in the way it rejected its key principle – the negation of negation. The use of dialectical phraseology created an illusion of continuity in method. Furthermore: such a formalized and degenerated dialectic was needed to prove that whatever existed in socialism was necessarily such as it was, i.e. that it was rational.

4

The humanist thought which has developed, within the frames of Marxist philosophy and outside it, during the past decade is to a great extent a revolt against Stalinism. This has given it a militant, polemic character, and has also set some of its limits.

In order to break one authority (Stalin), another, greater authority (Marx) is being used. A scholastic philosophy, for which a suitably selected quotation was considered a proof, is fought by the comments and explications of other, 'better' quotations. This is often very useful for practical purposes and even theoretically necessary to save the most valuable humanist elements of Marx's doctrine from the oblivion in which they have fallen at the hands of both his enemies and his successors. However, rethinking someone else's thoughts is a far cry from that concreteness for which a dialectician should strive.

Further, in its reaction to Stalinist positivism, modern humanism sometimes takes an anti-scientific attitude. It was typical Stalinist dogmatism to misuse science and to look for a quasi-scientific form for its doctrines. The party line had to be presented as the result of a 'scientific' examination of existing reality and an exact expression of social necessity. At the same time, the decisions of the party congresses and articles of the party functionaries were the starting points for the work of social scientists. The paradox was complete: on the one hand, there was a society in which all important decisions were said to follow from scientific insights into social necessity, which was so rational that no errors were possible; and on the other hand, there was the same society ruled by the arbitrary decisions of a few leaders, without social sciences in the proper sense, i.e. without objective and critical empirical examination of its structure, its centres of power, its inner tensions and conflicts, and the way of life, attitudes and morals of its various social groups.

However, the fact that science can be used for the justification of the existing social order in both capitalism and socialism does not mean that a humanist philosophy should eliminate science or that scientific results are irrelevant to philosophy. The fact that doctrines of determinism are sometimes used to rationalize the most irrational blunders and inhuman injustices does not mean that there are no general tendencies of social change and no necessary limits to various possibilities of historical action.

A genuine supersession of all kinds of misuse of science would be a wide integration of scientific results within the framework of a humanist philosophy. There is certainly no other kind of knowledge so objective and reliable as that provided by science. Whatever *has been*, *is* and *will probably happen* in the near future can best be known by using scientific methods. Only science can tell us the real possibilities of the future course of events and the approximate probabilities of various alternatives. But which one of these alternatives we choose to take depends upon our fundamental human needs, our conception of what kind of human life and society are good for man. Our values influence the procedure of our research and even our conception of what scientific facts and laws are. To this extent there is no pure science, no pure knowledge. On the other hand, if our choice of aims and values is to be realistic, it has to be based on knowledge. To decide rationally what man and society *ought* to be we should have at our disposal the most reliable account possible of what they really *are*.

This dialectic of fact and norm, knowledge and value, reality and ideal, science and philosophy is often neglected in modern humanist thought.

A particularly weak point in many contemporary humanist considerations is the treatment of the great theme of human freedom. We are often faced with a choice between two mutually exclusive theses: one, a vulgarization of Hegel's well-known formula: 'Freedom is the knowledge of necessity'; and, two, a belief that freedom is absolute and indivisible. From a dialectical point of view the dilemma is hardly tenable. It is easy to see that once necessity is conceived in a rigid way, as the existence of a set of laws which are independent of human action and determine the outcome of social processes in a unique way, any talk of freedom within such a context is at best a verbal game.

The opposite extreme leads to the same result. To talk about human freedom without any qualifications (as an essential element of human ontological structure, or as a condition of authentic existence, etc.) might make sense as poetry, or even have some practical value as an implicit criticism of a world in which there is still so much oppression and denial of elementary human rights, so many concealed forms of slavery. However, the cognitive value of most such 'odes to liberty' is rather insignificant. Upon serious consideration it becomes clear that freedom means something definite only under a set of conditions: A person is free while acting towards the realization of a certain goal if, and only if: (1) there is nothing in his objective surroundings that compels him to act in a given way; (2) the goal is an objective possibility, i.e. a state of affairs which is not excluded by the existing physical and social laws; (3) the proper means have been selected for the realization of the given goal; (4) the person in question knows the first three conditions; (5) his goal is a real value for him, that is, it corresponds to one of his genuine needs, and he is aware of it; (6) his needs are not merely a result of various external influences; he has accepted them after critical reflection as a part of his personality.

An analysis of this kind, no matter how sketchy and incomplete, indicates the multiple relativity of the concept of freedom; the reality to which the concept refers is contingent upon a number of factors, both objective and subjective. In fact, an essential feature of dialectical thinking is the thesis that any term has a definite meaning only in relation to a whole system of ascertainable conditions.

In a number of other issues, too, we are being offered humanist solutions which represent only the opposite extreme to Stalinist dogmatism. Once it was customary among Marxists to deny that it makes sense to speak of man in general; it was legitimate to speak only of a man who belongs to a definite class in a given historical epoch. Nowadays, many open-minded younger Marxists discuss anthropological problems and (for good reasons) assume the concept of man in general. However, the informative value of such discussions is not always discernible. The defect does not lie in the mere use of too abstract and too general concepts; philosophy, as such, has no limits in this respect. The question is how are the concepts used, how much empirical content is covered by them. Hegel's distinction between *abstract* and *concrete* generality is pertinent here. *Abstract* refers to those general terms whose meaning is constituted solely by a few common features of the denoted objects. *Concrete* refers to general terms that have a rich meaning embracing not only common features but also many specific and even individual characteristics of the denoted objects. Increasing experience and knowledge leads to the enrichment of general concepts and to the transition from abstract to concrete. In the light of this dialectical demand for the maximum available concreteness, no

85

humanistic theory is satisfactory which operates with concepts such as *human essence, human nature, generic being of man, alienation*, etc., without bothering about sociological, psychological, and other relevant scientific data, and without taking into account specific conditions of human life in various contemporary societies.

Good examples of one-sided humanist criticism are the treatments of such problems as: the effect of rapid technological progress on human life, the role of planning in society, the importance of future social ends. Bureaucracy in socialist countries has been insisting on strict planning in all spheres of material production, even in education and culture; it has been placing so much emphasis on technological progress that Marx's original conception of a human society has been reduced to the idea of an affluent society, and this impoverished ideal has been pressed on masses of people as a goal for the future which demands the most serious sacrifices in the present. This ideology is now rejected by many Marxist philosophers for excellent humanist reasons:

Strict planning destroys all individual initiative and leaves the workers in the position of men ruled by a new social group.

Fast technological progress is not a way to solve all social problems; in fact, while fighting material poverty and overcoming primitivism, it also causes certain forms of alienation and dehumanization similar to those in developed capitalist countries.

Sacrifices to be made by one generation for the sake of following ones is not something that can be decided by rulers alone, especially if they do not sacrifice anything themselves.

However, some humanist philosophers have gone to the other extreme in their criticism:

They have rejected not only strict bureaucratic planning, but any rational planning, in both social and individual life; they declare that genuine creative activity is free from *any* previous schemata to which our actions should conform. But this is not true even for artistic creation: the fact that a piece of music, a poem, or a ballet has a more or less rigid, previously determined form (fugue, sonnet, a well-known choreographic design) certainly does not decrease its creative value. In material production and other objective forms of social life one of the greatest problems contemporary socialism faces is how to build a social system in which self-management will be combined with flexible planning by some central, truly democratic, representative bodies. This may seem contradictory; that is why those who prefer a simple way of thinking and who are unhappy with one side of the contradiction between centralism and decentralization quickly jump to the other. However, the (dialectical) solution seems to lie in a transformation of both such that they can be reconciled and mutually adjusted. The experience of socialist countries in the last few decades indicates that there is no other way to secure both freedom and the initiative of individuals and small social groups on the one hand, and rationality of the system as a whole on the other.

Certain humanists, critical of the existing cult of technology, have also revolted against technology in general, without any qualifications. What they condemn is not primarily the manifold misuses of technology and its inhuman by-products, but technology itself as a metaphysical entity, an ontological structure of the present-day human being. This one-sided, unrealistic attitude disregards the instrumental nature of technology and the plurality of different, even opposite functions it plays in modern society. It liberates man from natural forces, but under certain conditions makes him a slave of his own products. It tends to eliminate his material poverty, but sometimes increases his spiritual poverty. It creates both an abundance of material goods and an overwhelming urge for property and consumption. It makes possible cultural growth of an unprecedented mass scale, but too often it provides only cheap cultural substitutes. Instead of over-emphasizing one or the other side of these contradictions, one should grasp them in their totality and, by all means, under given specific conditions (e.g. the attitudes toward technology must be different in a highly industrialized and in a backward country).

The practical point of the whole criticism should be a demand for a rational control of technological progress, for a practical annulment of its negative, inhuman consequences. In this way technology would be placed where it belongs – as an important *means* of human liberation and fulfilment but not an *end in itself*.

Some humanist philosophers often sound utopian when speaking about ends – which to a great extent is simply the consequence

87

of their method, especially their anti-scientific attitude and their systematic preference for pure speculative vision over prediction based on objective knowledge. They tend to imagine future man as free from all contradictions, all forms of alienation – an easy-going creature who constantly loves, plays and enjoys nature. However, the experience of those countries that have undergone successful social revolutions and made efforts to build a new world does not seem to confirm such an over-optimistic vision of the future. It is true that some of the crudest forms of human alienation have been more or less abolished. But some have survived, and new unsuspected ones have appeared, especially in connexion with the creation of new centres of enormous power, which are no longer based on economic wealth as in capitalism, but on unlimited political authority. The increasing power of state and political organizations in some socialist countries has brought to life new kinds of social contradictions on both the national and the international level: new forms of political oppression introduced by bureaucracy; new ways of grabbing the surplus product, even without possessing the means of production; new tensions between rich and poor; new conflicts between nations and countries within the socialist camp, etc. There is no reason to think that, however great the social progress, the forseeable future will bring complete elimination of old forms of human deformation and degradation without introducing some new conflicts and contradictions.

In each historical stage of such a world a philosophy is needed which will constantly keep in focus the essential problems of human existence, constantly give a sense of direction and help to realize the optimal possibilities of a free and rich human life in the given society. This philosophy must have a method of criticizing, not only of increasing positive knowledge – a method that will bring to light the main contradictions of the human condition in each epoch, especially those negative aspects that must be superseded by creative practical action in order to make the next step in the realization of fundamental humanist ideals possible. Thus humanist philosophy and dialectical method seem to presuppose each other.

NIRMAL KUMAR BOSE

⊛ ⊚ ⊛ ⊚ ⊚ ⊚ ⊚

Gandhi: Humanist and Socialist

NIRMAL KUMAR BOSE, an editor of the Bengali Encyclopedia, was Gandhi's personal secretary in 1946–7. Imprisoned several times in the course of the Gandhian
movement, he has written several books dealing with the
great leader, among which are *Studies in Gandhism, Selections from Gandhiji* and *My Days with Gandhi*. Mr Bose is
also an anthropologist. Born in 1901, he studied at the
University of Calcutta and taught there from 1930 to 1957.
The following year he spent at the Universities of Chicago
and California, after which he returned to direct the
Anthropological Survey of India at the Indian Museum in
Calcutta.

Introduction

The supreme problem which faces mankind today is the
problem of war. In spite of the fact that persistent efforts have
been made since the First World War to establish a forum where
nations can resolve their conflicts in peace, mankind seems to be
no nearer the formation of a single world community. All
nations wish to avoid war, yet do not see any way out of it, for
war still remains the most effective means of bringing about decisive results, even though the cost may be great.

Gandhi recognized very clearly that the human family may
perhaps never reach a state where there will be no conflict, or
where conflict will no longer have to be resolved by 'direct action'. So he tried to find a substitute for war which would be
equally effective, but which would not leave men debased, as
they now are, after a conflict. It was in the pursuit of this that he
invented the technique of *satyagraha*, by which conflicts could
be conducted at a civilized moral level.

Satyagraha

Literally the word *satyagraha* means 'insistence upon truth'. The basic assumption underlying it is that no man sees truth in its entirety, and that he therefore has no moral right to impose a particular view of truth upon others. However, it is his right and duty to live according to his own lights, and to oppose whatever seems to him wrong in the views of others.

The *satyagrahi*, or the man who practises *satyagraha*, refuses to cooperate with a social system based upon immorality. At the same time, he tries to build up a different way of life in terms of what he considers to be moral. *Satyagraha* has thus two aspects: one which is constructive, and the other which leads to militant, but civil, opposition to wrongs.

In the course of such resistance, the *satyagrahi* patiently and courageously bears all the violence which his 'opponent' may shower upon him, yet refuses to regard the opponent as an 'enemy', and aims at his conversion. For him, the human family can never be divided into those who are friends and those who are enemies.

In war, on the other hand, superior violence imposes one partial view of truth upon another. Victory does not necessarily mean that the victorious are more morally right than their adversaries, although victors have always made this claim. Striking ability in war does not depend upon the morality of one's cause, and has very little relevance to it.

In *satyagraha*, the *satyagrahi* not only tries to live according to his own lights, but also attempts to accept whatever may be right and just in the view of his opponent. *Satyagraha* therefore ends when the conflicting parties arrive at a solution which incorporates all that is 'true' in both sides. There is neither victory nor defeat, but an agreement to which both parties willingly subscribe, while institutions or practices proven wrong are destroyed during the conflict.

All his life, Gandhi tried to organize the masses of India for this 'collective practice of civil disobedience', so that they could eradicate the numerous weaknesses present in their social and political life.

Political aim

A correspondent once asked Gandhi if everything can be defended by means of non-violence. His answer was clear and emphatic.

> What is gained by violence can not only not be defended by non-violence, but the latter requires the abandonment of all ill-gotten gains.
> *Q.* Is the accumulation of capital possible except through violence, whether open or tacit?
> *A.* Such accumulation by private persons is impossible except through violent means, but accumulation by the state in a non-violent society is not only possible, but desirable and inevitable.[1]

In other words, a community must set its own house in order before it can prevent, by non-violence, an aggression upon its just rights.

What should be the character of such a community? What should be its economic aims, and how should it organize the State? We shall proceed to furnish an answer in Gandhi's own words as far as possible.

In 1904 Gandhi was deeply influenced by the thoughts of Ruskin. Later on, he produced a paraphrase of *Unto This Last* in the Gujarati language, which was his mother tongue. The central ideas derived by him were:

(1) That the good of the individual is contained in the good of all.
(2) That a lawyer's work has the same value as that of the barber, in as much as all have the same right of earning their livelihood from their work.
(3) That a life of labour, i.e. the life of the tiller of the soil and of the handicraftsman, is the life most worth living.[2]

In 1928, he further explained:

> According to me the economic constitution of India and for that matter of the world should be such that no one under it should suffer from want of food and clothing. In other words everybody should be able to get sufficient work to enable him to make ends meet. And this ideal can be universally realized only if

1. N. K. Bose, *Selections from Gandhi* (Ahmedabad: Navajivan Press, 1957), p. 39.
2. Ibid., p. 38.

the means of production of the elementary necessaries of life remain in the control of the masses. These should be freely available to all as God's air and water are or ought to be; they should not be made a vehicle of traffic for the exploitation of others. Their monopolization by any country, nation or group of persons should be considered unjust. The neglect of this simple principle is the cause of the destitution that we witness today, not only in this unhappy land but in other parts of the world too.[1]

In his political activities, Gandhi tried to work through the Indian National Congress in order to convert this democratic organization into an instrument of the collective exercise of non-violence. Incidentally, he once said about himself:

Violence is no monopoly of any one party. I know Congressmen who are neither socialists nor communists but who are frankly devotees of the cult of violence. Contrariwise, I know socialists and communists who will not hurt a fly but who believe in the universal ownership of the instruments of production. I rank myself as one among them.[2]

This was in 1938. We may therefore look upon him as a socialist who believed in the morality of non-violence. Gandhi had, however, strong leanings toward anarchism; for he believed in the supremacy of the individual rather than of the state. But he also recognized that, as long as human nature remains as it is, a state will be necessary. But that state is best which governs the least. He once wrote to a correspondent:

It is my firm conviction that if the state suppressed capitalism by violence, it will be caught in the coils of violence itself and fail to develop non-violence at any time.

The state represents violence in a concentrated and organized form. The individual has a soul, but, as the state is a soulless machine, it can never be weaned from violence to which it owes its very existence.

What I would personally prefer would be not a centralization of power in the hands of the state, but an extension of the sense of trusteeship, as in my opinion the violence of private ownership is less injurious than the violence of the state. However, if it is unavoidable, I would support a minimum of state ownership.

Q. Then, sir, shall we take it that the fundamental difference between you and the socialists is that you believe men live more by self-direction or will than by habit, and that they believe men

1. Loc. cit.   2. Ibid., pp. 38–9.

92

live more by habit than by will, this being the reason why you strive for self-correction, while they try to build up a system under which men will find it impossible to exercise their desire of exploiting others?

A. While admitting that man actually lives by habit, I hold that it is better for him to live by the exercise of will. I also believe that men are capable of developing their will to an extent that will reduce exploitation to a minimum. I look upon an increase in the power of the state with the greatest fear, because, although while apparently doing good by minimizing exploitation, it does the greatest harm to mankind by destroying individuality, which lies at the root of all progress. We know of so many cases where men have adopted trusteeship, but none where the state has really lived for the poor.[1]

Gandhi's definition of freedom also stemmed from this particular point of view, as well as from his belief that the Law of Bread Labour is the first moral law of human existence. Every man has to earn his bread by the sweat of his brow; and the precept is to be taken in a literal and not a metaphorical sense. So he defined Swaraj for India in the following terms:

By Swaraj I mean the Government of India by the consent of the people as ascertained by the largest number of the adult population, male or female, native-born or domiciled, who have contributed by manual labour to the service of the state and who have taken the trouble of having their names registered as voters. I hope to demonstrate that real Swaraj will come not by the acquisition of authority by a few but by the acquisition of the capacity of all to resist authority when abused. In other words, Swaraj is to be attained by educating the masses to a sense of their capacity to regulate and control authority.[2]

Economic aim

We have already described some of the economic ideals of Gandhi. He believed in the small community and face-to-face relationship, where men live in equality by sharing common labour.

This logically leads to the decentralization of production. At one time he disapproved of all heavy machines, for in his opinion they helped to swell profits, and made it possible for some to

1. N. K. Bose, *Studies in Gandhism*, 3rd edn (Calcutta: Merit Publishers, 1962), pp. 65–6.
2. Bose, *Selections from Ghandi*, p. 114.

live upon the toils of others. But, later on, he modified his views and would have as many machines as would lighten human labour. However, he was never prepared to barter away human freedom for the sake of productive efficiency.

When someone asked him if he was against all machinery, the reply was:

My answer is emphatically, 'No'. But, I am against its indiscriminate multiplication. I refuse to be dazzled by the seeming triumph of machinery. I am uncompromisingly against all destructive machinery. But simple tools and instruments and such machinery as saves individual labour and lightens the burden of the millions of cottages, I should welcome.[1]

Again,

What I object to is the *craze* for machinery, not machinery as such. The *craze* is for what they call labour-saving machinery. Men go on 'saving labour', till thousands are without work and thrown on the open streets to die of starvation. I want to save time and labour, not for a fraction of mankind, but for all; I want the concentration of wealth, not in the hands of few, but in the hands of all. Today machinery merely helps a few to ride on the back of millions. The impetus behind it all is not the philanthropy to save labour, but greed. It is against this constitution of things that I am fighting with all my might.

Q. Then you are fighting not against machinery as such, but against its abuses which are so much in evidence today?

A. I would unhesitatingly say 'Yes'; but I would add that scientific truths and discoveries should first of all cease to be mere instruments of greed. Then labourers will not be overworked and machinery, instead of becoming a hindrance, will be a help. I am aiming, not at eradication of machinery, but limitation.[2]

Gandhi favoured the small machine which lightens labour. But what about factories where this kind of machine is manufactured? Who shall own them, and who run them? The reply was as follows:

I am socialist enough to say that such factories should be nationalized, or state-controlled. They ought only to be working under the most attractive and ideal conditions, not for profit, but for the benefit of humanity, love taking the place of greed as the motive. It is an alteration in the conditions of labour that I want. This mad rush for wealth must cease, and the labourer must be assured,

1. Ibid., p. 66.   2. Loc. cit.

not only of a living wage, but a daily task that is not a mere drudgery. The machine will, under these conditions, be as much a help to the man working it as to the state, or the man who owns it. . . . The individual is the one supreme consideration. The saving of labour of the individual should be the object, and honest humanitarian consideration, and not greed, the motive. Replace greed by love and everything will come right.[1]

Summary

We may now try to summarize what has been said above. It is clear that Gandhi was inspired by the highest ideals of democracy and egalitarianism. He was a humanist even before he was a nationalist; and he refused to lay aside at any time his feelings about the undivided nature of the human family. He persevered in the faith that these feelings would prevail against every other, provided man was prepared to pay the highest price for Love and Unity.

In his experiments during the struggle for Indian independence, Gandhi tried to forge a tool which might be of service to all mankind. He knew the tool was not yet ready to take charge of international problems, but hoped that with growing experience in *satyagraha* man would one day be able to preserve a sense of human unity even when involved in conflict with those who denied it. When *satyagraha* had become perfected by intelligent application, then man would possess a real and moral substitute for war.

A year before the Second World War, when he sensed that the world was once more preparing itself for a blood bath, he spoke in humility about his personal efforts:

I am myself daily growing in the knowledge of *satyagraha*. I have no textbook to consult in time of need, not even the *Gita*, which I have called my dictionary. *Satyagraha* as conceived by me is a science in the making. It may be that what I claim to be a science may prove to be no science at all and may well prove to be the musings and doings of a fool, if not a madman. It may be that what is true in *satyagraha* is as ancient as the hills. But it has not yet been acknowledged to be of any value in the solution of world problems or rather the one supreme problem of war. It may be that what is claimed to be new in it will prove to be really of no value in terms of that supreme problem. It may be that what are

1. Ibid., p. 67.

claimed to be victories of *satyagraha*, i.e. *ahimsa*, were in reality victories not of truth and non-violence but of the fear of violence.

These possibilities have always been in front of me. I am helpless. All I present to the nation for adoption is an answer to prayer or, which is the same thing, constantly waiting on God.[1]

1. Ibid., p. vii.

HERBERT MARCUSE

⊚ ⊚

Socialist Humanism?

HERBERT MARCUSE has achieved a considerable reputation for his works *Reason and Revolution: Hegal and the Rise
of Social Theory, Eros and Civilization: A Philosophical Inquiry into Freud, Soviet Marxism* and *One-Dimensional
Man: Studies in the Ideology of Advanced Industrial
Society.* Since 1954, he has taught at Brandeis University,
with interruptions as *Directeur d'études* of the École Pratique des Hautes Études, Paris. Born in Berlin in 1898, he
studied at the University of Berlin and received a Ph.D.
from the University of Freiburg. After teaching a year in
Geneva, he was from 1934 to 1940 at the Institute of
Social Research, Columbia University. He spent nearly
ten years with the Office of Intelligence Research, Department of State, Washington, after which he returned to
Columbia as a research fellow in the Russian Institute; he
has also been at the Russian Research Center of Harvard
University.

Almost twenty years ago, Merleau-Ponty raised the issue of
socialist humanism with uncompromising clarity. Is the humanistic, non-terroristic construction of a socialist society in the
given historical period a real possibility? He rejected the alternative of humanism and terror: there is no choice between violence and non-violence, but only between two modes of violence
– capitalist and socialist.

> *En U.S.S.R., la violence et la ruse sont officielles, l'humanité est
> dans la vie quotidienne. Dans les démocraties, au contraire, les prin-
> cipes sont humains, la ruse et la violence se trouvent dans la pratique.
> A partir de là, la propagande a beau jeu.*[1]

(In the U.S.S.R., violence and deception are official, and
humanity is in daily life. In the democracies, on the other hand,

1. Merleau-Ponty, *Humanisme et Terreur* (Paris, 1947), p. 197.

97

the principles are humane, but deception and violence are found in practice. Beyond that, propaganda has a field day.)

The two social systems are locked in a global struggle in which the renunciation of socialist violence is found to strengthen the realm of capitalist exploitation. But socialist violence has the chance of breaking the infernal circle of terror and counter-terror as long as it is carried by the supranational solidarity of the only class which, *'selon la logique interne de sa condition'*, is capable of translating humanism from ideology into reality. Merleau-Ponty knew that precisely this condition no longer prevailed, and that the proletariat had ceased to be 'the term of reference' in communist thought and policy, but he refused to engage in an ideological rescue of humanism and to reject the actual development in the name of humanistic 'values':

Opposer ici au marxisme une 'morale d'abord', c'est l'ignorer dans ce qu'il dit de plus vrai et qui a fait sa fortune dans le monde, c'est continuer la mystification, c'est passer à côté du problème.[1]

(To oppose to Marxism the principle 'morality first' is to ignore that which is most true in the former and which has made its fortune in the world, is to perpetuate mystification, to bypass the problem.)

The solution:

Parler pour l'humanisme sans être pour le 'socialisme humaniste' à la manière anglo-saxonne, 'comprendre' les communistes sans être communiste, c'est apparemment se placer bien haut et en tout cas au-dessus de la mêlée. En réalité c'est simplement refuser de s'engager dans la confusion et hors de la vérité. Est-ce notre faute si l'humanisme occidental est faussé parce qu'il est aussi une machine de guerre? Et si l'entreprise marxiste n'a pu survivre qu'en changeant de caractère?[2]

(To speak of humanism without being for 'humanistic socialism', in the Anglo-Saxon manner, and to 'understand' the communists without being communist, is apparently to place oneself high above, or in any case above, the conflict. In reality, it means refusing to become entangled in confusion and falsehood. Is it our fault if Western humanism is rendered false because it is also an apparatus of war? And if the Marxist enterprise has only been able to survive by changing its character?)

1. Ibid., pp. x ff.   2. Ibid., p. 203.

The human reality is an 'open' system: no theory, whether Marxist or other, can impose the solution. The contingency of history, which today denies humanism, may also one day deny the denial. Meanwhile there are the enslaved human beings who must accomplish their own liberation. To develop their conscience and consciousness, to make them aware of what is going on, to prepare the precarious ground for the future alternatives – this is our task: 'our' not only as Marxists but as intellectuals, and that means all those who are still free and able to think by themselves and against indoctrination, communist as well as anti-communist.

Today, after the destalinization and under conditions of liberation and decentralization in the communist world, the 'solution' is no more visible than it was at the end of the war. The Soviet Union does not seem to become more 'humanistic' by making arrangements with the West, nor the West by accepting these arrangements. But the post-war development of the capitalist and communist societies in coexistence suggests that the prospects of socialist humanism should be re-examined with a view to the technical capability and productivity of these societies. This paper offers only a few remarks on the problems.

In the Marxian conception, socialism is humanism in as much as it organizes the social division of labour, the 'realm of necessity' so as to enable men to satisfy their social and individual needs without exploitation and with a minimum of toil and sacrifice. Social production, controlled by the 'immediate producers', would be deliberately directed towards this goal. With this rational organization of the realm of necessity, man would be free to develop himself as an 'all-round individual' beyond the realm of necessity, which would remain a world of want, of labour. But the qualitatively new organization of the realm of necessity, upon which the emergence of truly human relationships depends, in turn depends on the existence of a class for which the revolution of human relationships is a vital need. Socialism is humanism in the extent to which this need and goal pre-exist, i.e. socialism as humanism has its historical *a priori within* capitalist society. Those who constitute the human base of this society have no share in its exploitative interests and satisfactions; their vital needs transcend the inhuman existence of the whole towards the universal human needs which are still to

H

be fulfilled. Because their very existence is the denial of freedom and humanity, they are free for their own liberation and for that of humanity. In this dialectic, the humanist content of socialism emerges, not as value but as need, not as moral goal and justification but as economic and political practice – as part of the basis itself of the material culture.

This much for the Marxian conception. Its historical denominator is obvious. Socialism is 'objectively' humanism by virtue of its specific place in the development of industrial society, defined by the existence, interest and action of the class-conscious proletariat in its supranational solidarity. This historical constellation has been 'surpassed' by the actual development of the advanced industrial societies. To the degree to which their inherent contradictions have unfolded themselves, to the same degree have their rising productivity and power succeeded in suppressing the need for resolving the contradictions. As technical progress provides the instrumentalities for a rational organization of the realm of necessity far beyond anything Marx ever envisaged (the 'abolition of labour' does not seem to be the problem of the future, but rather how to avoid the abolition of labour), these instruments are used for perpetuating and even intensifying the struggle for existence, for total mobilization rather than for pacification. The increasing threat of leisure time is utilized by management to defend the *status quo* of repression. Technological rationality is geared to the requirements of the Cold War, which is waged not only (perhaps not even primarily) against the external enemy, but also against the enemy within the established societies – against a qualitatively new mode of existence which could free man from enslavement by the apparatus which he has built.

In terms of the established industrial societies, nothing is more sensible than the fear of that stage where technical progress would turn into human progress: self-determination of life in developing those needs and faculties which may attenuate the struggle for existence – human beings as ends in themselves. This fear is not only that of technological unemployment, but also that of boredom, of a void which has to be filled and which cannot be filled except by bigger and better management from above and outside. Not only the political but also (and primarily) the technical apparatus and production itself have become systems of domination into which the labouring classes are incorporated and incorporate themselves. The 'inner logic of their condition', according to which they were the historical agents of socialist humanism, is no longer *their own*. The objective identity of socialism and humanism is dissolved. It was never an *immediate* identity: it was real to the extent to which the objective condition was seized and transcended in the consciousness of the historical subjects and in their action. This mediation is suppressed by the overwhelming power of technical progress welded into an instrument of totalitarian domination, operating not only through the terrifying concentration of economic and military power, but also through the rising standard of living under the imposed conditions of living. As long as the established direction of technical progress prevails (and in the era of coexistence it is bound to prevail), change in the ownership and control of the means of production would be quantitative rather than qualitative change. Prerequisite for the liberation of the humanistic content of socialism would be a fundamental change in the *direction of technical progress*, a total reconstruction of the technical apparatus. This is the historical idea of humanism today.

Other ideas of humanism belong to the eighteenth and nineteenth century; they retain an image of man which has been surpassed by the development of society. This classical image still guides Marx's early writings; it finds expression in the notion of the all-round individual, the 'personality' which fulfils itself in a realm of freedom. But this notion pertains to a stage where the intellectual culture was still divorced from the material culture, not yet incorporated into mass production and consumption, where the mind and the soul were not yet taken over by scientific management, where time and space were not yet occupied, in their entirety, by organized business and organized relaxation – where there could still be a realm of freedom not correlated with that of necessity. Even so, it is difficult to envisage what Marx's all-round individual would or would not do – simply in terms of occupation or non-occupation. There is an unfortunate kernel of truth in the malicious denunciation of the vision of free individuals who spend their day in alternating between fishing, hunting and being creative. If this vision were to become reality tomorrow (and it could far more easily become reality than when

Marx wrote!), it would be the very denial of freedom and of humanity.

To be sure, Marx revised his early notions of human freedom by refraining from such positive visions and by examining the conditions of liberation rather than of liberty attained. However, the developed Marxian theory retains an idea of man which now appears as too optimistic and idealistic. Marx underrated the extent of the conquest of nature and of man, of the technological management of freedom and self-realization. He did not foresee the great achievement of technological society: the assimilation of freedom and necessity, of satisfaction and repression, of the aspirations of politics, business and the individual. In view of these achievements, socialist humanism can no longer be defined in terms of the individual, the all-round personality and self-determination. If these ideas are supposed to be more than the privilege of a few, if they claim universal validity, they seem dangerously void of meaning and substance. Their realization would call for conditions in which man would fulfil himself in his daily work, in which socially necessary labour would be 'attractive labour', a possibility which Marx emphatically denied: 'Labour cannot become play, as Fourier wants.'[1] Short of it, these images of humanism have the repressive connotation of pre-technological 'higher culture' which leaves the lower culture on which it is built unaffected. Marx recognized the ideological character of this humanism when he translated the 'metaphysical' terms of the early writings into those of political economy. The chance of humanism arises with the abolition of the exchange economy and its institutions; with the rational, socialist organization of labour; then, *man* may become free to build his own life and to be human with the others. Even then, the true realm of freedom, the *'menschliche Kraftentwicklung'* which is an end in itself begins only beyond this realm of necessity. But the socialist organization of labour has created free time, and 'the free time which is leisure time as well as time for higher activity has naturally [*sic!*] transformed man into a different subject (*in ein andres Subjekt verwandelt*) and, as this different subject, man also enters into the process of immediate production'.[2]

1. Marx, *Grundrisse der Kritik der politischen Oekonomie* (Berlin: Dietz, 1953), p. 599.
2. Ibid.

Today, advanced industrial society is creating free time, but the possessor of this free time is not a 'different subject'; in the capitalist and communist systems, the subject of free time is subordinated to the same norms and powers that rule the realm of necessity. The mature Marxian conception, too, appears idealistic and optimistic.

With the passing of the objective conditions for the identity of socialism and humanism, socialism cannot be made humanistic by committing socialist policy to the traditional humanistic values. In the situation of coexistence (which must be the framework for any non-ideological analysis), such humanization is bound to be ideological and self-defeating. Here, a distinction must be made between capitalist and socialist humanism. In the capitalist world, the fight for the rights of man, for freedom of speech and assembly, for equality before the law, which marked the beginning of the liberal era, is again a desperate concern at its end, when it becomes evident to what extent these liberties have remained restricted and denied. And this fight is hampered to the degree to which it respects, in its own action and suffering, the liberal values and the legality which the adversary meets with unpunished violence. In the communist world, the assertion of individual rights and liberties and of the initiative of the labouring classes would promote (and should promote) radical dissent and opposition to the economic and political repression on which the established régime depends, and which it considers as prerequisite for defence and growth in competitive coexistence. According to this logic, effective dissent and opposition within the communist societies would alter the precarious international balance in favour of capitalism – which would not necessarily brighten the prospects of socialist humanism. For the labouring classes are no longer those to whom the revolution once appealed, and their initiative is not likely to revive international socialist solidarity.

These are the given historical conditions which a discussion of the failures and chances of socialist humanism must face if it does not want to deal with mere ideologies. Advanced industrial society can take care of humanistic values while continuing to pursue its inhuman goals: it promotes culture and personalities together with toil, injustice, nuclear armament, total indoctrination, self-propelling productivity. The intensity with which the powers that be mobilize the underlying population against their liberation goes hand-in-hand with the growing capabilities of society to accomplish this liberation. Inasmuch as these capabilities are utilized (or suppressed) in the interest of domination, of the defence of the *status quo*, they remain technical capabilities, barred from their humanistic realization. As technical capabilities, they define the prospects of socialist humanism. Severance of the fatal link between technical progress and progress in domination and exploitation is the precondition. Humanism must remain ideology as long as society depends on continued poverty, arrested automation, mass media, prevented birth control and on the creation and re-creation of masses, of noise and pollution, of planned obsolescence and waste, and of mental and physical rearmament. These conditions and institutions are the social controls which sustain and extend the prevailing state of affairs. Consequently, their abrogation on behalf of humanism would be revolutionary subversion, and this subversion would also subvert the very needs and necessities of human existence. What appeared, in the pre-totalitarian era, as the precondition of freedom may well turn out to be its substance, its historical content. For the substance of freedom as well as humanism must be defined in terms of the human beings in their society, and in terms of their capabilities. Advanced industrial society is a society in which the technical apparatus of production and distribution has become a totalitarian political apparatus, coordinating and managing all dimensions of life, free time as well as working time, negative as well as positive thinking. To the victims, beneficiaries, and heirs of such a society, the realm of freedom has lost its classical content, its qualitative difference from the realm of necessity. It is the work world, the technical world which they must first make their own: the realm of necessity must become the realm of their freedom. The technical apparatus of production, distribution and consumption must be reconstructed. Technological rationality must be redirected to make the work world a place for human beings who one day may perhaps be willing to live in peace and do away with the masters who guide them to desist from this effort. This means not 'humanization' of labour but its mechanization and planned production for the emergence of new needs – those of pacification of the struggle for existence. Some aspects of the new technology can be delineated: the complete rebuilding of cities and towns, the reconstruction of the countryside after the ravages of repressive industrialization, the institution of truly public services, the care for the sick and the aged.[1]

The failure of humanism seems to be due to overdevelopment rather than backwardness; once the productive apparatus, under repressive direction, has grown into an apparatus of ubiquitous controls, democratic or authoritarian, the chances of a humanistic reconstruction are very poor. This situation accentuates the historical truth of the Marxian conception. The humanistic chance of socialism is objectively grounded neither in the socialization of the means of production nor in their control by the 'immediate producers' – although these are necessary prerequisites – but rather in the existence, *prior* to these changes, of social classes whose life is the very negation of humanity, and whose consciousness and practice are determined by the need to abrogate this condition. The totalitarian–technological stage has not altered this truth: no matter how 'technical' the basis of socialism has become, no matter how much it is a matter of the redirection and even reversal of technical progress and technological rationality – these are political tasks, involving radical changes in the society as a whole. Technical progress occurs as political progress in domination; thus it is progress in the suppression of the alternatives. The fact that, in the most advanced areas of industrial civilization, this suppression is no longer terroristic but democratic, introjected, productive and even satisfying does not change this condition. If suppression is compatible with individual autonomy and operates through individual autonomy, then the *Nomos* (norm) which the individual gives himself is that of servitude. This *Nomos*, which is the law of our time, outlaws the pacification of the struggle for existence, national and international, among societies and among individuals. Competition must go on – for profit and power, for work and fun, for the bigger and better deterrent, and it increases the productivity of the whole, which in turn perpetuates this sort of competition and promises the transformation of its victims into

1. For an elaboration of these propositions, see my *One-Dimensional Man: Studies in the Ideology of Advanced Industrial Society* (Boston: Beacon Press, 1964; London: Routledge & Kegan Paul), especially Chs. 9 and 10.

its beneficiaries, who will then do their best to make their contribution. And to the degree to which the other societies are forced into the same circle, the qualitative difference between socialism and capitalism is being obliterated by the sweep of a productivity which improves the standard of living through improved exploitation.

Socialist theory has no right to denounce, in the name of other historical possibilities, growing social productivity which allows a better life for more sections of the population. But the question here is not that of future possibilities; it is the present reality which is at stake. In this reality, the denial of humanity spreads through all achievements: it is in the daily preparedness for annihilation, in the equipment for a subterranean existence, in the ever more ingenious planning of waste, in the inescapable inanities of the Media, in the abolition of privacy, and – perhaps the most effective denial of all – in the helpless awareness of all this, in public acknowledgement and criticism, which are impotent and contribute to the power of the whole, if they are not crushed and silenced by force. Thus the need for liberation exists: it exists as universal need far beyond that of one particular class – but it exists only 'in itself', not *for* the individuals in need. Socialism appears again as an abstract idea; loyalty to its idea excludes the fostering of illusions. Its new abstractness does not signify falsification. The proletariat which was to validate the equation of socialism and humanism pertained to a past stage in the development of industrial society. Socialist theory, no matter how true, can neither prescribe nor predict the future agents of a historical transformation which is more than ever before the spectre that haunts the established societies. But socialist theory can show that this spectre is the image of a vital need; it can develop and protect the consciousness of this need and thus lay the groundwork for the dissolution of the false unity in defence of the *status quo*.

EUGENE KAMENKA

⊚ ⊚

Marxian Humanism and the Crisis in Socialist Ethics

EUGENE KAMENKA was born in Cologne in 1928 and taken to Australia in 1937. He was educated at the Sydney Technical High School and the University of Sydney, where he took first-class honours in philosophy under the late John Anderson. His doctoral thesis, *The Ethical Foundations of Marxism,* submitted in the Australian National University, Canberra, was published by Routledge & Kegan Paul and Frederick A. Praeger in 1962. Dr Kamenka has lectured in philosophy at the University of Singapore and has worked in Israel and London; he is now Research Fellow in the History of Ideas at the Institute of Advanced Studies of the Australian National University and lives in Canberra. He is currently completing a book-length study of Ludwig Feuerbach and then plans to take up again the examination of the connexion between German philosophy and sociology, with special reference to the concepts of *Gemeinschaft* and *Gesellschaft.*

I

'Man is born free; and everywhere he is in chains. One thinks himself the master of others, and still remains a greater slave than they.'[1] It was for the sake of liberating men from these chains (chains which Rousseau thought could be made 'legitimate') that Marx became a radical critic of society; it was in the name of freedom, and not of security, that Marx turned to communism. The vision before his eyes, from his youth onward, was that of the creative, self-determined man, master of his environment, of the universe and of himself, cooperating, spontaneously and harmoniously, with all other men as 'aspects' of the human spirit liberated within him. 'Dignity', the young Marx writes in a secondary school essay, 'can be afforded only by that

1. J.-J. Rousseau, *The Social Contract*, Book I, Ch. I.

107

position in which we do not appear as servile instruments'; 'the criticism of religion', he writes in the *Deutsch-französische Jahrbücher (Franco-German Yearbook)* nine years later, 'ends in the teaching that *man is the highest being for man,* it ends, i.e. with the categorical imperative to overthrow all conditions in which man is a debased, forsaken, contemptible being forced into servitude.' Communism, for Marx, meant neither the mere abolition of poverty nor that abstract application of fairness which he rejected so scathingly in his *Critique of the Gotha Programme* – the triumph of distributive justice in social affairs. Least of all did Marx see communism as a form of state socialism in which governmental or 'representative' power and authority replaced individual power and authority over men. Ultimately more consistent than Rousseau, Marx implicitly rejected any possible justification for the 'chains' that bind men together; in the belief that Rousseau's general, universal will could and would flower in history, Marx confidently predicted that all social chains would wither away. Communism would be the society of freedom, in which man became the subject and ceased to be the object of power. No longer would man's nature and actions be determined by something outside himself, either by the state, society, man's social situation, his animal needs or by other men. No longer would man's fellow human beings confront him as competitors, enslaving him and themselves to the inexorable demands of competitive economic life. For the first time in human history, society, technology and the whole range of human conduct and relations would become expressions of man's true being and cease to be limitations upon that being. In his own life, man would find that true and ultimate freedom which is the necessary destiny of man; in other men he would find partners in that spontaneous but cooperative creativity that distinguishes man as a universal and social being from the animal as a limited and particular one. Man would become praxis – the subject and not the object of history.

'The critique of society which forms the substance of Marx's work', Dr Maximilien Rubel correctly reminds us,[1] 'has, essentially, two targets: the State and Money.' The state, for Marx, was the visible, institutionalized expression of political power

1. Maximilien Rubel, *'Le Concept de democratie chez Marx'*, in *Contrat Social*, Vol. VI, no. 4.

over men; money, both the visible means and the secret but indispensable ground of the more fundamental and pervasive economic power over men. If Marx was concerned with the critiques of politics and economics, it was because he saw in these critiques the key to understanding the human condition and grasping the necessary foundations for the elimination of power over men.

In Marx's earlier works, especially in his contributions to the *Deutsch-französische Jahrbücher*, in his *Economic and Philosophical Manuscripts* of 1844, and in the *German Ideology* that he wrote with Engels in 1845-6, we are presented with an analysis of the nature and foundations of human dependence subtler and less dated than the crude class theory of human dependence which Marx's vulgarizing disciples have drawn out of his popular political pamphlets. In these earlier works, Marx makes it clear that he does not see man enslaved simply by other men: the citizen by a dictatorial police state, the worker by a greedy and grasping capitalist. All past and present social systems may resolve themselves, from one point of view, into systems made up of masters and slaves – but the masters are no more free than the slaves, both live in a relationship of mutual hostility and of insurmountable mutual dependence, both are governed by the system that makes them play out their allotted roles, whether they will or not. Marx sees this dependence as arising 'naturally' from the division of labour and the consequent introduction of private ownership. But the possibilities of intensifying dependence, of alienating man from his work, his products and his fellow human beings, are vastly increased with the rise of money as a universal medium of exchange. Money – into which everything can be converted – makes everything saleable, and enables man to separate from himself not only his goods, the product of his work, but even from his work itself, which he can now sell to another.

> Money lowers all the gods of mankind and transforms them into a commodity. Money is the universal, self-constituting value of all things. It has therefore robbed the whole world, both the human world and nature, of its own peculiar value. Money is the essence of man's work and existence, alienated from man, and this alien essence dominates him and he prays to it.[1]

1. Karl Marx, 'On the Jewish Question'; my translation from *Marx-Engels Gesamtausgabe* (M.E.G.A.; Frankfurt am Main: Marx-Engels-Lenin Institute, 1927 f.), Section I, Vol. 1-i, p. 603.

Man's alienation, for Marx, is expressed in the fact that man's forces, products and creations – all those things that are extensions of man's personality and should serve directly to enrich it – are split off from man; they acquire independent status and power and turn back on man to dominate him as his master. It is he who becomes their servant. As the division of labour, the use of money and the growth of private property increase, man's alienation becomes more acute, reaching its highest point in modern capitalist society. Here the worker is alienated from his product, from the work that he sells on the 'labour market', from other men who confront him as capitalists exploiting his labour or as workers competing for jobs, and from nature and society which confront him as limitations and not as fulfilments of his personality. It is this alienation – expressed in the intellectual field by the compartmentalization of the science of man and society into the 'abstract' study of economic man, legal man, ethical man, etc. – which Marx portrays vividly in his *Economic and Philosophical Manuscripts*:

> The more riches the worker produces, the more his production increases in power and scope, the poorer he becomes. The more commodities a worker produces, the cheaper a commodity he becomes. The devaluation of the world of men proceeds in direct proportion to the exploitation of the values of the world of things. Labour not only produces commodities, but it turns itself and the worker into commodities. . . .[1]

Not only the products of man's work, but the very activity of this work are alienated from man. The alienation *within* the worker's activity consists:

> First, in the fact that labour is external to the worker, i.e. it does not belong to his essential being, in the fact that he therefore does not affirm himself in his work, but negates himself in it, that he does not feel content, but unhappy in it, that he develops no free physical and mental energy but mortifies his body and ruins his mind. Therefore the worker feels himself only outside his work, while in his work he feels outside himself. He is at home when he is not working and when he works he is not at home. His work, therefore, is not voluntary, but coerced; it is *forced* labour. It is, therefore, not the satisfaction of a need, but only a *means* for satisfying needs external to it. . . .
>
> The result therefore is that man (the worker) no longer feels

1. M.E.G.A., Section I, Vol. 3, p. 82.

himself acting freely except in his animal functions, eating, drinking, procreating, or at most in his dwelling, ornaments, etc., while in his human functions he feels more and more like an animal. What is animal becomes human and what is human becomes animal.

Drinking, eating and procreating are admittedly also genuinely human functions. But in their abstraction, which separates them from the remaining range of human functions and turns them into sole and ultimate ends, they are animal.[1]

The source of all the distinctions between the savage and the civilized man, Rousseau writes, 'is that the savage lives within himself, while social man lives constantly outside himself, and only knows how to live in the opinion of others, so that he seems to receive the consciousness of his own existence from the judgement of others concerning him'.[2] Marx, in his early (and, I should argue, in his later) work seeks to show the necessary foundation of this alienation in economic life, in a division of labour organized on the basis of private property, in the use of money that makes it possible to convert all things, even labour and care and affection and love, into commodities that are bought and sold. For Marx the division of labour and private property is, of course, inevitable, even necessary, at a certain period of history – only through it can man develop his capacities and realize his limitless potentialities. The savage has not yet separated his labour from himself, has not yet learned to produce for any purpose but use; but in his desperate struggle to satisfy his basic (animal) needs, in his pitiful dependence on nature, he is also man in bondage. To master nature and to overcome human alienation – in these achievements lies the key to the freedom of man. Capitalism has done the former; socialism, Marx believed, would accomplish the latter.

At the end of his *Economic and Philosophical Manuscript* of 1844, Marx painted a picture of the communist society, the society of true and ultimate human freedom. Sympathetic critics have called it the picture of a society of artists, creating freely and consciously, working together in spontaneous and perfect harmony. In such a society, Marx believed, there would be no

1. Ibid., pp. 85–6.
2. *A Discourse on the Origin of Inequality*, in J.-J. Rousseau, *The Social Contract and Discourses* (London: Dent [Everyman's Library], 1913), p. 237. My colleague, Mr S. I. Benn, kindly drew my attention to the passage.

state, no criminals, no conflicts, no need for punitive authority and coercive rules. Each man would be 'caught up' in productive labour with other men, fulfilling himself in social, cooperative creation. The struggle would be a common struggle: in his work, and in other men, man would find not dependence and unpleasantness, but freedom and satisfaction, just as artists find inspiration and satisfaction in their own work and in the work of other artists. Truly free men rising above the very conception of property will thus need no rules imposed from above, no moral exhortations to do their duty, no 'authorities' laying down what is to be done. Art cannot be created by plans imposed from outside; it knows no authorities and no discipline except the authority and the discipline of art itself. What is true of art, Marx believed, is true of all free, productive labour. Just as true communism, for Marx, is not that crude 'communism' which 'is so much under the sway of *material* property, that it wants to destroy everything which cannot be owned by everybody as *private property*; it wants *forcibly* to cut away talent, etc.';[1] so 'free labour', for Marx, is not 'mere fun, mere amusement, as Fourier thinks with all the *naïveté* of a *grisette*. Truly free labour, e.g. composition, is damned serious at the same time, it is the most intensive exertion.'[2]

The vision of communism outlined here, I believe, remained with Marx all his life. It comes out clearly in the *German Ideology* of 1845–6, in the notes and drafts he made between 1850 and 1859, in his *Critique of the Gotha programme* in 1875. It runs through all three volumes of *Das Kapital*. It is a vision of freedom, of spontaneous cooperation, of men's conscious self-determination once they are freed from dependence and need. It is not merely a vision of economic plenty or social security. Engels may have seen communism that way; Marx did not. To the end of his life, through the 'economic filth' that he waded through so conscientiously and unwillingly, Marx remained the philosopher, the apostle and the predictor of freedom.

1. *Economic and Philosophical Manuscripts*, MEGA, Section I, Vol. 3, pp. 111–12.
2. From the draft notes (1857–8) that grew into the *Critique of Political Economy* and were first published in 1939; here cited from the German edition, Karl Marx, *Grundrisse der Kritik der politischen Oekonomie* (Berlin: Dietz Verlag, 1953), p. 505.

2

The intellectual crisis in the democratic socialist movement today is a crisis in socialist ethics: a crisis that stems from the tension between Marx's emphasis on economic rationalism and
material sufficiency, his interest in what he saw as the economic
preconditions of freedom, and his emphasis on a truly human
morality that would overcome the very conception of property
and the divorce between means and ends. Georges Sorel drama-
tized this conflict in Marxian thinking in his picture of the historic conflict between the ethics of the consumer, interested in
profits and returns, seeking security, seeing all things as means
to a commercial end, and the ethics of the producer based on
the 'heroic' values of disinterested creativity, cooperation,
emulation, and indifference to reward. The German sociologist
Ferdinand Tönnies, in part consciously influenced by Marx,
strikingly developed Marx's contrast between the commercial,
divisive society of capitalism and the unalienated society of
communism into a sociological category, the contrast between
the commercial, divisive *Gesellschaft* and the organic fellowship
of the *Gemeinschaft*. *Gesellschaft* is the bourgeois commercial
society in which the cash nexus tends to drive out all other social
ties and relationships, in which men become bound only by contract and commercial exchange, in which the city dominates the
country and the trading class converts the whole land into a
market, in which the 'common, social sphere' is based on the
fleeting moment when men meet in barter, when they have what
the law of contract calls 'a [transitory] meeting of minds'. The
'common sphere' of the *Gemeinschaft*, on the other hand, rests
on a natural harmony, on the ties of tradition, friendship, and
the common acceptance of a religious order; production is
primarily agricultural and for use, society is based on status relations that prevent any man from treating another 'abstractly'.
In the *Gemeinschaft* men are essentially united in spite of all
separating factors; they act on each other's behalf. In the *Gesellschaft* they are essentially separated in spite of all uniting factors;
here every man is isolated and by himself, other men confront
him as competitors and alien intruders. The distinction between
Gemeinschaft and *Gesellschaft*, for Tönnies, is intimately associated with the distinction between two kinds of will, each of

them characteristic of one of the two societies. The *Gemeinschaft* is based on the *Wesenwille*, the natural or integral will in which a man expresses his whole personality and in which there is no developed differentiation between means and ends. Against this stands the *Kürwille*, the rational but in a sense capricious will characteristic of *Gesellschaft*, the will in which means and ends have been sharply differentiated and in which what Max Weber calls *zweckrationale* (purposefully rational) behaviour prevails. In his pamphlet on property, published in 1926, Tönnies illustrates the difference. Property which is the object of the natural will is so closely bound to the nature of the person that any separation from it necessarily produces unhappiness: the owner and his property fuse together, the property becomes part of the owner, loved and cherished as his own creation. This is the way that men are inclined to behave towards living things that they own, towards their house and the yard, and towards the 'sod' which they and their forefathers have worked for generations. In the relationships that result from the natural will there is no sharp differentiation of pleasure and pain, satisfaction and dissatisfaction: the farmer finds in his land both sorrow and joy, duty and pleasure, obligation and privilege. The rational will, on the other hand, finds its paradigmatic expression in the relationship to money, to property that is expressed as credit or debit in a ledger, to 'hands' who cost so and so much in wages. The ultimate consummation of the property of the rational will is the commercial *share*, held by an owner who has not even seen the property it confers on him. It is in these relationships that joy and sorrow, satisfaction and dissatisfaction, are sharply differentiated: *profit* is *plus*, joy, satisfaction; *loss* is *minus*, sorrow, dissatisfaction. Here is the consummation of utilitarian morality: everything is abstracted, torn out of its living context, subsumed under an alienated end.

In the advanced Western society of industrialism, where social mobility and redistributions of wages, status and opportunity have hopelessly blurred and diffused the simple cleavages of traditional class conflicts and where growing affluence has destroyed the plausibility of linking the concept of alienation with that of poverty, some of the ablest of socialist thinkers have returned to the young Marx read in the light of Tönnies. The contemporary socialist critique of capitalism, they say, cannot rest any longer on allegations of the worker's impoverishment and material exploitation: it must focus instead on the failure of capitalism to provide a *Gemeinschaft*, a sense of community, and on the manipulation of human beings in the interests of commercial ends, on the way in which capitalism moulds man into seeking transitory material satisfactions. In the societies claiming to march towards communism, on the other hand, the ablest of the social critics – such men as Ernst Bloch and Leszek Kolakowski, supported by a number of Yugoslav philosophers – have used Marx's vision of communism as a true fraternity in which the opposition between individual and society would have been overcome as a way of criticizing the authoritarian concepts of *Gemeinschaft* and the emphasis on obedience and subservience preached by the Party theologues. It is in Marxian humanism, and not in the commercial morality of Fabianism and 'advanced' trade unions, that non-bureaucratic socialists see the greatest chances of an ethical renewal. There are admittedly those, in Portugal, in large parts of Italy, and in the 'underdeveloped' countries outside Europe, to whom classical Marxism still makes an appeal because the situation in their countries is not a 'twentieth-century situation'; because, like the men to whom the *Communist Manifesto* was addressed, they are still waging the struggle for political democracy, the abolition of seigneurial privileges and the freeing of economic development from the restraints, not of capitalism, but of traditional society. The paradox is that to most of these people Marxism is only a way of destroying conditions that stand between them and the twentieth century. Instead of leading man from the *Gesellschaft* of capitalism into the free, fraternal *Gemeinschaft* of communism, the class struggle in their hands becomes at best a means for leading man from the oppressive *Gemeinschaft* of pre-capitalist society into the *Gesellschaft* of the modern industrial age. It is deeply significant that our most realistic hopes for genuine political liberalization in the Soviet Union and – ultimately – in Communist China, rest on the growth of specialization, the comparative overcoming of chronic shortages and the rise of a consumers' market: in short, on the increasing permeation of some of the values that distinguish capitalist society from traditional, authoritarian society.

Here, then, lies the fundamental problem for socialist humanists. Classical Marxism welded together, in one tremendous act of force and faith, the affirmation of industrial development and the longing for the brotherhood and community of the feudal–agrarian village. The machines that robbed man of his individuality, it taught, had a historic mission: while they seemed to support and extend the naked divisiveness of commercial society, they would end by overthrowing it and leading to the Kingdom of Man. The paths to political and economic democracy, to material satisfaction and to freedom in the fullest possible sense, were all one and the same path. Today, the paths have divided, not in two or three, but in a hundred directions, and the world demands a new map from those who wish to erect a new signpost.

From the work of Marx and Tönnies, from the concepts of alienation and *Gemeinschaft*, it is possible, I believe, to construct a radical ethic: an ethic linked with the acquisition of knowledge, with the traditions of spiritual and material production and of political enterprise and democracy. But it will be an ethic of struggle and criticism, which carries with it no guarantee of success. History is neither the story of the progressive unfolding of a spontaneously cooperative human essence nor is it the inevitable march towards a truly just and human society. History is the battleground of competing traditions, movements and ways of life: it presents us with no total story and no final end. And what is true of history is equally true of society. The socialist humanist, like the exiled Trotsky, will have to recognize that 'history' and 'society' can confront us with one outrage after another; when they do, he will, like Trotsky, have to fight back with his fists.

Even in the formulation of a critical programme, there are problems that must be faced squarely. The work of Tönnies, in elaborating the concept of *Gemeinschaft*, runs together the brotherhood of a working team of equals and the paternalism of a feudal community in which everyone knows and accepts his place. The Promethean socialist vision of the non-commercial society is distinguished from the Romantic conservative vision by its rejection of *hierarchy* and by that alone; yet it is precisely on this point that socialist collectivist practice has failed when working on any scale but the infinitesimal. A great part of the heritage of democratic socialism, and of the socialist concept of freedom, rests on the 'open' society created by capitalist development: the *Gesellschaft* that freed men from the bonds of religious and feudal authority, created the ideal of individualism, cut the oppression of the extended family and vastly increased the area of the 'private' as opposed to the 'public'. The divorce of means and ends has multiplied to an incredible extent the scope and power of human production; the capitalist market, as Hayek and von Mises have emphasized, has created a model by which men find it possible to agree to common means while feeling that they can maintain their diverse individual ends.

This feeling is no doubt partly illusory. Capitalist means do shape the ends that people pursue and such ends acquire no special ethical 'sanctity' simply because they are pursued. But in developing a theory of freedom we can no longer follow Marx in his tacit reliance on the essentially cooperative nature of the human spirit, freed from economic bonds. Neither can we simply rely on the factory as the school of revolution: if modern industrial development has taught new forms of cooperation, it has also raised new and mightier forms of bureaucratization. If the growth of science and technology increasingly liberates man from physically unpleasant work and increasingly tends to eliminate the direct use of power in allocating material resources, it also constantly increases the need for management and direction and the subtler economic and social dependence of man. If we have to revise, to some extent, Marx's concept of man, we must revise, far more radically, Marx's view of industrial society. To this task, I hope, some of my fellow contributors will be addressing themselves.

UMBERTO CERRONI

◎ ◎

Socialist Humanism and Science

UMBERTO CERRONI has studied the institutions of socialism in two books, *Kant and the Foundation of the Juridical
Category* and *Marx and Modern Law*. He teaches philosophy of law at the University of Rome, where he completed his studies in 1947, is a member of the Italian
Society for the Philosophy of Law and of the Executive
Committee of the Antonio Gramsci Institute in Rome,
directs the publication of *Rassegna Sovietica* (*Soviet Review*), and has contributed to numerous cultural publications. He was born in Milan in 1926.

I

Words have a history, and the term 'socialist humanism' is
no exception to this rule. It has two principal meanings which
will be discussed. The first derives from social-democratic
tradition and has been updated by some existentialist interpretations of Marx's notions. A whole sector of theoretical 'revisionism' has proceeded to abandon revolutionary thought and
action itself, preaching the 'humanistic' characteristics of Marxism for the sake of which they have sacrificed their 'narrow'
classist characteristics, and have finished by integrating *Capital*
sometimes with the *Metaphysics of Fashion*, and sometimes with
the *Phenomenology of the Spirit*. This tendency is quite well represented by certain interpretations of Austro-Marxism, by
Léon Blum's socialism 'on human scale' or by other more recent ideas (Lefebvre, Hippolyte, Cálvez, Tucker, etc.).

A second meaning, current in the U.S.S.R. during the Stalin
era, has considered 'socialist humanism' as the moral output of
classical socialism. However, if the first tendency has striven to
liquidate the Marxist science theoretically, the second has
preached its moralistic principles precisely while executing in

practice the most dehumanized distortions of socialism. There is, therefore, reason enough to be on guard *vis-à-vis* both versions of the term.

Nevertheless, it would be unfair to distrust the term 'socialist humanism' itself; rather we should distrust the ideas previously associated with it, and subject them to criticism.

It seems to me that the defects of the term in question are derived from the traditional corruptions that the word 'humanism' has suffered, corruptions that consist substantially in rationalization and moralizing rhetorics. It should be noted that deformations of this type originated because a precise reference to the content and historical meaning of humanism had been lost. Among these meanings two seem essential: the first, ripened during the theoretical polemics that marked the dissolution of the old medieval theological culture, consisted in the secularization of thought, that is, in the construction of rationalistic perspectives which obtained their intellectual baptism from the awakening experimental sciences; the second, developed above all in the modern utopian way of thinking, originated in the intuition of the integration of the individual, mankind and nature, the 'perfectibility' of 'the earthly city', and therefore the transference of moral problems from the otherworldly sphere, or interiority, to the worldly sphere, or exteriority; man's problem was reduced from that of 'salvation' or purity of intentions to that of liberation, and, in the final analysis, of social emancipation. Outside this context and historical meaning, the term 'humanism' seems to lack any important cultural values.

It can therefore be said that the discussion of humanism is a discussion of the theoretical and practical consequences (gnosiologically and socially) of lay culture. (Attempts have been made – for instance those of Jacques Maritain – to extract a sort of humanism from the transcending vision of Christianity; but these attempts are, I believe, plagued with errors.) This is a discussion, therefore, of the consistency, vigour and historical adequacy of a rational programme scientifically founded on the knowledge of the human world (and therefore of the unification of knowledge) and of a social programme constituting the integration of the individual with society. If this is true, the importance of the struggles of Marxist theoreticians to construct a socialist humanism will easily be understood, at the moment when modern thought seems to have abandoned the two principles we have just outlined. Starting from a well-founded criticism of the dogmatic and moralist tradition, this struggle has progressively deepened the division between 'humanistic sciences' and natural and physical sciences. The separation of the 'human kingdom' from the 'kingdom of nature' implies the necessity of a Kantian 'teleological' integration of scientific knowledge, which must culminate in a Hegelian reduction of history to philosophy as a mere phenomenology of the Spirit, or it implies the necessity to conceive the structure of human knowledge as a non-causal structure (non-explanatory), or as 'comprehensive'. (Cf. the contrast between *Verstehen* and *Erklären* in modern gnosiology, Dilthey's historicism, neo-Kantianism, the 'sociology' of Max Weber, and Croce's transformation of history into philosophy.) Instead, the era of the most imposing progress of science is also the era of the renaissance of the most serious metaphysical tendencies in social sciences. Even the young sociological science has again requested the help of philosophy, and even of rationalism; it would be enough to recall the critical considerations of C. Wright Mills. On the other hand, ideal types have been considered as typical 'points of reference'; it might suffice, for instance, to think of the manner in which Kelsen deals with the problem of democracy.

It would be interesting, but too laborious, to analyse the historical components of these two sequences. We can see them, for example, in the fundamentally sceptical results which the critical examination of abstract rationalism (Kant) has come to, and in the progressing limitations of the problems inherited from the analyses of classic economy. In short, it seems that modern theoretical conscience has again brought to light the incapacity of the intellect to know simultaneously the world and the 'irregularity' (individuality, irrepeatability) in economic, social and political phenomena, and therefore the impossibility of transforming them. Even more interesting and urgent seems, therefore, the programme of a socialist humanism. But this programme will be fruitful only when it can be rid simultaneously of the two typical 'rhetoric' defects of humanism, i.e. abstraction and moralism. In short, if socialist humanism is to be freed from the dangers of agnosticism and irrationalism which we are denouncing in modern thought, it should also be liberated from the *abstractionism* of the old dogmatic rationalism, and from the *merely* utopian characteristics of social projections. The one, in fact, reduces thought to the empirical prison of things, while the other confirms man in his present social conditions. Only thus is it possible, I think, to reconquer, through the cognizance of the world, the scientific functions of the intellect, and, along with the notion of the transformability of society, its causal structure. In both fields, the gnosiological and the ethical–social, the most difficult and fruitful work theoretical Marxism can undertake is to recover either the hypothetic–experimental structure of thought, or the causal–objective foundation (*Gesetzmässig*) of the world and of society. A socialist humanism freed from all rhetorics – and therefore of all abstract assertions not confirmed by science, or by real transformations – needs above all to be constructed as a science. It is in this that its materialistic character must consist.

2

The scientific seriousness of this problem, and the momentousness of the tasks assumed by a social movement such as Marxism prevent us from forgetting criticism made not so much against Marx but against Marxists working in our time; this criticism tends to demonstrate the incoherence of a humanistic programme understood in the terms we have briefly recalled. This criticism has in essence sustained two theses:

(*a*) that on a theoretical basis, Marxism has developed a metaphysics, and therefore the dogmatism of a new laical theology which has become secondary to science;

(*b*) that in the practical sphere, socialism is to date very far from constructing an institutional system (economic–political) capable of injecting in science the need of a profound and direct social integration.

These are severe criticisms and it would be useless to pretend that they cannot be sustained by authentic evidence; Stalin's years are there to prove them. In fact, in these years, in the name of Marxism, something very serious that must worry us has happened: in the theorical sphere, a vilification of science and of its methods of investigation, founded on the free intellectual construction of hypotheses and their strict causal verification; and in the practical sphere, an almost inconceivable (at least for a Marxist) distortion of the scientific experimental foundations of the economic–social construction.

We cannot avoid the problem by counting the years that separate us from Stalin. We need rather to measure the critical distance separating the socialism of that era from the destruction effected today, by all the distortions of Marxism. I do not pretend to reopen here the discussion of such a complex phenomenon. I think however, that we must, for our purposes, recognize the criticisms we have mentioned, and examine them in order to arrive at a project for a socialist humanism that is not mere rhetoric. At this point, however, our talk must necessarily turn towards Marx: this thinker who is already the great phenomenon of world culture, this Aristotle of modern times.

My thesis is that among Marxists themselves there has existed, for a long time, a great misunderstanding regarding Marx. If synthesizing is permitted, this misunderstanding can be abridged as follows: too many Marxists still consider that the main task of the Marxist thought is to guide an 'exact' and 'scientific' philosophy before which the very natural and physical sciences would be considered simply as evidence or proof. Of that exact philosophy, which would preserve a dimension *qualitatively* differing from experimental science, dialectics would be the instrument. Not a few Marxist intellectuals – at least in Italy – have on the contrary articulated a different hypothesis: Marx has not elaborated a new philosophy unifying the world of knowledge and absorbing science, but has rather added to the knowledge of humanity the instruments of science; in short, Marx's dialectics do not regress science to philosophic reason, but introduce philosophic reason into scientific intellection.

It is of course not possible to discuss both theses analytically; but we can consider some thoughts which arise from our thesis regarding the development of the socialist movement, and particularly the problem of socialist humanism.

3

The humanistic tenets of Marx's thought can no longer be seriously doubted after the posthumous publications of essays such as *Criticism of the Hegelian Philosophy on Public Right, Economic and Philosophical Manuscripts of 1844* and *German Ideology*. Even those rejecting historical materialism subscribe to such tenets, and, what is more, they have constantly used them in opposition to the classic, economic and political results of Marx's investigations. In fact, it seems that the hazards in the publication of Marx's work, not to mention those of its diffusion and popularization, have created a peculiar situation: the political socialist movement which was based on the concept of the class struggles has remained largely ignorant, for a long time, of the problems of 'the young' Marx, while others, criticizing classic socialism, have often referred to the 'humanism' of his youthful works. We thus witness a tacit repudiation of his youthful humanistic principles, by precisely those forces which in practice have developed Marx's principles and should benefit from them.

An attentive examination of the intellectual biography of Marx constantly reiterates one problem: the group of his works commonly called 'youthful' constitutes the methodical transfer through which Marx's thought 'descends' from philosophy to political economy, from theorical criticism to practical criticism, and even from a design of criticism to one of struggle. If the 'youthful' thought is the road towards *Capital*, it should always be considered, either to explain the *methodologic* necessity of the reduction of philosophic criticism to economic–social criticism, or to enlighten the methodological connexions of this same investigation. Any other way of considering this early work is to risk impoverishing and denaturalizing the true thought of Marx, to graft it on to a traditional methodology, and to dissociate the economic–scientific criticism from the general theoretical problems.

4

We do not want, however, to pose a problem of sheer philology. It seems to me, on the contrary, that these notes (which should be developed later) will serve to focus on a strictly practical problem regarding the history of the socialist movement. First of all, despite the assumptions of certain self-appointed executors of the 'will' of Marxism, the ensemble of doctrines we call scientific socialism has been deprived of a scientific bond, of coherence and theoretical internal completeness, and the lack of these qualities has been substituted by the intrusion of theoretical elements, absolutely alien and even opposed to the true intellectual development of Marx. I refer to that 'dialectic materialism' which from Engels to Stalin has done nothing but ask help or credit from that lower form of Hegelianism which was discarded by serious thinkers after the adventures of social Darwinism and of nineteenth-century positivism. Marx has been clearly 'integrated', and therefore revised, following Hegel in a servile fashion, with consequences not less serious than those of neo-Kantian revisionism. During Stalin's régime, experimental science was forced to move along idealistic perspectives based on those 'prenotions' against which Bacon, the founder of the experimental method, had already fought. Philosophy was in this guise liberated again from science, and revolved once more round its axis, shrinking the social and political sciences into a dogmatic and utopian theory and finding in dialectics (Hegelian) a pass-key to open all doors – and therefore nothing. Once philosophy was restituted to its perennial sphere, it was logical that the so-much-talked-about 'humanism' would afterwards return to an anthropology fatally inclined to the old moralistic generalities. Socialist humanism therefore ended in the pure and simple rhetorical exaltation of its ends, and afterwards in the 'surrendering' of the individual to the community. Let us add that this community, necessarily opposed to the interaction of individuals, could not consist in anything but the present state; hence this surrendering resolved itself in a moralist reinforcement of the domination–subordination relationship of constituted authority over the worker. In this manner, all the 'humanistic' potentiality of socialism turned into statism; in the Hegelian manner, the socialist state became 'a substantial unity with a self-purpose, absolute, motionless, wherein liberty reaches its supreme right and whose final objective has a priority right against that of individuals, whose utmost duty consists in being components of the State' (Hegel).

It may well be that, even without knowing it, socialism was returning to the old path of statist moralism, searching for the mediation between the individual and the community, no longer in the naturalistic dimensions of the socialization of the means of production and consequently of social self-government, but precisely in that 'metaphysic power of the State' against which the young Marx had fought with Hegel. The socialization of man becomes then rather a pedagogic (moralistic) problem of the state, and not a real and practical procedure; and the activities of the state, instead of being specific *functions* of the association of producers, were on the contrary projected as *ends in themselves*, as 'formalities' or as 'rites' (Marx). From these ceremonial rites, all the traditional components were resurrected: bureaucracy, formalism, pedagogism, official truth, secrecy, mysticism of hierarchies and of the head of the state, and the subordination of real science to the formal 'science' of politics. Above all, the separation of society and state (of individual and community) was revived – a separation that socialism should have all but abolished and that, by its continued existence, resulted in persecution and ulterior theoretical sanction.

It is true that it was a 'new' state, the state of workers. Despite this, whoever theorized on this novelty evidently lost sight of the fact that neither the change in political personnel, nor the change of the state's objectives, can achieve by itself a change in the positive structure of the state as a 'merely delusory community' (Marx). In short, the unifying function of the socialist state can be developed only through the specific manner of its subordination to society, of the progressive transference of its functions to the community of workers and of the progressive transformation into communist self-government.

5

Certain conclusions can be drawn from what we have said. Socialist humanism must, in the first place, rid itself of that secular tradition of dogmatic rationalism which pretends to be above science, and arrive at conducting social investigation with the typical methods of science; that is to say, it must base knowledge on the examination of actual social relationships. Only in this way can the primacy of political economy make sense within the sphere of social disciplines. In the second place, socialist humanism must construct its own models of social transformation as functions of scientific criticism of the capitalistic social structure, avoiding in this way the pure mental (dogmatic) search of socialist construction. In the third place, it must accept the merely experimental nature of its models; thus these models

can be modified in accordance with their efficiency in the transformation of relationships inherited from the past. In the fourth
place, it must realize, in the special level of political theory, that
the authentic efficiency of its models should be measured, taking
into consideration not only a future of complete social homo-
genization (communism), but also the possibility of attaining the
consent of workers and stimulating their organization; in the
present it is only in this sense that communism can succeed as a
supreme achievement, even arriving at the dissolution of democracy.

Recapitulating briefly, we could adopt the formula: an authentic humanism (which can only be socialistic and therefore
materialistic, a socializer and emancipator of workers), must succeed in grounding all knowledge on science, in order to free itself
from the rationality of its 'autosufficiency' and its abstractionism. A science of society, while it cuts the abstract rationalistic
tradition from philosophy, and also liberates science (confined
to nature) from its 'scientist' anguish, organically grafts it on to
society, and connects at the same time the social development
(an area reserved to philosophical speculations) with science. In
short, it completely establishes that relationship of reason–consent–interest which has to date been separated into two 'king-
doms': that of the rationalistic–idealistic area of philosophy versus
science, of 'freedom' versus 'necessity'. Along this line, we do
not find it difficult to envision even the practical construction of
a society where, through the Marxist programme of a thorough
naturalization of man and a thorough socialization of nature, the
harmonization of individual and society would be absolutely
feasible. In reality, the individual would succeed in realizing
himself, all the more since his liberty would necessarily imply a
conscious and interested participation in society; on the other
hand, the human society would benefit more when its members
became thoroughly integrated on the basis of a hierarchy of
effective assets of each member. Neither reason above science
nor science above reason; neither the individual over society nor
the society over the individual. Once the critical requirements
we have outlined are satisfied, the programme for a socialist,
anti-rhetorical and historically efficient humanism seems to be
established.

Translated by T. Gil

II. ON MAN

ADAM SCHAFF

⊛ ⊛

Marxism and the Philosophy of Man

ADAM SCHAFF, born in Lvov, Poland, in 1913, studied law and economics in Lvov and at the École des Sciences Politiques et Économiques in Paris, and philosophy in Poland and the Soviet Union. In 1945, he received his doctor's degree at the Soviet Academy of Sciences, Institute of Philosophy. During his youth, he participated in the Polish underground Communist movement and is now a member of the Central Committee of the Polish United Workers' Party. As a philosopher, he specializes in epistemology and his principal publications in this field are *Concept and Word, Problems of the Marxist Theory of Truth, Introduction to Semantics* and *Language and Cognition*. He has also done research in the methodology of the social sciences in relation to Marxist theory and has published *Introduction to the Theory of Marxism, The Rise and Growth of Marxist Philosophy, The Objective Nature of the Laws of History* and *A Philosophy of Man*.

There is nothing new in the statement that the central problem of socialism – of *any* socialism, and Marx's socialism in particular – is the problem of man, with its most essental aspect of creating conditions for man's happiness and full development. For *any* socialism, whether ancient or modern, utopian or scientific, has its roots in rebellion against social evils, poverty and exploitation, slavery and oppression, and all other sources of human suffering. *Any* socialism, even if incapable of saying *what human happiness is*, is always ready to say what its obstacles are, and to imply in its programme ways and means of eliminating the sources of man's misery.

Marx's socialism – whose ideological expression is found in Marxism – is no exception to the rule. A product of the age of great social upheavals, Marxism was born out of an intensified autoreflection on the relationship between the individual and society. When the young Marx first became concerned with the problem of the human individual and the various forms of his alienation in a class society, his thinking already formed part of the great philosophical trends of the age. It was the merit of his genius that, although his point of departure was the same as that of his contemporaries, he could take a different road and go further than they did. The fact that Marx chose a different way was due, in the field of theory, to a number of reasons – all of which can be reduced to his different idea of the human individual. In any case, a philosophy of man was the cradle of Marxism.

The more important attempts at solving the problem of the individual and society can be placed between two extreme approaches: the heteronomous and the autonomous concepts of the human individual.

The former posits the existence of some superhuman forces of which the human individual is the product or emanation – not only in the physical sense but also, and perhaps primarily, in the sense of his attitude and behaviour, based on a system of values built from outside, from a superhuman world. This is a typically religious approach – and it does not matter whether it refers to a personal God, the Absolute Idea, Fate, etc. An example of this approach is Catholic personalism.

The autonomous conception, on the other hand, rejects the existence of any superhuman forces as responsible for the creation – physical and spiritual – of the human individual and his behaviour; as a result it believes in humanism. But there are two opposed varieties of this approach. One of them – exemplified, for instance, in Sartre's atheistic existentialism – by rejecting heteronomy and construing its humanistic autonomism, takes as its starting point the individual interpreted as a spiritual monad (a monad of will, conscience, emotion, etc.). In an extreme interpretation it is a typical Leibniz monad which 'has no windows'; the individual is lonely, isolated, 'doomed to freedom' or 'doomed to choice', and has no help or assistance. It is true that the metaphysical concept of heteronomy – which the modern, scientific mind cannot accept without renouncing all its habits of thinking – has been eliminated, but a mere trifle has been lost in the process – society and the bonds that arise within its framework. And it is no wonder that the purely subjectivist and asocial pattern of this type of existentialism has encountered enormous difficulties, for it expects from the modern mind an equally great, although different, sacrifice as its antagonist. Sartre, it is true, looks for a way out, and attempts to reconcile existentialism and historical materialism – but without success. The result is that the structure of his doctrine is far from coherent, and its 'original sin' remains.

A diametrically opposed approach is provided – within the framework of the anti-heteronomous conception – by the attempt to solve the problem based on society and social relations. A typical example of this position is represented by the vulgarized type of Marxism – in the form of economic materialism. Here, it is true, we do dissociate ourselves from both the need to look for the help of heteronomous, superhuman forces and voluntarist subjectivism – but in exchange, while regaining human society, which has been lost in the existentialist confusion, we in turn lose sight of the individual. From a history-maker, a master of his own choices, he becomes a *mere* product, a statistical average, an executor of historical laws which are independent of his will. Let me repeat: *this is not* authentic Marxism, it is only its crude interpretation – understandable as it is because of a psychological reaction, among other things, to the subjectivist or religious misinterpretation of the problem. Nevertheless, such an approach did exist for many years – and we must not overlook it now when trying to arrive at a correct view of the matter.

Marxism – at least in the interpretation that regards Marx's development from youth to maturity as a whole – adopts an attitude which is in a sense different from all the above-mentioned conceptions. Rejecting the heteronomous notion of the individual as metaphysical, Marxism chooses the empirical foundation of radical humanism: *men* are makers of their history and history discloses to us nothing outside their action. Everything else is speculation. But existentialist metaphysics is rejected by Marxism with equal emphasis as subjectivist–voluntarist speculation: what is given in experience is not individuals – but *social* individuals; while making history they are also its product. In its struggle against subjectivism Marxism continues Aristotle's old line – man is *zoon politikon*. But his *point of departure* is the human *individual* who, not only as a living organism but as an organism that acts on a plan conceived in *its* mind, is something separate in its individuality. Thus Marxism also vigorously opposes those theories which, while rejecting the anti-humanist, heteronomous vision of the individual, run to the other extreme of the equally anti-humanist, asocial vision of this individual, to whom they only concede the passive role of a product and whom they actually overlook in some abstract idea of society.

In investigating the relationships between the individual and society, our point of departure – only an *empirical* one – is the *individual* man; he thinks and acts and always cooperates with others, within some social framework, but is a *distinct* individual. When Marx insists that 'men create history' he opposes both those who maintain that history is created by some superhuman forces while man is only their instrument, and also those according to whom history is created, not by actual human individuals, but by some abstract social groups. But when the individual is treated as the starting point of our analysis we must not forget that his autonomy is only *relative*. This is not a mysterious monad of will and consciousness, isolated and deprived of contact with others; this is a *social* individual, because, unable to live with society, he is – since the moment of birth – shaped *by society* and is its product, physically and spiritually. The issue was once graphically expressed by Marx when, criticizing the narrow scope of Feuerbach's concept of the *generic* individual, he put forth his own idea of the individual as *the entirety of social relations*. This was one of Marx's greatest discoveries – and it contained the nucleus of his philosophy of man. But it later resulted in a formal departure from any direct interest in the philosophy of man, which had been so characteristic of Marx in his youth.

For if the individual is always *social* – that is, if he is a product of society which he creates – then he is in a sense dialectically involved in society; and if the problem of his happiness and development is to be interpreted as liberation from unhappiness and barriers to development, then the problem of the individual, and of his happiness and full development presents itself to us as a *social* problem. What will be of decisive importance is not moral self-improvement, the will of the hero as an arbitrary creator of history or prayers to some supernatural force, but the ability to set in motion those *social* forces which alone are capable of removing the *social* barriers to individual happiness.

Thus, although we begin with the *individual*, we are not only aware of his *social* aspects, but we also perceive the *social* way to the implementation of *individual* aims. The philosophy of man here becomes one with historical materialism as a *theory* of social development and a basis of the *practical* activity of men.

Consequently, the emphasis, particularly with regard to action, is shifted to society and to the material existence shaping its development. Marx, together with the young Hegelians, *began* with the problems of the individual. To the young Hegelians, this remained the central point: they thought that the subjective aspect of individual life could solve the problem of relationships between the individual and society. *Marx* also remained faithful to his original problem – the conditions of the individual's happiness and full development – but shifted its solution to the social plane. New categories appear – social class and class struggle, social formation and factors of its development, capitalism and socialism, bourgeoisie and proletariat – as the forces shaping society. But the problems of the individual and a philosophy of man are *implicit* in this new conception. What is more, without them Marxian socialism loses its supreme sense – since it loses its humanist meaning. And that is why all attempts at splitting Marx's homogeneous theory into his 'early' and 'mature' views, which are alleged to be not only different but opposed, are basically erroneous. This is the case both when the only 'true Marxism' is considered to be based on Marx's views in his youth and when these views are nonchalantly rejected as a survival of idealism or a young man's inconsistent step towards an idea later grasped by a mature man. The young Marx's thinking can only be understood from the viewpoint of its mature shape – for, in his own graphic phrase, the anatomy of man is a key to the anatomy of the ape; but the mature shape of scientific socialism cannot be understood unless it is conceived as the embodiment of the ideals which Marx cherished from his youth, and unless his scientific analysis is illuminated with socialist humanism.

Marx's change is obvious – not only in the choice of words but also in the approach to the question, both theoretical and practical. The numerous alienations and how to overcome them, the problem with which Marx was preoccupied in his youth, assumes the form of struggle against capitalist domination – a struggle which will put an end to class society and, with it, to exploitation, the state, religion, prejudice, etc. – and thus to basic forms of alienation. And this change of approach also means the shifting of emphasis – particularly in the practical struggle for the fulfilment of the desired ends. To ensure individual happiness the masses are roused. Their struggle is only a means to an end, but as long as the struggle goes on it is the centre of attention. This is only normal, for only in this way can the goal be reached. In propaganda, too, the struggle against capitalism gains ever more significance: the ultimate aim is implicitly understood – but what is really absorbing is the actual struggle, on which all efforts have to be concentrated.

The problem of the individual was overlooked in the later phase of Marxism for two reasons. The first is of an objective nature and is connected with the concentration of forces – poor as they were in comparison with the opponent's power – on what was the most important thing at that time – the struggle of the masses. The other reason is of a subjective character and was connected, particularly during the rapid growth of the movement and in view of the long struggle facing it, with the fact that many of those taking part in the movement began to forget about the difference between the actual aim of the struggle and the ways and means leading to this end. The process – which inevitably led to a debasement of the doctrine – was encouraged by a number of factors: the inadequate training of the leaders in theoretical problems, which was rather normal in view of the movement's rapid numerical growth; the pressure of current tasks, which tended to postpone matters not immediately connected with the practical requirements of the movement; the fact that the enemy, taking advantage of these difficulties, turned the problem of the individual into an ideological weapon in its struggle against Marxism; the sectarian and dogmatist distortions in ideology, etc. The result was a situation in which the humanist foundations of Marxian socialism were not only forgotten by many honest and devoted working-class revolutionaries, but even began to be considered by them as something alien to the revolutionary struggle. This is all the more astounding since their words sharply contradicted not only the roots of their own activities and devotion but also what they were actually doing.

The reversion of Marxists today to the problems of the philosophy of man is due to at least three concurrent factors.

First, there are the objective requirements of the movement that – after seizing power in a number of countries – is now not only confronted with tasks connected with the struggle against the old system, but, primarily, with the task of creating new ways of life. The problem of the individual will sooner or later make itself felt – even if it was overlooked for some time. Whatever we call it and in whatever form it presents itself to us, the 'philosophy of man' will force its way through, since with stabilization, when the enemy has been subdued and life is going on, the central problem – how to make people happy – will be of ever greater importance. Victory brings with it new complications and difficulties, partly because the errors committed by the builders of the new life are now visible. These errors have to be corrected, but it is also necessary to analyse their causes and effects – and this, as well as the creation of new forms of individual life, encourages reflection on the philosophy of man.

Second, these objective reasons result in greater needs in the field of theory itself. Although, in a sense, it reflects objective reality, theoretical thinking has a certain degree of autonomy. This is evidenced, among other things, by the tendency to arrive at a rounded philosophical system. The absence of certain elements in the picture of reality is regarded as a serious gap – particularly with the growing importance of some stimuli in the field of practice. It is not a coincidence that modern Marxist theoreticians regard the wants and deficiencies in the field of the theory of values, the philosophy of man, ethics, etc., as an important lack in their theoretical system. But that some twenty years ago the same gaps did not give rise to similar doubts and did not encourage a similar theoretical activity, while today they constitute important incentives, is due to a change in the objective situation and practical requirements.

Third, the intensified interest in the philosophy of man must be placed in the context of the new forms and meaning of ideological struggles. Marxists are now increasingly concerned with the philosophy of man – not only because of the pressure of practical needs, and not only because they want to fill in the gaps in the system – but also because they are interested in the ideological struggle. For the philosophy of man has recently become

– in the period of great upheavals and the ensuing reflection on the relationships between society and the individual – not only the subject but also an instrument of this struggle.

Political coexistence, enforced as it is by modern warfare techniques, is the only reasonable alternative to global destruction. But while technical development may in international relations make men renounce the use of force, it cannot – and does not – make them abandon their systems of values and the concepts and ideas of social life based on these systems. So long as these differences remain, conflicts and attempts to gain victory for one's own ideals are inevitable. If it is no longer possible to solve conflicts by the use of armed forces, only the possibility of *convincing* the opponents and the undecided by means of proper arguments remains open. When we say 'ideological struggle' we mean argumentation against the system of values opposed to ours; in doing this we must set forth our own system of values and our own ideas. This method of struggle must inevitably gain in importance in conditions of peaceful coexistence. Whether this leads to an ideological *rapprochement* as well is a different matter; it is an important issue worth separate treatment.

In conditions of coexistence the problems of the philosophy of man become particularly significant, not only theoretically but also in practice. For what they are primarily concerned with are such issues as the freedom of the human individual, the idea and guarantees of his happiness, his relationship to society and the consequent problem of moral responsibility, etc. These are problems which in capitalist countries form the strongest barrier between the 'man in the street' and socialism, which is undoubtedly the result of the 'free world's' propaganda machinery, but is also largely due to the socialists' errors and to their misinterpretation of the situation. These errors are primarily connected with their inability to shift from the nineteenth-century picture of capitalism to its present conditions. Capitalism still exists as a system, but its forms have thoroughly changed, and consequently the ideas of those who live under it have been modified. This is only natural with the rapid technological and economic transformations of the last decades and in view of the pressure exerted by the socialist world, which forces capitalism to counteract the revolutionary influence of socialism by resorting to proper measures. Unfortunately, in their theoretical analyses, Marxists pay little, if any, attention to this; on the contrary, since the supporters of capitalism say that because of these changes capitalism has ceased to exist, it is often asserted that nothing has changed in capitalism and Marx's formulations from a century ago are literally repeated. This is as false as to insist that capitalism no longer exists simply because it has changed. Capitalism still exists, often more cruel and more capable of exploitation than before. But it is a different capitalism, it has different forms of action and functioning. This is precisely why nationalization or planned economy is no longer an anti-socialist bogey for the 'man in the street' in the capitalist countries, and why this argument is now less often used in official anti-communist propaganda; it is even admitted that socialist economy is capable of considerable results. On the other hand, anti-communist propaganda makes an ever more militant use of the problem of the human individual, his freedom and development, etc. And it must be admitted that this is sometimes a more effective bogey.

What is inevitable in this sphere is not only struggle – which is already going on – but also a Marxist offensive, which must be done under the great threat of defeat in ideological struggle.

Success in the struggle for the minds and hearts of men in conditions of coexistence, particularly in what is known as the 'new world', will chiefly depend on the results of economic competition. But not only on this. Of no less importance to men are problems of liberty – especially in the case of the young nations of Asia and Africa; this is true both of national liberty and of freedom of the individual, with all the implications of the philosophy of man. Human choices and attitudes will naturally be affected first of all by facts. But not only by them. What will also be important is how these facts are presented and much will depend on a theory's ability to support and develop practice. Facts are not only born in a spontaneous way; they are also consciously shaped and encouraged.

Here is a new and different aspect of the philosophy of man – as an element of the ideological struggle and a factor influencing the formation of the practical relations between the individual and society.

MILAN PRŮCHA

◎ ◎

Marxism and the Existential Problems of Man

MILAN PRŮCHA, of the Institute of Philosophy, the
Prague Academy of Sciences, has taught at the State University in Moscow and studied in France. He has published
several essays in his field of interest, the critical analysis of
phenomenology and existentialism, including 'Philosophical Problems of the Existence of Man', and 'Cogito and
Prima Philosophia in Marxism'. He was born in Plzeň,
Czechoslovakia, in 1931.

Existentialism, Marxism and Christian philosophy conflict
over the concept of alienation. Is man thrust into an absurd
world in which the fact of mortality condemns all his aspirations?
Is man an unrepeatable product of the historical process, revolt-
ing against exploitation and against the alienated machinery of
social organization? Are the problems of life and death independent of social organization, or are they exclusively historical
problems which will find their final solution in the harmony
between the individual and society?

Although Existentialists and Christians radically oppose each
other, they are agreed in their interpretation of Marx. Hegel
conceived alienation in the following manner: the subject first
encounters the outer, to him alien, world, but later recognizes
himself in this object, thus reassuring himself of the identity of
consciousness and being. Marx, it is said, comprehends alienation (that is, the fact that man's creations become blind and
hostile forces to him) as a manifestation of transitory capitalist
relations, rather than deducing it from the existence of the objective world. From this interpretation it is easy for Marx's critics
to object that any social or human relationship will always end
in externalization: that technology (the means by which man

forms his world) or state administration (even a socialist one) becomes alienated; that love or any human relationship results in separation, or the realization of oneself outside oneself. This criticism is extended to a broader problem: Marxism encloses man within history, so that it is unable to confront man with the external world and thus can deal only with historical, not existential, problems.

This description of the differences between Marx's and Hegel's concepts of alienation is an oversimplification. Marx criticized Hegel on the ground that he could not comprehend the specificity of the alienation of social relations in capitalist society. But he also criticized him on the most general philosophical level:

> When Hegel conceives wealth, the power of the state, etc. as entities alienated from the human being, he conceives them only in their thought form. They are entities of thought and thus simply an alienation of *pure* (i.e. abstract) philosophical thought. . . . Alienation is . . . the opposition within thought itself . . . (*Economic and Philosophical Manuscripts*).

A critical examination of Marx's *Economic and Philosophic Manuscripts* shows that for Marx as well as for Hegel labour in its most general form *always* presupposes alienation and the overcoming of alienation. But this general analysis of labour is not identical with the concept of alienated labour that Marx later formulated in his critical study of capitalist society.[1] In *Grundrisse der Kritik der politischen Oekonomie* (1857–8) and in *Capital*, he speaks of *reified* (*verdinglicht*) relations and reification (*Verdinglichung*). He uses these concepts to express the alien character and the alienation of capitalist relations of production:

> The social character of activity . . . appears here as an alien object in relation to the individuals . . . their mutual relationship appears to the individuals themselves as something alien and autonomous, as an object. (*Grundrisse der Kritik der politischen Oekonomie* [Berlin, 1953], p. 75.)

Thus Marx did not reduce Hegel's complex conception to an analysis of man's position in history or to an analysis of the economic relations between men. Hegel limited alienation to the

1. Cf. T. J. Ojzerman, *Formirovanije Filosofii Marksizma* (Moscow, 1962), p. 260.

realm of thought and reduced the human drama to a spiritual drama, but Marx had a total conception of man which included his relations to the outside world. In order to compare Marx's viewpoint with that of Existentialism and Christianity, it is not enough to analyse the terminology; a thorough understanding of the concept of alienation in terms of philosophical materialism and atheism is necessary.

In Heidegger's conception the world is deprived of its independent qualities and meanings and possesses only those which it acquires through its contact with human subjectivity. There are no ideas in *Sein und Zeit* capable of expressing the resistance which matter offers to man. The intriguing formula which proclaims man as a being thrust into a world alien to him, and which calls for meditation on this tragic aspect of human life, turns out to be a disappointment. The extreme sharpening of the contradiction between being and consciousness in Sartre's philosophy results in the disappearance of contradictions between man and the world, because their mutual alienation becomes so absolute that subjective choices are detached from the material conditions within which they are possible. Existential philosophy, which meant to express the tragedy of man's situation, becomes a superficial optimism through its idealism.

Man is not the universal purpose of the world which religious illusion believes him to be. Man came into existence in a certain part of the universe, under certain favourable conditions, as a partial product of the development of matter. He must, therefore, assert himself through his practical activity against the world as a whole; 'rooted' in the world, he must carry into it a meaning given by human existential needs. The materialistic conception of the world, expressing the 'relatedness' and 'alienation' of man and the world, overcomes the onesidedness of Existential and Christian philosophy and forms the basis for solving the philosophical problems of man's existence.

There is neither absolute alienation, which prevents communication between man and world, nor total harmony, which presupposes the possibility of identifying man with the world. The world cannot be a pure object to man, nor can it be a pure *Erlebnis*.

The world is not a pure object because man must already be in the world, must live in reality, in order to make it his object.

Reality, however, cannot be a mere *Erlebnis*, because man can only live in the world by making it the object of his knowledge and of his transforming activity. In our opinion this is the significance of Marx's criticism of all previous materialist philosophies: they did not comprehend that 'things, reality, the sensible world are conceived only in the form of objects of contemplation, but not as human sense activity, as practice, not subjectively' (*Theses on Feuerbach*, Thesis I).

Philosophy after Marx cannot ask simply whether the world stands before man or against man in the form of an object. The perspective on problems of human existence has fundamentally changed and the inquiry has to be concerned with how man lives in the world. Mechanical materialism conceived man as a thing among things, as a machine, but it was not capable of erecting a spiritual dam against idealism. As a philosophy for which reality exists only in the form of an object, it unconsciously placed the philosophizing ego before the reality from which the ego observed and judged it. Thus it transformed the real ego into a de-realized and unreal ego, into pure self-consciousness. Reality degenerated into dead matter incompatible with any kind of subjectivity. Marx surpassed this concept of man by overcoming its naturalism and applying socio-historical criteria. But he also changed the entire perspective of philosophy. It ceased to be a philosophy of being prior to reality, a philosophy of contemplation, and became a philosophy leading to intellectual clarification of the position of the ego in the known reality and of the act by which the ego makes reality its object. The concepts of ego and reality are not abstractions, as in Hegel; the concepts relate both to a material, natural being and to nature. That is why Marx emphasizes that if real physical man posits his objective being and powers as alien objects, 'the *positing* is not the subject; it is the subjectivity of *objective* powers' (*Economic and Philosophical Manuscripts*). Man is a subject in that he exists in his natural forces and as his natural forces, and the only possible object of his life's manifestations are real sensuous objects. The being which has no object outside itself is not objective. The being which does not have its own naturalness outside itself is not natural because it is not part of nature's essence. The objective being has objects outside itself and is an object; it behaves objectively and its being is thus an objective being. The natural

141

being is a finite, conditioned, limited and suffering being because
the objects in which it confirms itself are independent of it.
Hunger, for instance, is an objective bodily need, a need for an
external object. 'Man as an objective sentient being is a *suffering*
being, and since he feels his suffering, a *passionate* being. Passion
is man's faculties striving to attain their object' (*Economic and
Philosophical Manuscripts*).

Marx's analysis of man as a material, objective, suffering and
passionate being stands as irrefutable proof of the superficiality
of those critics who accuse him of reducing all human problems
to that of man's condition in capitalist society.

The merits of the philosophical concept of man as an objective being are vindicated in the controversy between Marxism
and Existentialism. Heidegger, for instance, was incapable of
dealing with the problem of existence in terms of the corporeality
of the existing being; the latter is for him, as it is for Hegel, pure
subjectivity moving in a world of pure thought. Sartre formulates this problem only as an antinomy: I am my body because
self-consciousness is possible only as consciousness of a certain
facticity; at the same time I am not my body because the body is
exceeded by what I am. In his conception of unconditioned and
unmotivated freedom, however, he retreats even from these
controversial positions. Here man assumes the form of pure
'ego', of thought, of self-consciousness. He is completely excluded from reality, nothing conditions or determines him. The
inability to conceive man as an objective being and to place him
in the real world results in a conception of existence based on the
mutual alienation of the ego and the world. Hence the emptiness
of 'ego' which is the abstract negation of the world and all its
wealth. Hence the characterization of man's being as a 'being for
death', as a centre of feelings of anxiety, disgust, boredom.

No doubt credit must be given to Existentialism for reopening
the problem of death in its deep philosophical meaning, a problem which appears with brutal radicalism in every atheistic
philosophy. Existentialists have convincingly shown that death
means that chance and absurdity are ineradicable constituent
elements of human existence. Does this mean, however, that
mortality is the sole or determining factor of man's existence?
Does death devalue all human aspirations, all human desires,
relationships and feelings? The empty 'ego' of the subjectivistic

concept of man can have in fact no other problem but that of its bare existence. But if man is conceived as an objective being he ceases to move only within the abstract sphere of yes or no, and he becomes a being completely interested in the world. Just to preserve existence is not his sole interest. As an objective being he is universally passionate and craves the world; he experiences hunger, sex and the whole vast range of specifically human passions and feelings, not merely anxiety. The finitude of the objective being is thus not reduced to its mortality. It must, of necessity, realize itself outside itself in the objective world. This finitude is the exact opposite of the indifference to which, according to Heidegger, the comprehension of man as mortal must lead. Man is far freer than Existentialism would have him. Through his interest in the world and in the fate of other people he creates his human riches and the hierarchy of interests and values which deprive death of its character as the absolute arbiter. 'Positive' passions confirm the structure of human existence and are just as 'authentic' as anxiety, boredom or disgust. The natural structure of man as a finite being is thus the complete openness of the world, an interest in the world and not abstract negativity – death.

A more complex view of the problems of man's existence may be outlined on the basis of Marx's philosophy; and criticism of some over-simplified interpretations of Marx reveals the true meaning of the social determination of man.

The common denominator of the various philosophical concepts opposed by Marxism is the traditional view that the individual precedes society, which is expressed in such notions as the 'social contract'. The traditional view attempts to derive the social structure from the qualities of the individual. Human essence is seen as an abstraction common to each single individual, so that the methods for studying it consist in finding characteristics common to all individuals. The logic of this conception leads to a type of conclusion which may be illustrated as follows: because neither Mozart nor Aristotle was engaged in tool production, this activity does not belong to the human essence, but the soft earlap which is found only in man, and not in other animals, does belong.[1] Thus conceived, history is only

1. Cf. E. V. Iljenkov, *Dialektika abstraktnovo i Konkretnovo v 'Kapitale' Marksa* (Moscow, 1960), p. 29.

an external and accidental side show, manifesting an unchangeable human essence given by God or by nature (which must then be identified with human nature).

The 'naturalistic' interpretation of man operates deliberately with the method of an impoverishing reductionism: it cannot find within the sphere of 'natural' qualities an equivalent to the results of manifold human activity and therefore explains all this wealth by means of a few instincts. It cannot comprehend the freedom of human existence and therefore opposes to it a physiological or other primitive determinism.

Marx comprehends the essence of man as the result of specific human activity, in accordance with his concept of practical materialism. Man as a natural being creates social reality. This is a new reality in comparison with natural reality, in which the being of each individual achieves its content only in relation to other individuals, in relation to the social entity. In the Sixth Thesis on Feuerbach Marx wrote: 'the essence of man is not an abstraction inherent in each individual. In its reality it is the totality of social relations'. 'Sociability' as a determinant of the essence of man cannot be understood as a characteristic of the abstract individual, but as a reference to social reality. In the dynamics of social reality, which are more varied than the activity of each single individual, the data of an answer to the question 'What is man?' are being historically formed and concretized.

In this way it is possible to approach more concretely the study of human essence and to follow the actual historical process of its formation. The relevant questions concern the degree to which man has cultivated the variety of his social relations, the extent to which he has extricated himself from nature and developed his social essence, and the degree to which his individual existence has become a social one. Man's existence, at the same time, contains irreducible natural determinations which may be modified in various ways in history, but not abolished. Human naturalness – which Marx describes in these words: '. . . my own nature which is a unity of needs and impulses . . .' (*Grundrisse*) – is not identical with human essence. This is a necessary notion in the Marxist comprehension of man, which Marx uses both in his early works and in the *Grundrisse* and in *Capital*. It enables him to judge the mode of social existence in order to determine whether human naturalness confirms itself in it and develops, or is mutilated.

It is also necessary to examine the relationship of individual existence and the social essence of man to see (a) whether individual existence appears as an affirmation of the social essence, or as its negation; and (b) whether the social essence manifests itself to individuals as their own potency or as an uncontrollable force which subjugates and overwhelms them.

Marxism, because it differentiates between the existence of man and his social essence, differs profoundly from Existentialism. According to Sartre the human individual has no essence: I shall have an essence only after I am dead. Heidegger pays lip service to the essence of man: 'The essence of being is in its existence' (*Sein und Zeit*). But for him, as for other Existentialists, it is identical with human existence, which is conceived wholly uncritically in its bare immediacy, outside of history and other external determinants. This conception of existence is, on the intellectual level, a continuation of Kierkegaard's protest against a purely speculative overcoming of the individual's suffering in Hegel's system of philosophical abstractions. Existentialists passionately try to proclaim that human existence cannot be reduced to an idea, but they completely miss the mark as far as the Marxist conception of the relation between human existence and essence is concerned. In Marxist philosophy the human essence is not merely an 'ideal', a 'norm', a product of the intellect, but is a product of history. Marxism does not reduce the existence of man to its social essence, but it avoids an uncritical acceptance of the given existence. Unlike Hegel, who emphasizes essence, and unlike Existentialism, which emphasizes existence, Marxism does not *identify* existence with essence. By a critical concrete historical confrontation of man's existence with his social essence, it asserts itself as a philosophy of active humanism.

If we regard communism as the movement which forms itself in history as an answer to the question of the relationship between existence and essence, this is in accord with the views formulated by Marx as early as the *Economic and Philosophical Manuscripts*. Communism is 'the true solution of the conflict between existence and essence', 'the real appropriation of human essence through and for man', 'the whole movement of history is his real act of creation', 'Communism is humanism, a complete humanism' (*Economic and Philosophical Manuscripts*). It is not a question of opposing these ideas to Marx's later studies, but of avoiding the distortion of the humanist core of Marx's concept of communism, which a preoccupation with the later writings may produce.

The dynamics of history cannot be deduced from individual existence. The concept of total man expresses much more than the most general existential structures. It is a concept which cannot be determined speculatively because it formulates a historically arising perspective of the development of man.

Human existence is not excluded from history, and does not contain a dynamic not deducible from history. The question of the forms and modes of individual existence is thus a historical question. Marx refuted the sophistry of bourgeois philosophers and economists who presented capitalist social relations as the expression of the natural traits of individuals. To attempt to deduce the notion of total man from general existential structures would be to make the same mistake:

> The universally developed individuals, whose social relations are brought under their own control as their own communal interrelationship, are the products, not of nature, but of history. The level and the universality of the development of wealth, which makes *this* individuality possible, itself depends upon production on the basis of exchange value . . . (*Grundrisse*, p. 79.)

This does not mean that the concept of total man is wholly outside the existential problem. It constitutes a concrete historical solution although it does not abolish these problems. The existential structure of man as an objective being and as a being whose essence is not inherent in the abstract individual but is of a social nature has always determined the most general features of the mode of man's self-assertion: it has always been and will always be possible solely as an assertion of his essential powers, as an active and passionate relation of this finite being to the world, as the acquisition and development of the possibilities and values that society imparts to the individual. The self-assertion of man occurs in an alienated form for a long period. The active being of the individual is suffering, because it is exploited in exhausting and deadening work; his social being is alienated and thus transformed into an uncontrollable power which opposes him and reduces him to a slave. The conception of total man expresses a perspective through which to overcome this alienation. By abolishing exploitation, by subjecting the entire social process to the control of associated individuals, by overcoming the division of labour, through deliverance from the pressure of unsatisfied natural needs, through the development of scientific knowledge, by making art a living form, by the creation of a new type of social relationship, etc., the individual can gain new possibilities for liberating himself from his egocentric self-isolation and for participating in the being of all mankind.

If under alienated relations man's essence as a social being has been only a means for his existence, now the existence of man *is* in his universal, conscious and active being a human social essence.

Translated by T. B. Bottomore

KAREL KOSÍK

⊚ ⊚

Man and Philosophy

KAREL KOSÍK, head of the Department of Dialectical
Materialism at the Institute of Philosophy in Prague, has
contributed to the literature of Marxism with his books
The Czech Radical Democracy and *Dialectic of the Concrete*.
The latter book is being translated into Italian, Spanish
and Polish. Mr Kosík received his education at the Univer-
sities of Prague, Leningrad and Moscow. He was born in
Prague in 1926.

Since there are many areas of specialization which are concerned with man, ranging from those founded upon common-
sense knowledge of human nature all the way to the arts and
sciences, it is not at all clear at first glance whether man has any
further need of philosophy in order to know himself. Off-hand it
would seem that philosophy could attain a truly scientific level
only by the *exclusion of man* from its very foundations as a discipline, i.e. through the critique of anthropologism. Philosophy
arrives at the problem of man on the one hand too late, achieving
a synthesis or a generalization merely on the basis of some other
area of specialization, and on the other hand superfluously,
since the particular task could have been performed by some
other, more specialized discipline.

Common-sense knowledge of human nature is the practical,
prosaic refutation of anthropological romanticism, for it posits
man as being *at all times* a configuration of interests and invi-
dious attitudes. The lessons of a worldly utilitarianism are implied in this form of knowledge, whereby man perceives man as
competitor or friend, neighbour or master, fellow sufferer or
acquaintance, colleague or subordinate, and so on. Through
everyday utilitarian intercourse, a familiarity with the human
character, with its inclinations and habits, is built up, and this

148

knowledge then becomes established as folk wisdom or as practical and general truths, such as: men are deceitful, human nature is fickle, *homo homini lupus*. Machiavelli's advice to rulers as to how they are to govern rests in part upon this kind of knowledge:

> As for men, let the following be said of them in general: they are thankless, fickle, deceitful, cowardly, greedy; as long as you show yourself to be of worth to them they will be with you body and soul, and will offer you their blood, their property, their lives, and their sons, provided you have no need of any of these things; but as soon as you need them, they will rebel against you. (*The Prince*, Chapter 17.)

Hegel considered this kind of knowledge of human nature to be useful and desirable, particularly under poor political conditions, when the arbitrary will of an individual is governing and the relations among men are founded upon intrigues; but such knowledge is entirely without philosophical value, for it cannot rise up from shrewd observation of chance individual occurrences to a grasp of human character in general.

In this common-sense approach to knowledge of human nature, man does not become known, but rather his various *functions* are established and evaluated within the framework of a fixed system. It is not the character (the essence) of man that is made the centre of attention, but only his functionality. In his *System of Governing and Ruling*, Machiavelli deals with man as if with some manipulable entity, as modern science does when it views man in the modern industrial system from the standpoint of the technological process of production, and regularly depicts him as a component – the 'human factor' – in this process.

Such a way of viewing human nature cannot see through its own conditionality and relativity. The so-called worldly-wise, who calculate on the vanity and *naïveté*, the ambition and corruptibility, the timidity and indolence of the individual, and who enter into extended transactions with the human material on the basis of these calculations, have no idea that these qualities or functions really exist only within the general system of manipulations and manipulability, a system within which they too are inseparable components. Outside of this system the qualities of men undergo a transformation, and this so-called worldly wisdom loses its value and meaning.

Modern anthropological research posits the *complexity* of man as its basic assumption, thereby reflecting the spirit of scientific method and of the growing number of disciplines that are concerned with the study of man. Man is a complicated being, and cannot be explained by some simple metaphysical formula. Every one of his special interests is set up as the subject matter of an independent scientific discipline, so that it may be exactly analysed. The various specialized anthropological sciences have assembled an enormous mass of material, pouring forth invaluable findings about man as a biological being, a cultural being, a social being and so on. Yet, despite the force of these scientific achievements, man *qua* man has never been so great a problem as he is today.

This discrepancy is due to an improper conception of the role of scientific anthropology. The various human sciences are occupied with either one or the other special aspect of man. When they explain their observations systematically, these sciences proceed from their own special viewpoints to develop a conception of man as a whole. The problem to which they address themselves is summed up in the question, What is man? The answers they give add up to a depressing variety of definitions, since each one allows itself broader and broader range in positing man's fundamental characteristics. It is true that man is a living being who produces tools, but it is equally true to say he is a living being who employs symbols, who knows of his own mortality, who is capable of saying, No, who is a social being, and so on. One definition cannot dispute the assumptions of another, for *every* particular aspect of man is isolated, and *none* of them is capable, from its own particular standpoint, of providing a notion of the *whole* man, concretely and as a totality.

In the pursuit of the question, *What* is man?, the question, *Who* is man? is either left unanswered, or is set aside altogether.

As long as the relationship between these two questions – *What* is man? and *Who* is man? – is left unaccounted for, all attempts at achieving a synthesis of the data assembled by the various specialized branches of anthropology will remain fruitless. It is only on the basis of a distinct and established conception of man that a synthetic discipline will be able to draw together the data of the various partial sciences into an integral knowledge of man. The concept of man as a whole must be the premise of such a synthesis. Otherwise the synthesis would be one-sided, whether we were aware of it or not, for it would be undertaken on the basis of some specialized scientific pursuit, and man would accordingly be biologized, physicalized, sociologized, economicized, irrationalized or something of the sort.

If man, divided into races and nations, creating disparate cultures, governing with his understanding and yet governed by the unknown, is as such the subject-matter of science, why then should such distinct human concerns as happiness, the responsibility of individuals, the relationship between the individual and the collective, the sense of life and the like, all be neglected? The 'philosophy of man' came into being with the realization that Marxism had neglected precisely these problems, which, in the critical interval, had been taken up by existentialism. In this sense, the 'philosophy of man' is historically conditioned, and appears to be a protest against dehumanization, an endeavour to make man once again the centre of attention. But, on the contrary, this philosophy does not in any way conceive of man as a starting point, but looks upon him rather as an addition. Now, since the Marxist-existentialist critique of alienation is shallow at its very foundation, the 'philosophy of man' turns out to be subject to this same weakness, even though it was intended as an answer to those preceding philosophies.

The 'philosophy of man' does not really set out from the *philosophical* problem of the nature of man – if it did so, it would arrive at a new approach to reality in general, and hence form a new conception of it – but simply adds man to the uncritical rift that it sees in reality. Since its attitude is based upon the notion of man as a completion, its conception is necessarily one-sided. The 'philosophy of man' cannot rationally account for why *only* such questions as individual responsibility, morality and happiness belong to the problem of the nature of man, and not such questions as truth, world, matter, being, time and the like. It does not get to the heart of the matter; the most basic philosophical questions are exluded from its area of interest, and man is considered in isolation from fundamental philosophical problems. Thus man is at the same time split into innerness and outerness, into subjectivity and objectivity, with the result that the 'philosophy of man' really turns out to be concerned with only fragments or abstractions of real man, such as his innerness, his subjectivity, his individuality and so on.

Man can no more overlook the fact of his existence *in the world* than he can account for the world as a reality without including man. The gnosiological question as to whether and how the world can exist independently of man really presupposes man in the world, so that he can ask this question. Man is implicitly included in every conception of the world (reality); that this juxtaposition is not always clear is a source of frequent mystifications. To posit the existence of man is to make a statement, not only about man, but also about the reality outside of him: nature, out of which man developed and in which he exists, is in principle different from nature without man. Not only is nature so marked by the existence of man that it becomes humanized through history, but it also indicates through man's existence its dynamic character and productive capacity (particularly as seen in the philosophy of Schelling), a capacity to produce (necessarily or accidentally), under certain conditions and in definite stages, a 'highly organized material, equipped with consciousness'. Without the existence of man as a component of nature, the conception of nature as *natura naturans*, i.e. as productivity and activity, is unthinkable.

The definition, employed by natural science, of man as a 'highly organized material, equipped with consciousness', is not really without presuppositions, and does not have the manifest character of a timeless truth. If those who employ this definition do not concern themselves with its presuppositions, but simply place it within a scientific framework for the use of biologists, chemists, embryologists, geneticists and so on, this fact does not in any way speak out against philosophy, but rather is in its favour. The above quoted definition is not false, but rather it becomes false the moment it reaches beyond its bounds. For it presupposes a totality or a system which explains man through something that is *not* man, that stands outside of him and is not by its nature bound up with him. Man is seen herein as a component of nature, subject to the laws of the natural world. But if he is *solely* a component of this totality that he has not created (though he knows its laws and uses them for his own purposes), if processes penetrate him and the laws of nature govern him, and yet these things do not have man as a precondition, but merely impose themselves upon him, how is this fact to be reconciled with human *freedom*? In such a case, freedom is merely a recognition of necessity. Sartre argues against this conception:

> We must choose: man is first of all himself or first of all Other than himself . . . Heidegger starts out with Being in order to arrive at an interpretation of man. This method brings him close to that which we have called the materialist dialectic of the external: it, too, starts out with Being (Nature without the addition of anything alien to it) in order to arrive at man . . . (Sartre, *Critique de la raison dialectique*).

However right this argument might be in terms of Sartre's critique as a whole, in the positive sense it is problematical. In the choice *whether* to be first of all oneself *or* first of all something other than oneself, there is an implied abstraction or division of the original concreteness (totality) of man, who is first of all himself only because he is at the same time something else, and who is something else only because he is or can be himself.

In contrast with the question, *What* is man?, posed by specialized scientific research, the philosophical question, *Who* is man?, always implies another question as well, i.e. What is the world (reality)? It is only in this relationship of man–world that the problem of the nature of man can be grasped. Philosophy in the true meaning of the word is always concerned with the problem of the nature of man; in this sense, every philosophy is at the same time a philosophy of man. But, in order to shed light upon the problem of the nature of man and be a real *philosophy* of man, it must formulate itself unconditionally as a philosophy of *not*-man, in other words as a philosophical inquiry into the reality that is outside of man.

To say then that the question, Who is man?, is a complex one is not to refer to the notion that man has an ever-changing, Proteus-like nature. Rather, its complexity is due, in the first place, to the fact that it leads to other questions, and that the task of formulating it clearly, is a long process of demystification and getting rid of preconceived judgements.

And this question is complex, in the second place, because it is resolved by philosophy, unaided by any specialized fields of science, in terms of philosophy's proper and original subject: the relationship between man and the world. It is only within the framework of this philosophical problem that the question,

Who is man?, can be dealt with. If philosophy excludes man from its subject-matter, or reduces him, with respect to the reality outside of man, to either some aspect or product, then its efforts become misguided; following these lines, it sooner or later loses its genuinely philosophical character and transforms itself either into a logical–technical discipline or into mythology. It is noteworthy that such contradictory tendencies as the later philosophy of Heidegger on the one hand and modern positivism on the other end up either with the mythology of language (language as 'the house of Being' in Heidegger) or with the analysis of language (Carnap: 'A philosophical, i.e. a logical, investigation must be an analysis of language'). Since the Being of man consists in its relationships to man, to things and to reality external to man, these relationships can be released from this particular configuration and raised up to Being, which is 'itself', as Heidegger says; the explanation of man then proceeds on the basis of this mystification.

The so-called philosophy of man really *passes man by*, since it does not establish the connexion between the problem of his nature (among other problems) and the question of *truth*. On the other hand, the various theories of truth arrive at absurd conclusions when they do not take into consideration the connexion between truth and the problem of the nature of man. After all, did not Husserl, in his *Logical Inquiries* concerning the critique of psychologism and relativism, fall into an objective *idealism* because he did not clarify the relationship between objective truth and the existence of man? Husserl says rightly that truth loses its meaning when it is the content of a knowing subject, upon whose laws it is dependent. In such a case truth is transformed into a dependency of the knowing subject, so that the phrase, 'Other species, other laws of thinking, other truths' becomes valid. For Husserl, the relationship between man and truth is one between the *knowing* subject, with its limitations, and the *timeless* realm of ideal value. This ideal realm of truth exists independently not only of the intelligent being – either as the particular person or as the human species in general – but also of the realm of real time-space-existences. Even if *nothing existed*, the existence of truth would not essentially be different. The Newtonian laws exist independently of the existence of matter, even though its character and relationships are what give expression to these laws: 'Were all gravitating masses to be annihilated, the law of gravity would not thereby be done away with, but would only remain without the possibility of factual application.'[1] These idealistic consequences are not without relation to the problem of the nature of man, and they end up in a human world of arbitrariness and untruth, contrary to the intention of the philosopher. Since, according to Husserl, truth exists independently of man, who can realize the fixed and timeless truth only in his knowledge of it, then man in his own nature is not attuned to truth and is in practice excluded from it. According to this theory, truth can properly be pursued only in mathematics and in logic, whereas the realm of man and of history, excluded from this pursuit, becomes the prey of not-truth.

In his work Husserl does not pose the fundamental question as to whether the fact that man has a capacity to know objective truth (i.e. that truth whose content is independent of a perceiving individual and of humanity) does not indicate that man's very being has an *essential* relationship to truth. If man perceives objective truth (which Husserl does not doubt to be the case), then this very fact characterizes him as a being that has *access* to truth; thus he is not simply closed off within a subjectivity of race, of sex, of historical time, of contingency and of particularity. Who is that essence within whose Being are rooted, in a unique fashion, the processes both of social – human and of extra-human reality? Who is that essence whose Being is characterized through both the practical *production* of the social-human reality and the spiritual *reproduction* of the human and extra-human reality, of reality in general?[2]

It is in the uniqueness of man's Being that we can perceive the essential inner relationship between truth and man. The human reality is that point at which truth is not only revealed (perceived), but is also realized. For its very existence, truth needs man, just as man needs truth. This mutually dependent relationship means that man, in his relationship to truth, is no mere *perceiving* subject, but is also an essence that *realizes* truth. Since to speak of the objectivity of truth is not to identify it with

1. Husserl, *Logical Inquiries*, Vol. I (Halle, 1913), p. 149.
2. On this problem see the author's treatise, *Who is Man?*, Memorias del XIII Congresso Internacional de Filosofiía, Vol. II (Mexico, 1963), pp. 231–8.

objective reality, but rather simply to characterize it as an entity that exists, and, in its own terms, truth is seen to be not only the content of perception, but also the spirit of reality. Since mankind's Being has a kind of structure through which the Being of extra-human reality (nature) and that of human reality unfold themselves in a certain way, human history can be considered as a process in which truth differentiates itself from not-truth.

Translated by Ronald Sanders

MAREK FRITZHAND

⊚ ⊚

Marx's Ideal of Man

MAREK FRITZHAND, author of *The Ethical Thought of the
Young Marx* and *Man, Humanism and Morals*, is professor
of ethics at Warsaw University. He was born in 1913.

To understand the basis of Marxian humanism, we must comprehend the fundamental features of Marx's ideal of man. As
early as the *Economic and Philosophical Manuscripts of 1844*,
Marx equated humanism and communism and proclaimed the
latter to be the realization of humanistic ideals among the
masses. Marx never reduced communism to the radical transformation of only the *economic* conditions of human existence;
instead he saw in communism the radical transformation of the
whole of human existence. In communism Marx foresaw conditions which would correspond to man's rank of 'supreme being'.
For Marx, the ultimate legitimation of communism consisted in
its creation of a new free man living in accordance with his
human nature and his axiological status. By revealing Marx's
picture of man, we thus portray one of the most essential aspects
of Marxian humanism.[1]

Let us begin with a general discussion of Marx's ideal of man.
According to Marx, the man best fitting his model-man as he
should be is a man completely absorbed in this world and not in
'the next'; a man who does not brood over death, but fights for
a meaningful and valuable life.

Life is meaningful and valuable only when it is lived intensely
and thoroughly, only when the human being can realize himself
during his lifetime by developing all his human abilities and

1. A detailed analysis of Marx's works forms the basis of my reconstruction of Marx's ideal of man. This analysis can be found in my book
The Ethical Thought of the Young Marx, published in Warsaw in 1961.

satisfying all his human needs. The human being who lives a meaningful and valuable life is one who finds happiness and consummation in activities which transform nature and society. He seeks Truth, Beauty and the Good, seeks expression in and through culture and civilization, and absorbs everything new and valuable created in these spheres. He is an active, creative and wealthy man – rich in human riches. His wealth consists in the fullness of human life, the diversity of human needs and the variety of their satisfaction. It is the wealth of individuality and personality for ever developing, for ever growing richer. His talents never lie fallow; his abilities are never wasted.

Above all he is proud; he prizes his freedom and autonomy – not a freedom and autonomy outside society, outside the human community, but with people, by people and for people. Man can only achieve real happiness and perfection when he associates his own happiness and perfection with those of others. According to Marx, human self-realization can only be attained completely and generally if people treat one another as ends in themselves, as the highest human value. A man is, then, more of a human being, and closer to Marx's ideal of him, the more powerfully he is bound to others, the more he owes them and the more they owe him.

The human being that corresponds to Marx's ideal can never come to terms with a world which makes meaningful and valuable life impossible. Confronted with such a situation, he considers himself called upon to fight for a new and better life. He finds a happiness in battle he could never find in the evil reality surrounding him. He looks ahead and never behind – he is committed to progress and to an idea. Marx despised petty materialism. The creator of *contemporary philosophical materialism* was a passionate propagator of a sublime *moral idealism*.

It is now time to describe Marx's ideal of man in detail. The best procedure would be to elaborate the meaning of three terms Marx used to characterize his Ideal Man. According to Marx, people should be 'total',[1] 'personal' and 'auto-active' (*selbsttätig*).[2] What does Marx mean by these terms?

1. Of course, Marx's use of the term has nothing to do with the meaning imparted by Hitler's ideology.
2. *Selbsttätig* could best be rendered by the English term 'active' in the sense intended by Hannah Arendt. Cf. her distinction between 'be-

What did Marx intend when he proclaimed the ideal of a 'total' man? *First*, he meant the overcoming of the 'fractionalization', 'fragmentation' and 'functionalism' of modern man caused by the institution of private property and the social division of labour.

The majority of people cannot develop all their human abilities and capabilities, nor can they satisfy all their human desires and needs. Their lives are one-sided, partial, limited. They can realize only a minimum of the vast repertoire of human functions. They are bound to one field and one kind of activity.

The 'total' man is a complete man, whose self-realization knows no bounds. He is a human individual not separated by private property from the 'totality' of the world of culture and civilization. The 'totality' of that human being consists in his 'possession' of that total world – possession understood here as the fullest possible share in the creation and enjoyment of the goods of civilization and culture.

The 'total' man is independent of the division of labour which cripples, impoverishes and 'functionalizes' human beings. Marx was aware of the need for a division of labour and of its significance for the development of mankind. He was not against a voluntary division of labour which would do justice to the desires, inclinations, talents and individuality of human beings. He disapproved only of a compulsory division of labour which condemns people to work in the same treadmill, doing the same things and performing the same functions all their lives. This division of labour has 'assumed a life of its own'. It has alienated itself from human beings, constrained their powers, limited their lives and their possibilities of choice. Thanks to this division of labour, some people are always engaged in mental activities, others do physical labour; some enjoy products, others always make them.

The 'total' man is a man whose mental and physical activities form a whole during his lifetime. He does not know the distinction between work and enjoyment. He does not know the dichotomy of town and country created by the division of labour – a dichotomy which makes some men into 'narrow-minded town animals', others into 'narrow-minded country animals'.

---

haviour' and 'activity'. Inasmuch as this meaning of 'activity' has not yet been completely accepted, the word 'auto-activity' was preferred.

He does not know class division which limits the choices available to him, which defines his place in life and, in the overwhelming number of cases, predetermines his fate and mentality. The 'total' man will no longer have to confine himself to only one occupation. Marx even considers confining oneself to artistic activity to be inconsistent with his ideal of the total man. In communistic society there will be no painters as such, but only people who also paint. Marx deplores all limitations of man – even those levied by art, which he values so highly and whose representatives, the artists, in many ways serve him as a model for his ideal of man.

Secondly, the 'total' man is a homogeneous harmonious man who is never divided by activities inconsistent with one another or mutually exclusive. Marx's analysis of the alienation of labour of the worker provides us with an example of such men divided within themselves. Labour, in conditions of alienation, in a world in which the products of men become independent of their creators and become his enemies, is something external for the worker. It does not give him any satisfaction and is felt to be a bore and a torment. The worker finds himself outside of work, not within it. The human being is thus divided in two – the working man who does not feel at home in his work, and the man who feels himself outside of work.

This situation is not only a violation of the 'totality' of man. It makes the self-realization of the working people impossible, it makes their lives senseless and meaningless and dehumanizes them. For humanity, according to Marx, manifests itself in work, understood as a voluntary activity, a product of one's inclinations, a creative activity which gives life meaning and value. Alienated work, however, is compulsory work. It does not satisfy the need for work as such, but is only a means for the satisfaction of other needs. Alienated work divides the human soul, it degrades man to the level of a means to an end and makes the development and perfection of his powers and talents impossible.

Marx gives yet another example of a division of humanity inconsistent with the principle of 'totality': i.e. the division between the economic and moral existence of man, between the demands of economics and the demands of morality. This bifurcation produces uneasiness and the feeling that one is being torn in half.

From an economic point of view, there is nothing wrong in prostitution or deception, but morality condemns these activities. Should man place his trust in morality or in economics? In the world of alienation, where man's products and relations become independent of their creator and contradict one another, economics and morality exclude one another. Instead of man's welfare being the measure of their value, instead of serving man, each integrated into the whole of his life, man's products and relations alienate themselves and are transformed into destructive powers which divide his life into separate spheres. Then there is only one thing to do. Man must transform social conditions so that the human being can live like a 'total' man, create a society where the various aspects of his life are in equilibrium and harmony, and life is not deprived of its many-sidedness.

We can shed more light on Marx's ideal of man by analysing the concepts of the 'personal' and 'auto-active' man, concepts which explicate the 'total' man conception further. For Marx, 'personal' man is man in that sphere of life where he feels 'himself', 'at home', in which he acts consistently with his own will, proclivities and needs, and in accordance with his abilities and talents. The 'accidental' man – on the contrary – is man in that sphere of life foreign and even hostile to him. It is a sphere of life in which he feels limited and enslaved, in which he acts against his own inclinations and despite his lack of real interest.

Marx could only condemn a situation in which there were two separate spheres, the personal and the accidental, and where the latter gradually overwhelmed the former. This is a situation which contradicts his postulate of the 'total' man. It leads to a partial, one-sided development of the personality and signals the bifurcation of the individual. This new division, contrary to the ones discussed previously, cannot be liquidated by a synthesis of opposite poles, but only by a destruction of one of them – by the destruction of 'accidentality'.

The 'personal' man, for Marx, is a man who is 'himself', who manifests his personality traits, and develops his individuality and character harmoniously. This ideal man knows no contradiction between his personal life and his life in society, no distinction between what he is or can be and what compulsive division of labour and class division make him.

He is an 'active man' whose 'activity' is of his own doing and springs from his own needs (*selbstbetaetigung*). Creative work is just such an activity. Marx finds it best exemplified in artistic activity. The artist's activity is an end in itself, not a means to an end. It elevates the artist, perfects him, and gives him pleasure. All human work, especially manual labour, should become that kind of activity. Once the spirit of creativity permeates this labour, once physical and mental effort become one, labour will be able to develop people and make them happy. It will lose those characteristics which caused its neglect, and will become one of the most valued forms of human activity.

'Auto-activity' is, then, nothing less than freedom, freedom in the sense of the voluntary and unconstrained activity stimulated by one's own profound internal needs. Free activity, according to Marx, is a creative manifestation of one's life that comes from an unconstrained development of all of one's abilities. This free activity is a very important feature of Marx's ideal of man.

This freedom can only be obtained through the human control of nature and society, but this poses the question of what relation man should have to his surrounding world. According to Marx, it must never be a relation of submission, in which people are controlled by the inhuman world of things. But in fact people *are* the victims of general alienation: they do not control their products; their products control them. For instance, the products of labour confront the labourer as products independent of him and alien to him – as capital, a power which enslaves him. It is not people but capital which runs bourgeois society. Contrary to all appearances, it even controls the capitalist. The character traits of the capitalist do not make him a holder of capital; it is the capital held by him which makes him what he is and determines what he can become.

In an alienated society apersonal factors determine what a man is and what he can become. The most abstract of these factors is money. The members of society in their respective social classes are slaves to a dead material. They are slaves of their own products, of the social relations and division of labour created by them. In such a situation, the bigger and better the human world created by them, the more developed culture and civilization, the smaller they become, the more they depreciate, and the more fear they experience in looking upon the world. Not only the oppressed, but the suppressors as well are subordinate to the foreign power of things (although the latter are satisfied with the situation as it is). Everyone is controlled by destructive 'inhuman factors'.

Marx's ideal men reorganize social relations along socialist principles and thus consolidate and extend their control over nature and society and subordinate it to the good of all. These ideal men are capable of conscious control over the forces of society and nature. They are guided by reason and by science. These people will feel at home in the world around them; it will no longer be a mysterious force for them. Instead, it will become the source of their well-being, and material for their creative activity.

Marx not only desired control over things for his ideal men, but he demanded that they cease treating one another as things. Their mutual relations were not to be determined by their relations to things. One can best illustrate the meaning of Marx's conception of 'immediate' inter-social relations, relations unmediated by the forces and values of things, by examining Marx's criticism of the role money plays in the mutual relations of human beings.

It is money which destroys the 'immediate' relations between human beings *qua* human beings. Friendship and love lose all connexion with the personality of the partners and become dependent on money. Human feelings and values are commercialized. Everything can be bought and sold, even virtue, honour, knowledge and conscience.

People cease talking to one another in a human language and speak the language of things. They are able to communicate to one another about things, but when they themselves are at stake, when their own happiness is at issue, they have increasingly more difficulty reaching an understanding, let alone an agreement.

'Human language,' writes Marx, 'is conceived either as a "request", a "plea", an "impudence" or as "nonsense".' To meet this situation, Marx demands that people converse in a human language; that they cease letting money and other material factors determine mutual human relations, that they permit personal qualities and inclinations to hold sway in this domain. People must treat human beings as persons and not as things, they must consider them the highest value in life.

M

The arguments presented until now fully justify the claim that Marx's model of man is a moral model, and that his man acts according to moral principles. But we must go into the matter in more detail, because there are certain statements in Marx's work which have been used to justify the thesis, so often propounded, that Marx preached amorality. The most important of these statements are given below.

'For the Proletariat,' writes Marx in the *Communist Manifesto*, 'law, morality and religion are bourgeois prejudices which conceal the specific interests of the bourgeoisie'. In the *German Ideology*, we read:

> Communists do not preach morality. They do not turn to people with the moral imperative 'love one another, do not behave like egotists and the like'. On the contrary they know quite well that both egoism and self-sacrifice are necessary forms of the developing individual in certain circumstances.

These statements and similar ones do not prove that Marx's doctrine was an amoral one. They are not inconsistent with the whole of his ethical doctrine. In the *Communist Manifesto*, the very context shows that Marx was not talking about morality in general but about the bourgeois morality he always condemned. In the *German Ideology*, Marx was not disputing morality as such, but only moralism, the moral sermons (*Moralpredigt*) which spread the illusion that propaganda and moral persuasion alone can change people and the world.

In both passages Marx uses the term 'morality' in the same way he uses the word 'work'. He often demands the 'elimination of work', but it is clear that he is not speaking about all work, only about the compulsory labour which denigrates man – alienated work. He criticizes morality in the same fashion. He is criticizing a specific kind of morality – the morality which serves the interests of the oppressing classes. In a broad sense, he is talking about 'alienated morality'.

According to Marx, alienated morality is every form of morality which has 'alienated itself' and become 'independent of man'. The alpha and omega of this morality is not human happiness and perfection. It reveals itself to man as an alien force which turns against his human needs and inclinations.

Marx did not condemn *human morality*, the morality which recognizes no mediator between man and man, no mediation by

God, by the supernatural or by things. Man consistent with Marx's ideal is moral in the human sense, not in the alienated one. But would that morality transcend 'egoism' and 'altruism',[1] by forbidding mutual love and devotion? How are we to understand this notion of Marx?

'Altruism' in the traditional sense of the word – a meaning Marx had in mind in the context above – required 'self-sacrifice', the giving up of oneself. But this is not a characteristic of Marx's ideal of man and is altogether unnecessary in the society envisioned by him.

The morality of human beings in this new society will not be alienated morality which makes an *obligation* of mutual love, or treats love as *self-sacrifice*, as contrary to the real interests of the individual. According to the new morality, love is a natural phenomenon of human life; it is the *self-affirmation* of man in his relations with other people. *The attitude of Marx's ideal man is beyond the alternative of egoism or altruism. He feels the welfare of others as his very own.* This is an attitude which expresses *the unity of the human species and best corresponds to Marx's ideal of man.*

Translated by A. Ross

1. Marx himself does not use the word 'altruism' in the context referred to above.

BRONISLAW BACZKO

⊚ ⊚

Marx and the Idea of the Universality of Man

BRONISLAW BACZKO heads the Department of History
of Modern Philosophy and Social Ideas at the Institute of
Philosophy and Sociology in Warsaw. Born in Warsaw in
1924, he received his doctor's degree in philosophy in
1955 and is professor of the history of modern philosophy
at Warsaw University. His main writings include *The
Social Ideas of the Polish Democratic Society, Philosophy of
the French Enlightenment* and *J.-J. Rousseau – Solitude and
Community*.

It is a difficult task to reconstruct the contents of the idea of
the universality of man in the philosophical anthropology of
Marx. Difficulties lie on the side of the author as well as on the
side of the reconstruction of the idea. Marx wrote no work dedicated specifically to this idea. Yet at the same time, the entire
work of Marx is concerned with it. The recognition of man as a
being of universality and the explanation of the meaning of this
universality is the starting point of the work of the young Marx,
and constitutes the philosophical premise of his later writings.
'The root of man is man himself,'[1] wrote Marx. The universality
of man is for Marx a fact that is revealed in history, as well as a
value that permits the grasping of history as meaningful. The
complete reconstruction of the idea of the universality of man in
Marx, its contents and its significance, would properly require
the recapitulation of the entire Marxist philosophy from exactly
this point of view; such a recapitulation, obviously, transgresses
the boundaries of this essay.

But difficulties lie also on the side of the reconstruction of the

---

1. 'Toward the Critique of Hegel's Philosophy of Right', Introduction,
Marx–Engels: Collected Works, Abt. I, Bd. 1, Part 1, p. 614. (I was unable
to find an English translation of this work. The original German reads:
'*Die Wurzel für den Menschen ist aber der Mensch selbst.*' – *Translator*)

idea – its historical changeability, many-sidedness and multiplicity in meaning. The idea of the universality of man is a typical example of what A. Lovejoy called a 'unit idea' – an idea woven out of many different threads, which, consequently, gives itself with difficulty to detailed analysis without serious damage being done to its unity and meaning. Many philosophical efforts were made in the attempt to bestow human meaning on the world in which man lives and which he creates; these efforts were evident in the unceasingly renewed exertions to reiterate the idea of the universality of man anew, and in the affirmation of the universality of man as a value, but also in the questioning of that value. But, at the same time, in the history of that idea, there were also found contradictions of human existence and the struggle of human thought with the awareness and the transcendence of those contradictions.

The genealogy and the history of the idea of the universality of man is inseparable from the history of the ideal of humanism. For in this idea there were synthesized various notions which in the course of history helped to enrich the ideal of humanism.

In the history of ideas, the beginnings of the contemporary concept of the universality of man should be sought, perhaps, in the Renaissance conviction that man is a being distinguished from God and from nature by his possession of a relative and an unstable place in the midst of other, more stable, beings. In God, essence is identical with existence; and the chief characteristic of beings which belong to the world of nature is that their existence is described by God-given boundaries. Man, however, as Pico della Mirandola formulated it, was created when God had already exhausted all archetypes, when 'his treasure-chest was empty'. Man, therefore, is neither an earthly being nor a heavenly being, neither mortal nor immortal. He is a creation of man himself, who can and must choose the mode of his own life; he is a being that alone among all other beings is self-determining.

The Renaissance experience of the status of the ontological man in the world was of particular significance. During the Renaissance the feeling of man's autonomy and of his responsibility for himself, the general versatility of his generic and individual relations with the world, and the marked tendency towards self-affirmation in these relations went frequently hand-in-hand with the feeling of loss of security and loss of stability; feelings such as these did not exist in the medieval ages, because the basic world-view of that time provided man with at least the appearance of a stable and hierarchical universe where the place and the meaning of his own existence were clearly defined.

One of the aspects of the history of the contemporary idea of the universality of man in the seventeenth and eighteenth centuries was the transcendence of those significant feelings of the Renaissance man. Various ideas, often heterogeneous, crossing with each other and supplementing each other, culminated in that optimistic notion of the universality of man which was adopted by the philosophy and the world-view of the Enlightenment.

The idea of the universality of man, as a species and as an individual, was enriched by drawing upon contents from the higher spheres of human activity – intellectual, as well as practical – in all areas in which man had proved himself a free and a rational being. The idea of the universality of man, therefore, absorbed the conviction that man is a responsible being, and that, consequently, he experiences his own particular individuality as a value and not as a guilt or a sin. It also absorbed the conviction that man is capable of bringing into being creations whose sole cause and meaning of existence is to be found in the autonomous activity of man. Man's ability to treat the entire world as an object that can be changed, and his ability to transform it with the aid of science and technology, was, moreover, often acknowledged by the rational Enlightenment as defining the entirety of his postures. But the idea of the universality of man also absorbed another characteristic conviction of the Enlightenment, namely, that the efficacy of human endeavours is guaranteed by nature itself and by the fact that man belongs to and is part of the world of nature. This conviction concerning the possibility of humanizing nature by turning it into an object of human needs and aspirations repeatedly drew – in a paradoxical manner – sanctions for itself from the naturalistic understanding of man. One of the contents of the idea of the universality of man became also the conviction of the fundamental harmoniousness of the various, specifically human, needs and aspirations. The guarantee of this harmony was supposed to be the uniformity of human nature and of human reason in all individuals, this uniformity revealing itself in the homogeneity of culture. Man's ability to individualize, to experience, and to give value to the world in various ways through separate individuals was not considered a contradiction of the impersonal and universal character of human reason, as this reason objectifies itself in science and in practical collective endeavours. A culture created by men and reflecting their rationality was considered to be a world fundamentally approachable for each individual. In the course of progress the uniformization of culture was to furnish a premise for the development of diversity and autonomy of individuals. The rational nature of man was acknowledged as a guarantee of the rationality of the world that man created. This world – if superstition, ignorance and a mistaken understanding by people of their interests were removed from it – would have been a world in which man would have affirmed himself as an individual and as a species.

In the naturalistic and scientific understanding of progress, the idea of the universality of man celebrates its triumph in its unproblematic stature. The universality of man is acknowledged, not as a problem, but as a fact inseparable from man's existence, inseparable also from the possibility of the unlimited development of man's reason, and from the biological necessity of man's adaptation to the world.

But to the history of the contemporary idea of the universality of man belongs also the crisis – here schematically described – of the present conception of man and of progress. The crisis, in its consequences, leads to the crisis of the idea of the universality of man. Not so much the universality of man as a fact, is questioned, but of man as a value. The sociological context of the critique of the idea of the universality of man, especially in the forms that this critique adopted from the beginning of the eighteenth century, posed objections to middle-class culture, as well as – treating the matter more broadly – to the price which man paid for the moral and physical cost of urbanized and industrialized civilization, and to the domination of the technological attitude towards the world in that culture. These objections, connected with the critique of culture, created out of the universality of man a problem for man himself. They undermined the universality of man as a value, although, at the same time, they aided its enrichment. The feeling of a cultural crisis, even though finding expression in the form of a radical negation of cultural values, nevertheless performed creative cultural functions by overcoming and transcending the inertia of cultural models, systems of values and models of behaviour. Also, the crises through which the idea of the universality of man passed caused it to become more complex, and aided its adjustment to new cultural forms. The revelation of 'uneasiness in the culture' enriched the idea of human universality, and pointed to the possibility of conflict between the diverse aspects of mankind. However, what is more important, this revelation disclosed a certain particular paradoxical aspect of that idea. The paradox consists in the fact that the idea of the universality of man contains also – or perhaps above all – the conviction that man is able to problematize himself, that he is able to transcend his everyday, actual existence. Questioning himself even in the most general definitions, man unceasingly renews his efforts of value-creating, of giving meaning to himself and to the world, to his own existence and to his own history.

This paradoxical character of the idea of universality finds a distinct expression in the status of that idea in the contemporary world, a status that is particularly complicated and varied in meaning. This paradoxicality permeates not only the ideas of our time, but its reality constitutes the essence of our everyday life.

From one point of view, it could be said that only our everyday life has remained filled with the universality of man. Yet at the same time this universality of man is a banality – albeit a cruel one – because for the human epoch that gave birth to concentration camps and to atomic bombs, the universality of man is not – and cannot be – only a fact, but above all a problem. It is possible to say that in our time the universality of man celebrates its bitter, ironic triumph by placing man – in the scale of a species – before the final problems of his existence. For in the previous history of the idea of the universality of man, it was tacitly assumed that man's existence – as a biological species – is something unquestionable, a fact located beyond the borders of man's responsibility. A problem could have been only, *What meaning* should man give to himself and to his history? or, What meaning should he infer from his existence in the world? For us, no matter how much in our everyday life we may drive this into our subconsciousness, the very existence of man has shown itself to be relative and secondary to his universality. It has become dependent upon what man will contrive to do with the forces that he himself has set into motion, and upon whether he will manage to realize and to preserve himself in the world that he has created. The problem of the universality of man does not lie only in what meaning man can give to the world, but in the fact that he can – destroying himself – remove from it all meaning.

The universality of man was not inherent either in the plan of nature or in the plan of history. It arose as a result of many un-coordinated processes in nature and history. But, whatever may be its genesis, the universality of humanity, today more than ever, constitutes our human reality, and is an active force in this reality. It was not the design of history that we should be able to plan our history, nor was it its intention that we should be re-sponsible for it. Still, today we can think of history only on the condition that we extend the universality of man to its total re-sponsibility for all humanity. We can think about humanity and mankind only as our own affair, for which we alone are respon-sible, or otherwise we could not think of it at all. The desire to escape from this responsibility, and the feeling of solitary help-lessness in the face of such responsibility, conceal themselves behind a tendency of thought, characteristic of our age, which separates everyday life from history, existential time from his-torical time.

Writing all this, we make no pretence either to describe the history of the idea of the universality of man and the change-ability of its various contents, or to create a typology of its various historical forms. A separate topic also would be the des-cription of the place of Marx in the history of that idea, and still another topic would be the place of Marxism.

Marx lived in a world without concentration camps and atomic bombs and many of our questions were not his questions. Marxism, in time, was confronted with transformations charac-teristic of the entire European culture and it is impossible to understand its history and the contradictions of its development outside of this context, although Marxists themselves were not, and are not always, conscious of this context and of their own involvements. Marxism in the course of its history absorbed scientific and technological contents, but it also experienced its particular anti-positivistic break. It is reacting to changes even today, absorbing into itself (again sometimes consciously and sometimes unconsciously) problems and contradictions of our age and its culture, as well as the confrontations of various cultures that come to fruition in it. Nonetheless, the basic questions of Marx remain the fundamental questions of our age as well.

This outline restricts itself to the reconstruction of certain starting points of the idea of the universality of man as this idea is understood by Marx. What interests us above all is the extraction of those *questions* relating to human universality which are contained in Marxist thought. Like every important humanistic world-view, the thought of Marx is not only and not so much a set of *answers* as a structure of *questions* and *tensions* that problematize man.

We start with the question concerning the ontological status of man, and the connexion of that status with the universality of man as a species. 'The whole character of a species – its species character – ' writes Marx in the *Economic and Philosophical Manuscripts*, 'is contained in the character of its life-activity; and free, conscious activity is man's species character. Life itself appears only as a *means to life*.'[1] The specific feature of man is not simply that he is an active being with a particular instrumental cleverness. Man does not dissolve into one of his life's activities – rather he makes his own activity an object for himself, for his consciousness, and for his activity.

Viewing the matter biologically, the universality of man is expressed in his ability to extend the sphere of the world of nature – the world on which he depends. The universality of man reveals itself in the universality of his needs and in the possibility of extending those needs to the whole of nature.

The notion of need has a meaning in Marx that transgresses the feeling of 'want'. Man transforms things into objects of his needs, gives them human meaning, and endows them with values. Needs for Marx are not only – and not mainly – biological needs, or reducible to biological needs. The spiritual needs connected with man's striving towards a comprehension of the world, towards self-affirmation, etc., are specifically human. The universality of man is based on the fact that he

1. 'Economic and Philosophical Manuscripts', *Marx–Engels: Collected Works*, Abt. I, Bd. 3, p. 88. [*Karl Marx: Economic and Philosophic Manuscripts of 1844* (Moscow: Foreign Languages Publishing House, 1959), p. 75. – *Translator*]

applies to the world his specific, human standard of values. For example, Marx recognizes the fact that man structures his world not only in conformity with his biological needs, but also in accordance with his values and his aesthetic needs, as a mark of human universality. Needs, therefore, are for Marx inseparable from man's possession of subjectivity. Man experiences the world as having meaning; but the meaning is based not only on things, but is also grounded in man's value-creating relations with the world. Man is a being who, on the basis of his activity, grasps the world of nature and the world of his own history as a totality that is for him a meaningful structure.

The individual has a need for other men, as *men*, and therefore as beings with respect to which he enjoys a specifically human, personal relation, beings which could be for him – speaking in the words of Kant – not only means but also and always ends. Marx speaks in connexion with this about the 'plenitude of human need' opposing it to economic wealth – the collecting of things for oneself. The 'plenitude of human need' reveals itself in the fact that man '*needs* a complex of human manifestations of life, and [that he is a man] whose own self-realization exists as an inner necessity, a *need*'.[1] In the above understanding of the 'plenitude of need' and the 'wealth of needs', the idea of the universality of man is joined in Marx with the *Faustian idea of man* as a being never content, a being for whom self-realization is an unending process, a being who constantly transcends himself and continuously creates his own new and as yet unfulfilled possibilities.

In Marx's description of the status of the ontological man in nature there is a certain ambiguity. Sometimes Marx appears to tie the universality of man with the total autonomy of the ontological man as a value-creating being. At other times, Marx appears to proclaim a particular naturalism, in the sense of a conviction that nature and man make up an ontologically homogeneous reality and that in nature a harmony is established between man and things – a peculiarly 'natural' relation of man to objects, but also a 'human' relation of objects to man[2] (Marx's

---

1. Ibid., p. 123. [Erich Fromm, *Marx's Concept of Man* (New York: Frederick Ungar, 1962), p. 137. – *Translator*]

2. Ibid., p. 119. [*Karl Marx: Economic and Philosophic Manuscripts of 1844*, p. 107. – *Translator*]

understanding of the value of an object of utility is characterized by this point of view). Marx also seems to hold the belief that in man, as a 'species-being', there does not exist any discord between the natural-biological and the historical-consciousness aspects of his existence, but that they mutually complement each other in human universality. The analysis of the above ambiguity is a distinct question into which we are not able to penetrate here. Abstracting from the difficulties connected with it, however, it is possible to affirm that the universality of man is for Marx inseparable from the *historicity of man*.

Man creates himself as a universal being by living and acting in history. When Marx speaks about the universality of man, he also has in mind the universal character of the tasks that history places before man. History is, at the same time, a fact, a reality that man encounters, and a set of problems to be unravelled, a field of man's activity, of human praxis. 'Mankind', proclaims a thesis of Marx, 'always takes up only such problems as it can solve, since, looking at the matter more closely, we will always find that the problem itself arises only when the material conditions necessary for its solution already exist or are at least in the process of formation.'[1]

Still, history for Marx is never an independently active force that contains within itself provisions for an inevitable automatic development, or a meaning not dependent upon the activities of the men acting in it. Marx never writes 'History' with a capital letter. He writes, rather that

> history does not do anything, it 'does not own any wealth', it 'does not cause any struggles'! It is not 'history' but *man*, real, living man who does everything, who owns everything, and who is the cause of all struggles. 'History' does not utilize man as a means for the attainment of *its* own ends – as if history were some type of a distinct person. History is nothing other than the activity of man aspiring towards his aims.[2]

1. 'A Contribution to the Critique of Political Economy', *Marx–Engels: Works*, (Berlin, 1961), Vol. 13, p. 9. [*Karl Marx and Frederick Engels: Selected Works* (Moscow: Foreign Languages Publishing House, 1958), Vol. I, p. 363. – *Translator*]
2. *The Holy Family*, in *Marx–Engels: Collected Works*, Abt. I, Bd. 3, p. 265. [I was unable to obtain an English translation of this work. The original German reads: '*Die Geschichte tut nichts, sie "besitzt keinen ungeheuren Reichtum", sie "kämpft keine Kämpfe"! Es ist vielmehr der Mensch, der wirkliche, lebendige Mensch, der das alles tut, besitzt und kämpft; es ist*

The fact that man participates in a history which he does not choose but only finds does not absolve him of the responsibility for the historical meaning of his own activities, and for the meaning that he gives to history, in which his participation is not partial but total. Mankind takes up only such tasks as it can solve – but (as Merleau-Ponty accurately observed) this does not mean for Marx that history is a logical construction containing, together with the tasks, only one necessary resolution of these tasks, which is supposed to pre-exist in history and which would exclude human choice. We find that in the course of history there is constantly renewed and enriched the fundamental problem which men alone place before themselves and solve in history, namely, What is man and what is his manner of life, what can he make of himself, what is he as a process of his own activities and of the creation of his own unfulfilled possibilities?

In history there also arises and is solved the problem of the relation of the individual, as an individual, with the human species. Humanity is not the starting point of history – the premises for humanity are produced in the course of history; it is a problem and a task of human culture. Similarly, man as an individual does not pre-exist either in human nature or in the positivistically understood evolutionary process, or in the determinisms of the 'logic of history'. 'Man,' wrote Marx, 'individualizes himself in history.' Also, the synthesis between the development of the universality of man as a species and the evolution of the feeling of individuality is not, for Marx, a fact that is established in history. It is a problem that comes into existence in the course of history.

For Marx, the measure of human universality is the degree of individualization of mankind. Individuality, for him, is neither the particularization of the species nor the epiphenomenon of history. It is for Marx a *concrete* phenomenon that is not reducible to any exterior conditions related to it, even though the premise of the entire diversity of individuality is the opportunity that history and society provide for the development of the 'plenitude of individuality'.

The authenticity of individual existence is not a product that

nicht etwa die "Geschichte", die den Menschen zum Mittel braucht, um ihre – als ob sie eine aparte Person wäre – Zwecke durchzuarbeiten, sondern sie ist nichts als die Tätigkeit seine Zwecke verfolgenden Menschen.' – Translator]

is born out of anonymous social forces and offered as a gift to the individual. It always remains a problem for the individual, a problem that is dependent upon the choice of values; it is only when the individual does decide on a set of values that meaning is given to the biological–social process of his existence. But *mass unauthenticity*, the depersonalization of human existence, of inter-human relations, and of the individual's relation to himself is a phenomenon of social determinants that gives itself to analysis and solution on a historico-social scale.

The above question, in conjunction with the idea of the universality of man, places before us the central problem of the entire Marxist conception of philosophy – the problem of alienation. The blending of the concept of the universality of man with the various aspects of the problem of alienation constitutes the most original, specifically Marxist contribution to the long history of the idea of human universality. Alienation is defined by Marx differently, depending upon the aspect that he is analysing, and upon the basis of that social *concrete* fact which Marx knew, i.e. the industrial-capitalistic culture of the second half of the nineteenth century. It is not our task and it would transgress the boundaries of this outline to reproduce even the most salient points of that analysis. We limit ourselves to the recollection of the most important aspects of the matter in relation to the Marxist understanding of the universality of man.

Speaking in the most general terms, the reign of alienation means that man's species-universality, which is objectivized in his culture and in the forms of human collective activity, appears before the society of real, concrete individuals as an alien, hostile and destructive force over which they have no control, which they do not understand, which destroys and impoverishes them physically and morally, and degrades and depersonalizes them. And alienated situation signifies that 'man's species nature is estranged from him, . . . that one man is estranged from the other, as each of them is from man's essential nature'.[1] Men do not have control over their own social activities; they find themselves in the situation of the sorcerer's apprentice, who forgot the adjuration with which he had set dead objects into motion. The progress of humanity, for which one of the measures used

1. 'Economic and Philosophical Manuscripts', op. cit., p. 89. [*Karl Marx: Economic and Philosophic Manuscripts of 1844*, p. 77. – *Translator*]

by Marx is the development of human universality, assumes the form of 'that hideous pagan idol, who would not drink the nectar but from the skulls of the slain'.[1]

The reign of alienation means the materialization of man, the degradation of man to the status of a thing, and the rule over him of things, relations and institutions created by him. 'With the *increasing value* of the world of things proceeds in direct proportion the *devaluation* of the world of men.'[2] If the measure of universality of man is the degree of his individualization, then the alienating processes produce on a mass scale the uniformization and standardization of the individual. A world in which man is reduced to features that can be measured by money, that can be bought and sold, accomplishes the ultimate deformation of human consciousness and individuality. The qualitative distinction of an authentic human experience of the world and of one's own existence remains falsified and reduced to the *duration in time* which money creates and which has become money. 'We should not say', wrote Marx, 'that one man's hour is worth another man's hour, but rather that one man during an hour is worth just as much as another man during an hour. Time is everything, man is nothing; he is at the most time's carcase. Quality no longer matters. Quantity alone decides everything; hour for hour, day for day.'[3]

Individuality remains reduced to a set of social roles that are in contradiction to each other and yet demand conformity; consequently individuality succumbs to disintegration. Interhuman relations become reduced to relations between the representatives of anonymous functions, and individuals to the role of exchangeable elements. The relations of the individual remain repressed to the margin of social life, to the partial sphere of privacy, and give way to degradation and falsification. The alienated world imposes upon man the reversal of the relation of ends to means – his biological functions and needs are no longer

1. 'Future Results of British Rule in India', *Marx–Engels: Selected Works* (Moscow, 1962), Vol. I, p. 358.
2. 'Economic and Philosophical Manuscripts', op. cit., p. 82. [*Karl Marx: Economic and Philosophic Manuscripts of 1844*, p. 69 – *Translator*]
3. 'The Poverty of Philosophy', *Marx–Engels: Collected Works*, Abt. I, Bd. 6, p. 138. [Karl Marx, *The Poverty of Philosophy* (Moscow-London: Foreign Languages Publishing House; Lawrence and Wishart), p. 59. – *Translator*]

the means for the realization of specifically human functions. Human biological needs are severed from the remainder of human functions and are opposed to these functions as an autonomous aim; thus human functions become degraded to animal functions. If the universality of man expresses itself in his activity, then, when human activity, human work in the broadest sense of that word, is not a sphere in which man is confirmed as man, when it is *only* something imposed upon him and external to him – then his own activity becomes for him an alien and a hostile force.

Although he connects the reign of alienation with the capitalistic-industrial world, Marx is also opposed to the romantic tendency encountered in the sociological meaning of that term. He does not relate the overcoming of alienation to the ideal of a return to small, closed communities, in which the individual character of inter-human relations and the internal harmony of the individual are paid for by the impoverishment of the individual and by the constraint of individuality through authorities and institutions. The overcoming of alienation cannot mean the impoverishment of man – either of the individual or of collective activity. Marx accepts the world of industrial civilization as a fact and a value, as a world that enriches human possibilities and provides opportunities for the development of the 'plenitude of needs'. The alienated character of industrial civilization gives rise to a longing for a return to – as Marx described it – 'the unnatural simplicity of the poor',[1] a longing for the pre-individualistic stages of human development.

An alienated situation, for Marx, is not an ontological determinant of the human condition, rather it is a socio-historical problem created by men in history. 'Not the gods, not nature, but only man himself can be this alien power over man.' The emancipation of man from the forces of alienation that rule over his life and consciousness is for Marx a problem of the reconstitution of human relations, and thus it is inseparable from the realization in collective practice of the socialistic model and ideal of society.

We wish to emphasize two other aspects concerning the

1. 'Economic and Philosophical Manuscripts', op. cit., p. 112. [*Karl Marx: Economic and Philosophic Manuscripts of 1844*, p. 100. – *Translator*]
2. Ibid., p. 90. [Ibid., p. 79. – *Translator*]

understanding of man's emancipation from the social forces of alienation in connexion with Marx's concept of the idea of the universality of man.

One of these aspects is the problem of the emancipation of work from alienation, by giving it a character of human activity which would not deform man physically and spiritually. The idea of the humanization of work has a twofold form in Marx. From one side, Marx underscored the possibility of a humanization of the process of work itself, both through the overcoming of the division of labour, and through the humanization of the technical–productive and institutional forms of work by the maximum approximation of the process of work to instinctive, spontaneous creative work. (It appears, therefore, that the young Marx, by placing a particular accent on the general philosophical aspect of the emancipation of work, was inclined to identify the realization of the idea of the universality of man with the possibility of a complete identification of *all work* with *spontaneous creative activity*, on the model of artistic creativity.)

But, at the same time, Marx was opposed to the absolutization of work as a value. He considered the subordination of the complex of human needs and activities to productive work to be a characteristic feature of middle-class industrial culture, which by force had made work into a virtue. Marx stressed the fact that for the individual the idea of the universality of man is inseparable from the *time free from labour*, which the individual disposes of as a sphere of his own free cultural choices. (The entire complexity of sociological questions related to the problem of leisure time and the alienated situations that arise within the sphere of leisure time, belongs already to our contemporary epoch and not to the epoch of Marx.) The second aspect of the matter is that the universality of man is for Marx linked with the problem of man's emancipation from the alienating processes, is related to *freedom* – freedom on the historical scale, in the sense of the rule of man over his own historical destiny, and on the individual scale, in the sense of the maximization of individual choices in the determination of one's own life.

It is not the elimination of choices or contradictions that is important in the idea of the universality of man. In Marx, especially in his earlier works, there sometimes indeed do appear prophetic tones connecting the realization of the idea of the universality of man with the disappearance of all contradictions of individual and social life. But it is not here that the pulse of Marxist thought beats. Emancipation from alienation is not for Marxism a final state – but a process.

For Marx, the premise for man's liberation from alienation is the socialistic reconstruction of society, a reconstruction understood as a human, historical undertaking aimed at the control of collective life and at the conscious resolution of its contradictions. But meaning to this undertaking is given not by the attainment of maximum technical efficiency, but by the complex of values which Marx joins with man's conscious effort to overcome everything that may be a cause of alienation.

The results of human activities in history always diverge to a certain degree from their intentions. In the process of history in which man is a participant something always remains unrealized. However, Marx does not bind the destiny of the idea of the universality of man to an absolute of human history, which would be its end, but rather to the human endeavour of constantly making history more meaningful for the men who create it.

Translated by Walter Odajnyk

DANILO PEJOVIĆ

◎ ◎

On the Power and Impotence of Philosophy

DANILO PEJOVIĆ, who has translated the works of
Lukács, Bloch, Heidegger, Sartre, and others into Serbo-
Croatian, has also written articles about these men. His
books include *French Philosophy of Enlightenment*, *The Real
World* and *Why Philosophy?* He was born in Ludbreg,
Yugoslavia, in 1928 and studied philosophy at Zagreb
University, where he received his Ph.D. in 1958. Subse-
quently, he spent two years studying at the University of
Freiburg and in New York on a Ford Foundation fellow-
ship. Since 1955, he has been teaching philosophy at the
University of Zagreb.

'Philosophy and Revolution' is a frequent theme in our
philosophical discussions, a theme not only in currency as a
reminder of our celebration of the twentieth anniversary of the
popular uprising in Yugoslavia, but also decisive in the highest
sense to the entirety of Marxism, indicating as it does the vitality
of the relationship between Marx's thought and the existing
world and embodying the essence of the intellectual and practical appeal of Marx's thought in modern history.

Indeed, 'Philosophy and Revolution' is only another way of
expressing Marx's well-worn catch phrase about the 'realization
of philosophy', beginning as a revolution in philosophy in order
to end as a revolutionary philosophy in the form of the philosophy of the revolution.

What is involved here is not just a revolutionary rhetorical
phrase from the pen of the young Marx, or a striking stylistic
effect, or an exaggerated literary metaphor that paraphrases 'a
compound of Hegel and Feuerbach' in the eyes of those interpreters and critics who are happy to point at the 'mature crea-

tions of the old Marx' as leaving behind illusory youthful romanticism, and revealing a 'definitive' abandonment of philosophy
in favour of politics.

No, the idea of the 'realization of philosophy' remained Marx's
central thought from the moment of its original formulation in
Contribution to a Critique of Hegel's Philosophy of Law through
the so-called 'middle Marx', the political writer, all the way to
the final pages of the posthumous third volume of *Capital*,
which continue, despite all 'realistic' anti-philosophers, to work
with such 'long since abandoned' categories as 'alienation' and
'realization'. Incidentally, the notion of the realization of philosophy is actually the basis for Marx's renowned analysis of the
'fetishism of goods' in the first volume of *Capital*, for Marx's
struggle to shorten the working day, and for the major components of Marx's *Critique of the Gotha Programme*.

Hence, what is involved here is nothing less than Marx's central idea. The entirety of the magnificent intellectual structure of
Marxism stands or falls on it. Nevertheless, we should immediately recognize that the way in which this idea is formulated
does change in the course of Marx's writings. For this reason,
and because of the unexemplary language throughout the later
works, the concept is not always entirely clear. But there is no
reason why our *intellectual* interpretation of Marx's works as a
whole cannot be everywhere acknowledged as fundamental.

The idea of the 'solemnization of philosophy' to the effect
that philosophy ought to be taken *seriously* and that only in this
way can philosophy become capable of *changing* the world (cf.
the Eleventh Thesis on Feuerbach) is thus Marx's central idea
as a thinker, clearly indicating his *supreme intellectual ambition*
to be no more nor less than *Promethean*. Marx had cited the
image of Prometheus as 'the greatest in the entire philosophical
roster' as early as his doctoral dissertation on 'The Difference
Between the Philosophies of Nature of Democritus and Epi-
curus', seeing in him the personification of the concept of philosophy immanent in the entire history of the West. Originating
as critical thought in Greece, as part of an effort to free man
from fear, philosophy had been anti-mythic from the start and
had introduced *reason* instead of miracles as the explanation of
the world. The historic mission of philosophy had thus been to
lead to the *liberation* of the world in the process of uncovering

the truth about man and being as a whole. Prometheus initiated heresy in stealing fire from the gods to give it to men that they might inhabit the earth warmed; that is why Marx saw in him the first philosopher.

In other words, true philosophy could justify its existence only by keeping faith with its Promethean mission. In modern times, in Marx's opinion, philosophy had *betrayed* its Promethean mission and its *raison d'être* by becoming an exact science of things, i.e. by being transformed into the economics of the bourgeois world.

The turnabout in philosophy in modern times and the rise of the bourgeois economics of the production of goods and of the exploitation of man and nature for profit were for Marx the *same* process of the perversion of philosophy from an idea of liberation into the science of exploitation and enslavement.

The prime task of philosophy in the eyes of Marx as a thinker was to *turn itself around again*, to revolutionize itself, and return to its origins in the grand humanistic tradition of the ancient world. This would be possible only if the world that had transformed people into things were destroyed, that world of which the most objective alienated expression had been obtained in modern philosophy through the Hegelian scheme.

Serious consideration for philosophy and the solemnization of the essence of philosophy, in Marx's view, must take the form of the abolition of the real world that in its thoroughgoing alienation transformed philosophy into unserious twaddle and exiled it to the realm of the pure thoughts of a purely intellectual imagination. The mutual alienation between unserious philosophy and the real (serious) world is therefore not only a philosophical problem but indeed primarily a problem of the world.

However, since Hegelian philosophy was no more than the perfected intellectual expression of the senselessness of the bourgeois world, the widest possible gap had opened up between philosophy as rationality and the world as senselessness. The two could be reconciled only through the realization of the sense of philosophy that had been wholly lost in the world. Marx's concept of revolution dovetails in this way with his idea about the realization of philosophy.

On the other hand, in view of the fact that Marx was Hegel's disciple, the question arises as to whether the realization of philosophy may not have meant for Marx primarily the realization of Hegelian philosophy.

Yes and no! Yes, to the extent that Hegelian thought remains philosophy. But no, to the extent that Hegelian thought is the most grandiose reflection of the loss of philosophy as a means of liberating the world.

Marx's concept of the realization of philosophy, precisely to the extent that it is the *philosophical thought* of the revolution, is therefore essentially *ambiguous*. This essential ambiguity in Marx's message carries within it the clear possibility of a *dual interpretation*. The realization of philosophy takes place primarily as the realization of Hegelian philosophy, but *also as something else*, far more concealed and hence more difficult to understand.

The possibility of a dual interpretation is thus present within Marx's thought itself. Marx's thought is capable of being understood *solely* as a demand for the realization of modern philosophy as compressed into the Hegelian programme, while the other aspect can be forgotten. Such has in fact been the case.

This is precisely why it was possible for the realization of philosophy to be comprehended as no more than the fulfilment of the Hegelian demand for a thoroughgoing rationalization of the world. Yet the world has already been rationalized in the modern era in the sense of modern technology and economics. At the same time, the other aspect of Marx's thought was forgotten, i.e. the realization of the Promethean function of philosophy. On this basis, Marx also looked upon Hegel as a *positivist*, as an interpreter of the real world that must be eliminated in its reality and returned to the free habitat of mankind.

Many today interpret this very idea about changing the world as an expression of Marx's dissatisfaction with Hegelian conservatism, as a demand for the radicalization of Hegelianism, and as an effort to fulfil the master's programme. Marx is therefore a *technologist*, say these interpreters, and everything that has happened to his thought in the twentieth century is inevitable, and could not have been otherwise.

The whole difficulty of understanding Marx's fundamental thought originates in this speculative ambiguity. Marx knew that his idea of the realization of philosophy could not be realized *apart* from the fulfilment of the Hegelian programme,

i.e. the rationalization of the world in terms of modern technology and economics. Yet Marx by no means thought that the
latter would mark the fulfilment of his own programme or that
the realization of philosophy as the Promethean idea of liberation would be no more than the realization of modern philosophy.

Marx knew that 'there can be no returning to the old days'
and that his vision could be realized only along with the realization of Hegelian philosophy. Yet in that which *had been,* not
everything had passed away; it was contained in the essence of
the future. Only in this way can we explain those frequent
'romantic digressions' in Marx's writings, in which he expresses
admiration for the medieval craftsman as an artist in contrast to
the mechanized modern worker dismembered as a personality
and transfigured into a piece of machinery by the division of
labour.

This ambiguity in relation to the realization of philosophy
makes it possible to regard Marx *solely as a technologist,* and
this remains one possibility of interpretation.

Marx was understood in this fashion by Social Democracy,
which first broke up the whole of his thought into 'purely scientific' and 'ideological–ethical' components. Marx's thought was
then dissolved into an 'objective scientific pattern', comprehended after the fashion of the natural sciences and complemented by a pure 'ethical imperative'. The theory and practice
that followed are a matter of record.

Many contemporary interpretations of Marxism, including
that of the Polish philosopher Leszek Kolakowski (1956), still
try to separate Marx the scholar from Marx the ideologist. Much
more importantly, however, such 'reworkings' have had the
effect of clearing the ground for interpretations that have not
simply remained in the realm of theory but have also pene-
trated into the practice of politics on a grand scale.

Who is the greatest interpreter of Marx in this sense? Who
built on this misinterpretation a whole system of ideas as the
foundation of a political practice?

None other than the 'greatest genius of mankind', long – too
long – renowned as the 'greatest philosopher, economist, politician, strategist, linguist, aesthetician, etc., etc.' – Stalin!

What does Stalinism mean *in philosophical terms?*

Nothing else but an interpretation of Marx's idea about the realization of philosophy in a strictly Hegelian sense, i.e. the *realization of philosophy as technology*, fulfilled to the maximum extent in Stalin's version of 'socialism in one country'.

But we should not seek the sources of this interpretation in Stalin's 'philosophical' writings, nor even in his political speeches, much less in the official Soviet edition of this 'gem' or in the police persecution of academic philosophy. At best, the data in such sources would provide only partial and peripheral descriptions of what Stalin accomplished in the course of his rule in the practice of the planned 'technification' of Russia.

This feat in actuality was possible only on the basis of a *total* or *absolute organization* of politics, economics and all spheres of Soviet life generally. Everything had to be planned and calculated from a single centre, everything had to be objectified in the light of a rational arrangement of the world as a technical system. All 'sectors' of reality were to function as the component parts of a single mechanism, with the motive force and drive fused in the person of the Leader.

Absolute technological organization is feasible in practice somewhere on this earth in our times only because technology is not just the characteristic feature of present-day life but rather *is* in itself *contemporaneity* in the sense of bare present-day life, the *current era in the world*. For technology originates in the essence of the course of modern history.

In this sense, Stalin 'had right on his side' when he demanded that everything must be sacrificed in the name of this goal, and he possessed exemplary knowledge of how to execute his policies in practice. This knowledge, which broaches no disagreement and which knows everything earlier and better than anyone else, is the only possible knowledge in an absolute organization. This is the renowned Hegelian *absolute knowledge* that concludes the *Phenomenology*.

This is why Stalin was everywhere and always 'the most' this and that, and why no one could know more than he. More precisely, all the lower forms of knowledge were only pre-stages of the absolute and acquired their sanction, justification and dignity only when the Leader nodded his head, depriving his subjects of their essential nature and deigning them a suitable place within the system of the closed circle of absolute knowledge.

This is the metaphysical speculative–dialectical secret of Stalinism. But how did Stalinism appear in empirical terms?

Exactly as the opposite. As the servant of the people and of technology, Stalin was depicted in ascetic tones as the most devoted of modest clerks in the organization.

In essence, however, Stalin's metaphysical image and empirical image originate in the same essential configuration. Even he in all his power is the very picture of an *implement*, for the instrumentality of technology spares no man, and Stalin could thus be only the implement at the disposal of some higher element that had been built into the system of absolute organization.

Having transformed all into implements and equipment, Stalin then proceeded to execute his programme of industrialization and succeeded in Europeanizing Russia into a mighty technological power. He was extending the work of Ivan the Terrible and Peter the Great in this sense and became, however strange it may seem, the *greatest continuer of the bourgeois world*. He is the philosopher of the technological revolution *par excellence*. Through his efforts, peasant Russia acquired the capacity to conquer the cosmos and to fire missiles into the heavens, once the habitat of gods now dead.

Why, then, is it possible and even justifiable today for Stalin's continuers to criticize Stalinism?

Because Stalinism is after all a *romantic phase* of the technological revolution, and Stalinist methods are becoming a barrier to further technological advance. Criticism of Stalinism in the Soviet Union today therefore amounts primarily to a destruction of the hindrances to the further realization of philosophy as technology, for Stalinist methods have become outmoded in present-day Russia. This does not mean that such methods will cease to play a role in countries with a stage of development such as China's at the moment. 'Chinese Communism' may even outstrip Stalinism in time, drawing closer and closer to the 'bestial form' that Marx saw before him in the possibility of such a realization of philosophy:

> *Communism* is after all the *positive* expression of abolished private ownership, is first and foremost *general* private ownership. By virtue of the fact that this relation is comprehended in its *generality*, communism is in its primary form only the generalization and extension of such ownership. In this way, communism

manifests itself in a dual form. The authority of property owner-ship is so strong in opposition at first that primary communism will want to liquidate everything that is not capable of being pos-sessed by everybody as private property, to purloin talent, and so forth. Direct physical possession is the only goal of life and exis-tence. The status of worker is not abolished, just extended to cover all men. The private-property relationship remains the rel-ationship of the community with the objective world. Finally, the tendency to counterpose general private ownership to private ownership comes to be manifested in such a bestial form that the community of women is counterposed to the marital state (which is surely a form of exclusive private ownership), with woman be-coming social and common property. It can be said that this idea about the community of women is the proclaimed secret of such a terribly crude and unintellectual communism. Just as woman passes from the marital state to common prostitution, so also does the entire world of wealth, i.e. of the objective human being, pass from a relationship of exclusive marriage with a private owner to a relationship of universal prostitution with the community. Such communism, by everywhere negating the human personality, is only the consequential expression of private ownership, which latter is a negation itself. General envy, which becomes consti-tuted as a force, is only a form of concealment in which avarice is installed and given satisfaction in a different way. The spirit of all private ownership as such is at least directed against any richer private ownership in the sense of envy and proclivity to a process of levelling-off, which latter attributes may be said to make up the essence of competition. The primitive communist is simply an extension of this envy and of this levelling-off process in terms of a foreordained minimum. His horizon is specific and limited. How little this abolishment of private ownership has to do with the genuine acquisition of property is evidenced precisely by this abstract negation of the whole world of education and civilization, by this return to the unnatural simplicity of the man who is poverty-stricken and without needs and who has not yet reached the stage of private ownership, much less overcome it.

The community is only a community of labour and equality of wages, which are paid by the joint capital, i.e. by the community as the common capitalist. Both sides in this relationship are raised up to a foreordained generality, labour as a compulsion assigned to everyone, capital as the recognized generality and as the power of the community.[1]

1. Marx and Engels, 'Economic and Philosophical Manuscripts', in *Rani radovi* (Early Works), 2nd edn (Zagreb, 1961), pp. 239–40.

Can there be a better description of the 'Chinese road to socialism'?

Yet this Chinese road to socialism is only an Asiatic form of Stalinism, an extension of Stalinism in the form of a caricature of the omnipresent total senselessness of existence.

If Stalinism is thus one of the stages in the technological revolution and one of the ways to realize philosophy in the Marxian sense as the exclusive realization of Hegelian philosophy, then its place in history has been defined at the same time, its boundaries and transience. Hence, Stalinism is not just false; it is *part of the truth*. The development of the productive forces, as the chief task of the present, creates part of the future but is not itself the future. There can be no leisure in the midst of poverty, and philosophy begins out of leisure in the sense of contemplation (the luxury of contemplation is possible, says Aristotle in his *Metaphysics*, when physical needs have been satisfied) and of a search after the sense of human existence in the world and in the wholeness of being.

A revolution in human relations and a turnabout in man himself are therefore the goals of socialism, not the build-up of the productive forces.

This is exactly why Stalinism did not humanize relations in production, much less social and human relations generally. Having subordinated all to industrialization, Stalin destroyed much in this respect, if not indeed culture in the final analysis. Though music, the most abstract of the arts, flourished during Stalin's reign, poetry and the pictorial arts did not.

Stalin neither knew nor wanted to know about the Promethean aspect of the matter, of course, much less deal with it, but it remains the essential task of democratic socialism. Political power is not needed for this job. Nor can the goal ever be attained in its totality, for this concealed sense of being is the *truth of the world*, which can be grasped only in fragments in time as a reflection of its transience. The goal of history, the full sense of history can never be realized in its totality. We can only approach it more closely.

What does philosophy have to contribute to this end?

As power, philosophy has already been realized in technology. As powerlessness, philosophy may be defined as the creative powerlessness to determine the full sense of the movement that reveals itself to a limited extent in various eras of history. In history, therefore, the world is directed towards something that *surpasses* it, evidencing the impotence of philosophy and of the world itself. Yet to realize the lost sense of the world still 'makes sense', for this is an approach and a conscious movement in the direction of this lost sense so that man may be at peace with himself, feel at home, and return from an alien land to his home country and true habitat. This is a process that lasts as long as history itself, since time equals transience in motion towards the higher sense of human life on this earth that is realized only in stages.

All *utopias* therefore appear to be burdened with exaggerated pretensions, originating as they do not in the Greeks' Promethean understanding of the mission of philosophy but rather in the biblical faith of salvation. Technology is thus perverted from a means of shortening the working day and increasing leisure time into an attempt to deliver us from the curse of labour (cf. Adam's exile from paradise), leading to extremely dangerous consequences and to the negation of transience as the essence of history.

But if the goal of history is understood to be not salvation, but rather a freer and more sensible life on this planet, then philosophy has the task envisaged by Marx, viz. to be sensible (and not calculating) and capable of helping people to live more sensibly and of leading them to freedom. If this essential *other* interpretation of Marx should be forgotten, in contrast to Stalinism, all is lost.

Dual interpretation, as well as misinterpretation, is always a possibility with every great idea. This is why Stalinism 'was possible', this is why our struggle for the *humanistic* dimension in Marx's thought is of the greatest significance at this moment in history. Philosophy can prove nothing, but it can point the way if we are willing to listen to it.

In an essential and most profound sense, therefore, philosophy and revolution remain interrelated as two aspects of a single process that is to last as long as history itself. In the simplest terms, Marx wanted to *turn* man's life away from concern with things and towards greater concern with himself and with his own meaning, which had been lost in the world of labour, economics and technology. This is the *essential revolution* that is supposed to take place inside us.

Otherwise, the danger exists that Marx will continue to be regarded as a technologist and as the prophet of the technological revolution leading to mythical high living standards.

This Marx *did not* want. If we fail to take this other side of his message about the solemnization of philosophy seriously, or if we do not hear him out to the end, or mishear, then philosophy will be devoid of any sense. And Stalin will be the greatest modern and sole true Marxist.

Translated by William Hannaher

MAXIMILIEN RUBEL

◉ ◉

Reflections on Utopia and Revolution

MAXIMILIEN RUBEL is master of research at the French National Centre of Scientific Research and has written widely on Marx and Marxism. Born in Czernowitz, Austria-Hungary, in 1905, he became a naturalized French citizen in 1936 and holds a *Licence* in law and a Doctorate of Letters. Among his books are: *Bibliographie des œuvres de Karl Marx; Karl Marx, pages choisies pour une éthique socialiste; Karl Marx, essai de biographie intellectuelle;* and *Karl Marx, Selected Writings in Sociology and Social Philosophy* (with T. B. Bottomore).

Two ideas of great importance are to be found at the very core of socialist thinking: Utopia and Revolution. Yet they are seldom examined in their reciprocal relation. It is as if Revolution were held to imply the rejection or exclusion of Utopia, and Utopia to imply the banishment or denial of Revolution. Such appears to be, summarily described, the general approach of nineteenth-century socialist thinkers. In the twentieth century, up to the First World War, the debate – although restricted to the ideological disputes cropping up periodically between Marxists and non-Marxists, or Marxists and anarchists – was somewhat livelier. But since then there is only silence, as if the turmoil of contemporary history had muted all voices daring to urge a resumption of the debate.

Back to the Sources

Marxism is not the sum total of all socialist ideology. Nor does it embody all socialist thought. Its ethics and theories go back to the industrial revolution which took place in England during the last third of the eighteenth century. From the very start, socialism appears with all the characteristics of a new Gospel – a message of worldly liberation and salvation. However visionary they may have seemed to others, the early socialists or communists of the industrial age did not conceive their ideals as being inconsistent with the practical means of carrying them into effect. For William Godwin, Reason is the means to achieve the desired social transformation; for Gracchus Babeuf, violence – i.e. unreason – is the means. At first declared to be a legal movement, Revolution – due to the closing of the Panthéon Club – becomes the business of a 'secret directory' empowered to act 'by and for the people'. Babeuf's idea is to seize power in order to 'restore it to the people'; but there are obstacles to be overcome. Called to the ballot boxes, the masses were quite capable of restoring tyranny: prior to exercising sovereignty, they had to be taught their lesson.

Irresistibly, once started on the slope of impatience and 'provisional' authority, the Babouvists transform social revolution into organized war, with all the rules of the game: hierarchy, discipline, obedience, commandments, specialization, etc. It is Revolution managed from above by a general staff or a committee of experts, until it is time for the masses to act by themselves – once the enemy has been defeated and power conquered. This ambiguity of Babouvism is to be found also in Auguste Blanqui and his followers: honesty and good intentions are tokens of devotion offered the people – a people still ignorant, reduced to mere inert matter, or more exactly to a main striking force on the battlefield. The essence of Babouvism is outer-directed organized violence. Its humanism is in the intention, the aim, the Utopia: it is not to be found in the means – unless one considers vengeful acts perpetrated by the rebellious masses to be manifestations of their will to achieve freedom. In this case it would be the purpose of violence to 'humanize' violence, since it aims at establishing a society devoid of violence. The danger and weakness of such a conception reside in the impossibility of foreseeing and appraising, choosing and evaluating actions in a humanist perspective.

The so-called Utopian socialism goes back to a tradition of humanist rationalism prior to the French Revolution. With Saint-Simon, spiritual heir of the Encyclopedists, political power plays only an accessory part. The 'New Christianity' is the ethical basis of a power which is not political but administrative (managerial). The essence of this socio-economic Christianity is a science of production. Politics is replaced by industrial organization for human well-being and security, whose only objective is – in the words of Saint-Simon on his deathbed – 'to assure to all men the greatest freedom in developing their faculties'.

The utopians intend to reform society in the name of reason and science. In the view of Robert Owen, cooperation is the key to solving social problems. Owen has none of Charles Fourier's passion; he has no imagination; his doctrine amounts to a few elementary ideas, the basic one being that man is the product of his environment. Still, that pioneer of cooperative socialism was always ready to advocate *spontaneous* effort, distrust, and even hostility towards the powerful, the rich, the ruling classes. If socialism means cooperation, then Owen is the first of contemporary socialists; and if in the last analysis Marx's socialism is simply a system or method of cooperative production, then Marx is Owen's disciple.

Karl Marx

Marx did not abolish Utopia. On the contrary he rejuvenated it and enlarged its scope. With him, Utopia becomes one single movement in two stages: Revolution–Creation. Before Marx the utopians thought and imagined creation independently from the very men who were supposed to build the new City. Man was Marx's first and foremost concern. 'We know that for the new-fangled forces of society to work well, they only need to be mastered by new-fangled men – and such are the working men.' (*Speech at the Anniversary of the 'People's Paper'* 14 April 1856.)

Initially Fourier's and Owen's disciple, soon deeply involved in political struggle, Marx was never to break the spiritual bonds that linked him to utopian socialism. It suffices to read on that score a statement which he prepared, two years before his death, for the Russian Populists who sought his opinion about the chances and perspectives of the peasants' communes in the context of the development of capitalism in Russia. Not once, during that lengthy and arduous reflection, does Marx dwell upon political questions properly speaking – such as class structures or party organization. All his thought bears upon the original nature of the archaic institution of the rural commune and its importance as a 'regeneratory element in the Russian society, [an] element of superiority over the countries enslaved by capitalist régimes'.

In that apologia for a 'localized microcosm', as Marx calls the Russian commune, it is easy to see a last tribute which he pays to Robert Owen, pioneer of cooperative and communal socialism. Like his utopian predecessor, Marx puts all his confidence in the creative spontaneity of those who produce the wealth of nations without enjoying it themselves. He bestows upon the primitive commune the virtues of a social microcosm. One may recognize in this idealizing of an as yet ill-known institution a projection into the future of a wish-image. Yet, it is no accident that Marx felt a sympathy with Owen's Utopia. The cooperative commune which Marx imagined meets the equation we mentioned earlier – that of the opposition between the Jacobin (political) concept and the one we shall now call for the sake of clarity the communalist concept of the workers' movement. In the first, initiative of action and consciousness of purpose are conferred on political *avant-gardes* heading large and easily manoeuvrable masses; in the second, the small size of action groups makes it possible to do away with lasting and hence 'professional' leaders, and all political élites are deemed superfluous. Here, delegating power does not mean the relinquishment of a right, but the conferring of a temporary and imperative mandate for a strictly circumscribed task.

In a sense Marx is the most utopian of the utopians: caring little about the City to be, bending his mind on destroying the existing order, he elevates Revolution to the level of an absolute requirement. It is the mechanics of this imaginary and imaginative Revolution that partake of Utopia: it supposes men thoroughly conscious of their 'gilded miseries', men capable of thinking the entire gamut of social and socialist reality. In fact, Marx lays down an economic law of pauperization which is more difficult to grasp than plain and naked want. He grafts the Utopia to be on to the actual daily struggle and formulates a dialectical clue to the proletarian revolution: let the workers will and make *their* revolution, and they shall get socialism in the bargain. In other words, for the workers to become conscious of their alienation (in the deepest meaning Marx ascribes to this Hegelian term) is *eo ipso* to become capable both of destroying

o

capitalism and building Utopia – a classless, stateless, moneyless society. Thus Marx's concept contains an odd paradox: it is at the culminating point of their destitution that the workers are presumed to become conscious of the dire necessity of advancing towards a social rebirth through a *total* revolution. A strange 'materialism' indeed, which envisages such a metamorphosis of the slave who has been turned into a mere cog of a profit-making industrial machine.

According to Marx, 'communist consciousness' is supposed to 'emanate' from the dispossessed masses, not at all from an intellectual élite (*The German Ideology*). Bourgeois intellectuals cannot become communists prior to reaching the level of revolutionary consciousness which is that of the enslaved workers. Therein lies the paradox of the workers' movement. Yet Marx makes the distinction between socialist consciousness and socialist science. The latter is both possible and necessary in relation with the double-edged concrete movement of the proletariat: class consciousness and political action.

In appointing their own political spokesmen, the workers voice their will to upset the existing order from within – or depending on circumstances – from outside the established institutions. 'The proletariat constitutes itself into a class and, consequently, into a political party,' states the *Communist Manifesto*, showing thereby that instead of joining political parties outside their own ranks the workers awake spontaneously and creatively to the consciousness of their selfhood. Whereas interest and profit cement into a unit the bourgeois class, the proletariat's cohesion as a class is hammered out in the daily struggle for bread and the consciousness of pursuing a revolutionary goal. What Marx – and before him, in 1843, Flora Tristan – thus formulated in one single proposition, namely, that 'The emancipation of the working class must be conquered by the working class itself', remains the implicit postulate of all genuine socialist thought.

Unions, parties, councils and other forms of labour organizations are true to their aims only if they are the conscious and spontaneous creation of the workers themselves. As a class whose very being takes on the form of organized struggle, the workers must not commit their initiative to the hands of a corporate élite that claims to prescribe and guide their social and political action. No other meaning can be ascribed to the formula which Marx and Engels repeated again and again as they censured the bourgeois intelligentsia for professing to educate the working class politically. No doubt, intellectuals do play a part in the workers' movement; but the part they play is adequate and effectual only inasmuch as they bring into the movement 'elements of culture' and not ready-made theories, philosophies, esoteric doctrines concerning the ends and means of history, a dialectic of revolutionary action, etc. True, as a man of action and a party 'leader', Marx did not always himself conform strictly to the principle of the workers' self-emancipation. But at least both he and Engels recognized the fact and found fault with themselves each time they searched their souls.

Marxism Judged by Marx

The real problem is not the opposition Utopia–Marxism, Marxism–Reformism, Marxism–Revisionism, but Jacobinism–Self-Emancipation. The point in question is whether, at the same time as they entrust to chosen and/or elected bodies the representation and defence of their interests, social classes and men as such can retain the autonomy of their consciousness and actions.

There is a dangerous ambiguity looming here: is a social class able to have *one* consciousness, *one* will, *one* action? In other words, is it possible for a social class to think, will, act, except through the instrumentality of 'democratically' elected mandataries appointed to *represent*, i.e. to *voice* the will and thought of a community? In that case, is not the group's formal or tacit approval regarding their delegate's doings and decisions the *sole* evidence there is as to the congruency of their will with his comportment? But if, thus formulated, the question carries its own answer, the answer does not exhaust the *whole* question. Indeed, a further question arises, which demands a rejoinder: what are the most efficient conditions in which a delegation of mandates would result in representing the real interests of those concerned?

Socialist thinking prior to Marx was very much preoccupied with this question. The answer consisted in describing and defining an 'ideal' society. Marx inherited and enriched this legacy. His challenge is aimed not at the *fundamentals* but at some of the aberrant aspects of the so-called utopian socialism. Producers' commune, cooperative enterprise, oneness of work and culture – in short Utopia's stateless and moneyless City represents in Marx's view the resurrection, alongside modern technology, of the archaic rural commune and the cradle of primitive communism.

The historical experience of the last sixty years carries a clear, unequivocal lesson: in both its reformist and revolutionary forms, the Jacobin conception of the labour movement has met with failure. When Lenin broke the ties he had kept until the First World War with Karl Kautsky's ideas, he proclaimed the ineffectiveness of the labour movement in the industrially developed countries, whose proletariat had been 'betrayed' by an aristocracy which issued from its own ranks. On the other hand, he argued, the material and moral conditions for a revolutionary movement did exist in an industrially underdeveloped and mainly rural country, such as Tsarist Russia. It was there – according to the so-called theory of 'Permanent Revolution', then common to Trotsky and Lenin – that the socialist revolution could be set in motion, if not carried through.

Actually, in theory and practice Lenin and his party were an élite of bourgeois radical intellectuals artificially grafted on to a stirring social mass whose genuine revolutionary aspirations were readily manipulated by an apparatus of professional revolutionists. The results were soon to be felt. After winning the confidence of the spontaneously formed Soviets who opposed the Kerensky government, the Bolshevik party succeeded in establishing itself as a state power. Just as in the countries of capitalist tradition, a political aristocracy conscious of its interests and objectives had taken the place of the 'social microcosm' which – according to Marx's theory and Utopia – surges spontaneously from the soil of every society in a state of historical evolution and transformation.

Marx may have overestimated the political element in the workers' movement; but he never supposed that the working class had to abandon itself to the dialectical wisdom of a party or an élite of political experts. For Marx the *Utopia of the Revolution is an ethic of revolutionary behaviour*. The workers' destitution is the central motivation of the revolutionary act, as well as the creative force of the new social order. As the direct subject of this revolutionary transformation, the worker is also its object – since he abolishes himself as a *wage earner*.

Conclusion

Utopia and Revolution are the two historical coordinates of the socialist movement. That is to say, in order to materialize, the socialist movement must regard itself as both Utopia and Revolution. It means also that, to become a socialist, one must be at the same time a utopian and a revolutionary: one must will and desire Revolution *and* Utopia, will the abolition of our society and desire the creation of the New City.

The ethic of Revolution and Utopia is that of a socialist humanism. Socialism is a historical necessity only inasmuch as it is thought and willed as an ethical necessity. That is what Marx had in mind when he offered the following dilemma: the proletariat is either revolutionary, or it is nothing. To restore its full meaning to the concept of socialist ethics, let us add that socialism is either consciousness of Utopia, or it is nothing.

Translated by J. Malaquais

ERNST BLOCH

⊚ ⊚

Man and Citizen According to Marx

ERNST BLOCH was professor of philosophy at the University of Leipzig until he was forced to retire after the events in Hungary and Poland in 1956 and the law-suit against Wolfgang Harich in East Berlin, when his philosophy was attacked as 'counter-revolutionary' and 'revisionist'. In 1961 he was invited to the University of Tübingen, where he is now teaching.

Born in 1885, he studied philosophy, physics and music and received his Doctor of Philosophy degree in 1908. During the Nazi régime, he lived in Switzerland, France, Czechoslovakia and the United States. His books include *Traces, The Inheritance of the Present, The Principle of Hope, Natural Law and Human Dignity.*

Before the middle class acceded to power, it was or seemed to be more humane than any other class in all of history. It championed individual freedom, love of country, and the universality of humanity. Of course, there was a catch to individual freedom, while love of country could turn into narrow nationalism, and the concept of humanity could be understood in increasingly abstract ways. But ideals that seem to have been so pure, at least when first launched, may be weakened, or even perverted, in practice; as a rule they are most glowing in retrospect. Often attempts are made to start afresh, to begin again at the beginning, as though originally everything had been perfect. It is as though the only thing wrong were the failure to follow the line as originally formulated. And since only that which came later is looked upon as the root of present evils, it alone is called to account.

In the present context, however, the ideal was not entirely different from its realization. We must keep this in mind when the preservation of the revolutionary heritage is in question, especially where the ideal of 'the citizen' is concerned. Though not so obviously, *le citoyen* contained from the first the seeds of the future, and served the same economic and social trends that later produced the emancipated bourgeois. The latter's features, too, though very different from, and incomparably less attractive than, those of the progressive citizen – expressing as they did nothing but mere freedom of enterprise – were a necessary part of the original image, or at least an important element of the framework within which it was conceived. Indeed, as early as 1791, when the Rights of Man were still being confidently proclaimed, the spring-time yearnings of the French Revolution which were never to materialize already contained a considerable amount of bourgeois aspirations, and these, as we know, in the end materialized on a grand scale. Clearly, the bourgeois – not the citizen possessing real freedom, equality and fraternity – was the more up to date, in economic terms, for it was he who supplied the driving power to industrial production. In the Declaration of the Rights of Man and of the Citizen, 'property' occupies a prominent place among the four 'inalienable rights of man': it comes before 'security' and 'resistance to oppression'. As for liberty, private property was the primary determinant of its content in the French Constitution of 1793. Article XVII reads: 'The right of property is that right which belongs to every citizen to enjoy and dispose of according to his pleasure his property, revenues, labour and industry.'

Even before Thermidor, this conception of the *citoyen* was in line with capitalist interests, in so far as the people had not yet produced a soil in which the flowers of real freedom could take root – or, as Marx put it, in so far as the people had not discovered, in the idea of the interest of the French Revolution, the idea of its own real interest. Thus Marx sharply distinguishes the selfish content in the Rights of Man as first proclaimed, from the political – still abstract and idealistic – image of the citizen. The special inducement to draw this distinction so sharply was supplied in such condescending observations as those by Bruno and Edgar Bauer, who wrote that 'the pure idea' of the French Revolution was spoiled by the 'uncritical masses'. Instead, Marx and Engels pointed out that the revolution had been fully successful in emancipating the middle class and launching a profit economy such as was economically necessary at the time. To discern this they had to subject the ideology of the Rights of Man to sharp criticism. And indeed, quite apart from this special case, every bit of mankind's heritage must be treated critically if it is to be taken over by socialism, not treated as sacrosanct. So long as the bourgeois freedoms are more bourgeois than free, it is quite natural to test the rights of man against their ideological content; from the first Marx treated them with caution, partial negation, and a number of reservations. Thus, in *The Jewish Question* (1844), Marx says that

> the so-called rights of man, as distinguished from the rights of the citizen, are nothing but the rights of a member of civil society, i.e. of the normally selfish man, viewed apart from his fellow men and from the community as a whole. . . . Thus, man was not liberated from religion, he was granted religious freedom. He was not liberated from property, he was given property rights. He was not liberated from the self-seeking of private enterprise, but accorded freedom of enterprise.

And in *The Holy Family* (1845), he wrote:

> It is the very slavery of bourgeois society which seems to constitute the greatest freedom, because the seemingly complete independence of the individual, who mistakes for personal freedom the unrestrained control of his alienated vital elements – property, industry, religion, and so on – is no longer checked by ties to the community, no longer subject to social control . . . his personal freedom is actually complete servitude, total inhumanity. . . . What a colossal illusion is modern bourgeois society, the society of industry, of universal competition, of private interests, of anarchy, of self-alienated natural and spiritual individuality! This society is forced to recognize and sanction human rights while at the same time destroying its own vital manifestations in individuals, and it attempts to give political power in this society the form of the ancient republics.

In the opening pages of *The Eighteenth Brumaire of Louis Bonaparte* (1852), Marx called the same self-deceptions the 'conjuring up of the dead of world history'. However, now criticism yields significant positive results – concerning not the rights of man in general, but 'the rights of the citizen': in the opening pages of the same work, Marx says that Robespierre's self-deceptions (and, a century earlier, Cromwell's as well) were such as 'they needed in order to conceal from themselves the bourgeois limitations of the content of their struggles and to keep their enthusiasm on the high plane of the great historical tragedy'. Thus, 'the awakening of the dead in those revolutions served the purpose of glorifying the new struggles . . . of magnifying the given task in imagination. . . of finding once more the spirit of the revolution'. The spirit of the revolution: the rights of the citizens were indissolubly bound up with it, and, after all the criticism Marx levels against them in *The Jewish Question*, he concludes that this spirit is realized 'only when the real individual man has reabsorbed the abstract citizen into himself . . . only when man has recognized his *forces propres* as social energies, and has organized them as such, no longer isolating social power in the form of political power as something apart from himself'. The abstract citizen, divorced from the 'secular man' (though contained in the latter), is the *citoyen* of the Declaration of the Rights of Man, but – and this is the point – he is citizen also as the political power, the vehicle of a freedom that has become 'socialized'. Accordingly, one's fellow men no longer, as in the egoistic terms of the *droits de l'homme*, constitute limitations upon one's own freedom, but represent the common realization of freedom. Be that as it may, the image of the citizen suffered damage already, as it were, in the bourgeois womb, the effects of which were felt only later, because not originally recognized. On the other hand, despite the pernicious uses to which the image was eventually put, it could, even as a mere slogan, serve to combat its more successful counterpart, and indeed – as Hölderlin for example shows – remain capable of purifying itself.

From this point of his analysis Marx views the rights of man in more glowing terms. Though exposing the bourgeois class content with unsurpassable sharpness, he goes on to bring out intimations of the future, which were as yet without foundation when he wrote. He discovered that the right to private property dominated the other rights of man, but he perceived how thereby the other rights stand out the more saliently. In his denunciation of private property as a bourgeois limitation upon the rights of man, did Marx reject freedom, the right of the people to resist oppression and to insure its own security? Not at all! Marx's aim, rather, was to carry the idea of freedom further, to develop its logical consequences freed from the checks and hindrances of private property and the latter's increasingly destructive incursions. He is so far from being a critic of freedom that, on the contrary, he views freedom as a glorious human right, indeed the foundation of his own criticism of private property. Hence the conclusions he draws: not freedom of property, but freedom from property; not freedom of trade, but freedom from the self-seeking anarchy of unregulated trade; not emancipation of the egoistic individual from feudal society, but the emancipation of mankind from every type of class society. He restores to liberty, as distinct from property, its truly radical prestige among the rights of man, and we have all seen how, as an end in itself, it is still historically relevant, a real weapon against fascism and also against dictatorship. Consequently, the rights to freedom of assembly, freedom of association, freedom of the Press, and to individual security are today more important than ever, as also the right of workers to resist exploitation and oppression. Under socialism, once exploitation and oppression of the workers have disappeared, human rights are no less alive, no less militant; however, they take on more positive meaning as rights to inexorably objective, practical criticisms for the furthering of socialist construction, within the framework of solidarity. Accordingly, socialist solidarity means that man no longer represents the selfish individual, but the socialist individual who, in the terms of Marx's prophetic formula, has transformed his *forces propres* into social and political energies. In this way 'the citizen' has advanced beyond the abstract–moralistic never-never land to which the ideology of the French Revolution consigned him, and belongs to a socialized humanity in the here and now. In every country, the workers raise the same banner of the rights of man: in the capitalist countries as the right to resist exploitation, and in the socialist countries as the right to criticize – even the duty to criticize – as part of the task of building socialism. Without it, socialism would be authoritarian – a contradiction in terms – whereas, in point of fact, the International fights for the rights of Man: for organized maturity.

In Delacroix's famous painting, *Liberty Leading the People*, progress is conceived purely and simply as a road into the future. It denotes the freedom which, in a single progressive act, wrenches us free from the dead past and transports us into new realms, daylight ahead of us, the night behind. It is the conditions of production, primarily, which are outdated, which have become fetters; this was why, in 1791, the new roads at first revealed consisted in the sway of the emancipated egoistic individual, freedom of competition, the open market, in short, the rising capitalist mode of production and exchange. The bourgeoisie, intrinsically a class anything but heroic, had all the more need for heroic illusions on the model of classical antiquity. So far as the Jacobin illusions went – their belief that they were doing away with all oppression – these derived their force from something altogether unlike the Roman virtues. That something was their anticipation of a vastly improved kind of *polis*, their sense of human progress as within the bounds of historical possibility; this was what endowed their cause with so much greater moral grandeur than any mere emancipation of the Third Estate. Such was the sense of 'human rights' that made Beethoven keep a bust of Brutus in his home, and which makes the music of *Fidelio* and the Ninth Symphony a hymn to the imminence of a joyful new day; the revolutionary struggle of that time held the promise of total liberation. It was to all this that Marx referred when he spoke of the 'spirit of revolution', which he felt it was necessary to rekindle through magnifying the given task in imagination, in defiance of the 'bourgeois limitations of the content of the struggles'. However different the social tasks of earlier revolutions may have been, and however unmistakably the proletarian–socialist revolution, abolishing class society as such, differs from all those before it, all revolutions are nevertheless related in their typical common tendency – that of a leap into freedom. Jacobinism was especially close in spirit – at least in anticipation – to this leap, and the French Revolution itself, by going far beyond the liberation of private enterprise, disclosed its approximation to socialist–humanistic progressive content logically and necessarily.

The same Marx who so penetratingly exposed the capitalist purport of the eighteenth century's Rights of Man tells us in *The Holy Family* how much else was implied in Jacobinism:

> The French Revolution brought forth ideas that led beyond all older conceptions of the human condition. The revolutionary movement which began in the Cercle Social in 1789 and in mid-career had Leclerc and Roux as its chief representatives, and which was defeated when Babeuf's conspiracy failed, gave rise to the communist idea; Babeuf's friend Buonarotti reintroduced it

in France after the revolution of 1830. This idea, logically developed, is the idea of a new human condition. . . . Just as Cartesian materialism culminates in true natural science, so the other current of French materialism leads directly to socialism and communism.

Thus, there was already more than a little red in the old tricolour, introduced by the so-called Fourth Estate – the red of irreversible progress. Marx directed it against the emasculation of his epoch, against political alliances with the 'age-old powers of life' represented by the Church and the Nobility, and against a nihilism which had lost all sense of the *Ça ira* of the French Revolution. Whereas Marx criticized what was partly undynamic, partly abstract in the natural-law slogans of the time, he did so to carry the Revolution further, in order to make it socialist. Man conceived as 'egoistic individual, divorced from his fellow men and his community' was undynamic; the citizen conceived as mere imitation of the ancient ideal in a new polis, as 'an allegorical, moral person' was abstract and static, anything but a vehicle of social freedom. What still remains to be done is to transform the 'liberty, equality and fraternity' of the purely political citizen into living energies of living men; only then, says Marx, will human emancipation be achieved. Then our fellow men will no longer be, as in the egoistic, bourgeois phase of the Rights of Man, checks and hindrances upon our freedom, but all men will live together in community of freedom.

Translated by Norbert Guterman

ERICH FROMM

⊚ ⊚

The Application of Humanist Psycho-analysis and Marx's Theory

ERICH FROMM, is well known for his writings and lectures on psycho-analysis, philosophy, political science and religion. He has lectured at Columbia and Yale Universities and at the New School for Social Research and has been on the faculties of the William Alanson White Institute of Psychiatry, Psycho-analysis and Psychology, Bennington College, Michigan State University. He is professor of psycho-analysis at the Medical School of the National University of Mexico and teaches at New York University. His writings include *Escape from Freedom, The Forgotten Language, The Art of Loving, The Sane Society, Man for Himself, Marx's Concept of Man, May Man Prevail?, The Dogma of Christ* and *The Heart of Man.* He was born in Frankfurt-am-Main in 1900 and completed his studies in psychology, sociology and philosophy in Germany. He was trained in psycho-analysis at the Berlin Institute of Psycho-analysis.

M arxism is humanism, and its aim is the full unfolding of man's potentialities; not man as deduced from his ideas or his consciousness, but man with his physical and psychic properties, the real man who does not live in a vacuum but in a social context, the man who has to produce in order to live. It is precisely the fact that the whole man, and not his consciousness, is the concern of Marxist thought which differentiates Marx's 'materialism' from Hegel's idealism, as well as from the economistic–mechanistic deformation of Marxism. It was Marx's great achievement to liberate the economic and philosophical categories that referred to man from their abstract and alienated expressions, and to apply philosophy and economics *ad hominem.*

Marx's concern was man, and his aim was man's liberation from the predomination of material interests, from the prison his own arrangements and deeds had built around him. If one does not understand this concern of Marx one will never understand either his theory or the falsification of it by many who claim to practise it. Even though Marx's main work is entitled *Capital*, this work was meant to be only a step in his total research, to be followed by a history of philosophy. For Marx the study of capital was a critical tool to be used for understanding man's crippled state in industrial society. It is one step in the great work which, if he had been able to write it, might have been entitled *On Man and Society*.

Marx's work, that of the 'young Marx' as well as that of the author of *Capital*, is full of psychological concepts. He deals with concepts like the 'essence of man', and the 'crippled' man, with 'alienation', with 'consciousness', with 'passionate strivings', and with 'independence', to name only some of the most important. Yet, in contrast to Aristotle and Spinoza, who based ethics on a systematic psychology, Marx's work contains almost no psychological theory. Aside from fragmentary remarks like the distinction between fixed drives (like hunger and sexuality) and flexible drives which are socially produced, there is hardly any relevant psychology to be found in Marx's writings or, for that matter, in those of his successors. The reason for this failure does not lie in a lack of interest in or talent for analysing psychological phenomena (the volumes containing the unabridged correspondence between Marx and Engels show a capacity for penetrating analysis of unconscious motivations that would be a credit to any gifted psycho-analyst); it is to be found in the fact that during Marx's lifetime there was no dynamic psychology which he could have applied to the problems of man. Marx died in 1883; Freud began to publish his work more than ten years after Marx's death.

The kind of psychology necessary to supplement Marx's analysis was, even though in need of many revisions, that created by Freud. Psycho-analysis is, first of all, a *dynamic* psychology. It deals with psychic *forces*, which motivate human behaviour, action, feelings, ideas. These forces cannot always be seen as such; they have to be inferred from the observable phenomena, and to be studied in their contradictions and transformations.

To be useful for Marxist thinking, a psychology must also be one which sees the *evolution* of these psychic forces as a process of constant interaction between man's needs and the social and historical reality in which he participates. It must be a psychology which is from the very beginning social psychology. Eventually, it must be a *critical* psychology, particularly one critical of man's consciousness.

Freud's psycho-analysis fulfils these main conditions, even though their relevance for Marxist thought was grasped neither by most Freudians nor by Marxists. The reasons for this failure to make contact are apparent on both sides. Marxists continued in the tradition of ignoring psychology; Freud and his disciples developed their ideas within the framework of mechanistic materialism, which proved restrictive to the development of the great discoveries of Freud, and incompatible with 'historical materialism'.

In the meantime, new developments have occurred. The most important one is the revival of Marxist humanism, to which the present volume bears witness. Many Marxist socialists in the smaller socialist countries especially, but also those in the West, have become aware of the fact that Marxist theory is in need of a psychological theory of man; they have also become aware of the fact that socialism must satisfy man's need for a system of orientation and devotion; that it must deal with the questions of who man is, and what the meaning and aim of his life is. It must be the foundation for ethical norms and spiritual development beyond the empty phrases stating that 'good is that which serves the revolution' (the worker's state, historical evolution, etc.).

On the other hand, the criticism arising in the psycho-analytic camp against the mechanistic materialism underlying Freud's thinking has led to a critical re-evaluation of psycho-analysis, essentially of the libido theory. Because of the development in both Marxist and psycho-analytic thinking, the time seems to have come for humanist Marxists to recognize that the use of a dynamic, critical, socially oriented psychology is of crucial importance for the further development of Marxist theory and socialist practice; that a theory centred around man can no longer remain a theory without psychology if it is not to lose touch with human reality. In the following pages I want to point to some of the principal problems which have been dealt with or which ought to be treated by humanist psycho-analysis.[1]

The first problem which should be dealt with is that of the *'social character'*, the character matrix common to a group (nation or class, for instance) which determines effectively the actions and thoughts of its members. This concept is a special development of Freud's character concept, the essence of which is the *dynamic* nature of character. Freud considered character as the relatively stable manifestation of various kinds of libidinous strivings, that is, of psychic energy directed to certain goals and stemming from certain sources. In his concepts of the oral, anal and genital characters, Freud presented a new model of human character which explained behaviour as the outcome of distinct passionate strivings; Freud assumed that the direction and intensity of these strivings was the result of early childhood experiences in relation to the 'erogenous zones' (mouth, anus, genitals), and aside from constitutional elements the behaviour of parents was mainly responsible for the libido development.

The concept of *social character* refers to the matrix of the character structure *common to a group*. It assumes that the fundamental factor in the formation of the 'social character' is *the practice of life as it is constituted by the mode of production and the resulting social stratification. The 'social character' is that particular structure of psychic energy which is moulded by any given*

---

1. Unfortunately there are so few authors who have attempted to apply revised psycho-analysis to the problem of Marxism and socialism that I must refer mainly to my own writings since 1931. Cf. especially *Das Christusdogma* (Vienna: Psychoanalytischer Verlag, 1931; republished in an English translation, *The Dogma of Christ*, New York: Holt, Rinehart & Winston, 1963; London: Routledge & Kegan Paul); *Die psychoanalytische Characterologie und ihre Bedeutung für die Sozialpsychologie* (Leipzig: Hirschfeld, Zeitschrift für Sozialforschung, 1932); *Escape from Freedom* (New York: Holt, Rinehart & Winston, 1941); *The Sane Society* (New York: Holt, Rinehart & Winston, 1955; London: Routledge & Kegan Paul); *Marx's Concept of Man* (New York, Frederick Ungar, 1961); *Beyond the Chains of Illusion* (New York: Pocket Books: Credo Series, ed. R. N. Anshen, 1962) deals explicitly with the relationship between the theories of Marx and Freud. Among other writers writing from a psychoanalytic–Marxist standpoint the most important is Wilhelm Reich, even though there is little in common between his theories and mine. Sartre's attempts at developing a Marxist-oriented humanist analysis suffers from the fact that he has little clinical experience and, on the whole, deals with psychology superficially even though in brilliant verbiage.

society so as to be useful for the functioning of that particular society. The average person must *want* to do what he *has* to do in order to function in a way that permits society to use his energies for its purposes. Man's energy appears in the social process only partly as simple physical energy (labourers tilling the soil or building roads); and partly in *specific* forms of *psychic* energy. A member of a primitive people, living from assaulting and robbing other tribes, must have the character of a warrior, with a passion for war, killing and robbing. The members of a peaceful, agricultural tribe must have an inclination for coopera-tion as against violence. Feudal society functions well only if its members have a striving for submission to authority, and respect and admiration for those who are their superiors. Capitalism functions only with men who are eager to work, who are disci-plined and punctual, whose main interest is monetary gain, and whose main principle in life is profit as a result of production and exchange. In the nineteenth century capitalism needed men who liked to save; in the middle of the twentieth century it needs men who are passionately interested in spending and in consuming. The social character is the form in which human energy is moulded for its use as a productive force in the social process.

The social character is reinforced by all the instruments of in-fluence available to a society: its educational system, its religion, its literature, its songs, its jokes, its customs, and, most of all, its parents' methods of bringing up their children. This last is so important because the character structure of individuals is formed to a considerable extent in the first five or six years of their lives. But the influence of the parents is not essentially an individual or accidental one, as classic psycho-analysts believe; the parents are primarily the *agents of society*, both through their own characters and through their educational methods; they differ from each other only to a small degree, and these differ-ences usually do not diminish their influence in creating the socially desirable matrix of the social character.

A condition for the formulation of the concept of the social character as being moulded by the practice of life in any given society was a revision of Freud's libido theory, which is the basis for his concept of character. The libido theory is rooted in the mechanistic concept of man as a machine, with the libido (aside from the drive for self-preservation) as the energy source, governed by the 'pleasure principle', the reduction of increased libidinal tension to its normal level. In contrast to this concept, I have tried to show (especially in *Man for Himself*) that the various strivings of man, who is *primarily* a social being, develop as a result of his need for 'assimilation' (of things) and 'socialization' (with people), and that the forms of assimilation and socialization that constitute his main passions depend on the social structure in which he exists. Man in this concept is seen as characterized by his passionate strivings towards objects – men and nature – and his need of relating himself to the world.

The concept of the social character answers important questions which were not dealt with adequately in Marxist theory.

(*a*) Why is it that a society succeeds in gaining the allegiance of most of its members, even when they suffer under the system and even if their reason tells them that their allegiance to it is harmful to them? Why has their *real* interest as human beings not outweighed their *fictitious* interests produced by all kinds of ideological influences and brainwashing? Why has consciousness of their class situation and of the advantages of socialism not been as effective as Marx believed it would be? The answer to this question lies in the phenomenon of the social character. Once a society has succeeded in moulding the character structure of the average person in such a way that he likes to do that which he has to do, he is satisfied with the very conditions that society imposes upon him. As one of Ibsen's characters once said: He can do anything he wants to do because he wants only what he can do. Needless to say, a social character which is, for instance, satisfied with submission is a crippled character. But crippled or not, it serves the purpose of a society requiring submissive men for its proper functioning.

(*b*) The concept of the social character also serves to explain the link between the material basis of a society and the 'ideological superstructure'. Marx has often been interpreted as implying that the ideological superstructure was *nothing but* the reflection of the economic basis. This interpretation is not correct; but the fact is that in Marx's theory the nature of the relation between basis and superstructure was not sufficiently explained. A dynamic psychological theory can show that society produces the social character, and that the social character tends to produce and to hold on to ideas and ideologies which fit it and are nourished by it. However, it is not only the economic basis which creates a certain social character which, in turn, creates certain ideas. The ideas, once created, also influence the social character and, indirectly, the social economic structure. What I emphasize here is *that the social character is the intermediary between the socio-economic structure and the ideas and ideals prevalent in a society.* It is the intermediary in both directions, from the economic basis to the ideas and from the ideas to the economic basis. The following scheme expresses this concept:

$$\downarrow \quad \begin{array}{c} \text{ECONOMIC BASIS} \\ \text{SOCIAL CHARACTER} \\ \text{IDEAS AND IDEALS} \end{array} \quad \uparrow$$

(c) The concept of social character can explain how human energy is used by a society, like any other raw material for the needs and purposes of that society. Man, in fact, is one of the most pliable natural forces; he can be made to serve almost any purpose; he can be made to hate or to cooperate, to submit or to stand up, to enjoy suffering or happiness.

(d) While all this is true, it is also true that man can solve the problem of his existence only by the full unfolding of his human powers. The more crippled a society makes man the sicker he becomes, even though consciously he may be satisfied with his lot. But unconsciously he is dissatisfied, and this very dissatisfaction is the element which inclines him eventually to change the social forms that cripple him. If he cannot do this, his particular kind of pathogenic society will die out. Social change and revolution are caused not only by new productive forces which conflict with older forms of social organization, but also by the conflict between inhuman social conditions and unalterable human needs. One can do almost anything to man, yet only almost. The history of man's fight for freedom is the most telling manifestation of this principle.

(e) The concept of social character is not only a theoretical one lending itself to general speculation; it is useful and important for empirical studies which aim at finding out what the incidence of various kinds of 'social character' is in a given society or social class. Assuming that one defines the 'peasant character' as individualistic, hoarding, stubborn, with little satisfaction in cooperation, little sense of time and punctuality, this syndrome of traits is by no means a summation of various traits, but a structure, charged with energy; this structure will show intensive resistance by either violence or silent obstructionism if attempts are made to change it; even economic advantages will not easily produce any effects. The syndrome owes its existence to the common mode of production which has been characteristic of peasant life for thousands of years. The same holds true for a declining lower middle class, whether it is that which brought Hitler to power, or the poor whites in the South of the United States. The lack of any kind of positive cultural stimulation, the resentment against their situation, which is one of being left behind by the forward-moving currents of their society, the hate towards those who destroyed the images which once gave them pride, have created a character syndrome which is made up of love of death (necrophilia), intense and malignant fixation to blood and soil, and intense group narcissism (the latter expressed in intense nationalism and racialism).[1] One last example: the character structure of the industrial worker contains punctuality, discipline, capacity for teamwork; this is the syndrome which forms the minimum for the efficient functioning of an industrial worker. (Other differences – like dependence–independence; interest–indifference; activity–passivity – are at this point ignored, although they are of utmost importance for the character structure of the worker now and in the future.)

(*f*) The most important application of the concept of the social character lies in distinguishing the future social character of a socialist society as visualized by Marx from the social character of nineteenth-century capitalism, with its central desire for possession of property and wealth, and from the social character of the twentieth century (capitalist or communist), which is becoming ever more prevalent in the highly industrialized societies: the character of *homo consumens*.

Homo consumens is the man whose main goal is not primarily to *own* things, but to *consume* more and more, and thus to compensate for his inner vacuity, passivity, loneliness and anxiety. In a society characterized by giant enterprises, giant industrial, governmental and labour bureaucracies, the individual, who has

1. Cf. the detailed discussion of this point in E. Fromm, *The Heart of Man, Its Genius for Good and Evil* (New York: Harper and Row: Religious Perspectives Series, ed. R. N. Anshen, 1964).

no control over his circumstances of work, feels impotent, lonely, bored and anxious. At the same time, the need for profit of the big consumer industries, through the medium of advertising, transforms him into a voracious man, an eternal suckling who wants to consume more and more, and for whom everything becomes an article of consumption: cigarettes, liquor, sex, movies, television, travel, and even education, books and lectures. New artificial needs are created, and man's tastes are manipulated. (The character of *homo consumens* in its more extreme forms is a well-known psychopathological phenomenon. It is to be found in many cases of depressed or anxious persons who escape into overeating, overbuying or alcoholism to compensate for the hidden depression and anxiety.) The greed for consumption (an extreme form of what Freud called the 'oral-receptive character') is becoming the dominant psychic force in present-day industrialized society. *Homo consumens* is under the illusion of happiness, while unconsciously he suffers from his boredom and passivity. The more power he has over machines the more powerless he becomes as a human being; the more he consumes the more he becomes a slave to the ever-increasing needs which the industrial system creates and manipulates. He mistakes thrill and excitement for joy and happiness, and material comfort for aliveness; satisfied greed becomes the meaning of life, the striving for it a new religion. The freedom to consume becomes the essence of human freedom.

This spirit of consumption is precisely the opposite of the spirit of a socialist society as Marx visualized it. He clearly saw the danger inherent in capitalism. His aim was a society in which man *is* much, not in which he *has* or *uses* much. He wanted to liberate man from the chains of his material greed, so that he could become fully awake, alive and sensitive, and not be the slave of his greed. 'The production of too many useful things,' he wrote, 'results in the creation of too many useless people.' He wanted to abolish extreme poverty, because it prevents man from becoming fully human; but he also wanted to prevent extreme wealth, in which the individual becomes the prisoner of his greed. His aim was not the *maximum* but the *optimum* of consumption, the satisfaction of those genuine human needs which serve as a means to a fuller and richer life.

It is one of the historical ironies that the spirit of capitalism, the satisfaction of material greed, is conquering the communist and socialist countries which, with their planned economy, would have the means to curb it. This process has its own logic: the material success of capitalism was immensely impressive to those poorer countries in Europe in which communism had been victorious, and the victory of socialism became identified with successful competition with capitalism, *within* the spirit of capitalism. Socialism is in danger of deteriorating into a system which can accomplish the industrialization of poorer countries more quickly than capitalism, rather than of becoming a society in which the development of man, and not that of economic production, is the main goal. This development has been furthered by the fact that Soviet communism, in accepting a crude version of Marx's 'materialism', lost contact, as did the capitalist countries, with the humanist spiritual tradition of which Marx was one of the greatest representatives.

It is true that the socialist countries have still not solved the problem of satisfying the *legitimate* material needs of their populations (and even in the United States forty per cent of the population is not 'affluent'). But it is of the utmost importance that socialist economists, philosophers and psychologists be aware of the danger that the goal of *optimal* consumption can easily change to that of *maximal* consumption. The task for the socialist theoreticians is to study the nature of human needs; to find criteria for the distinction between *genuine* human needs, the satisfaction of which makes man more alive and sensitive, and *synthetic* needs created by capitalism, which tend to weaken man, to make him more passive and bored, a slave to his greed for things.

What I am stressing here is not that production as such should be restricted; but that once the optimal needs of individual consumption are fulfilled, it should be channelled into more production of the means for social consumption such as schools, libraries, theatres, parks, hospitals, public transportation, etc. The ever-increasing individual consumption in the highly industrialized countries suggests that competition, greed and envy are engendered not only by private property, but also by unlimited private consumption. Socialist theoreticians must not lose sight of the fact that the aim of a humanist socialism is to build an industrial society whose mode of production shall serve the fullest development of the total man, and not the creation of *homo consumens*; that socialist society is an industrial society fit for human beings to live in and to develop.

(*g*) There are empirical methods which permit the study of the social character. The aim of such study is: to discover the incidence of the various character syndromes within the population as a whole and within each class; the intensity of the various factors within the syndrome; new or contradictory factors which have been caused by different socio-economic conditions. All such variants permit an insight into the strength of the existing character structure, the process of change, and also what measures might facilitate such changes. Needless to say, such insight is important in countries in transition from agriculture to industrialism, as well as for the problem of the transition of the worker under capitalism or state capitalism, that is under alienated conditions, to the conditions of authentic socialism. Furthermore, such studies are guides to political action. If I know only the political 'opinions' of people as ascertained by the opinion polls, I know how they are likely to act in the immediate future. If I want to know the strength of psychic forces (which at the moment may not yet be manifest consciously) such as, for instance, racism, war- or peace-mindedness, such studies of character inform me of the strength and direction of the underlying forces which operate in the social process and which may become manifest only after some time.[1]

There is no space to discuss in detail here the methods that can be used to obtain the character data mentioned above. What they all have in common is avoidance of the error of accepting ideologies (rationalizations) for expressions of the inner, and usually unconscious, reality. One method, which has proved to be very useful, is that of an open-ended questionnaire, the answers to which are interpreted as to their non-intended or unconscious meaning. Thus, when the answer to the question, 'Who are the men in history whom you most admire?' is: 'Alexander the Great, Nero, Marx and Lenin,' while another answer is: 'Socrates, Pasteur, Marx and Lenin' the inference is made that the first respondent is an admirer of power and strict

1. Thus, for instance, the destructiveness present in the German lower middle class became manifest only when Hitler gave it the opportunity to express itself.

authority, the second an admirer of those who work in the service of life and who are benefactors of mankind. By using an extended projective questionnaire it is possible to obtain a reliable picture of the character structure of a person.[1] Other projective tests, the analysis of favourite jokes, songs, stories, and of observable behaviour (especially of the 'small acts' so important for psycho-analytic observation) help in obtaining correct results. Methodologically, the main emphasis in all these studies is on the mode of production and the resulting class stratification, on the most significant character traits and the syndromes they form, and on the relationship between these two sets of data. With the method of stratified samples, whole nations or large social classes can thus be studied by including less than a thousand persons in the investigation.

Another important aspect of analytic social psychology is what Freud called the *unconscious*. But, while Freud was mainly concerned with individual repression, the student of Marxist social psychology will be most concerned with the '*social unconscious*'. This concept refers to that repression of inner reality which is common to large groups. Every society must make every effort not to permit its members (or those of a particular class) to be aware of impulses which, if they were conscious, could lead to socially 'dangerous' thoughts or actions. Effective censorship occurs, not at the level of the printed or spoken word, but by preventing thoughts from even becoming conscious, that is, by repression of dangerous awareness. Naturally the contents of the social unconscious vary depending on the many forms of social structure: aggressiveness, rebelliousness,

1. This method was first applied by myself together with Dr E. Schachtel, Dr P. Lazarsfeld, and others at the Institute of Social Research (Frankfurt University) in 1931 and later at Columbia University. The goal of the investigation was to find the incidence of authoritarian *v.* anti-authoritarian characters among German workers and employees. The results corresponded pretty closely to the facts as shown by subsequent historical development. The same method has been employed in a psychosocial study of a small Mexican village, supported by the Foundations Fund for Research in Psychiatry, under my direction, with the assistance of Dr Theodore and Dr Lola Schwartz and Dr Michael Maccoby. The statistical methods of Dr Louis McQuitty make it possible to handle the hundreds of thousands of single data in such a way that, by using electronic computers, syndromes of typically related traits appear with all clarity.

dependency, loneliness, unhappiness, boredom, etc., to mention only a few. The repressed impulse must be kept in repression and replaced by ideologies which deny it or affirm its opposite. The bored, anxious, unhappy man of today's industrial society is taught to think that he is happy and full of fun. In other societies the man deprived of freedom of thought and expression is taught to think that he has almost reached the most complete form of freedom, even though at the moment only his leaders speak in the name of that freedom. In some systems love of life is repressed, and love of property is cultivated instead; in others, awareness of alienation is repressed, and instead the slogan is promoted 'there can be no alienation in a socialist country'.

Another way of expressing the phenomenon of the unconscious is to speak of it in the terms of Hegel and Marx, that is, as the totality of forces which work behind man's back while he has the illusion of being free in his decisions or, as Adam Smith put it, 'economic man is led by an invisible hand to promote an end which was no part of his intention'. While for Smith this invisible hand was a benevolent one, for Marx (as well as for Freud) it was a dangerous one; it had to be uncovered in order to be deprived of its effectiveness. Consciousness is a social phenomenon; for Marx it is mostly false consciousness, the work of the forces of repression.[1] The unconscious, like consciousness, is also a social phenomenon, determined by the 'social filter' which does not permit most real human experiences to ascend from unconsciousness to consciousness. This social filter consists mainly of language, logic and social taboos; it is covered up by ideologies (rationalizations) which are subjectively experienced as being true, when in reality they are nothing but socially produced and shared fictions. This approach to consciousness and the repression can demonstrate empirically the validity of Marx's statement that 'social existence determines consciousness'.

As a consequence of these considerations, another theoretical

1. It is interesting to note that Marx used the term repression—'Verdrängung' – in The German Ideology. Rosa Luxemburg spoke of the unconscious (the logic of the historic process) coming before the conscious (the subjective logic of the human being) in Leninism and Marxism, recently published in English in The Russian Revolution and Leninism or Marxism? (Ann Arbor: University of Michigan Press, 1961; London: Cresset).

difference between dogmatic Freudian and Marxist-oriented psycho-analysis appears. Freud believed that the effective *cause for repression* (the most important content to be repressed being incestuous desires) is the fear of castration. I believe, on the contrary, that, individually and socially, man's greatest fear is that of complete isolation from his fellow men, of complete ostracism. Even fear of death is easier to bear. Society enforces its demands for repression by the threat of ostracism. If you do not deny the presence of certain experiences, you do not belong, you belong nowhere, you are in danger of becoming insane. (Insanity is, in fact, the illness characterized by total absence of relatedness to the world outside.)

Marxists have usually assumed that what works behind man's back and directs him are economic forces and their political representations. Psycho-analytic study shows that this is much too narrow a concept. Society consists of men, and each man is equipped with a potential of passionate strivings, from the most archaic to the most progressive. This human potential as a whole is moulded by the ensemble of economic and social forces characteristic of each given society. These forces of the social ensemble produce a certain social unconscious, and certain conflicts between the repressive factors and given human needs which are essential for sane human functioning (like a certain degree of freedom, stimulation, interest in life, happiness). In fact, as I said before, revolutions occur as expressions of not only new productive forces, but also of the repressed part of human nature, and they are successful only when the two conditions are combined. Repression, whether it is individually or socially conditioned, distorts man, fragments him, deprives him of his whole humanity. Consciousness represents the 'social man' determined by a given society; the unconscious represents the universal man in us, the good and the bad, the whole man who justifies Terence's saying 'I believe that nothing human is alien to me'. (This incidentally was Marx's favourite motto.)

Depth psychology also has a contribution to make to a problem which plays a central role in Marx's theory, even though Marx never arrived at its satisfactory solution: the problem of the essence and nature of man. On the one hand Marx – especially after 1844 – did not want to use a metaphysical, unhistorical concept like the 'essence' of man, a concept which had been used for thousand of years by many rulers in order to prove that their rules and laws corresponded to what each declared to be the unchangeable 'nature of man'. On the other hand, Marx was opposed to a relativistic view that man is born a blank piece of paper on which every culture writes its text. If this were true, how could man ever rebel against the forms of existence into which a given society forces its members? How could Marx use (in *Capital*) the concept of the 'crippled man' if he did not have a concept of a 'model of human nature' which *could* be crippled? An answer on the basis of psychological analysis lies in the assumption that there is no 'essence of man', in the sense of a *substance* which remains the same throughout history. The answer, in my opinion, is to be found in the fact that man's essence lies in the very contradiction between his being *in* nature, thrown into the world without his will, and taken away against his will, at an accidental place and time, and at the same time of *transcending* nature by his lack of instinctual equipment and by the fact of his awareness – of himself, of others, of the past and the present. Man, a 'freak of nature', would feel unbearably alone unless he could solve his contradiction by finding a new form of unity. The essential contradiction in man's existence forces him to seek a solution of this contradiction, to find an answer to the question which life asks him from the moment of his birth. There are a number of ascertainable but limited answers to the question how to find unity. Man can find unity by trying to regress to the animal stage, by doing away with what is specifically human (reason and love), by being a slave or a slave-driver, by transforming himself into a thing, or else by developing his specific human powers to such an extent that he finds a new unity with his fellow man and with nature (the latter is very important to Marx's thought) by becoming a free man – free not only *from* chains but free *to* make the development of all his potentialities the very aim of his life – a man who owes his existence to his own productive effort. Man has no innate 'drive for progress', but he is driven by the need to solve his existential contradiction, which arises again at every new level of development. This contradiction – or, in other words, man's different and contradictory possibilities – constitutes his essence.

There are other basic concepts of Marx's to which depth psychology can make significant contributions. It can show that

Marx – like Spinoza and Freud – was neither a determinist nor a non-determinist. He was an *alternativist*. Man at every step of his individual and historical life is confronted with a number of 'real possibilities'. These possibilities, as such, are determined, being the result of the totality of the circumstances under which he lives, but man has a choice between alternatives as long as he is *aware* of them and of the consequences of his decision early enough so that his personality is not yet completely inclined towards what is against his human interest; once this has happened, the time for choice has irrevocably passed. Freedom, in this sense, is not 'acting in the awareness of necessity', but is based on awareness of real possibilities and their consequences, in contrast to belief in fictitious and unreal possibilities which are an opiate, and destroy the possibility of freedom.

Another topic of fundamental importance in Marxian thought to which psycho-analysis can make a significant contribution is the phenomenon of *alienation*. Limitations of space do not permit entering into a discussion of this topic here. Only one word may be said. The concept of alienation has often been used in Marxian literature as a purely intellectual concept, separate from the discussion of the psychological data related to the *experience* of alienation. I believe that one cannot speak meaningfully of alienation unless one has experienced it in oneself and in others. Furthermore, one has to examine the phenomenon of alienation in its relation to narcissism, depression, fanaticism and idolatry to understand it fully and to be able to study the degree of alienation in various social classes and the social conditions which tend to increase or decrease it. Psycho-analysis has all the tools to accomplish this.

To sum up: this article is a plea to introduce a dialectically and humanistically oriented psycho-analysis as a significant viewpoint into Marxist thought. I believe that Marxism needs such a psychological theory and that psycho-analysis needs to incorporate genuine Marxist theory. Such a synthesis will fertilize both fields, while the emphasis on positivistic Pavlovism, even though it has many interesting data to offer, will only lead to the deterioration of both psychology and Marxism.

III. ON FREEDOM

BERTRAND RUSSELL

⊚ ⊚

In Praise of Idleness[1]

BERTRAND RUSSELL has gained a world-wide reputation
for his work in philosophy and the cause of peace. Born in
1872, he became a Fellow of the Royal Society in 1908,
was awarded the Royal Society's Sylvester Medal in 1934,
the British Order of Merit in 1949 and the Nobel Prize
for Literature in 1950. Some of the best known of his
numerous writings are *Principia Mathematica* with Alfred
North Whitehead, *Roads to Freedom*, *The Conquest of
Happiness*, *In Praise of Idleness* and *Common Sense and
Nuclear Warfare*.

Like most of my generation, I was brought up on the saying:
'Satan finds some mischief still for idle hands to do.' Being a
highly virtuous child, I believed all that I was told, and acquired
a conscience which has kept me working hard down to the
present moment. But although my conscience has controlled my
actions, my *opinions* have undergone a revolution. I think that
there is far too much work done in the world, that immense
harm is caused by the belief that work is virtuous, and that what
needs to be preached in modern industrial countries is quite
different from what always has been preached. Everyone knows
the story of the traveller in Naples who saw twelve beggars lying
in the sun (it was before the days of Mussolini), and offered a
lira to the laziest of them. Eleven of them jumped up to claim it,
so he gave it to the twelfth. This traveller was on the right lines.
But in countries which do not enjoy Mediterranean sunshine
idleness is more difficult, and a great public propaganda will be
required to inaugurate it. I hope that, after reading the following
pages, the leaders of the Y.M.C.A. will start a campaign to

1. Written in 1932.

induce good young men to do nothing. If so, I shall not have lived in vain.

Before advancing my own arguments for laziness, I must dispose of one which I cannot accept. Whenever a person who already has enough to live on proposes to engage in some everyday kind of job, such as school-teaching or typing, he or she is told that such conduct takes the bread out of other people's mouths, and is therefore wicked. If this argument were valid, it would only be necessary for us all to be idle in order that we should all have our mouths full of bread. What people who say such things forget is that what a man earns he usually spends, and in spending he gives employment. As long as a man spends his income, he puts just as much bread into people's mouths in spending as he takes out of other people's mouths in earning. The real villain, from this point of view, is the man who saves. If he merely puts his savings in a stocking, like the proverbial French peasant, it is obvious that they do not give employment. If he invests his savings, the matter is less obvious, and different cases arise.

One of the commonest things to do with savings is to lend them to some Government. In view of the fact that the bulk of the public expenditure of most civilized governments consists in payment for past wars or preparation for future wars, the man who lends his money to a government is in the same position as the bad men in Shakespeare who hire murderers. The net result of the man's economical habits is to increase the armed forces of the state to which he lends his savings. Obviously it would be better if he spent the money, even if he spent it in drink or gambling.

But, I shall be told, the case is quite different when savings are invested in industrial enterprises. When such enterprises succeed, and produce something useful, this may be conceded. In these days, however, no one will deny that most enterprises fail. That means that a large amount of human labour, which might have been devoted to producing something that could be enjoyed, was expended on producing machines which, when produced, lay idle and did no good to anyone. The man who invests his savings in a concern that goes bankrupt is therefore injuring others as well as himself. If he spent his money, say, in giving parties for his friends, they (we may hope) would get pleasure, and so would all those upon whom he spent money, such as the butcher, the baker and the bootlegger. But if he spends it (let us say) upon laying down rails for surface cars in some place where surface cars turn out to be not wanted, he has diverted a mass of labour into channels where it gives pleasure to no one. Nevertheless, when he becomes poor through the failure of his investment he will be regarded as a victim of un-deserved misfortune, whereas the gay spendthrift, who has spent his money philanthropically, will be despised as a fool and a frivolous person.

All this is only preliminary. I want to say, in all seriousness, that a great deal of harm is being done in the modern world by belief in the virtuousness of *work*, and that the road to happiness and prosperity lies in an organized diminution of work.

First of all: what is work? Work is of two kinds: first, altering the position of matter at or near the earth's surface relatively to other such matter; second, telling other people to do so. The first kind is unpleasant and ill paid; the second is pleasant and highly paid. The second kind is capable of indefinite extension: there are not only those who give orders, but those who give advice as to what orders should be given. Usually two opposite kinds of advice are given simultaneously by two organized bodies of men; this is called politics. The skill required for this kind of work is not knowledge of the subjects as to which advice is given, but knowledge of the art of persuasive speaking and writing, i.e. of advertising.

Throughout Europe, though not in America, there is a third class of men, more respected than either of the classes of workers. There are men who, through ownership of land, are able to make others pay for the privilege of being allowed to exist and to work. These land-owners are idle, and I might there-fore be expected to praise them. Unfortunately, their idleness is only rendered possible by the industry of others; indeed their desire for comfortable idleness is historically the source of the whole gospel of work. The last thing they have ever wished is that others should follow their example.

From the beginning of civilization until the Industrial Revo-lution, a man could, as a rule, produce by hard work little more than was required for the subsistence of himself and his family, although his wife worked at least as hard as he did, and his chil-dren added their labour as soon as they were old enough to do so. The small surplus above bare necessaries was not left to those who produced it, but was appropriated by warriors and priests. In times of famine there was no surplus; the warriors and priests, however, still secured as much as at other times, with the result that many of the workers died of hunger. This system persisted in Russia until 1917,[1] and still persists in the East; in England, in spite of the Industrial Revolution, it remained in full force throughout the Napoleonic wars, and until a hundred years ago, when the new class of manufacturers acquired power. In America, the system came to an end with the Revolution, except in the South, where it persisted until the Civil War. A system which lasted so long and ended so recently has naturally left a profound impress upon men's thoughts and opinions. Much that we take for granted about the desirability of work is derived from this system, and, being pre-industrial, is not adapted to the modern world. Modern technique has made it possible for leisure, within limits, to be not the prerogative of small privileged classes, but a right evenly distributed throughout the community. The morality of work is the morality of slaves, and the modern world has no need of slavery.

It is obvious that, in primitive communities, peasants, left to themselves, would not have parted with the slender surplus upon which the warriors and priests subsisted, but would have either produced less or consumed more. At first, sheer force compelled them to produce and part with the surplus. Gradually, however, it was found possible to induce many of them to accept an ethic according to which it was their duty to work hard, although part of their work went to support others in idleness. By this means the amount of compulsion required was lessened, and the expenses of government were diminished. To this day, ninety-nine per cent of British wage-earners would be genuinely shocked if it were proposed that the King should not have a larger income than a working-man. The conception of duty, speaking historically, has been a means used by the holders of power to induce others to live for the interests of their masters rather than for their own. Of course the holders of power conceal this fact from themselves by managing to believe that their interests are identical with the larger interests of humanity.

1. Since then, members of the Communist Party have succeeded to this privilege of the warriors and priests.

Sometimes this is true; Athenian slave-owners, for instance, employed part of their leisure in making a permanent contribution to civilization which would have been impossible under a just economic system. Leisure is essential to civilization, and in former times leisure for the few was only rendered possible by the labours of the many. But their labours were valuable, not because work is good, but because leisure is good. And with modern technique it would be possible to distribute leisure justly without injury to civilization.

Modern technique has made it possible to diminish enormously the amount of labour required to secure the necessaries of life for everyone. This was made obvious during the war. At that time all the men in the armed forces, all the men and women engaged in the production of munitions, all the men and women engaged in spying, war propaganda or government offices connected with the war, were withdrawn from productive occupations. In spite of this, the general level of physical well-being among unskilled wage-earners on the side of the Allies was higher than before or since. The significance of this fact was concealed by finance: borrowing made it appear as if the future was nourishing the present. But that, of course, would have been impossible; a man cannot eat a loaf of bread that does not yet exist. The war showed conclusively that, by the scientific organization of production, it is possible to keep modern populations in fair comfort on a small part of the working capacity of the modern world. If, at the end of the war, the scientific organization, which had been created in order to liberate men for fighting and munition work, had been preserved, and the hours of work had been cut down to four, all would have been well. Instead of that the old chaos was restored, those whose work was demanded were made to work long hours, and the rest were left to starve as unemployed. Why? Because work is a duty, and a man should not receive wages in proportion to what he has produced, but in proportion to his virtue as exemplified by his industry.

This is the morality of the slave state, applied in circumstances totally unlike those in which it arose. No wonder the result has been disastrous. Let us take an illustration. Suppose that, at a given moment, a certain number of people are engaged in the manufacture of pins. They make as many pins as the world needs, working (say) eight hours a day. Someone makes an invention by which the same number of men can make twice as many pins as before. But the world does not need twice as many pins: pins are already so cheap that hardly any more will be bought at a lower price. In a sensible world, everybody concerned in the manufacture of pins would take to working four hours instead of eight, and everything else would go on as before. But in the actual world this would be thought demoralizing. The men still work eight hours, there are too many pins, some employers go bankrupt, and half the men previously concerned in making pins are thrown out of work. There is, in the end, just as much leisure as on the other plan, but half the men are totally idle while half are still overworked. In this way, it is insured that the unavoidable leisure shall cause misery all round instead of being a universal source of happiness. Can anything more insane be imagined?

The idea that the poor should have leisure has always been shocking to the rich. In England, in the early nineteenth century, fifteen hours was the ordinary day's work for a man; children sometimes did as much, and very commonly did twelve hours a day. When meddlesome busybodies suggested that perhaps these hours were rather long, they were told that work kept adults from drink and children from mischief. When I was a child, shortly after urban working-men had acquired the vote, certain public holidays were established by law, to the great indignation of the upper classes. I remember hearing an old Duchess say: 'What do the poor want with holidays? They ought to *work*.' People nowadays are less frank, but the sentiment persists, and is the source of much of our economic confusion.

Let us, for a moment, consider the ethics of work frankly, without superstition. Every human being, of necessity, consumes, in the course of his life, a certain amount of the produce of human labour. Assuming, as we may, that labour is on the whole disagreeable, it is unjust that a man should consume more than he produces. Of course he may provide services rather than commodities, like a medical man, for example; but he should provide something in return for his board and lodging. To this extent, the duty of work must be admitted, but to this extent only.

I shall not dwell upon the fact that, in all modern societies outside the U.S.S.R., many people escape even this minimum amount of work, namely all those who inherit money and all those who marry money. I do not think the fact that these people are allowed to be idle is nearly so harmful as the fact that wage-earners are expected to overwork or starve.

If the ordinary wage-earner worked four hours a day, there would be enough for everybody, and no unemployment – assuming a certain very moderate amount of sensible organization. This idea shocks the well-to-do, because they are convinced that the poor would not know how to use so much leisure. In America, men often work long hours even when they are already well off; such men, naturally, are indignant at the idea of leisure for wage-earners, except as the grim punishment of unemployment; in fact, they dislike leisure even for their sons. Oddly enough, while they wish their sons to work so hard as to have no time to be civilized, they do not mind their wives and daughters having no work at all. The snobbish admiration of uselessness, which, in an aristocratic society, extends to both sexes, is, under a plutocracy, confined to women; this, however, does not make it any more in agreement with common sense.

The wise use of leisure, it must be conceded, is a product of civilization and education. A man who has worked long hours all his life will be bored if he becomes suddenly idle. But without a considerable amount of leisure a man is cut off from many of the best things. There is no longer any reason why the bulk of the population should suffer this deprivation; only a foolish asceticism, usually vicarious, makes us continue to insist on work in excessive quantities now that the need no longer exists.

In the new creed which controls the government of Russia, while there is much that is very different from the traditional teaching of the West, there are some things that are quite unchanged. The attitude of the governing classes, and especially of those who conduct educational propaganda, on the subject of the dignity of labour, is almost exactly that which the governing classes of the world have always preached to what were called the 'honest poor'. Industry, sobriety, willingness to work long hours for distant advantages, even submissiveness to authority, all these reappear; moreover authority still represents the will of the Ruler of the Universe, who, however, is now called by a new name, Dialectical Materialism.

The victory of the proletariat in Russia has some points in common with the victory of the feminists in some other countries. For ages, men had conceded the superior saintliness of women, and had consoled women for their inferiority by maintaining that saintliness is more desirable than power. At last the feminists decided that they would have both, since the pioneers among them believed all that the men had told them about the desirability of virtue, but not what they had told them about the worthlessness of political power. A similar thing has happened in Russia as regards manual work. For ages, the rich and their sycophants have written in praise of 'honest toil', have praised the simple life, have professed a religion which teaches that the poor are much more likely to go to heaven than the rich, and in general have tried to make manual workers believe that there is some special nobility about altering the position of matter in space, just as men tried to make women believe that they derived some special nobility from their sexual enslavement. In Russia, all this teaching about the excellence of manual work has been taken seriously, with the result that the manual worker is more honoured than anyone else. What are, in essence, revivalist appeals are made, but not for the old purposes: they are made to secure shock workers for special tasks. Manual work is the ideal which is held before the young, and is the basis of all ethical teaching.

For the present, possibly, this is all to the good. A large country, full of natural resources, awaits development, and has to be developed with very little use of credit. In these circumstances, hard work is necessary, and is likely to bring a great reward. But what will happen when the point has been reached where everybody could be comfortable without working long hours?

In the West, we have various ways of dealing with this problem. We have no attempt at economic justice, so that a large proportion of the total produce goes to a small minority of the population, many of whom do no work at all. Owing to the absence of any central control over production, we produce hosts of things that are not wanted. We keep a large percentage of the working population idle, because we can dispense with their labour by making the others overwork. When all these methods prove inadequate, we have a war: we cause a number of people to manufacture high explosives, and a number of others to explode them, as if we were children who had just discovered fireworks. By a combination of all these devices we manage, though with difficulty, to keep alive the notion that a great deal of severe manual work must be the lot of the average man.

In Russia, owing to more economic justice and central control over production, the problem will have to be differently solved. The rational solution would be, as soon as the necessaries and elementary comforts can be provided for all, to reduce the hours of labour gradually, allowing a popular vote to decide, at each stage, whether more leisure or more goods were to be preferred. But, having taught the supreme virtue of hard work, it is difficult to see how the authorities can aim at a paradise in which there will be much leisure and little work. It seems more likely that they will find continually fresh schemes, by which present leisure is to be sacrificed to future productivity. I read recently of an ingenious plan put forward by Russian engineers, for making the White Sea and the northern coasts of Siberia warm, by putting a dam across the Kara Sea. An admirable project, but liable to postpone proletarian comfort for a generation, while the nobility of toil is being displayed amid the ice fields and snowstorms of the Arctic Ocean. This sort of thing, if it happens, will be the result of regarding the virtue of hard work as an end in itself, rather than as a means to a state of affairs in which it is no longer needed.

The fact is that moving matter about, while a certain amount of it is necessary to our existence, is emphatically not one of the ends of human life. If it were, we should have to consider every navvy superior to Shakespeare. We have been misled in this matter by two causes. One is the necessity of keeping the poor contented, which has led the rich, for thousands of years, to preach the dignity of labour, while taking care themselves to remain undignified in this respect. The other is the new pleasure in mechanism, which makes us delight in the astonishingly clever changes that we can produce on the earth's surface. Neither of these motives makes any great appeal to the actual worker. If you ask him what he thinks the best part of his life, he is not likely to say: 'I enjoy manual work because it makes me feel that

I am fulfilling man's noblest task, and because I like to think how much man can transform his planet. It is true that my body demands periods of rest, which I have to fill in as best I may, but I am never so happy as when the morning comes and I can return to the toil from which my contentment springs.' I have never heard working men say this sort of thing. They consider work, as it should be considered, a necessary means to a livelihood, and it is from their leisure hours that they derive whatever happiness they may enjoy.

It will be said that, while a little leisure is pleasant, men would not know how to fill their days if they had only four hours of work out of the twenty-four. In so far as this is true in the modern world, it is a condemnation of our civilization; it would not have been true at any earlier period. There was formerly a capacity for lightheartedness and play which has been to some extent inhibited by the cult of efficiency. The modern man thinks that everything ought to be done for the sake of something else, and never for its own sake. Serious-minded persons, for example, are continually condemning the habit of going to the cinema, and telling us that it leads the young into crime. But all the work that goes to producing a cinema is respectable, because it is work, and because it brings a money profit. The notion that the desirable activities are those that bring a profit has made everything topsy-turvy. The butcher who provides you with meat and the baker who provides you with bread are praiseworthy, because they are making money; but when you enjoy the food they have provided, you are merely frivolous, unless you eat only to get strength for your work. Broadly speaking, it is held that getting money is good and spending money is bad. Seeing that they are two sides of one transaction, this is absurd; one might as well maintain that keys are good, but keyholes are bad. Whatever merit there may be in the production of goods must be entirely derivative from the advantage to be obtained by consuming them. The individual, in our society, works for profit; but the social purpose of his work lies in the consumption of what he produces. It is this divorce between the individual and the social purpose of production that makes it so difficult for men to think clearly in a world in which profit-making is the incentive to industry. We think too much of production, and too little of consumption. One result is that we attach too little importance to enjoyment and simple happiness, and that we do not judge production by the pleasure that it gives to the consumer.

When I suggest that working hours should be reduced to four, I am not meaning to imply that all the remaining time should necessarily be spent in pure frivolity. I mean that four hours' work a day should entitle a man to the necessities and elementary comforts of life, and that the rest of his time should be his to use as he might see fit. It is an essential part of any such social system that education should be carried further than it usually is at present, and should aim, in part, at providing tastes which would enable a man to use leisure intelligently. I am not thinking mainly of the sort of things that would be considered 'highbrow'. Peasant dances have died out except in remote rural areas, but the impulses which caused them to be cultivated must still exist in human nature. The pleasures of urban populations have become mainly passive: seeing cinemas, watching football matches, listening to the radio, and so on. This results from the fact that their active energies are fully taken up with work; if they had more leisure, they would again enjoy pleasures in which they took an active part.

In the past, there was a small leisure class and a larger working class. The leisure class enjoyed advantages for which there was no basis in social justice; this necessarily made it oppressive, limited its sympathies and caused it to invent theories by which to justify its privileges. These facts greatly diminished its excellence, but in spite of this drawback it contributed nearly the whole of what we call civilization. It cultivated the arts and discovered the sciences; it wrote the books, invented the philosophies, and refined social relations. Even the liberation of the oppressed has usually been inaugurated from above. Without the leisure class, mankind would never have emerged from barbarism.

The method of a hereditary leisure class without duties was, however, extraordinarily wasteful. None of the members of the class had been taught to be industrious, and the class as a whole was not exceptionally intelligent. The class might produce one Darwin, but against him had to be set tens of thousands of country gentlemen who never thought of anything more intelligent than fox-hunting and punishing poachers. At present, the universities are supposed to provide, in a more systematic way, what the leisure class provided accidentally and as a by-product. This is a great improvement, but it has certain drawbacks. University life is so different from life in the world at large that men who live in an academic *milieu* tend to be unaware of the preoccupations and problems of ordinary men and women; moreover their ways of expressing themselves are usually such as to rob their opinions of the influence that they ought to have upon the general public. Another disadvantage is that in universities studies are organized, and the man who thinks of some original line of research is likely to be discouraged. Academic institutions, therefore, useful as they are, are not adequate guardians of the interests of civilization in a world where everyone outside their walls is too busy for un-utilitarian pursuits.

In a world where no one is compelled to work more than four hours a day, every person possessed of scientific curiosity will be able to indulge it, and every painter will be able to paint without starving, however excellent his pictures may be. Young writers will not be obliged to draw attention to themselves by sensational potboilers, with a view to acquiring the economic independence needed for monumental works, for which, when the time at last comes, they will have lost the taste and the capacity. Men who, in their professional work, have become interested in some phase of economics or government, will be able to develop their ideas without the academic detachment that makes the work of university economists often seem lacking in reality. Medical men will have time to learn about the progress of medicine, teachers will not be exasperatedly struggling to teach by routine methods things which they learned in their youth, which may, in the interval, have been proved to be untrue.

Above all, there will be happiness and joy of life, instead of frayed nerves, weariness and dyspepsia. The work exacted will be enough to make leisure delightful, but not enough to produce exhaustion. Since men will not be tired in their spare time, they will not demand only such amusements as are passive and vapid. At least one per cent will probably devote the time not spent in professional work to pursuits of some public importance, and, since they will not depend upon these pursuits for their livelihood, their originality will be unhampered, and there will be no need to conform to the standards set by elderly pundits. But it is not only in these exceptional cases that the advantages of leisure will appear. Ordinary men and women, having the opportunity of a happy life, will become more kindly and less persecuting and less inclined to view others with suspicion. The taste for war will die out, partly for this reason, and partly because it will involve long and severe work for all. Good nature is, of all moral qualities, the one that the world needs most, and good nature is the result of ease and security, not of a life of arduous struggle. Modern methods of production have given us the possibility of ease and security for all; we have chosen, instead, to have over-work for some and starvation for the others. Hitherto we have continued to be as energetic as we were before there were machines; in this we have been foolish, but there is no reason to go on being foolish for ever.

IRING FETSCHER

⊛ ⊛

Marx's Concretization of the Concept of Freedom

IRING FETSCHER was for three years editor of *Marxist Studies*, published in Tübingen, Germany, and is author of *From Marx to Soviet Ideology, Marxism, Its History in Documents* and *Rousseau's Political Philosophy*. Born in 1922 in Marbach-am-Neckar, he studied philosophy, and romanticism and sociology at the Universities of Tübingen, Paris and Frankfurt. His doctoral dissertation was on 'Hegel's Anthropology'. At present he is professor of political science at the University of Frankfurt-am-Main.

The young Marx encountered the question of individual freedom in society in two conceptual forms: the liberal concept, most concisely formulated philosophically by Kant, and Hegel's metaphysics of freedom. Both conceptual forms appear as expressions of historically concrete thought within the limitations of a given social and political reality. From the very outset, Marx's theoretical structure and political intention were to surmount, theoretically and practically, the limitation of these conceptions and their complementary abstraction. It is therefore impossible to understand adequately Marx's original political aim without a grasp of how he analysed these concepts as 'bourgeois conceptions of freedom'.

For Kant, the principle of political freedom is

> that no one can force me (in so far as he considers another person's welfare) to be happy in his way, but *each must seek his own happiness* in the way that suits him best provided that he permits *another the freedom* to pursue a similar goal; it is therefore possible to *formulate* a universal law for *the freedom of all* which does not interfere with *the freedom of each*.[1]

1. Kant, *On the Maxim: Good in Theory, but Bad in Practice*, in *Werke* Vorländer ed., Vol. IV, pp. 87 ff.

Freedom is thus the scope for the individual's pursuit of happiness, which is limited only by another individual's equally legitimate pursuit. The obvious deficiency of this concept is that it refers only negatively to one's fellow man, viewing him solely as the unavoidable legal *barrier* to one's own individual whim or caprice. This concept necessarily follows if, as with Hobbes and Kant, thought starts from the assumption that man's 'unsocial social existence' is an unyielding fact. If we proceed from the supposition that spontaneous, natural man is necessarily hostile to others until a state law forces him to consider the voice of conscience that leads him to respect the freedom claims of his fellow men, then we can find no other but this restrictive relationship between men.

For Marx, however, this antagonism of individuals – imputed to 'nature' since Hobbes – is the characteristic only of capitalistic competitive society. Jean-Jacques Rousseau preceded Marx in recognizing the historical nature of '*homo lupus*' when he explained that Hobbes's statements could be legitimately applied only to contemporary man and not to man in general.[1] In contrast to Rousseau, however, Marx saw that the free development of the human individual in all societies is tied to the active cooperation of the other individuals. A recognition of this could not break through to full consciousness until the advent of modern, highly specialized society with its division of labour. Whereas Rousseau yearned to turn back to an earlier age, to escape from the mercantilist division of labour of the precapitalist society of essentially self-sufficient rural families which he knew, Marx looked ahead to a cooperative civilization in which each man would take satisfaction in his own accomplishments because they contributed to the gratification of others and would accept the work of others as contributing to his own gratification. Instead of dissolving the mutual relations which corresponded to the ideal of the city-state, Marx preferred their universalization, and a radical transformation of their character.

Marx was not, however, the first to stress the limitations of

1. Cf. Rousseau's expression in the fragment *State and War:* 'Hobbes's error . . . is to confuse natural man with the men under his eyes. . . .' (Vaughan, *Rousseau's Political Writings*, Vol. I, p. 305). C. B. Macpherson, in his recent book *Political Theory of Possessive Individualism* (Oxford: O.U.P., 1962), convincingly traced the relationship between antagonistic market society and political theory from Hobbes to Locke.

Kant's conception of the liberal state. Whereas Kant developed the position that the function of the liberal state is to help the individual fulfil himself by securing the peaceful coexistence of naturally egoistical individuals, Hegel sought the freedom of rational citizens not in laws guaranteeing individual freedom of opportunity, but in the state structure itself.

In the *Philosophy of History* Hegel turned specifically against all liberal concepts of freedom, as Marx did later, and condemned them as mere 'negativity' and formalism: The state is

> not an assemblage of people *wherein the freedom of all individuals must be limited*. Freedom is only negatively comprehended when it is represented *as if the individual* in his relations to other in-individuals thus limited his freedom in order that this universal limitation – the mutual constraint of all – might secure a small space of liberty for each.[1]

Already in the *Jenenser Realphilosophie* Hegel explained 'formal freedom' as that 'whose substance is external to itself'.[2] The substance of freedom, for Hegel, is the 'Spirit', or, more precisely, what is objective in the living spirit of the commonwealth's institutions and laws. Although idealistically and mystically embellished, these thoughts were nevertheless perceived by Marx as an essential advance over the Kantian standpoint.

To see this, one has only to define 'Substance' as the real society of cooperating people, where the individual's truly human development can occur. The positive relation of the individual to all his fellow men (first of all incorporated into a state) becomes, with Hegel, a mere identification of the 'subjective Spirit' of each man with the 'objective Spirit' of the state. With Hegel, dialectical identification, which does not exclude the independent existence of both the individual and the state as fixed poles in relation to each other, remains merely a thing of ideal dimensions. The living man and the living society (Hegel's 'necessary and rational state') remain below this lofty sphere 'in insubstantial appearance'. Fundamentally, Hegel has only exchanged one abstraction for another. Whereas the liberal concept of freedom is based on the positive relationship between

1. Hegel, *Philosophie der Weltgeschichte*, Bd. I, ed. Lasson, p. 90. [The translation used here is from the last revision of the Sibree translation as given in *Philosophy of History* (New York: Dover, 1956). – *Translator*]
2. Hegel, *Jenenser Realphilosophie*, ed. Hoffmeister, Vol. II, p. 28.

people and expresses the restraints determined by the psychic demands of people in competitive society, the Hegelian state metaphysic says that man finds and can exercise freedom in the Ideal realm, not in his workaday personal relationships. Indeed, Hegel asserted, the 'state is the reality in which the individual has his freedom',[1] but the ideal state is not the human environment; in real 'civil society', it is the world of production, exchange and industry and here man must seek his freedom.

Marx's critique demonstrated the historical basis of the liberal concept of freedom and showed that it remained confined within the socially and temporally limited horizon of bourgeois thought. In the case of the Hegelian concept, Marx indicated that its illusory and complementary character becomes apparent against the reality of bourgeois society. His most thoroughgoing critique of the bourgeois thesis of freedom and the rights of man is found in *Capital*:

> This sphere [of circulation and commodity exchange] that we are deserting, within whose boundaries the sale and purchase of labour-power goes, is in fact a very Eden of the innate rights of man. There alone rule Freedom, Equality, Property and Bentham. Freedom, because both buyer and seller of a commodity, say of labour-power, are constrained only by their own free will. They contract as free agents, and the agreement they come to is but the form in which they give legal expression to their common will. Equality, because each enters into relation with the other, as with a simple owner of commodities, and they exchange equivalent for equivalent. Property, because each disposes only of what is his own. And Bentham, because each looks only to himself. The only force that brings them together and puts them in relation with each other, is the selfishness, the gain and the private interests of each. Each looks to himself only, and no one troubles himself about the rest, and just because they do so, do they all, in accordance with the pre-established harmony of things, or under the auspices of an all-shrewd providence, work together to the mutual advantage, for the common weal and in the interest of all.[2]

Marx showed that the freedom and equality guaranteed in the French Constitution as the Rights of Man, and taken over in

1. Hegel, *Philosophy of History*, ed. Lasson, Bd. I, p. 89 ff.
2. Marx, *Capital*, Kerr edn., p. 195 [in the original the citation is from *Das Kapital* (Berlin: Volksausgabe, 1947), Vol. I, p. 184. – *Translator*]

similar form by all liberal democratic constitutions, was an adequate expression of human relations in a market society, where
no one's social condition is fixed by the privileges of birth, and
everyone, as a 'commodity owner', is free to dispose of his goods
and is bound only by the terms of the contract to which he agreed.
But the sale of the labour-power commodity, this apparent
equality and freedom, is actually false. The actual inequality
of ownership lies in the fact that the owners of labour-power
have nothing to sell but their labour-power and are therefore
compelled, although not by law, to part with it, or – as German
so graphically puts it – 'to contract oneself out' [*sich zu
verdingen*]. Their labour-power, unlike the objective goods a
craftsman brings to market, is not an objective part of their being
but objective *ability* itself. Man's essence is his ability to transform Nature creatively and to shape it to his wishes and ends.
When he is forced to sell this ability he renounces his humanity
and an alienated relationship to mankind and humanity results.
The liberal conception of freedom is limited because it attributes
man's calculated special interests to his essence, whereas, in
actuality, this characterization only reflects man in competitive
society and may be wrong about both the past and the future.
Marx shows Hegel's metaphysics of the state as the abstract
complementary of the idea of freedom already expressed by
bourgeois *democracy* in the Constitution of the French Revolution.

Marx's criticism of the Hegelian Philosophy of Right was that
it explained the bourgeois democratic state which Hegel, as a
German, first encountered only in its theoretical (ideological)
form. The superiority of the Hegelian conception over the liberal
was, as we have already seen, its ability to grasp the dialectical
relationship of the individual to society. We find the same
recognition again in Marx – no matter whether he gained it from
Hegel or from the experience of social reality itself:

> It is above all necessary to avoid postulating 'society' once again
> as an abstraction confronting the individual. The individual *is*
> the *social being*. The manifestation of his life – even when it does
> not appear directly in the form of a communal manifestation,
> accomplished in association with other men – is therefore a
> manifestation and affirmation of social life.[1]

1. Marx–Engels–Gesamtausgabe, I/iii, p. 117. [The translation used

As we have already seen, for Marx the Hegelian conception fails because it presents the social individual only in the idealistic abstract form of subjective and objective Spirit and relegates concrete man (the sensuous real being), as well as the civil society formed by him, to a sphere of lower rank. Man as a socially related being is suspended in an illusory and imaginary sphere beyond civil society with its calculated intelligence, its private egoism, its work, its law and its competition. But Marx realized that the abstraction of Hegelian philosophy from concrete daily life was no accident: it was only possible for 'German thought to abstract its notion of the modern state from natural man while, and in so far as, the modern state was itself abstracted from actual people, or the whole man gratified himself only in an imaginary manner'.[1] Man lived in this 'modern state' only in the abstract form of *citizen* (*citoyen*) during the course of his real sensuous existence as a member of the bourgeois (competitive) society. As a citizen he might be part of the civil society and imagine himself dialectically united with the rest of the citizens in the community, but in his real sensuous existence he is unfree and isolated, subject to alien laws ('contingency'), and can relate himself to his fellow men only negatively (e.g. as competitor).

The completed political state [Marx writes in 1843], is in its essence the *species-life of man* in opposition to his material life. All presuppositions of his egoistical life continue to exist *outside of the state sphere* in civil society. Where the political state has reached its true development, man leads a double life, heavenly and earthly, not only in thought, in consciousness, but in actuality, in life, life in the political community *in which he recognizes himself as a social being*, and life in civil society where he acts as a *private person*, looks upon *other people as means*, and is *himself degraded into a means* and becomes the plaything of alien forces.[2]

Man's 'true life' should be in community with his fellow men, each fulfilling himself and relating to the others in enriching accomplishment; but this 'true life' exists in the modern world

---

here is from T. B. Bottomore's translation of Marx's essay, *Private Property and Communism*, as it appears in *Marx's Concept of Man*, by Erich Fromm (New York: Frederick Ungar, 1963), p. 130. – *Translator*]

1. Marx–Engels, *Werke* (Berlin, 1955 ff.), Vol. I, pp. 384 ff.
2. Ibid., p. 354 ff. [except from 'On the Jewish Problem' – *Translator*].

only as the illusory and transcendental form of the community
of citizens that is first tangibly experienced when it closes ranks
and is brought into hostile relations with the community of
citizens of *another* state.[1] In their real daily existence, on the
other hand, individuals lead an 'untrue life', a life of deliberate
isolation and hostility against their fellow men: 'actual man is
first recognized in the form of egoistical [untrue] individuals,
true man, in the form of abstract [unactual] citizen'.[2] This
analysis posed the task of developing the actual (untrue) person
of civil society into a true person (conscious of his dialectical
relationship with his fellow men).

In his early writings Marx formulated the task in this way:

> Only when actual man takes back into himself the abstract citizen
> of the state and, *as individual man in his empirical life, in his in-
> dividual work, in his individual relations*, has become species-
> essence, only when man has recognized and reorganized his
> *forces propres* as social powers, and therefore no longer separates
> from himself social power in the form of political power, *only
> then is human emancipation completed.*

In his works of the 1840s and 1850s, particularly in the *Extracts* (*Exzerptheften*) and in the *Outline to the Critique of Political Economy* (*Grundrisse der Kritik der politischen Oekonomie*),

---

1. Hegel drew this consequence, and in *Philosophy of Right* he elaborated on this very point of the higher ethical nature of the idealistic concept of the state as against the civil state: 'An entirely distorted account . . .
results from regarding the state as a merely civil society and from regarding its final end as only the security of individual life and property. . . .
The ethical moment in war is implied in what has been said. . . . War is
not to be regarded as an absolute evil. . . . War is the state of affairs which
deals in earnest with the vanity of temporal goods and concerns. . . . This
is what makes it the moment in which the ideality of the particular attains
its right and is actualized. War has the higher significance that by its
agency . . . the ethical health of peoples is preserved in their indifference
to the stabilization of finite institutions; just as the blowing of the winds
preserves the sea from the foulness which would be the result of a prolonged calm . . .' (*Rechtsphilosophie* §324, in *Werke*, Jubiläumsausgabe,
Vol. VII, p. 434. [*Philosophy of Right*, §324. The translation used here is
by T. M. Knox, O.U.P., 1942. – *Translator*]). Hegel saw empirical confirmation of his philosophical deduction of the usefulness of foreign war
in the fact that 'successful wars have checked domestic unrest and consolidated the power of the state at home'. (Loc. cit.)

2. Hegel, *Rechtsphilosophie*, in *Werke*, Jubiläumsausgabe, Vol. VII, p.
379.

Marx left us detailed information about this concrete free man who, 'in his individual work, in his individual relations, has become species-essence'. Man is 'species-essence' when he no longer projects his inherent qualities into an otherworldly Being – as, according to Feuerbach, happened with religious reification – or, as in political alienation, no longer poses a world beyond the existing everyday bourgeois 'state'. According to his natural abilities, then, every individual has acquired *all-roundedness* which, for him and with him, living humanity has realized by humanized work. Only when he is liberated from the 'idiocy' of lifelong fixation to a trade, and from the slavery of wage labour, will such all-rounded appropriation of species-life by the individual be possible. Only when this is realized can the state (and religious ideology) wither away as the necessary complement to the incomplete actuality of society and its members. The state's becoming superfluous is specifically linked, above all, to the abolition of economic class privileges; with their abolition the necessity for the forcible protection of the privileged against the underprivileged is also abolished. The superfluity of the (democratic) state is dependent on the rise of a society in which the individuals have become 'species-beings' (*Gattungswesen*) who relate themselves totally and positively to their fellow men.

The barriers to individual freedom in the 'political state' were and remain necessary so long as real inequality in the opportunity for individual development remains, and the 'alienation' of all is not overcome. With the elimination of property privileges a decisive step is taken but the end not yet attained. As long as it is not yet possible to reduce working time so that the necessary tasks of all can be fulfilled voluntarily and the productivity of all suffices to satisfy the total needs of each, inequality remains the real prospect and therewith the 'unfreedom' of the concrete individual remains. As long as the gratification of my needs remains mediated not through my claim as man but through my purse – and this is surely the case today even in the 'socialist states' – there can be no talk that the human development of which the young Marx spoke has come true.

In the *Excerpts* as well as the *Economic Essays*, originating in the years 1844 and 1845, Marx opportunely worked out the idea of alienated, commodity-producing society pregnant with the future, unalienated human society. In these formulations one

245

can clearly gather the sense which the concept of 'human emancipation', the liberation of concrete man, had for Marx. Division of labour in the technical sense is the prerequisite of both forms of society; but in the one it is tied to the egoistical isolation of each individual, and in the other to the loving relationship of each for all. The following description is valid, according to Marx, for commodity society:

> I have produced for myself and not for you, as you have produced for yourself and not for me. The result of my production has, in and of itself, just as little direct relation to you as the result of your production has to me, i.e. our production is [*not*] *production of people for people as people*, i.e. not social production. As human beings thus, none of us has a relationship of gratification to the product of the other. *Our mutual production has no existence for us as people.* Our exchange can therefore also not be the mediating movement wherein it is acknowledged that *my product* is for you, at the same time as it is *a materialization of your being, your needs.* For not the human essence is the bond of our production for each other.[1]

The simple commodity system, and even more the expanding capitalistic one, is already exposed here as one in which the universal dependence of all on the products of work, differentiated by division of labour, does not appear as a spontaneous joyous, beneficent working of each for the others, the actualization of the 'fundamental nature of man' for the human needs of other people, but as an egoistical working of each only for himself. Only indirectly – through the compulsion to exchange on the market – and 'behind the back', does production also become production for others. It is certainly not a relation between people, but only between 'solvent buyers'. Every single person (or group of people) satisfies the human needs of other people according to 'aesthetic laws' and other such characteristically established rules: great poetry is meaningful to the poetic understanding, a symphony to the musical ear, painting to the cultured taste, etc. But these appropriate attributes of people, the ability to enjoy, hear and see, do not mediate their 'appropriation' but only the disposition of money. Specific products are not for me or you as people, but for you and me only in so far as we are commodity owners, money owners. They are also not

1. Marx–Engels–Gesamtausgabe, I/iii, p. 544.

created for us, but for our money, not for socially related men, but for the objectified embodiment of society: money.

In a truly 'human' society, where individuals are not mutual barriers to their freedom, but discover their essence as fulfilled and enriched beings, the following description would become valid:

Granted, we have produced as people: in his production each of us has *twice affirmed* himself and the other. 1) In production I found my individuality, and my particularity materialized, and therefore, in the course of the activity I enjoyed a personal expression of life as well as a sense of the individual joy in the contemplation of my personality as objective, sensually perceptible and indubitable power. 2) *In your satisfaction*, or your use of my products, I had immediate *satisfaction as well as consciousness that my* work satisfied a human need. Therefore I, as an *objective human being*, have produced an object corresponding to another human being's need. 3) I became, *for you, the mediator between you and the species*, thus I became a necessary, self-conscious and sentient part of your fulfilment of your essence. Thus, *I knew I was affirmed in your thought as well as in your love.* 4) In my individual expression of life I directly created your expression of life. Thus, my true essence, my *actualized species-essence*, was confirmed *in my immediate individual activity.* Our productions were so many mirrors reflecting our being.[1]

Here the evil magic of commodity-producing society, of exchange mediated through egoism, of products fragmented and losing their specific character (even disregarding the real transformation in labour itself) is dissolved. The variegated world of human products is transformed from a distorted mirror, where alienated man meets his likeness as a materialized commodity, into a true mirror of social humanity. The effort of all men becomes dependent upon the needs of others as is the effort of the lover who composes a song for his beloved.

Marx was no dreamer who expected the immediate realization of his ideal of the human world. But I am convinced that, despite many cautious remarks at a later period, he always held fast to that concept of human potential. The mastery of nature by associated mankind and the increase in labour productivity are certainly necessary preconditions for such emancipation from

1. Ibid., p. 546.

the alienated and reified world, but they are not yet liberation itself. Never did Marx see in the mere mastery of man over nature the meaning of history and the essence of liberation to which socialism summons. One may almost cite the biblical phrase: 'For what is a man profited, if he shall gain the whole world and lose his own soul?' Also for Marx, it would have helped little to achieve a perfect mastery of nature without bringing about the society in which freely associated people remould their nature. The mastery over nature is not 'anti-nature', but 'prohumanity'. The goal is the elimination of egoism and of the rule of man over man.

However, as long as freedom and happiness have *not yet* become concrete realities, the two abstract concepts of freedom retain an actual importance, notwithstanding the valid reservations we have become acquainted with. In all countries – including the socialist countries – an inevitable bit of democratic metaphysics lies hidden, inevitable ideology. Precisely because individual labour output results, not from joyous spontaneity and love of fellow man, but from 'material interest', the picture of an antagonistic society, the state, must appear as the complement of the still unsocial society. Nor may it be identified with that communistic society which alone connects spontaneous human beings producing for each other. Each state, including the 'Peoples' Democracies', remains an 'illusory social essence' that can 'become superfluous' and then 'wither away' only when a true social essence, in the sense Marx outlined, originates underneath. But the liberal conception, to which we were introduced in the classical Kantian formulation, retains its relative significance during this entire time. It appears necessary and correct because it secures a scope of freedom for egoistical unsocial individuals. It appears in optimal form when an enforceable law separates the freedom of the individual, not only from another individual, but also from the superior power of the government. The liberal ideology which believes the maximum of human freedom to be attained with this kind of guarantee must certainly be opposed. Hegel and Marx clearly enough stressed the narrowness and abstractness of this concept of freedom. But as long as the human society described by Marx is not realized and the majority of individuals, even in the 'socialist countries', are driven by egoistical motives in the performance of their work, those liberal guarantees can in no way be dispensed with. They need, above all, to be concretized by supplementary measures guaranteeing the right of usufruct (education, medical care, universal social security, etc.). These measures are not superfluous as long as competitive envy and real inequality continue as essential characteristics of society. Misuse of freedom must also be prevented by the suitable interpretation of the Kantian formula. Freedom for the economic enslavement of fellow men does not belong to those actions 'which can coexist with the freedom of the will of each and all according to a universal law'.

As long as concrete freedom is not realized, the two complementary abstract forms of freedom retain their restricted and historically limited validity.

Translated by R. Dunayevskaya

GAJO PETROVIĆ

⊚ ⊚

Man and Freedom

GAJO PETROVIĆ, associate professor of philosophy at the
University of Zagreb, Yugoslavia, is author of *English
Empiricist Philosophy*, *Philosophical Views of G. V. Plekhanov*, *From Locke to Ayer* and *Philosophy and Marxism*.
Born in Karlovac, Yugoslavia, in 1927, he studied philosophy in Zagreb, Leningrad and Moscow, and spent two
years studying in Great Britain and the United States.

I. What makes man man is not some property or activity peculiar to him (or a sum of all such properties or activities), but a
structure of being peculiar to him which is common to all really
human properties and activities – that is, praxis. Man is the being that exists through and as praxis.

2. Praxis is a mode of being essentially different from any
other mode of being. Freedom is one of the essential constituents
of that mode. As the being of praxis man is the being of freedom.
There is no freedom without man and no humanity without
freedom.

3. Freedom is the essence of man, but that does not mean that
man is always and everywhere free. The 'escape from freedom'
is widespread in the contemporary world. However, this does
not refute the thesis that man is the being of freedom; it only
confirms that contemporary man alienates himself from his
human essence, from what he as man can and ought to be.

4. There are various 'kinds', 'forms' and 'aspects' of freedom.
One speaks of metaphysical, ethical, psychological, economic,
political, national, religious freedom; of freedom of the spirit, of
the will, of thought, of conscience, of movement, of action; of
freedom of the Press, of radio and television, of assembly, of
speech, of association; of freedom from exploitation, oppression,

hunger, war and fear; of freedom from tradition, convention, vice, passion, weakness, prejudice; of freedom of art, science, education, teaching; of free behaviour, free love, free time, etc. But listing various kinds or forms of freedom does not solve the question, What is freedom? Before we answer this question we cannot be sure whether the kinds of freedom mentioned are really freedoms, or only pseudo-freedoms.

5. If freedom is understood as the non-existence of external obstacles to movement, then it is nothing specifically human; such freedom can appertain to a beast, bird, fish, even to water or a stone. But freedom is not the absence of external obstacles or, more generally, the sum of the external conditions under which something exists; freedom is a specific mode of being peculiar to man.

6. If freedom is conceived as the knowledge and acceptance of fate, destiny, universal necessity, then freedom is only another name for voluntary slavery. But freedom is not passive submission or adaptation to 'external' or 'internal' necessity. A free action can only be one by which a man changes his world and himself.

7. Mere intensity of activity or the degree to which activity has proved successful is by no means a measure of freedom. Even the most intensive and successful activity, if it is determined from the outside, is not free. Disciplined soldiers, obedient employees, well-paid policemen may be extraordinarily active and successful; nevertheless their activity is anything but free. An action is free only when a man determines his deed by himself.

8. However, not every activity which is determined 'from within' is free. Spontaneous activity in which a man's needs, inclinations, desires or passions directly determine his acts is very often not free. Only that self-determined activity in which a man acts as an integral many-sided personality, in which he is not a slave of one or another individual thought, feeling or aspiration, is truly free.

9. Those who are seemingly freest are really farthest from free activity. Tyrannical dictators, ruthless conquerors, insatiable exploiters are all slaves of their inhuman fixed ideas and ambitions. Their activity is the destruction of humaneness; a man is really free only when what is human in him determines

his actions, and when he, by his deeds, contributes to humanity.

10. The theory according to which knowledge of necessity is a precondition of free activity is, at best, incomplete. If everything were necessary, human activity would not be free either. The knowledge of necessity (if by this word we mean that which is outside human power) is only a recognition of the limits of freedom. A positive condition of freedom is the knowledge of the limits of necessity, the awareness of human creative possibilities.

11. The ingenious but contradictory definition of freedom as control over nature founded on the knowledge of natural necessity is an adequate expression of the basic orientation of modern man, who is interested in something only as a possible object of subjection and exploitation. However, freedom does not consist in the reckless exploitation of nature, but in the ability of man to humanize it and to participate in its blessings in a human way.

12. The concept of freedom as control over oneself presupposes the split of man into one part which controls and another part which is controlled. But domination is a negation of freedom. The idea of freedom as control over oneself serves frequently as a disguise for efforts to repress man's aspiration for freedom and to justify reconciliation with 'external' unfreedom.

13. The above two conceptions and their synthesis, the idea of freedom as the control of man over external nature and over himself, presuppose that man and nature are a sum of ready-made forces which one only has to harness, subject and use. However, the essence of freedom is not in the subjection of the given, but in the creation of something new, in the development of man's creative abilities, in the broadening and enriching of humanity.

14. The being of freedom (man) is never absolutely free (a completely unalienated man) or absolutely unfree (a completely inhuman being). Man is always, to a greater or lesser degree, free. Hence freedom is 'relative', but this relativity does not form the essence of freedom.

15. The aim of human freedom is a free person in a free society. This 'ideal' has not been thought up arbitrarily. There can be no free society without free persons, or any free person outside a social community. But this does not mean that in a free society all are free, or that in an unfree society all are unfree.

16. Even in a free society an individual may not be free.

Society can be so organized as to enable and encourage the development of free personalities, but freedom cannot be given as a gift to or forced upon anyone. An individual becomes a free human person only through his own free activity.

17. Even in an unfree society an individual can be more or less free. The external obstacles erected by an unfree society may make free human activity more difficult or limit it, but they cannot prevent it entirely. An unwavering revolutionary in chains is freer than the jailer who guards him, or the torturer who tries in vain to break him.

18. An unfree society strives to crush and destroy free personality; a free society enables and helps its blossoming. Hence the struggle for a free society is a component part of the struggle for the freeing of personality. When this part wants to become the whole of it, it becomes the reverse of what it ought to be. The struggle for a free society is not a struggle for a free society unless through it an ever greater degree of individual freedom is created.

19. The problem of freedom is 'eternal', but in every epoch it assumes a different form. In our time it has been shown, for example, that a free society is not created merely by the 'expropriation of the expropriators', or merely by the raising of living standards, or by a combination of the two. In a society from which exploiters have been eliminated, man's freedom is threatened by the means by which he communicates with nature and with other men (technology) and by the social forms in which that communication takes place (social organizations and institutions). The question of freedom faces us today primarily as a question of freedom with socialism, and as a question of freedom with technology.

The above theses can be divided into three groups: theses 1 to 4 are introductory – they try to explain and to locate the question concerning the essence of freedom; theses 5 to 14 are central – they attempt to answer the question raised; those in the third group (15 to 19) are perhaps the most important – they discuss an essential aspect of the question, an aspect with far-reaching consequences.

I begin with a few summary statements on man and praxis. The first two theses are very incomplete; I have said more about

the subject elsewhere.[1] That I start from man and praxis is to
show how the question of freedom inevitably emerges when one
wants to solve the question of man. In trying to elucidate the
sense of the question of freedom, I criticize the view that the
question can be answered by a classification of the forms of freedom, or by a description of the development of freedom. I also
reject the view that it can be solved by a linguistic study, or
simply by preaching. The question of freedom is first and above
all the question of the essence of freedom. So what is most important in theses 1 to 4 can be expressed briefly: the question of
freedom is an essential part of the question of man, and the question of the essence of freedom is the central part of the question
of freedom.

It is impossible to say what freedom is without saying what it
is not. Therefore, in discussing the question of the essence of
freedom (theses 5 to 14), I criticize some of the unacceptable
theories of freedom. First is the theory – advocated by Hobbes
in the seventeenth century and still held by a number of philosophers (including some 'Marxists') even in the twentieth century – according to which freedom is something outside the free
man, namely, the mere absence of external impediments to
motion. The second is the theory which regards freedom as
something 'external' which has become 'internal', as an external
'necessity' known and accepted, or somehow used, by the free
person. Found in ancient Greeks, Spinoza, Hegel, Engels, it is a
theory developed in several variants which, at first glance,
might seem quite different. Compare, for example: 'freedom is
the knowledge of necessity', 'freedom is adjustment to a known
necessity', 'freedom is power over nature and over oneself based
on the knowledge of the external and internal necessity'. The
third main theory which I briefly touch and criticize reduces
freedom to a pure internal self-determination, to a mere 'precondition' of free activity, a theory which has also been developed in many different variants (compare, for example, Kant

1. 'Pitanje o covjeku i Karl Marx', Našeteme (Zagreb), No. 4, 1961, pp.
536–76; 'El Concepto del hombre en Marx', Cuadernos Americanos (Mexico
D.F.), No. 4, 1962, pp. 112–32; 'Marx's Theory of Alienation', Philosophy and Phenomenological Research (Philadelphia), No. 3, 1963, pp.
419–26; 'Man as Economic Animal and Man as Praxis', Inquiry (Oslo),
Vol. 6, 1963, pp. 35–56.

and Sartre). In criticizing the above three theories, I try to state and explain different aspects of a theory the core of which is the view that freedom is something 'internal' becoming also 'external', namely the self-determining creative activity, the creative deed of enlarging and enriching humaneness. A possible misunderstanding concerning the 'absolute' and the 'relative' character of freedom is dispelled in thesis 14.

Although the question of the essence of freedom is the major question about freedom, it is not the only one which can be raised. To ask about the different forms or aspects of freedom is not only legitimate; it is indispensable. In theses 15 to 18 I restricted myself to only one part of the question about the forms of freedom: the relationship between the free person and the free society. What is perhaps most important in these theses is to understand the asymmetrical character of the relations between 'personal' and 'social' freedom: there can be no free society without free persons (which does not mean that *all* individuals in a free society are free persons), but there *can* be a free person without a free society (which does not mean that a person can be free outside any social community, or that the degree of the achieved social freedom is irrelevant to personal freedom). If one grasps the exact character of that fundamental asymmetry, which has important consequences both for personal responsibility and for social action, the rest of the theses on free person and free society become easy to understand.

The concluding thesis (19) touches the difficult aspect of freedom as an 'eternal' and 'historical' problem. It serves as a concluding remark here; it could serve as an introductory remark elsewhere (for example, in a text on freedom today).

There is no mention in the theses of the thinker who mainly inspired them. This is not in order to conceal the origin, but simply because it is not difficult to see that they were inspired by the man who wrote: '*Die Lebensgefahr für jedes Wesen besteht darin, sich selbst zu verlieren. Die Unfreiheit ist daher die eigentliche Todesgefahr für den Menschen.*'[1] ('The mortal danger for each person consists in the danger of losing himself. Hence, lack of freedom is the true mortal danger for man.')

1. Karl Marx: '*Debatten über die Pressefreiheit*', *Rheinische Zeitung*, No. 135 (15 May 1842). In Karl Marx and Friedrich Engels, *Werke* (Berlin, 1957), Vol. 1, p. 60.

I subscribe to most of Marx's theses on freedom such as they stand, or with certain corrections. As concerns the one just quoted, I am inclined to correct it slightly: Unfreedom is not merely the death-*danger* for man, it is man's *death*.

RUDI SUPEK

⊛ ⊛

Freedom and Polydeterminism in Cultural Criticism

RUDI SUPEK, professor of sociology at the Faculty of Philosophy, Zagreb, Yugoslavia, has written on such contemporary issues as *Existentialism and Decadence, The Psychology of Bourgeois Poetry, Public Opinion Research* and *Youth on the Road of Fraternity.* He was born in Zagreb in 1913 and received a doctor's degree in psychology in Paris in 1953.

Culture is very likely one of the most sensitive areas of social criticism. Nowhere else can the inadequacy or absurdity of theoretical presuppositions or methodological procedures be uncovered so rapidly, nowhere else can human creative activity overwhelm erroneous premises and conclusions with such promptitude and nowhere else can such harm be inflicted upon the creative potentialities of human beings as when a dogmatic theory is imposed on cultural policy by means of social compulsion. Hence, we are going to dwell for a moment on certain aspects of cultural criticism in contemporary Marxism, pointing out how the erroneous use of certain cognitional categories has led to wholly distorted theoretical conclusions. The creative nature of man, the mode of human participation in social life, the relationship between the collective *élan* and individual creative potentialities, the establishment of certain social limitations on creativity, and individual ability to overcome personal and social limitations in the service of one and the same ideal, are all most prominent in the field of culture. It is precisely in the realm of culture in our times that the contradiction between society and the individual, between the collective consciousness

257

and the individual consciousness, and between the concrete totality represented by society and the ideal totality represented by the individual, begins to sharpen in the most obvious way.

We have just encountered, in *the concept of totality*, the first category that is a source of certain ambiguities and one-sided interpretations in social criticism.

This category is interpreted in the social sciences generally, and in sociology in particular, in terms of the concept of society as such, either in the spirit of *ontological realism* or in the spirit of *ontological nominalism*. Society in the former sense is some sort of higher, organic and closed entity to which the individual is subordinated in every respect; society in the latter sense is no more than a chance accumulation, an aggregation of interests or the locale in which individual wills and interests are operative (or join together, or compete, or struggle). Both concepts have deeply permeated the thought, philosophy and sociology of bourgeois society. While classic liberalism (Smith, Hobbes, Bentham) held to nominalism, romantic philosophy interpreted society and the people in the light of ontological realism. The latter conception thus carried over from Hegel and Schelling to the theoreticians of the 'folk soul' (Lazarus and Steinthal) and organic positivism (Comte, Spencer, Durkheim) and thence to the most recent totalitarian doctrines of the fascist and Stalinist varieties.

However, on this occasion we will treat only certain theories in the realm of culture, and in particular the Marxist application of the category of totality to the interpretation of culture and cultural policy. In this field, we must face up to *three well-known conceptions in the spirit of ontological realism*, which involve the complete subordination of the creative individual to the social totality.

The first conception in this series falls within the range of *theory of reflection*. By analogy with the reflection of 'objective reality' in the subject, this theory assumes that the cultural superstructure is only a reflection of the material foundation of society, with the entire 'social reality' being considered as something more real and more primary in terms of value and with cultural creation being regarded as nothing but a more or less adapted reflection of reality proper. This theory falls back on the Platonist idealization of 'objective reality' and affirms the inferiority of culture and the art that can only reflect (not to say imitate) this reality. Art necessarily lags behind reality. The best compliment that art can possibly receive is that it has succeeded in conveying an impression of social reality 'as faithfully as possible' or 'as characteristically as possible'. Cultural creation, along with the whole realm of aesthetics, thus becomes in ontological terms just an epiphenomenon of material reality.

Within the bounds of historical dynamics, the material social foundation becomes something not only objective but also causative, the cultural superstructure being something subjective and consequential. Since the social and political correlative of the material foundation is in the ruling class, culture is always the spiritual expression of a single class. When the foundation changes, the superstructure also changes. When the foundation disappears, the superstructure likewise disappears. Culture thus retains the characteristic features of an epiphenomenon, even when the inverse effect of the superstructure on the foundation is mentioned out of respect for the dialectic. It is important in a methodological sense at this point to keep in mind that the foundation and the superstructure are the *correlatives of the same historical entity*. The cultural superstructure in this view, thus remains closed within the bounds of a given foundation and incapable of transcending this foundation in any way, i.e. incapable of shifting to another historical epoch in terms of value.

Such a grasp of the whole, or totality, of a given historical situation leads to certain consequences in the theory of culture. First, the search is on for the class correlatives or 'social equivalents' of particular cultural themes and artistic styles. Second, attempts are made to explain changes in cultural creation *exclusively* in the light of changes in the social foundation.

The theory of the *progressive and decadent development of society* as a historical entity is our second example of the erroneous application of the category of totality. This theory is really just a sub-variety of the first, which introduces the ideas of the progressive and decadent development of particular phases into the relationship between the foundation and the superstructure. By applying the foundation-superstructure scheme one-sidedly to the realm of culture, this theory projects the political and social decadency of a society on to cultural creativity. To be sure, this theory soon encounters certain small difficulties. It cannot explain why the most valuable cultural achievements have so often been produced in such decadent epochs as the Athenian era after Pericles, the Roman era after Caesar and the Middle Ages after Dante, not to mention the decadence that is supposed to have set in with the appearance of impressionism in bourgeois society.

This theory has also created another difficulty by introducing a purely gnosiological criterion alongside the historical criterion of progress and decadence. Under the theory of reflection, the progressive is that which is more objective or realistic and the decadent that which provides a more subjective reflection, i.e. a reflection which is subjectivistic or expressionistic. The gnosiological criterion being lasting and unalterable, realism must necessarily be progressive and impressionism or expressionism decadent or even reactionary, the latter art forms being expressions of a subjectivistic attitude towards reality. From Lukács to Timofeev, the theoreticians of socialist realism have confused historical dynamics with the postulates of cognitional theory that are otherwise applicable only to scientific cognition. It is a genuine riddle to them why the revolutionary bourgeoisie expressed itself at one time in a pronouncedly subjectivistic art and the revolutionary proletariat during the time of the October Revolution likewise made use of a subjectivistic art in the expressionism of Mayakovsky, Piscator, Meyerhold and so many others. The 'cultural superstructure' obviously fails completely to respect certain of the fundamental principles of the theory of reflection. How else are we to explain the fact that the bourgeoisie expressed itself in a romantic and subjectivistic manner during its progressive phase, with realism making an appearance only by the time of the first serious social crisis after 1818 as a symptom of crisis and thereby of the beginning of decline?

If we assume that decadence set in immediately after the era of realism in painting and literature, i.e. with the appearance of impressionism and naturalism, then the only conclusion to be drawn is that every further cultural creation so long as this decadence lasts (a whole century thus far!) will amount to one step further into decadency. Expressionism will be more decadent than impressionism, surrealism more decadent than expressionism, and non-objective or abstract art the extreme mode of decadence. The longer the decadence lasts, the more profound will be the decline in values, and the greater the dehumanization. For these reasons, the more recent cultural achievements of bourgeois society will always be less acceptable than the older achievements, which are then transformed into 'the classics'. In this way, so far as the cultural inheritance is concerned, the theory leads to traditionalism and to the sole acceptance of old and outmoded cultural values. Such an orientation in relation to the cultural inheritance in a socialist society must necessarily 'go always against the stream and against the era' and make fresh forces old before their time.

We have already pointed out that this theory leads to a variety of difficulties in the interpretation of cultural dynamics and often to absurd conclusions. And the adherents to this theory themselves frequently contradict each other. Lukács thus considers that bourgeois art was progressive only during its earliest phase, e.g. in the Flemish landscapes, and then fell into decadence with the onset of romanticism (even though the latter amounted to a 'French revolution in poetic form'!). On the other hand, the idea is much more common (shared alike by Plekhanov, Hausenstein and Hamann) that decadence set in with the appearance of impressionism, through which 'the petty bourgeoisie attained its culminating position'. Plekhanov nevertheless noted the joyous aspect of this art and considered it to belong to the society of the future by virtue of its hedonist unconcern. On this basis, the Soviet theoretician Matsa has been impelled to doubt that impressionism is decadent art and to ascribe the beginning of decadence to expressionism, which 'deforms the external world'. As we have already seen, the question then arises as to how the October Revolution could have been echoed in expressionism. The answer is simple. The shout, the cry, the slogan and the directive are always going to be compact in the expressionistic mode like action itself, for narration is unfeasible in the course of the action. Yet such an uncomplicated psychological explanation is not accepted by the adherents to socialist realism. To be sure, there have been some recent attempts to consider non-objective art alone as genuinely decadent art. This opinion has been expressed by the Soviet critic Lifshits on only one occasion but seems to be acquiring a multitude of adherents, although it has not yet become 'official'.

The *theory of reification* is our third example of the erroneous application of the category of totality in the field of culture. Much more subtle than the others, this theory has attracted large numbers of contemporary Marxists, for it undeniably contains a fragment of the truth. The weak side of this theory is its historical relativism, conditional upon the enclosure of the cultural–historical situation within the bounds of a specific totality.

Like the other theories, the theory of reification lays stress on the foundation, i.e. on the economic relationships or modes of production in capitalist society. We know that the idea of reification means to Lukács what Marx termed 'the fetishism of commodities' – the idea that the value of a particular commodity is to be regarded as its objective characteristic, devoid of any specific social relation created by value itself. Reification occurs in such a way that concrete individual labour is transformed into an abstract amount of labour, the amount that can be considered socially necessary. The latter is no more than an abstraction from the former, and amounts to the reduction of an original qualitative unity to a quantitative continuum determined by value or price. The process of reification thus consists essentially of the transformation of qualitative relations into quantitative magnitudes. The roots of reification naturally lie in a whole conglomeration of secondary phenomena that are inseparable from a system of hired labour, e.g. the reduction of the working men to a bare work force, the separation of the producers from their products and from the means of production, the determination of the value or prices of goods through the haphazard effect of the capitalist market relations that amount to a force outside man and raised above man's will, and in sum the entire goods-and-money and technical–utilitarian superstructure of the capitalist economy (particularly in its liberalistic and pre-statist form).

The process of reification amounts to the foundation of bourgeois society in so far as the creation of market values is concerned, and must inevitably be generalized or reflected in the superstructure of this society, in science, philosophy, law, morals and art. Just as the capitalist mode of production has a tendency to expand and gradually to overwhelm all areas of social production, so also does consciousness as the reflection of this process come gradually to imbue all such fields. Since Marx, Max Weber and George Lukács, and recently Erich Fromm and Lucien Goldmann, have been particularly insistent on the fact that goods-and-money production is not only the configuration of the economy in a bourgeois society but also the 'soul' of such a society. Usefulness, profit, money, quantification, rationalism and instrumentalism have thus saturated all realms of social life and thought. Rationalism along with science in this same circle has become the enemy of humanism, instrumentalism along with technology the chief source of human alienation. Likewise, mass production entails mass consumption and is the main source of the other-than-human or 'artificial' needs that are generated by means of advertising and with the lure of false social prestige, as Erich Fromm has pointed out. Rather than assuming reification to be the sole or fundamental process operative in bourgeois society, to be sure, Fromm adds the dimension of the human personality.

In fact, the application of the category of totality in the social criticism of bourgeois society under the theory of reification does not go beyond the dependence of the superstructure upon the foundation, i.e. the dependence of the social totality upon a *universal process* termed reification, so far as the essential determinism of social phenomena is concerned. The starting point is a historically closed system, viz. bourgeois society, the analysis of which comes down to a kind of phenomenological reductionism of delusive phenomena to a fundamental and essential process of change. No determinism capable of transcending this particular historical situation has been taken into consideration, either as a preceding series or as a future series.

In what manner ought these theories to be subjected to correction?

First, it is necessary to transcend social, economic, class, cultural and historical totalitarianism, and thus relativism in two senses, viz. in individual or personal terms, and in terms of world history. In the first instance, the category of social totality deserves to be interpreted in relation to 'total social facts' (Marx, Mauss, Gurvitch). Let us recall no more than the following definition from Marx:

263

Hence, however much a human being should be a *separate* individuum, and it is precisely his separateness which makes him an individuum and an actual *individual* being in the community, he is likewise a totality, the ideal totality, the subjective existence of an imagined and experienced society in itself, just as he exists in actuality at the same time as the perception and genuine spirit of social existence and as the totality of the human manifestation of life. (Karl Marx, *Der historische Materialismus* [Leipzig: A. Kroener Verlag], Vol. I, p. 298.)

Obviously, Marx has kept in mind the fact that both society and the personality are 'total social facts'; i.e. the whole social reality can be encompassed if we proceed from the one to the other and vice versa. This reciprocity of perspective is based in any event on a dialectical relationship that imparts full independence to the personality in the sense of an ability to identify with any other personality in the society (any reduction of the art of a given artist to his class origins being thus illusory), and an ability to identify with the entire society as a whole (to transcend in consciousness narrower class or group interests), and an ability to transcend the present-day state of society – to anticipate the future as the 'totality of the human manifestation of life', not only in the name of the negation of that which is in existence, but also in the name of the *entire historical experience of mankind*. Positivistic organicism is not only incapable of comprehending the role of the personality in cultural creativity, but also finds *geniuses* to be an enigma. No less a figure than Lukács himself naïvely explains the survival of works of genius solely in terms of selection on the part of the ruling class from whatever in the past should serve the immediate interests of this class! In point of fact, great cultural works live on despite all barriers of history and class for the sole reason that such works have been created by personalities distinguished for greatness or genius, i.e. such individualized social totalities as have encompassed a maximum of 'human totality' in a personal creative act. The limitations of class and history that affect every creative personality – even those of the greatest genius – cannot affect the cultural and human values of a great work. Such a work reflects the constant endeavour of the individuum as the 'ideal totality of society' to penetrate and express the essential aspects of human existence in terms of duration in space and time. The result is always limited but on a universal human scale, for man as creator is always outgrowing himself through his work, and not only himself but also the concrete mankind that he represents.

In other words, the individual represents a specific determinant of cultural creation precisely because as an individual he deserves to be a part of the analyses of the culture of a society. For example, in terms of the universal process of reification, it is wholly incomprehensible why romanticism should have ignored the process of reification while the realism that followed with Balzac did not ignore these processes. Was it only because romanticism was 'more reactionary' or less progressive than realism, or was it because the romantics as human beings were less progressive than the realists (e.g. Victor Hugo as opposed to Balzac)?

The answer to the question indicates that to ask it is wrong. Romanticism had no need to reflect reification, for its aim was to express what was vital after the bourgeois revolution, viz. a new conception and a new expansion of the human personality, Promethean and autonomous. This personal and sentimental expansion of a grand sensitivity proved very soon to be illusory when confronted with social reality, but lost nothing thereby of its universal human and cultural value. Let us remember that Romain Rolland went to combat in behalf of socialism via Beethoven. Marx conducted himself in the same way with Phidias or Shakespeare, even though the social organization inhabited by these geniuses could scarcely have been pleasing to him.

In other words, we are obliged to keep track of the fate of human creation equally in the dimension of the class struggle and in the dimension of the human personality, at the level of human sociality and at the level of the artistic liberation of the personality.

Second, cultural phenomena transcend the foundation-superstructure scheme and historical relativism in the sphere of *world history*, by which we understand a continuous curve with all its internal contradictions throughout the historical epochs up to the present. Such a curve is assumed to be wholly natural where advances in science or technology are concerned. It is considered entirely understandable and even inevitable in these fields of endeavour for new discoveries to be linked together with the older ones and for such new discoveries to multiply increasingly, with the general curve of discoveries or cognition appearing in an exponential form, i.e. as a curve with positive acceleration. Positivistic organicism, historical relativism, and the theory of the rise and fall of cultures as worlds of their own are nevertheless incapable of encompassing such a kind of progressive alteration with constant upsurge within the bounds of their mode of thinking.

We know that aestheticians are opposed to the idea of progress in art, but we also know that they have in mind in this connexion solely the perfection of certain forms or the perfection of the aesthetic experience itself. In this sense, we truly cannot say that aesthetic expression actually advanced in terms of 'the beautiful' and 'the perfect' from the neolithic caves to the classical Greeks and from the classical Greeks to contemporary modernism. On the other hand, even if we have not advanced aesthetically, we have not necessarily failed to improve steadily in terms of the *creative act proper*, in the discovery of creative potentialities, in the analysis of expressional devices, in the discovery of the various laws under which dead matter is configurated. We would not find it difficult to show that man has advanced as steadily in art as he has in technology, which some so mystically counterpose to art, forgetting that art is inseparable from craftsmanship. Like the dance, primitive art is frequently incapable of aesthetic error, but is nevertheless wholly enslaved like primitive realism by a subject that has not yet become the object of critical reflection and is entirely bound up with a syncretic world of magic and mythology. Only with the Greeks did beauty begin to be discovered as a separate object of experience and thereby as a separate theme of human creativity. Only then were the laws of proportion, symmetry and rhythm discovered. Did not the Renaissance discover the laws of perspective for the first time, just as the Baroque period was to discover light and shadow as the medium of the spiritual existence of an object devoid of sheer mass? And what of today's discovery that 'what is deserving of being depicted is not the object but rather the impression which the object makes upon us' in the form of impressionism, cubism and abstract art? More careful analysis would show us that *we are constantly witnessing genuine discoveries* in relation to human modes of expression and to the way in which objects are represented throughout the entire evolution of European art, and that such discoveries have increasingly multiplied in modern times (we need only remind ourselves of contemporary 'applied art'), to the extent that the kind of exponential curve found by the sociologists in the field of science and technology could easily be constructed in the artistic realm as well.

There can be no doubt that the cyclic phenomena of cultural upsurge and stagnation, of progressive *élan* and decadency, amount to no more than a separate rhythm within a more general and more universal process of change. For this reason, we obviously will not have exhausted the meaning of a particular phenomenon by simply placing it within the framework of a process of progress and decadence. We must instead interpret such a phenomenon *within the framework of the general process of historical change,* i.e. in terms of world history. For example, a phase of decadence in bourgeois art set in with symbolism and impressionism in the light of the earlier ideo-affective expansion of humaneness, yet the same phase no less surely marks the beginning of one of the most fruitful periods of cultural and artistic creativity in terms of *the discovery of new potentialities* and in terms of the constant enrichment of human sensitivity and imagination. And the development of human potentialities, the development of all the most diverse and many-sided of human capabilities, should be considered the fundamental law of historical evolution (cf. Marx).

Third, the historical relativism of the theories of culture under discussion is incapable of explaining an extremely significant phenomenon in the process of cultural change, viz. *the many-sided complexity of historical determinism.* Specifically, *certain* cyclic processes of change are totally *exhausted* in the course of a single historical epoch, while *certain other* cyclic processes of change can be said to *transcend* a given epoch. In other words, there are cyclic processes of change *within* a given historical epoch (*endogenous* cyclic processes of change) and cyclic processes of change *above* a given historical epoch (*exogenous* or *transcyclic* processes of change). For example, the process of change in terms of world history can be conceived as a constant uncovering and deepening of human expressional potentialities.

267

To illustrate this phenomenon, however, we must take up an example which is close to us and can be easily understood.

In our *Psychology of the Bourgeois Lyric* (*Psihologija gradjanske lirike*, Zagreb, published by Matica Hrvatska, 1952), we described a cyclic process of change that began with romanticism and ended with surrealism. The ideo-affective attitudes that led in romanticism to an expansion of sympathy towards humanity and the cosmos led in symbolism to stagnation and in surrealism to radical negation. A dead end had eventually been reached, justifying those writers who reflected deeply on this process of change and who arrived at the conclusion that the surrealists must be 'the last romantics'! The attempt to depict *lettrisme* as an imitation of abstract art is a kind of intellectual weakness, for such an attempt mistakenly identifies technology with humaneness, whether affirmed or negated. To be sure, a new cycle of cultural change set in with the appearance of impressionism. Impressionism comprised a certain amount of 'technological interest', both in terms of thematic material (locomotives, the St-Lazare railway station, the Eiffel Tower) and in terms of procedures (spectrum analysis, complementary colours, the granular fusion of colours, etc.), and we find something kindred in the poetry of René Ghil and Paul Valéry. A certain constructivism and instrumentalism had evolved. Since impressionism, this tendency has dominated modern art in all varieties of expression up to and including contemporary abstract or concrete art, electronic music and *lettrisme* in poetry. This 'technological interest', subordinated to a greater extent in the beginning to certain humanistic preoccupations, has grown increasingly independent in the course of time, and recently even dominates some areas of endeavour. However, with reliance on concrete space in the field of architecture and in the manufacture of useful objects, this 'technological interest' is going to acquire a real foundation and is going to free itself of its romanticist and metaphysical proclivities.

Abstract art, although closest in time to surrealism, is immeasurably remote from it psychologically and is incomparably far away from romanticism and in particular from the 'night', 'hallucinatory' and 'grotesque' varieties of romanticism. This circumstance only serves to confirm the fact that the cycle is discontinuous and closed if we have the development of the romanticist component in mind, yet continuous and open if we have the 'technological component' in mind. Is it not clear by now that a cycle in art is already ending in bourgeois society? This society is necessarily continuing with its technological and cultural potentialities, while the 'technological cycle' in art that derives its inspiration from science and technology will necessarily be continuing apart from all limitations imposed by the class make-up of society, for which reason the resistance of socialist realism in some countries to abstract art is as purposeless as it is futile and is bound to end in the same way as have kindred attitudes towards modern architecture, urban planning and cybernetics.

We can draw the conclusion from this example that courses of development and values with a multitude of meanings and senses come to light within the bounds of a given historical epoch, like all organic creations. While one conception or stylistic form is dying out, another is already being born and is present to be able to continue along the path of its own and uniquely different fate.

Fourth, these theories are not capable of explaining the role of the *unconscious* in artistic creation, especially in instances of *stylistic change* where the influence of a kind of *collective unconscious* is of particular significance. Psycho-analysis has succeeded in explaining the influence of the unconscious only in relation to the content or theme of an artistic work, not in relation to stylistic changes. What is involved at this point is the fact that the unconscious in creation is not only a complex function of the intermediacy of experience in terms of the symbolization, projection or dramatization of specific materials, but also a direct influence upon the very *functional structure* of the experience.

If we desire to defend the thesis that the evolution of artistic sensitivity from romanticism to surrealism comprises a closed cycle that has been exhausted and resolved on the basis of its own premises, then we must take the *internal dynamics* of this evolution into account. These internal dynamics presuppose not only a change in specific experiential materials but also certain functional changes in the creative imagination, in which the unconscious plays a vital role as an intermediary. For example, we have already pointed out that romanticism represents a certain expansion in sympathy in human and cosmic terms, yet we also know that symbolism and impressionism mark a diminution of this affective expansion due to a general or collective state of mind which can be described as resignation. The question thus arises as to what the significance and consequences of this diminution in the affective expansion may be.

So far as functional changes are concerned, we are in a position to observe the course of two simultaneous processes in symbolism. The first is the *diminution of the humanistic expansion* along with the transferral of this expansiveness to the realm of the beautiful, the disinterested and the formalized. This is why the symbolists call themselves 'cultivators of form', 'stylists' or 'the dispassionate ones'. The second such process involves the *sensory or sensual component* of the creative imagination, which becomes stronger or *more independent*. The ideo-affective expansion that had taken place during the romantic era in the realm of humanism withdrew in symbolism and impressionism to the level of sensual relations with nature and things. Friedrich Hebbel was right in remarking that this sensual expansion was based on a kind of 'passive love' and on an ironic or Manichaean stance towards reality, described so dramatically and so accurately by Baudelaire and Nietzsche. The shift of the humanistic expansion to the realm of sensuality occurred unconsciously, being much more the product of the general spirit of the epoch than of any rational reflection on the part of an artistic creator. And yet this change is the key to an understanding of essential changes in artistic expression, for this diminution in the humanistic expansion gave rise to a whole series of other characteristic changes in sensitivity, e.g. a feeling of intimacy and presence, ambivalence of feeling, sensory plasticity, a tendency towards synesthesia, hyperintellectualism in the creative process, and a return to the past in its naïve and childlike aspects. This metamorphosis in sensitivity has resulted in corresponding changes in artistic style in such a way that an interdependence can be said to exist between structural changes in sensibility and artistic expression. We could also show a similar metamorphosis to have taken place in the transition from symbolism to surrealism.

Fifth, if it is correct to say that some cyclic processes transcend a given historical epoch, socio-economic arrangement or class society, while others do not, then an important methodological principle follows, viz. *some contradictions within the bounds of a given social system are resolved in the course of time, but other contradictions arise to take their places.* Some contradictions become simple differences under the law of the progressive differentiation of society and culture, while other differences become new contradictions. In other words, it is a mistake to make use of such simple contradictions as those between materialism and idealism, subjectivism and objectivism, progressivism and reaction, and the like, in the interpretation of culture. We must instead follow the development of every established contradiction to see whether it is being resolved in the course of time within the bounds of a given social system or not. Marx had already noted in connexion with economic development that some contradictions are resolved within the bounds of capitalism. We ought therefore to anticipate that such would be an even commoner occurrence in the realm of culture, which is more autonomous and is distinguished by a higher coefficient of individual factors. We are thus faced with a peculiar dialectic that transforms contradictions into contrarieties and contrarieties into contradictions. Let us attempt to illustrate with an example:

An extremely ferocious campaign is being waged in some socialist countries today against abstract art as the last, 'most radical' and most distorted expression of bourgeois decadency in art. This campaign takes into account only certain of the spiritualistic speculations of the early Kandinsky, Malevich and Mondrian. No consideration is given in this campaign to the actual context and function of the art that is involved, particularly in connexion with the appearance of the Weimar Bauhaus and with the analysis of the modern conception of space and pictorial matter. Nor do these criticisms take note of the fact that abstract art protests against misuse in the name of its *concreteness.* The real reason for this failure of understanding is that this campaign and these criticisms are unaware of the fact that a contradictory cultural situation, in the form of an attempt to flee the concrete world, has *undergone a transformation* contrary to its own original intentions by becoming involved in the concrete world and in the ecological (urban-planning) problems of this concrete world. Abstract art has thus ceased to be a negation of any world, bourgeois, socialist, or whatever. On the basis of contemporary spatial and pictorial concepts, abstract art has become a part of the most real world possible; that is, it has become wholly neutral so far as differences of class are concerned. In this way, abstract art may equally be the concern of Catholics and Protestants, socialists and communists. Against the wishes of its initiators, abstract art has become only 'one among others'. The most intelligent theoreticians of abstract art would not defend its exclusiveness in the name of 'progress', going no further than to mention abstract art as one possibility among many.

Sixth, modern cultural criticism in general has not yet acquired the habit of examining the significance or sense of cultural goods from the standpoint of the actual function of these goods in relation to man. Abstract–aesthetic, ideological–utilitarian, or economic–commercial criteria are commonly taken into consideration. These criteria, which have a somewhat longer tradition in our civilization, are easier to define. The problem of actual human needs and of determining the values of cultural goods in relation to human needs remains open, although contemporary social and psychological anthropology is beginning to touch on it on an increasing scale, primarily in the form of criticism of contemporary industrial and capitalist civilization in its extreme commercial and metropolitan forms.

Our objections to these theories up to this point suggest that the determinism of cultural phenomena is far more complex than it appears at first glance. In a very general way, it may be said that the existence of differences in historical rhythms points the way to the existence of *three fundamental systems* in the determinism of cultural phenomena: society in its structuralism; the personality as a separately individualized and universal system of functions and needs; and finally, the cultural areas proper with their own unique laws of development (science, philosophy, technology, language, art, etc.). There is no dispute today among researchers into culture about the existence of these three specific factors in cultural development. The argument begins when we attempt a closer examination of the significance and interrelations of particular systems. Our research is only now getting under way, but it is already clear that the existence and operation of these three systems will demand a *polydeterministic interpretation* of cultural evolution.

Seventh, if it is correct that various cycles and rhythms of historical development exist and that these three systems require a polydeterministic interpretation, then we are faced with the problem of defining the *methods* of cultural research and cultural criticism more accurately. Although space does not permit us to go into this problem, let us at least point out that every one-sided and simplified treatment of cultural phenomena must be excluded. The problem likewise excludes any vulgar–materialistic limitation to the foundation–superstructure scheme, any enclosure on the part of the positivistic organicism within an exclusive course of progress and decadency and any phenomenological reductionism to a universal basic process such as reification.

In what way ought we to approach the analysis of cultural phenomena? Above all, no doubt, a phenomenological survey of the totality of the phenomena in a given cultural–historical situation is in order. The phenomenological application of the category of totality for purposes of distinguishing the essential from the inessential, the profound from the superficial, and the fundamental from the secondary should naturally be the *first step* in such research. Yet a panoramic review of this kind will cease to be adequate the moment we ask ourselves the meaning of a given phenomenon in terms of duration in time. The problem will then have arisen of the complexity of the determinism of the given phenomenon – more profound study will undoubtedly discover, behind the statics of phenomenology, an increasing number of *generic* forms, which can be grasped only by means of *functional–structural analysis*. Just as the structure of the cultural and social situation has changed in the course of time, so also has the function of particular phenomena changed, and along with it the significance of such phenomena in the life of society and of individuals. The direction in which the functions, sense and values of particular phenomena are changing can be determined only by *historical–comparative* study of the development of society and culture. In other words, these are three different methodological standpoints which necessarily complement rather than exclude each other. However, the mastery of these methodological viewpoints entails a thorough acquaintance with actual social and cultural happenings. Petty criticism and methodological one-sidedness are commonly the offshoots of insufficient knowledge concerning various fields of culture, concerning the dependence of such fields of culture upon concrete social situations and concerning the place of such fields of culture in the general currents of historical change. The superficiality which we encounter so often in this area in everyday criticism, as well as in more serious discussions, results partly from inadequate study of the cultural materials, but no less from a lack of the dialectical spirit that is based equally on comprehensive intuition and the logical elaboration of methodological procedures.

Translated by William Hannaher

IV. ON ALIENATION

PREDRAG VRANICKI

⊚ ⊚

Socialism and the Problem of Alienation

PREDRAG VRANICKI, professor of philosophy at the
University of Zagreb, fought with the Army of National
Liberation against the fascist forces that occupied Yugoslavia during the Second World War. Born in 1922, he
received his diploma in philosophy from the University of
Zagreb in 1947. He has expressed his interest in the
problems of humanism, history and freedom; philosophy
and revolution; and socialism and culture in his books
*Karl Marx: Development of His Thought, Dialectical and
Historical Materialism, Philosophical Studies and Criticism*
and *History of Marxism*.

I

The phenomenon of alienation is very complex and has not
been sufficiently studied. Philosophical and sociological analysis
must still face up to a number of problems, viz. what the concept
of alienation encompasses, what the dynamics of alienation have
been in the course of history, the functions of identical forms of
alienation in different eras, whether alienation is overcome by a
continuous and unilateral process, etc. Leaving aside all of these
issues for the moment, I feel compelled to stress one factor that
I consider essential to the concept of alienation: While all of
human history and all historical creations (the state, culture, religion, etc.) are man's work and the expression of man's own
potentialities and powers, man has been capable of existing only
by separating these powers from himself, and by finding these
same powers counterposed to himself as specific material, social
or ideological forces.

So long as man's own work continues to exist as something
external to him (the political sphere, religion, the market, money,
etc.) and to oppose itself to him in the form of a superior
authority, we will encounter the phenomenon of alienation.

Man's world up to now has always been a world divided against itself – a world in which man, the creator of history, has been largely powerless, disfranchised and debased in historical terms. History is a constant tyranny over man to this day.

However, every form of alienation is distinguished by a specific historical content and function, for which reason different forms of alienation cannot all be evaluated in the same way. Furthermore, every form of alienation identified thus far has been superseded by some other form of alienation. A particular 'alienational situation' becomes intolerable only when new opportunities arise for the development of human forces and relationships. Regardless of the fact that human progress has always taken place within the confines of various forms of alienation, some forms of alienation have been more permissive than others towards the development of man as a 'polyvalent' being and the further generation of the richness of the human being, and have abolished the various social restrictions interfering with man's freer historical movement.

Hence, certain forms of alienation have been of historically progressive significance under certain historical circumstances. When new historical prospects open up in the course of this development for the liberation of man from some forms of alienation, the old forms of alienation become intolerable. Some of these forms will disappear in the course of this process (e.g. slavery and various forms of ideological alienation).

The historical process thus far has consisted just as much of a process of the creation of various forms of alienation as of a process of *de-alienation*. This process is in evidence, among other ways, in the increasing emphasis given to man himself and in the increasing preponderance ascribed to human rather than 'trans-human' political forces. The processes of de-alienation will be all the more powerful when this orientation of man towards 'man proper', and man's creativeness, become primary and essential factors, and when people so associated come to regulate their relationships with each other and with nature in this way.

Alienated historical situations have not only presupposed man's division against himself but have also been essentially characterized by the isolation of man from man by virtue of racial, national, class or other hostilities. These antagonisms have dragged contemporary man to the brink of disaster. Only the terrifying prospect of self-destruction has begun to have some effect in the sense of overcoming all the narrow-minded and anachronistic consequences of the contemporary alienated world.

The essential import of socialism derives from just such a historical legacy as this and from the specific historical structure known as bourgeois society. This is not the place to analyse all the grand accomplishments of bourgeois society, the achievements that are so significant an accretion to human creativity. Likewise, there is no room here to analyse all the limitations of bourgeois society. Such analysis has been performed often enough, sometimes well and sometimes not so well, from the time of Marx to our own day. To understand the foundations and historical traditions from which contemporary socialism springs, however, we must take note of at least those characteristics by which bourgeois society no longer corresponds to contemporary human requirements and potentialities.

Bourgeois society has carried the development of man to unheard-of heights, but only by transforming man within the framework of the wage–labour relationship into a component part of an omnipotent piece of machinery. The classic society of commodity production has converted everything into a commodity, into a thing. The worker in such a society sells his ability to work just as everybody else sells whatever is at his disposal – a commodity, his mind, his ideas, a trade, his body or his talent. Relationships have clearly been deprived of the fundamental characteristics of humanity if the entire society amounts to a relationship of buying and selling, if man has become a statistical cipher and if man is regarded as though he were part of a mechanism. A man who in ordinary life has become no more than a commodity producing other commodities and part of a value-producing mechanism can with equal ease become part of a mechanism which sees an enemy in another man or nation.

This alienation of contemporary man's everyday life is the foundation and source for all the other forms of his alienated condition. Just as the owners of commodities and the entire technocratic mechanism counterpose themselves to him as forces controlling his work and very existence, so also do the commodities which he produces counterpose themselves to him as either a power or a challenge. The *fetishism of commodities* has long

279

been a familiar phenomenon, along with a number of its consequences. Even if the most recent contemporary processes of bourgeois society succeed, through scientific and statistical organizational arrangements, in modifying the extreme consequences of the market mechanism, the commodity is acquiring increasingly magical power. Man comes to believe that the possession of certain commodities alters his qualities as a man and that wealth in commodities can be identified with enrichment as a human being. Man becomes wholly oriented in the direction of this externality, and thus impoverishes himself.

The 'thingification' of man, as one of the essential forms of man's alienation in bourgeois society, also dehumanizes a number of his other relationships. If the politico-technocratic mechanism relates to man as to a thing, man's active role will then be confined to the pursuit of well-being or political voting, and man will eventually relate to another man as towards a thing. The extreme and drastic forms of inhumanity that have come to light in the past thirty years are no more than the consequences of a more fundamental constellation.

The 'polyvalence' of the human being in the midst of this extremely 'thingified' and compartmentalized relationship becomes so distorted that the very process of work itself proves unbearable. All the efforts on the part of psychologists and sociologists to solve this impersonal situation for modern man, whatever improvements may have taken place, have ended in failure. Any such efforts are nothing more than serviceable palliatives, for the problem is not primarily psychological or technological, but rather a matter of the philosophy of history.

Man may be more or less aware of his alienated condition, but the end result is the division of his personality against itself and the formation of the *homo duplex*. As a man, he does not feel himself to be part of the broader community. As an official being, he does not feel himself to be a man. And this characteristic feature of the alienated man, so long familiar, has consequences of the most tragic kind in the field of human relationships.

2

If the contemporary society of private ownership and wage-labour relationships can be characterized in terms of the aforementioned factors – and the history of the last few centuries has confirmed this to be the case on innumerable occasions (e.g. wars, economic crises, concentration camps, gas chambers, etc.) – then the struggle to overcome such a state of affairs as this is surely the struggle for socialism as well.

At one time, at least in general terms, the problem of socialism was phrased more simply and appeared less complicated. Today, after many experiences, not devoid of tragedy, the problem of socialism must be considered primarily within these philoso-phico-sociological horizons. The revolution and revolutionary authority have often been regarded as sufficient guarantees that man would be liberated not only from the hired-labour relation-ship but also from all other forms of alienation. The problem of alienation thus becomes 'superfluous'. For example, the concept of alienation did not crop up at all in theoretical discussions dur-ing the decades of Stalinism. Even today, many theoreticians of socialism consider alienation to be incompatible with socialism, as though socialism were immune by nature to this disease.

Historical experiences offer an entirely different picture, for they have served to shatter numerous illusions and myths, especially those of the Stalinist era.

Stalinism failed to grasp that the time to put the revolution into effect is after the revolution has taken place, in so far as it exists at all. Only then can such social forms of relationships as will lead to the constant liberation of man and to the creation of a new historical personality be created on a permanent basis. In a word, the fundamental principles of philosophical and humanistic thought must be implanted in the deepest possible way. To be sure, socialism, to reach this goal, must continue on the basis of a number of alienated forms that cannot be imme-diately abolished or leaped over (state, classes, party, nations, bureaucracy, religion, commodity production, the market, etc.). Such is the case despite the fact that these forms in genuine socialist development must acquire other symbols and meanings and play a new role, as we shall see.

By virtue of their very existence, however, certain aspects of these alienated forms can (but need not) manifest themselves in the most negative fashion. So long as man under whatever system (socialism included) generates, senses and experiences his powers as a set of factors apart from himself, the possibility will exist for such factors to act towards him as a superior authority and to obstruct historical creations that deserve to be measured against the level of contemporary human development.

Therefore, contrary to the thesis of the superfluity of the problem of alienation under socialism, we must advance the thesis in the most decisive manner possible that the problem of alienation is the central problem of socialism.

This problem could not have been the central problem of bourgeois society for the simple reason that the basic historical task of bourgeois society was never, nor is it now, to liberate man from all the forms of his alienation. Bourgeois society accomplished its historical task by superseding feudal forms of dependence and subordination and by evolving certain limited forms of democratization in the realm of economic democracy. To the extent to which there is a tendency within bourgeois society to overcome certain of the negative consequences of bourgeois private ownership, the classic bourgeois order is going to give way to statist tendencies; yet bourgeois society did not and could not have the historical duty of abolishing economic and political, and hence ideological, *authority*. The basic task of bourgeois society was to make this authority function and not to abolish it, to solidify the position of the ruling class and not to eliminate it, and to separate authority from the people and not to transform the people into an 'authority'. Bourgeois society is a political society *par excellence* in the sense that 'political' is a synonym for the authority of a particular group of people over another.

Hence socialism cannot be based on those categories which are essential to bourgeois society. Since the task of socialism is to overcome those forms of human existence which create the alienated man, the dissolution of the alienated forms of man's social life becomes the central problem of socialism.

If the problem of socialism is not comprehended in these terms, the end result may be the evolution of political forms into paroxysms of dehumanization.

Stalinism is a typical instance of failure to consider the essential problems of socialism. Historically, Stalinism meant that the various forms of human alienation inherited directly from the former class societies were relied upon and strengthened. Instead of putting its trust in man – the historical creator of social life itself – Stalinism offered the major role in the formation and development of the community to the state and to various 'transmission belts'.

Having lost sight, on the intellectual horizon, of the true import of the socialist transformation, i.e. the gradual effort to abolish the system of political society and hence the forms of economic and political alienation, Stalinism based the evolution of this political society on extremes of power. The omnipotence of the political apparatus of the state was necessarily accompanied by the universal powerlessness of the individual, the human being, the personality – precisely the objects of the import of this radical historical endeavour.

Man as producer finds himself again in the alienated position of hired labour if he has been wholly deprived of participation in the management of production and in the distribution of the resultant product under such a system, which consists not only of total state planning but also of the disposal of surplus value by the state. The only difference in this instance is that capitalist monopoly has been supplanted by the universal monopoly of the state. The Marxist idea of planned production as opposed to the haphazardness of the capitalist market has been transformed into its own contradiction. Man as producer, not having become himself the planner, has become part of a plan, i.e. 'planned out'. We need not waste many words about the fact that numerous other characteristics of alienated labour have also manifested themselves in the process.

Instead of superseding the hired-labour relationship that is the fundamental characteristic from which all the other deformations of bourgeois political society originate, socialism in its Stalinist phase of development evolved new forms of this very relationship. The problem of economic and thereby political alienation, far from ceasing to exist, has thus become socialism's real and vital problem.

Very understandably, the historical illusion that socialism has been accomplished as the first phase of communism on the basis of such a relationship has given rise to a variety of other myths and obfuscations. We should not forget the truism that obfuscation is one of the fundamental forms of ideological alienation. Like every other form of alienation, of course, this form should not be comprehended in unhistoric and abstract terms. During certain periods of primitive awareness and a low level of social development, man has been able to advance only with the help of such alienated forms of consciousness. Man's very existence often depended on them. However, though mankind was capable at one time of progressing with this type of ideological consciousness, the contemporary evolution of man and his high level of development in knowledge and philosophy are incompatible with such a structure. This is especially true of a socialist evolution, in which man's relationships towards man, society and nature should become more lucid, more rational and more comprehensible. Man in socialist society must become increasingly aware of himself as the sole creator of his life and his destiny.

One of the myths already mentioned is that of the socialist state as the fundamental driving force and lever behind socialist advancement. Since the state consists primarily of a particular apparatus, this attitude has inevitably exalted the political sphere. The worker, instead of being recognized as the basic actor in this new historical transformation, has again found himself opposed by an institution which is essentially inaccessible to him and which has been managing all spheres of his life. Thus the foundations for the development of the bureaucracy and of all bureaucratic pretensions and mystifications has been created. It is but a step from this myth – that the problem of freedom has been solved by abolishing the bourgeois state – to the concurrent myth that a working-class state cannot generate a force which under certain circumstances dominates the working class, and espouses the primitive cult of the personality. The realm of state arbitration thus comes to encompass not only political and economic processes and relationships but also all others – scientific, philosophical and artistic. Whereas philosophy and science at one time had been the ancillaries of theology, in this case all these spheres became the ancillaries of politics.

The cult of personality and all the other alienated forms are therefore not just accidents of circumstance but rather expressions of a definite structure that rests on a concept of socialism as the absorption of all spheres of social life into the state.[1] This concept reached a culminating point in Stalinist theory and

1. By 'state' we are naturally referring in the Marxian sense primarily to a particular organizational arrangement and apparatus serving a given class or group in its exercise of authority over another. Aside from this, the concept of the state encompasses a number of other constituent parts.

practice in the thesis of 'completed socialism' once state ownership and arbitration came to predominate in society.[1]

This ideological fascination with bureaucracy and technocracy
established an extremely alienated theoretical credo. A number
of facts were lost sight of in the process. First, to give such great
power to political institutions necessarily meant to diminish in
practice the real freedom of the workers and the intellectuals.
Second, the import of socialism cannot consist of the evolution of the alienated forms of bourgeois society to still greater
power. Third, the dissolution of these alienated forms necessarily
presupposes the creation of new relationships that will supersede
all the forms of authority and force inherited by socialism.
Fourth, socialism is a development of these new relationships
which enable the working man to have an increasing influence
on the direction and organization of his own life.

The thesis of 'completed socialism' is consequently a *contra-
dictio in adjecto*, for anything involved in a constant transforma-
tive process can never be completed. It is impossible to build on
the old political forms (state, party, bureaucracy) due to the
reasons mentioned, but it is also impossible to build on new
forms, for the old ones cannot be abolished all at once. In
other words, socialism is the initial phase of communism during
which these contradictory processes evolve, while the pre-
dominance of new forms of a specifically communist nature will
mean that the first phase has been overcome.

3

The problem of alienation is thus of vital and historical importance to socialism, not only because practical experience has
shown that many deforming aspects of alienation are possible
under socialism, but also because socialism must continue on the
basis of various social forms which in themselves represent forms
of alienation. Furthermore, as we shall see, the very level of
economic and cultural development in contemporary society
generates various other forms of alienation which socialism can
not get rid of all at once. The entry of socialism on the world
stage is not the appearance of some magic wand to convert all

1. I have given a critique of this thesis of 'completed socialism' in my
dissertation on 'Marginalia on Humanism' in the collection entitled *Socija-
lizam i humanizam* (*Socialism and Humanism*; Zagreb: Naprijed, 1963).

evils into good and to resolve all human problems in the twinkling of an eye.

If our desire is to contribute more fully to human liberation, i.e. to the overcoming of various forms of alienation, then socialism must place its fundamental stress on man, and the free personality must be considered a prerequisite to social freedom, in theory and in practice. This means the permanent creation of those relations which will enable the working man to govern himself and his work process in economics, culture, education and all other sectors of social life. The opposite of the absolutization of political factor is to strengthen the power of the entire community rather than just the political segment thereof. Another aspect of this social management (in the form of workers' councils and various other councils) is for the state to wither away and die out as a power over man.[1]

We dare not close our eyes to these facts, or to the fact that socialism is not a magical leap from an alienated to a de-alienated society; on the contrary, it is a new historical process which also contains certain alienated forms; nor can one ignore the fact that its historical import and mission is precisely the conquest, not the increase, of alienation.

In terms of the contemporary level of human development, regardless of specific countries, socialism is also a hierarchical society. In view of this circumstance, and of the forms in which socialism evolves, bureaucracy is a constant accompaniment to socialism. Particular hierarchies in all spheres of life invariably endeavour to make themselves as independent as possible in relation to the lower levels. This again means that the tendency to create new forms of alienation is a permanent process that

1. These forms of management are known as 'social self-management' in Yugoslav terminology, and display a variety of specific features characteristic of Yugoslav society. The frequency of the disputes over the problem of the 'withering away' of the state only serves to show that the essence of the problem is not understood. The state is capable of 'withering away' in connexion with a number of extremely significant functions in the field of economics or culture, leading to the elimination of certain forms of alienation. At the same time, however, no socialist society can weaken or abolish its armed forces so long as international antagonisms have not been resolved. Socialism is therefore in the vanguard of the struggle for coexistence and general disarmament, for to supersede this historical anachronism (the existence of armies) would mean that man had made a great stride forward in his development.

socialism must thwart and overcome. Socialism is thus a process in which the evolution of forms of self-management permeates and opposes statist and bureaucratic tendencies. What is involved is not a linear process devoid of conflict, but rather a genuinely dialectical and contradictory process. *In other words, the political forms in which socialism evolves are essentially particular forms of alienation and are wholly positive and historically progressive only if they tend to dissolve themselves.*

However paradoxical it may seem, the socialist forces accomplish the process of de-alienation precisely by means of different forms of alienation, alongside de-alienated forms. This is a unique, wholly new, original and profoundly humane process and historical task of its own kind. While every authority in the past has endeavoured to make itself absolute and eternal, socialist forces use their power to eliminate themselves.[1]

Socialism from this philosophico-sociological standpoint is a process by which the previous forms of human alienation are to be overcome.

Socialism has emerged thus far in the less developed countries, and therefore increases in production and industrial development have appeared to be its prime tasks. This is just one aspect of the problems of these countries, an everyday concern and reality, without whose solution higher forms of human relationships cannot evolve. Yet this problem is not in itself a specifically *socialist* one, since increases in production are likewise the problem of capitalism. The vital problem of socialism is to be found in the realm of social relationships.

Without wishing to underestimate the significance of economic and cultural factors, I must conclude that such measures (rising production, industrial development) fail to strike their historical target unless accompanied by profound social transformation in the sense of self-management by man himself.

In view of the complexity of the domestic and international situations during the initial phases of development, however, even these forms of self-management are not by themselves absolute despite their essentially de-alienated structure. In the same way as political forms tend in themselves to develop into

1. I might point out that socialism in Yugoslavia has developed in precisely this way and that a great deal of historical experience has already been accumulated on the basis of workers' and social self-management.

bureaucracy and to dominate politically, various forms of particularism and localism (which are also forms of alienation) may develop in the same way in the field of self-management. The activities of the most progressive forces of socialism to overcome both bureaucracy and localism, along with all the other deformations, are of such great importance for precisely this reason. Such is indeed the fundamental import of the endeavours of the socialist and communist parties and leagues, wherever they happen to exist.

Alienation inevitably persists under socialism in other areas of social life which are generally similar in contemporary developed societies. Socialism has not as yet abolished the production of commodities, hence the market, money, or any of the fetishes which inevitably appear at this level of economic and cultural development of mankind. Regardless of the possibility of much stronger intervention on the part of the socialist state or society itself to prevent the occurrence of the various deformations originating from such a pattern, the occult power of the market and of money, and the hierarchy of status, are bound to have an alienating effect on the unstable structure of contemporary man. Egocentricity, the division of the personality into an official and a private component, and various other resultant moral aberrations are nothing more than manifestations of human alienation, even under socialism. The *homo duplex*, that characteristic phenomenon of contemporary civilization, has not disappeared as a problem under socialism. The effect of the external, the superficial and the ephemeral in the form of the living-standard, prestige or only shallow amusement is at work in the period of socialism. The structure and physiognomy of contemporary man is still primitive in many respects, burdened with a variety of negative characteristics inherited from the past, and hence quite unstable. Many people run away from themselves after having failed to find genuine contentment within themselves or in their creative relationship to socialism. Such people find their vital contentment outside themselves in the external and the incidental, rather than in the essential problems of their own personalities and communities.

Another problem of socialism is modern industrial production, which has led to extremes of specialization and the division of labour, thus alienating workers from their jobs, which are monotonous, uncreative and boring. Under socialism as elsewhere, of course, various palliatives will naturally be used to alleviate the situation. However, the historical solution is not to be found in any such palliatives, but rather in those measures which characterize socialism as a new historical form of the social organization of labour, i.e. of social relationships generally. The abolishment of those relationships in which the worker is cut off from participation in the entire organization of labour, production, planning and the distribution of surplus labour is the *conditio sine qua non* to any solution of this fundamental problem of contemporary civilization. But self-management on the part of the working-man begins as a process of abolishing the wage–labour relationship, that alienated relationship in which man is no more than a means. The whole hierarchy of values shifts with the transformation of the working man from a tool into an active factor in society.

But this factor alone is not sufficient to solve the entire problem. With the ever-growing process of creating a society in which the centre is man's self-government, with the ever-increasing abandonment of the political forms of his existence, the structure of productive forces, including man himself, must be changed simultaneously. The perspectives which are opened up by automation and the other achievements of modern science, along with the drastic shortening of the working day and, eventually, the abolition of the present division of labour into physical and mental, will extend the range of human freedom simultaneously with the transformations of social relationships.

However, there is still another prerequisite to be met if this 'free time' is to be used creatively. A new, 'polycultural', critical and historically responsible personality is needed, a personality requiring no intermediaries or alienated forms to sense a unity with history, a personality with horizons not confined to family or tribe or nation. Therefore this entire transformation period of socialism is the period of developing a new personality which will, in its entirety, become conscious of history as its personal creation, so that there will be no need for the idea of transcendence in order to explain its own existence and its own purpose.

Summing up, we may state again that alienation is not the problem of bourgeois society, because that society may itself exist as an alienated society. Alienation becomes the central problem of socialism, since socialism may exist and develop only under the condition that it overcomes and eliminates alienation.

Translated by William Hannaher

OSKAR SCHATZ
AND ERNST FLORIAN WINTER*

⊚ ⊚

Alienation, Marxism and Humanism
(A Christian Viewpoint)

OSKAR SCHATZ, director of the scientific department of
Radio Salzburg and of the 'Salzburger Night Studio' since
1959, is a free-lance political writer for newspapers in
Austria and elsewhere. He was born in Salzburg in 1924,
and upon graduation from the Salzburg Realgymnasium in
1942 did military service, spending two years as a British
prisoner of war. After the war, he studied natural sciences
at the University of Vienna and then took up law and
political science at the University of Innsbruck. He subsequently worked towards his doctorate in law, with
special interest in natural and political law, at the Philosophical Institute in Salzburg. From 1961 to 1963 he participated in a Marxist seminar of the Eastern Institute in
Salzburg under the direction of Professor E. F. Winter.
He is currently preparing a thesis on alienation in the
early writings of Marx.

ERNST FLORIAN WINTER was born in Vienna in 1923,
the eldest son of Dr Ernst Karl Winter, a well-known
Catholic sociologist. He emigrated to the United States
after the *Anschluss* in 1938, received his B.A., M.A. and
Ph.D. degrees at Columbia University, and did Japanese
studies at the University of Michigan. Since his return to
Austria, he has taught history and political science, speciali-
zing in Central and Eastern Europe and the Far East.
Co-founder and former co-editor of *Cross Currents*, he has
contributed to various journals of opinion and is the
author of, among other books, *Austrian Neutrality: Origin,
Content, Outlook* and *The Politics of Neutrality*.

* This essay is the result of a seminar on Humanism, Socialism and
Christianity held from March 1962 to March 1963 at the Ostinstitut,
Internationales Forschungszentrum für Grundfragen der Wissenschaften,
Salzburg, Austria, with Professor A. Auer, Doctors L. Maresch, Planty-
Bonjour and O. Schatz, and Professor E. F. Winter, chairman.

I

What legitimate interest could a Catholic Christian take today in socialism and humanism and their mutual relationship?
Or, to state it less ambitiously, what contribution to the present
discussion might be expected from a Christian viewpoint concerning a humanist socialism?

The concern for man's 'alienation' seems to offer itself as a
most useful connecting link between socialism and humanism
and between Christians and non-Christians. For every serious
analysis of the phenomenon 'man' meets sooner or later the
category 'alienation', in itself a complete concept touching all
kinds of human behaviour.

That man has become alienated in the process of his self-
realization was part of the revolutionary message of Karl Marx.
More than a hundred years after Marx, alienation has lost none
of its burning actuality; in fact, it has become a global phenomenon. After the conceptual and analytic beginnings in Rousseau, Fichte, Schelling and Hegel, it was primarily, and paradoxically, the Marxist version of socialism – and not the reflective thought of classical humanism or the practical witness of
Christianity, called love – that continued to analyse concretely
the modern dimensions of the problem of human alienation, and
also proposed a cure for it.

Marx recognized the phenomenon of alienation – which developed into the decisive anthropological aspect of the industrial
society – more clearly than any of his contemporaries. This he
owed first of all to an intensive critique of Hegel's apparently
abstract and idealistic theory of alienation. Secondly, however,
from this analysis and critique, Marx arrived at his own concep-
tualization and suggested a utopia as the means of concretely
solving the existential problem of human alienation. This nonetheless theoretical conclusion constitutes the personal greatness
as well as the tragedy of Marx's position. Besides, this his solution
has become of the greatest significance for the subsequent evolution of the category alienation because the latter is now increasingly suspected of being merely a subjective, arbitrary and
even ideological concept.

This suspicion came to be focused mainly on the act of '*annulment*' ('*Aufhebung*'), that is, the dictatorship of the proletariat, the violence of class struggle, the communist society – from which Marx expected the final solution of the problem of alienation. Marx sees the total character of the '*annulment*' as necessarily related to the totality characteristics of his alienation concept itself. Only thus can alienation be totally annulled and the total creative freedom of man realized. Yet the fact that the alienation of man has not only persisted but also appeared in a new, and for Marxist socialism unforseen, intensity, and has led to a deep longing for more humaneness, humanity and socialist humanism, invites basic reconsiderations. Perhaps the solution Marx so passionately desired has not gone deep enough, has remained on the periphery of the phenomenon – despite or perhaps because of its radicalism. It appears to us that its radicalism was not radical enough (in the original sense of the term). A radical theory of alienation must not stop at the social involvement of man but must push right through to his innermost anthropological dimensions.

The necessary corrective complement to Marx's 'real humanism' does not, therefore, lie in an exaggerated positivist sociology, which is incapable of grasping man anthropologically and thus falls away behind Marxist sociology, but rather in a humanist philosophical anthropology which includes the problem of human alienation explicitly as an integral part of its vigorous theorizing about man. Moreover, once this new and deeper reflection about man's being and nature is established, it also becomes necessary to encourage the study of those concrete conditions, set by modern man himself, which compromise his being and which tend to alienate him from his works and the outer world, from fellow man and from himself. This means clearly that today there can no longer exist a potent humanism without a serious appreciation of the category alienation. Even more important is Christianity's need for a clarification, inclusion and mastery of the phenomenon of alienation, which, as Erich Thier has noticed, has already become part of the 'European vocabulary'.[1] We must finally add the common observation that the phenomenon of the 'alienated man' is no longer

1. Erich Thier, *Das Menschenbild des jungen Marx* (Göttingen: Vandenhoeck und Ruprecht, 1961), p. 4.

restricted to the highly industrialized capitalist as well as socialist countries of the Western world extending from San Francisco to Vladivostok, but really reaches as far as does the impact of the modern technical civilization on the non-Western world. During the second half of the twentieth century, the alienated man is no longer a so-called 'European' or 'Western' or 'capitalist' or 'socialist' problem, but a global, universally human problem. Therefore it must be analysed as fully as possible and without ideological prejudices.

All this by no means implies that the Marxian category of 'alienation' has lost its validity. But it does mean that Marx's genuine insight is too peripheral and offers no final explanation. Rather it is subject to the same changes and modifications as all social phenomena today. Helmuth Plessner characterized this recently, when he said that alienation today concerns those very peculiarities of modern society

> which it has been gaining through its striving against becoming proletarian and against class-warfare; namely its high grade of organization and its rational compartmentalization for the purpose of a smoothly operating system. With the figure of speech 'alienated man', one characterizes ... the single individual in that social role which is being thrust upon him by an administered world. Man has become the bearer of functions.[1]

Thus alienated man also becomes the 'outer-directed' one (David Riesman), a category which, especially in its existential version, seems to share with the Marxist category alienation solely the name. True, Marx also applied alienation to the concrete, individual human being. Yet, he precisely defines this individuality as species-being (*'Gattungswesen'*). Although directly concerned with the individual, alienation was for him a process and phenomenon within man as species-being, that is to say within human society taken as totality. Persisting against this view is the existentialist alienation theory with which, by stressing not only the individuality but also the uniqueness and singularity of each individual existence, every form of human socialization (*'menschliche Vergesellschaftung'*) is in principle incommensurable.

While Marx recognized the cause of alienation more in the too

1. Helmuth Plessner, *Das Problem der Oeffentlichkeit und die Idee der Entfremdung* (Göttingen, 1960), p. 12.

low degree of human socialization and therefore expected salvation from the 'socialized man' of the future, the existential notion of alienation considers a totally socialized man equal to a total loss of man's nature. In view of the possibility of such a change into the opposite extreme, we say with Helmuth Plessner[1] that the appeal of existentialism to seek freedom and individuality internally has the same impact on the process of man becoming an externally alienated mere thing ('*Verdinglichung*') as does Marxist eschatology, which either places human self-realization at the end of pre-history, or states categorically that there will be no alienation in the socialist system.

In both cases, the concrete, present-day suffering and hoping man seems in his completely unpretentious humanity woefully unrealistic and out of place. Ours is precisely this concern for the concrete man, embedded in mankind. It is for his sake that we must hold fast to the category alienation, but to a de-ideologized category which can further our search for a social-political order *à la taille de l'homme*.

For this purpose we propose now, in Part 2, to analyse the historic alienation concepts, and in Part 3 to present a possible contemporary Christian viewpoint.

2

Wherever the search for an understanding of man and the striving for an illumination of the human condition predominates today, a thorough analysis of the notion of alienation, as a key category, forces itself upon us. This category is by no means simply a more or less esoteric notion, but presents itself rather as 'a real category indispensable for the description of social reality, as well as contemporary conditions'.[2] The category therefore neither denotes an imaginary space of pure interiority, nor relates to a world of massive exteriority, devoid of subjects, where it would become senseless. The interior and the exterior cannot be severed one from another, if man – as was self-evident to the fathers of the alienation concept – is to be considered identical with the 'world' and with the 'life' of man (the latter

1. Ibid., p. 20.
2. Cf. Arnold Gehlen, '*Über die Geburt der Freiheit aus der Entfremdung*', *Archiv für Rechts-und Sozialphilosophie*, XL/3 (1952), p. 338.

again pointing to a central interiority). Hegel says in the famous preface to his *Phenomenology of the Spirit* that the strength of the Spirit is only as great as its unfolding. While the Spirit unfolds itself into its exterior manifestation, this very process already offers the possibility and even the reality of alienation.

Alienation, moreover, does not refer to a specific form of the subjective or objective Spirit, to state, religion or economics. Rather the possibility of alienation is present wherever man, actively or passively, relates to the surrounding and objective world in order to find his identity with his self in his difference from this world. Modern cultural anthropologists explain how this imperative process of continuous self-identification is rooted in the very nature of man. Unlike the animal, with its fixation on a determined and biological environment with which it merges and blends into a uniform Nature, man must regain his original harmony and unity every moment of his existence, without ever completely reaching it. Man does so by surrounding his kind with an artificial and man-made milieu which becomes a kind of 'second nature' to him, joining his original organically equipped nature. This principally unfixed relation to a concrete environment makes man what he really is; namely, an open, universal, historical, but also endangered being which can also lose itself in the course of its self-realization, i.e. become alienated – a process completely unthinkable in organic nature. An animal is always what it is. It cannot therefore alienate itself. Man, on the contrary, can alienate himself because he possesses consciousness and self-consciousness, confirming his being only through self-communication to his fellow men, and thus discovering his identity.

This is a perception from the viewpoint of transcendental philosophy. However, in its absolute form it became decisive both for German Idealism and for the beginnings of the modern alienation theory.

If we call this second nature of man his 'culture', one recognizes that the alienation of man is related essentially to 'civilization'. And, since civilization is a social phenomenon, alienation also relates, in the last analysis, to the sociology of man. In the thoroughly unorganic and artificial world of culture and civilization, of community and social life, we describe alienation as an eminently social situation. Rousseau was the first to express its importance.[1]

His critique of culture and society contains two points relevant for the category alienation. First, culture is a system of behavioural models claiming to be binding on human attitudes. Man, who has placed his life under the coercion of behavioural models and standards is, however, no longer himself. He lives a life not decided by himself, but determined externally. Alienation therefore becomes synonymous with heteronomy, even though the human life determining the cultural and social milieu is a man-made product. Alienation can thus be overcome solely by identifying the exterior laws confronting man with the natural laws of reason. Reality must become rational. Rousseau's answer to the problem of alienation is not the myth of the eternal return but the myth of revolution, anticipating an essential theme of Marxism. Since consciousness is always determined by social existence and not vice versa, this existence must be made reasonable. Only thus can this axiom of historical materialism signify the determination of reason through reason itself.[2]

Second, man living in the original state of nature is a being of integrity. Being and appearance coincide in his existence. Man is reconciled with himself. Social man, on the other hand, has lost this original harmony. He is always alienated. A break between that which one is and that which one appears to be exists. This rupture is a symptom of the misery and travail of our contemporary epoch.

Rousseau's deep pessimism reveals a new life sentiment diametrically opposed to the progress–optimism of the early eighteenth century. It is a very dark and unhappy consciousness that no longer binds confirmation in Time and is thus able to understand its own epoch only antithetically as one of decline, confusion and absolute depravity. Herein lie the roots of a new understanding of history, which subsequently came to influence the classical German humanism of Lessing, Herder and Schiller.

1. Cf. Rousseau, *Discours sur les sciences et les arts* (1750); also Hans Barth, *'Die Idee der Selbstentfremdung bei Rousseau'* in *Wahrheit und Ideologie* (Zürich: Rentsch, 1961), and Iring Fetscher, *Rousseaus politische Philosophie* (Neuwied: Luchterhand, 1960).

2. Herbert Marcuse, *Reason and Revolution* (New York: Humanities Press, 1941; London: Routledge & Kegan Paul), p. 319: 'Reason, when determined by rational social conditions, is determined by itself.'

This peculiar feeling for those times remains the obscure backdrop to that glowing enthusiasm with which the best minds greeted the epochal events of the French Revolution. Like a photographic negative, this sure sense of corruption and of alienation accompanies the increasingly passionate demand for a final 'realization' and 'reintegration' of man. And these demands were primarily understood in terms of realizing human freedom.

In Fichte's notion of the lost and regained freedom one recognizes, though in abstract form, the core concept of the modern alienation theory, which, despite its thoroughly idealistic character, underlies the naturalistic theories of both Marx and Freud. Both are primarily concerned with freeing man from the determinism of those blind forces that man's productivity has produced and objectivized. Whether these forces operate with the vigour and efficacy of laws of nature in the present economic conditions or in the drives of the unconscious becomes a subordinate question. What remains decisive is the idea that man can become lord over his self again only when he makes the determining economic or psychological infrastructures rational. Any other form of freedom is illusory. The domination of being by consciousness is wrong. It must be overcome before the true relationship can emerge. The original affinity between Fichte's formula for lost freedom and Marx's and Freud's definitions of freedom as conscious necessity is not altered by the naturalistic and materialistic point of departure of the latter two, because in both cases the materialistic thesis can become true only in its negation. The customary labels 'idealism' and 'materialism' become irrelevant in view of the 'substantial idealism' which holds that the ideality manifest inside man can be externalized as direct subjectivity.

Hegel, like Schelling, gave abstract developments greater concreteness. The Spirit in Hegel produces his exteriority only from its interiority and against it, in order to annul the dialectic antithesis and rearrange the exteriority back into the new identity, a movement which he defined as 'identity of the identity and non-identity'. This process transpires in a multitude of concrete negations and rearrangements, giving witness to a historic fabric of unheard-of richness. Here the transition from the 'subjective spirit' to the 'objective spirit' was achieved.[1]

1. Cf. Wilhelm Seeberger, *Hegel oder die Entwicklung des Geistes zur Freiheit* (Stuttgart: Klett, 1962).

Since Descartes, thinking had been turning more and more from an objective to a subjective world. Hume's denial of the causality principle and Kant's stressing of criticism had helped sever consciousness from the world. On the contrary, Hegel's system strove to liberate the 'subjective spirit' from an empty formalism and lead it back from mere self-certainty to the objective world. He wanted to force man to part with himself, to 'alienate' himself, in order to regain himself.

Hegel's *Phenomenology* contains this central idea of a dialectic process in which alienation constitutes the negative moment. It is the negative of the position, yet not an absolute negative, for in the negation of the negative it is annulled *and* preserved in a higher synthesis. Alienation becomes thus the motor, the living pulse of this powerful epoch of the Spirit.

Although Marx relies directly on the *Phenomenology* in his Parisian manuscripts, his starting position is a completely different one, characterized by the destruction of the absolute Spirit and the concommitant change of speculative philosophy into philosophical anthropology. The primary tendency of this new direction, culminating in Feuerbach's criticism of religion, is the critical return to man as such. The proper goal becomes the establishment of a 'real humanism'.

In his *Economic and Philosophic Manuscripts*, 1844, Marx critically discusses the speculative alienation concept of Hegel from the point of real humanism. He criticizes mainly that 'spirituality' which reduces concrete man to an abstract self-consciousness. What about that realm which has become alienated to man, the state, wealth, etc.?

> It is precisely abstract thought from which these objects are alienated and which they confront with their presumptuous reality. The philosopher, himself an abstract form of alienated man, sets himself up as the measure of the alienated world.[1]

1. Marx, *Economic and Philosophical Manuscripts, 1844*, translated by T. B. Bottomore, in Erich Fromm's *Marx's Concept of Man* (New York: Frederick Ungar, 1961), p. 174. For the concept of alienation in Marx consult in particular: J. Y. Cálvez, *La Pensée de Karl Marx* (Paris: Seuil, 1956); Karl Löwith, 'Man's Self-Alienation in the Early Writings of Marx', *Social Research*, XXI (1954); Georg Lukács, *Geschichte und Klassenbewusstsein* (Berlin, 1923), and *Der junge Hegel und die Probleme der kapitalistischen Gesellschaft* (Berlin, 1954); Herbert Marcuse, '*Neue Quellen zur Grundlage des historischen Materialismus. Interpretation der unveröffentlichten Manuskripte von Marx*', *Die Geschichte (Internationale*

In order to identify 'alienation', non-alienated and true reality, against which alone the fall and loss can be measured, must be presupposed. For Marx this measure is not the ego and 'self' – this abstract man – but rather the

> real corporeal *man*, with his feet firmly planted on the solid ground, inhaling and exhaling all the powers of nature.

Self-consciousness is solely a quality of man's nature and not the reverse, as speculative thinking cares to maintain. This error calls forth weighty consequences for the concept of alienation.

> It is not the fact that the human being objectifies himself in-humanely, in opposition to himself, but that he objectifies himself by distinction from and in opposition to abstract thought, which constitutes alienation as it exists and as it has to be transcended.[1]

Marx's critical energy is thus directed primarily against the relationship between objectivity and alienation, as he thought Hegel saw it.

> Objectivity as such is regarded as an alienated human relationship which does not correspond with the essence of man, self-consciousness. The re-appropriation of the objective essence of man, which was produced as something alien and determined by alienation, signifies the supersession not only of alienation but also of objectivity; that is, man is regarded as a non-objective, spiritual being.[2]

This fundamental confusion between alienation (*Entfremdung*) and objectivity (*Gegenständlichkeit*) has wide-ranging consequences for the appropriation of an alienated human being.

> We have already seen that the appropriation of alienated objective being, or the supersession of objectivity in the condition of alienation (which has to develop from indifferent otherness to real antagonistic alienation), signifies for Hegel also, or primarily, the supersession of objectivity, since it is not the determinate character of the object but its objective character which is the scandal of alienation for self-consciousness. The object is therefore negative, self-annulling, a nullity.[3]

Revue für Sozialismus und Politik), IX (1932); Heinrich Popitz, *Der entfremdete Mensch: Zeitkritik und Gesellschaftsphilosophie des jungen Marx* (Basel, 1953); Robert Tucker, *Philosophy and Myth in Karl Marx* (Cambridge: C.U.P., 1961).

1. *Marx's Concept of Man*, p. 175.   2. Ibid., p. 178.   3. Ibid., p. 184.

Marx reproaches Hegel for not taking real alienation seriously enough, for being guilty of an 'uncritical idealism' which can easily turn into an 'uncritical positivism', ready to vindicate the real alienated life at the very moment when it believes it has been subdued intellectually. For when self-conscious man recognizes the general existence of his world as self-alienation, when he annuls it and 'claims to be at home in his other being',[1] he affirms this real life in its alienated shape, passing it off as its true being.

> Thus reason is at home in unreason as such. Man, who has recognized that he leads an alienated life in law, politics, etc., leads his true human life in this alienated life as such. . . . But in actuality private right, morality, the family, civil society, the state, etc., remain; only they have become 'moments', modes of existence of man, which have no validity in isolation but which mutually dissolve and engender one another. They are moments of movement.[2]

Marx is not simply in favour of the mere annulment of alienated institutional forms, but of the liquidation of the alienated being, the alienated objectivity. The insignificant difference in nuance between 'annulling' and 'liquidating' clearly shows the difference between a contemplative-oriented appreciation of the world and the practical revolutionary ideology of Marx. When Marx speaks of alienation (both as *Entäusserung* and *Entfremdung*), he means not only a negation in the sense of logical opposition, but the fall into a sphere of wickedness, ruin and profligacy.

An undercurrent foreign to idealism exists in all of this, and also the upside-down variety of Feuerbach already apparent in the cultural criticism of German classics. Fichte speaks of his age as the age of consummated sinfulness. But, while Lessing, Herder and Schiller were quite sceptical as to the final abolition of contemporary alienation, and escaped into schematic historic constructs, Marx was quite confident of the imminent breakthrough into a new aeon – a breakthrough, moreover, which would be solely the deed of mankind. This new age would be determined not by the law of alienation and confusion, but exclusively by the factors of totality, entirety and universal harmony. Marx obviously attached the conceptually logical and

1. Ibid., p. 185.   2. Ibid., p. 186.

complete, unequivocally defined Hegelian concept of alienation
to a precise historic period which, in the full sense of the word,
has not even become 'history' as yet. Marx called it pre-history
in the formation of man. But also for him this human pre-history
was stamped by the rhythm of the inner laws of alienation, by
the negation of the negation.

> In conceiving the negation of the negation, from the aspect of
> the positive relation inherent in it, as the only true positive, and
> from the aspect of the negative relation inherent in it, as the only
> true act and self-confirming act of all being, Hegel has merely
> discovered an abstract, logical and speculative expression of the
> historical process, which is not yet the real history of man as a
> given subject, but only the history of the act of creation, of the
> genesis of man.[1]

It was perhaps Marx's most ingenious accomplishment to define
this thoroughly negative act through which man, during the
hitherto existing course of history, could confirm himself as
man, namely as labour, toil, work. Yet even in this achievement
he was able to relate directly to Hegel's *Phenomenology*.

> The outstanding achievement of Hegel's *Phenomenology* – the
> dialectic of negativity as the moving and creating principle – is,
> first, that Hegel grasps the self-creation of man as a process, ob-
> jectification as loss of the object, as alienation and transcendence
> of this alienation, and that he therefore grasps the nature of
> labour, and conceives objective man (true, because real man) as
> the result of his own labour.[2]

In the last analysis, it is work, and particularly the modern
form of wage-labour, which has become the basis for the total
alienation of modern man. The intrinsic nature of work itself
constitutes and determines that. The product of work confronts
man as a strange being and as an independent power. In other
words, the realization of work appears as the irreality of the
wage-labourer, as loss of, as well as servitude under, the object.
If, therefore, man is to be set free against his own objective products and if alienation is really to be overcome, the proper cause
and source of every type of human alienation, namely work,
must be eliminated and raised into a new, positive form of
human self-activity, in which there will be no more room for any
kind of negativity. Alienated work can be overcome, because it

1. Ibid., p. 172.   2. Ibid., pp. 176–7.

is only a relativity, an historically limited condition for human existence. Alienated work must not be considered an essential part of human nature. As different as Hegel and Marx might be in their last spiritual intentions, their thinking stood challenged by the same contradictory, antagonistic reality of an early capitalistic society. According to their innermost intentions, however, they answered this challenge differently: Hegel with the philosophical gnosis of absolute knowledge and with rational mysticism; Marx with the utopia of a healed and integrated world in which the original myth of a happy, paradisical life continues to resound.

3

Has the crisis of alienation really found for us its focus in work?

Obviously, during the past two hundred years Western philosophically-oriented, and later also socially-oriented, thinking has been increasingly reflective and differentiated in its search for an understanding of the phenomenon of alienation. Marx saw also the moment near at hand to do something concrete about its solution.

Yet, it appears that theory and practice, while becoming more integrated, are also becoming more ambivalent. Two extreme fronts can be observed. The one, older and traditional, which is usually identified with religious sentiment and philosophical speculations, prefers to solve the problem by seeing alienation as primarily, if not exclusively, related to interiority, even to sin and original sin. Man must be converted to a toilsome interior purification. All energies are concentrated on this process with patience, humility and perseverance. The world and mankind and the products of human creativity are of only indirect concern. Theologically speaking, the concepts and the efficacy of 'soul' and 'grace' are needed for the reintegration of man, for love, for peace, and the regaining of true freedom. This liberation of man must never be the work of malediction and violence. Rather, mankind's fate is a long-drawn process of individual transformation and collective illumination. Actually, everyone knows that this has been the religious and philosophical wisdom of East and West throughout the ages. And Christianity in particular has attempted to institutionalize the reform of interiority and the practice of love. The philosophers in the Western tradition, from Socrates to Kant, have also made progress, even though often slow and painful, in the direction of giving social life ethical foundations. Christianity, humanism and socialism have participated in this ethical momentum. However, it appears that an overwhelming concentration on the interiority of the problem will not be sufficient to solve the problem.

The other, more recent and revolutionary, approach is an extreme call for exteriority, for the liquidation of alienation. The objectivity must be liquidated, in order to transform and liberate man. The development of concrete forms of human alienation forces this alternative upon man. The sole concentration on making men better by spiritual means comes too late in view of the surging masses of mankind and the awesome products of their alienation. From the original interior alienations of man from God, from himself and from his fellow men, emphasis has shifted the exterior social and economic forms of alienation. While the former appear elusive, the latter submit to practical manipulation. Thus Marx, who ran through the gamut of alienations, finally concentrated his attention on the realm of economics. However, it is clear that even Marx's view cannot be equated with a simple 'materialization' of the concept alienation, as if man were solely motivated by greed for material things. On the contrary, Marx wanted to liberate man from the fetters of blind economic determinisms.[1] Thus Marx's shift from an abstract philosophical-personal occurrence, as alienation was conceived traditionally, to the person–peripheral realm of material production certainly contributed to our more differentiated understanding and increased our appreciation of the anthropological dimension and the key role of work. Yet in the prophetic stipulation that alienation must be liquidated exclusively through atheism, class struggle, dictatorship and revolutionary measures in political economy lies the undifferentiated one-sided tragedy of the Marxist utopia.

How can these two extreme views be reconciled in view of the manifest urgency of resolving alienation on this earth without violence? A brief reference to two present phenomena will help

1. Cf. L. Landgrebe, 'Hegel und Marx', Marxismusstudien, I (1954), pp. 39–53; Landgrebe, 'Das Problem der Dialektik', ibid., III (1960), pp. 1–65; and J. Habermas, 'Eine philosophische Diskussion um Marx', Philosophische Rundschau, V, pp. 165–235.

304

us to see the possible direction of common Christian, humanist and socialist action.

Alienated work and labour is a more gigantic factor today, in both so-called capitalist as well as socialist countries, than could ever have been foreseen during the time of Marx. Nowhere has the so-called achievement of socialism fulfilled its promise, i.e. the liquidation of alienation and the realization of man's freedom. Everywhere the increase in the number of wage-labourers and the qualitative changes through scientific revolutions and enormous growth of productivity have increased alienation. The changes everywhere from an agrarian to a beginning-industrial and subsequently advanced-industrial and early atomic structure have been accompanied by a progressive alienation, in all types of political economy. The trend has clearly been towards an anthropological alienation of widest dimensions. Plainly, alienated modern man can attribute his alienated condition to the economic and social life released through industrial production, automation, consumption and atomic society, rather than to the polarization of rich and poor, still decisive for Hegel and Marx. Thus the creativity of man has suffered not only a spiritual alienation at the very height of its colossal achievements, not only an economic one at the time of plenty and productivity, but more recently, in addition, an anthropological, existential one. What *is* the ultimate sense of man, his life, his work?

Before the contemporary leap into the realm of free time, work had increasingly become the realm of necessity. With leisure, a new chance for realizing man's eternal longing, the possibility of a non-alienated creative being has appeared. However, for far too many the result has been the alienation of leisure time. Man can be freed from labour (and thus alienation) more than ever before. Yet, in a consumer, entertainment and welfare society, alienated leisure time, analogous to alienated labour, becomes the anthropological problem. For what, then, does man have leisure?

The practical humanism of Christianity can meet the humanism of responsible neosocialism through a common concern for the humanization of man, work and the world. There can be no final solution to history in this world. Rather, a Christian concentrates with eschatological hope on the immediate phase of human history at hand. This unfolds itself plainly in a labour of love, and the overcoming of concrete appearances of alienation today, instead of adding further manifestations of alienation.

Projection remains one of the direct consequences of alienation. To hypostatize an exterior enemy that must be destroyed – whether the capitalist, the Jew, the socialist, the religious man, the Negro, the communist, etc. – is not ending alienation, but accelerating its fatality. In its place, and in place of utopia at an inhuman price, and idealistic prognostication spiritually justified, many social, economic and anthropological dimensions of alienation could be concretely reduced. This is obvious in respect to colour line, poverty, servitude, occupational emptiness, work motivation, occupational therapy, racial prejudice, war, leisure-time programming, institutionalized freedoms, inalienable human rights, co-determination in decision-making processes, teamwork and the like – to mention only a few possibilities.[1]

A Catholic Christian can take a genuine interest in humanism and socialism today, precisely because together they could attempt to answer the questions posed so far. Marx started with religious alienation, and proceeded via political and social alienation to economic alienation, which he felt to be the root of all human alienation. Modern Christian thinking starts with the typical concrete alienation phenomena of an advanced – industrial and beginning – atomic society, recognizing in them a most acute expression of the deep frustration of man's creativity, and his longing for purpose and community life, and proceeds finally to a self-critical awareness of the problems posed by religious alienation, as the basic form of human alienation *per se*. Contrary to Marx's criticism and many Christians' defence, we do not limit this religious alienation to theoretical interior consciousness, but rather extend it to a phenomenon for which Christians are responsible. No institutionalized religion possesses in itself a guarantee against man's alienation from God,

1. Many of these concrete mobilizations of the resources of humaneness have been successfully experimented with in the United States. The challenge of Marxist–Leninist theory should, in this connexion, not be overlooked. Cf. H. R. Schlette, *Sowjet-Humanismus* (Munich: Kösel, 1960); Leo Kofler, *Der proletarische Burger* (Vienna: Europa-Verlag, 1964); as well as Arnold Künzli, *Das entfremdete Paradies* (Vienna: Europa-Verlag, 1963). The contributions of Africa and Asia will grow in importance as the world becomes one.

from himself, from his fellow men, from his work and its products and from the world. In other words, it would be unrealistic simply to point uncritically to religion as the solution of the problem. It appears to us a special duty to proclaim this, because without this recognition there can be no understanding of the insoluble interdependence between alienation in so-called profane and secular realms and the spiritual crisis within the great religions, including Christianity. Christianity, since the birth of Christ, has been no bystander, but a responsible actor in history. As Christians we must call for reform inside Christianity and the Church wherever they appear co-responsible for the alienation of man. The connexion between alienation, idolatry and fanaticism has become more than obvious today. These aberrations are quite possible within Christian ranks, though genuine Christian thinking will always, together with *'mea culpa'*, have to warn against the opposite extreme of deifying human spontaneity and liberty. In short, wherever one is seriously concerned about the humanity of man, God's care concerning man cannot be excluded and dismissed as irrelevant.

It is this care concerning man which in a modern, pluralistic world unites the Christian with all those, whatever their *Weltanschauung*, who are moved to humanize man and the human condition. That the Christians' involvement is for the sake of God's incarnation is their affair. The common concern, and not the dividing lines, is what matters.

Only one question remains: how can Christians recognize their proper tasks? In the great, universal community of life and love we call the Church, there are above all the lay people, dedicated to life and witness in the world, who know themselves to be united to all those working on the step-by-step overcoming of exterior alienation. The priests of God are dedicating themselves increasingly to help resolve interior alienation. With John XXIII, this inner-churchly division of labour has been entering a new stage of experimentation, opening new vistas for a new age of world-immanent hope. To close the gap between the two extreme positions discussed earlier, the people of the Church can be of great help, for on the Way of the Great Reconciliation we find that indeed institutions must be altered and souls must be healed; two tasks that must not be exercised one at the expense of the other or be structurally confused, but rather undertaken simultaneously. We therefore plead that the beginnings of a reconciliation of traditional polarity be recognized as the most workable basis for reconciling the basic antithesis between matter and spirit. Thus let us start forthwith to resolve that central modern problem of work.

MATHILDE NIEL

⊚ ⊚

The Phenomenon of Technology:
Liberation or Alienation of Man?[1]

MATHILDE NIEL has in recent years devoted herself to the
critique of the *mores* and social institutions of alienated
society. In connexion with this research she has lectured
regularly at the Sorbonne and has published numerous
papers, among which are *The Humanistic Psychoanalysis of
Erich Fromm, The Failure of Love, Microphysical and
Metaphysical Ebb* and *Boris Pasternak in Search of an Overt
Humanism.* Born in 1915, she had to interrupt her higher
studies because of her activity in the French Resistance
movement during the Second World War. In collaboration
with André Niel, she resumed her research after the war
and analysed the processes of creative conscience and
alienated conscience.

The problem I intend to discuss is certainly the most serious
which confronts modern man. *What is to become of the individual
in a technological civilization?* After a period of crisis are we going
to be turned into automatized robots, or finally liberated?

No one doubts that the phenomenon of technology dominates
our age. Up to the nineteenth century techniques evolved very
slowly: their transformation was hardly perceptible in the course
of an individual's life. At present, technological development is
accelerated and invades not only working life, but also family
life and leisure time; war and peace depend upon it; it transforms our natural surroundings and our living condition. Moreover, it takes hold of our very souls: present techniques – such
as advertising and propaganda – manipulate and condition the
human mind.

There are those who rejoice at this influence of technology

1. A lecture delivered at the Sorbonne on 24 November 1962.

upon the life of the individual; they expect human salvation to follow technological progress. Others are alarmed and see in this progress the final enslavement of mankind. Whom shall we believe? *Is technology a factor of alienation or of liberation of the individual? Is it a humanizing or a dehumanizing influence?* This, in its simplest form, is the question I shall try to answer.

Liberated Man and Alienated Man

What exactly is to be understood by *liberated man* and *alienated man*? One might say that the liberated man is the generous and disinterested man; he is also a creative man, who can express his personality and his talents in a creative action without constraint, whether in manual, intellectual or artistic work, or in his relations and friendship with other men. The free man is one who feels himself at the same time fully himself and in accord with other men. He is an individual without idols, dogmas, prejudices or *a priori* ideas. He is tolerant, inspired by a profound sense of justice and equality, and aware of himself as being at the same time an *individual* and a *universal man*.

The alienated man, on the contrary, never succeeds either in being himself or in living in a state of creative synthesis with other beings or things. He does not live in the present, whose wealth he fails to appreciate; he is interested only in the future, which draws him in quest of some kind of absolute, or in his desire to conform with a model or ideal. The alienated man does not think or act by himself; he always refers to something or someone outside himself, to tradition, a creed, an ideology, a transcendent being or a superior. He does not know how to live either in a dialogue with others or in an interior peace; he always needs someone to worship or to serve, to hate or to fight. He spends his life in *pursuing* something, either a *material end* which has been turned into an *absolute* (desire for wealth, comfort, the symbols of prestige), or a *spiritual end*, also turned into an absolute, which leads him to disdain life and the world. Sometimes he believes he has attained this absolute good, and then he is joyful and exalted; at other times he feels frustrated, and then he is miserable and depressed. His life is passed in desiring, hoping, despairing, worshipping and despising. The alienated man is tense, embattled, violent; he is narrow, intolerant and authoritarian; he is the passionate man. But he is also the pusillanimous man who fears authority, who is afraid of not thinking and acting like everyone else; he is cowardly, timorous, conformist; the *gregarious man*.

The liberated man, generous and creative, is not utopian, nor is he an abstract model to follow; *he is in us*. Without this creative man, there would never have been any sciences, any art, any acts of solidarity, any tolerance or social progress. There would never have been any close-knit families or faithful friends. But we have to admit, unfortunately, that in the individual, as in society, the forces of liberation have always encountered the forces of alienation, and that the latter have usually triumphed. At the present time, the forces of dehumanization are so strong that the individual and the whole human species are in danger. But, at the same time, the number of people who are becoming educated, who read good books and listen to good records, is increasing, and human solidarity is growing; alongside contempt for man, there is respect for man. We have to consider whether the development of technology will be undertaken with respect for man or with contempt for him.

Technology as a Factor of Humanization

It cannot be denied that the development of technology has made possible an improvement in the standard of living of great numbers of men, the relief of much physical suffering, the liberation of man from unpleasant tasks, and the prolongation of human life. A man who is hungry, cold or in pain cannot be himself. From this point of view, then, technology has been a liberator.

Many economists claim that technology awakens intelligence, and stimulates initiative and creativity. This is the view of the French economists Jean Fourastié and Louis Armand. They believe that the modern world demands creative minds capable of inventing and improving machines and organizations. In order to handle and repair the growing number of delicate and complex machines, workers are needed who have a ready intelligence and who are expert in their own special field.

'The ideal limit towards which the new organization of labour is tending is one where work will be limited to a single type of action: initiative,' writes Fourastié.[1]

1. Jean Fourastié, *Le Grand Espoir du XXᵉ siècle* (Paris: P.U.F.), p. 184.

MATHILDE NIEL

These economists even consider that workers will be trans-
ferred increasingly from the agricultural sector and the technically advanced, industrial sector of the economy (the primary
and secondary sectors) to the tertiary sector of more individualized services. For example, automation will require few
workers and technicians, while the demand for hairdressers,
laundry workers, painters, repairers, dentists, doctors, teachers,
bank and insurance clerks and civil servants will increase. Because the demand for consumer goods cannot grow indefinitely,
a point of saturation will soon be reached, and people will
demand relatively less in the way of foodstuffs and domestic
appliances, and more in the way of such objects as paintings,
records, furniture and works of art. Thanks to the nature of
work in the tertiary sector and to the universal spread of culture,
man will be able to develop completely as an individual; at least,
this is what the future seems to promise.

Moreover, the development of technology should permit a
considerable reduction in working hours and an extension of
leisure time in which each individual can exercise his preferred
activity, whether it is pottering about the house, gardening,
painting, reading or listening to music. The cultural use of
leisure is certainly aided by the growing diffusion of good records
and books at low prices.

But above all, technology should contribute to making social
relations more amicable and lead towards social justice and
equality. Comfort is being democratized; clothes and dwellings
are becoming more alike; rich and poor use the same roads go to
the same places on vacations, read the same papers, see the
same television programmes. Thanks to the speed of transportation, the same foods are becoming available to everyone. Customs are increasingly homogeneous;[1] one might even argue that
the worker is becoming bourgeois, while the bourgeois is becoming more democratic, and that the social classes are losing
their ritualistic character. Some believe that, as a result of technological development, capitalism will expire of its own accord.
It has been observed that when a country begins to industrialize
the barriers between classes break down. Nehru said that the
caste system becomes impossible in a train or on a factory
conveyor belt.

1. Edgar Morin, *L'Esprit du temps* (Paris: Grasset).

312

Since work is now carried on by teams, in factories and laboratories, scientific discoveries and technical inventions result very often from a creative cooperation which demands from each member of the team a disinterested attitude and a spirit of give and take.[1]

Finally, the modern techniques of transmitting information allow individuals to take an interest in men and events throughout the whole world. Science, television, literature, music and film cross national frontiers, which tend to be increasingly unimportant. Louis Armand considers that, in a technological civilization, 'international cooperation becomes more and more imperative', and that 'everything urges us towards sharing on a planetary scale'.[2]

In other words, *a world civilization in which individuals, feeling their unity, and no longer hounded by need or crushed by work, could become autonomous and creative* – this is the wonderful prospect which technology offers.

However, we need only look around us to see that we are still far from this golden age. What, in fact, does a technological civilization offer us in the mid twentieth century? Sprawling towns in which the air is polluted, vast business enterprises and impersonal government departments, a Press and radio that exploit the lowest human sentiments and the most vulgar tastes of the public, and colossal sums of money spent in preparing the most monstrous kind of war;[3] everywhere, anguish and increasing mental illness, and the general retreat of democracy in the face of totalitarianism and dictatorship. It is this hostile and menacing face which our technological universe presents.

We have the right to ask then, *why it is that technology, which could liberate the individual and break down barriers in the world, contributes, on the contrary, to the alienation of man.*

Technology as a Factor in Alienation

Ever since the eighteenth century, but especially in the nineteenth and twentieth centuries, scientific and technical discoveries have provoked a decline of the old religious, moral and

1. Louis Armand, Michel Drancourt, *Plaidoyer pour l'avenir* (Paris: Calmann-Lévy).
2. Ibid., pp. 97, 225.
3. Gaston Bouthoul, in *Sauver la guerre* (Paris: Grasset), speaks of a *quaternary sector*, that of destructiveness.

social values. In the words of Jacques Ellul, they have eliminated the sacred from the world.

Unfortunately, *man has made technology sacred*. Instead of being treated as a means to make life more human, it has become an end in itself. The objects created by technology – whose workings are not understood by most consumers – have become mysterious, the objects of a new cult. The occupation of a technician has a quasi-religious attraction. Like the priests of the ancient civilizations, the technocrats, physicists, engineers and economists constitute a ruling class which dominates the ignorant masses by its mysterious knowledge, its power and its high rewards.

The development of technology has given rise to a new morality. Useful research, submission to the needs of production and output, concern with quantity and efficiency have become the *virtues* of the new morality, the *technological morality*. On the other hand, disinterested research, art, poetry, philosophical thought, etc., have become the new mortal sins. Professor Roubault, of the faculty of sciences in the University of Nancy, boasts of feeling a real contempt for the human sciences: 'What is needed above all,' he writes, are 'genuine mathematicians, physicists, chemists, biologists and geologists, and *nothing else*.[1] All the rest is only dangerous and sterile palaver.'[2] As Jacques Ellul has shown very well, the technological totalitarianism which already exercises such a strong religious and moral influence is insinuating itself into our family life, leisure and education. Technological totalitarianism dominates political life itself and threatens the liberty of the citizen; propaganda, even in the democratic countries, makes abundant use of radio, television and the Press, and increasingly conditions the electorate; moreover, the police employ more and more advanced techniques for discovering opponents of the régime. By being placed in the service of the state and of ideologies, technology has become even more threatening.

The combination of *technology–state–ideology* constitutes a *super-Absolute* which aims to dominate the world and eliminate its opponents. It is in the name of this collective super-Absolute, raised to a tyrannical god, and disregarding the profound needs

1. Our italics.
2. Marcel Roubault in *Le Monde*, 20 November 1958.

of individuals, that the state formulates its plans for expansion. Like other religions, technology promises a paradise for the individual, a paradise which is no longer in heaven, but on earth, in the future. 'Let us take an interest in the future rather than the present,' Louis Armand proposes.[1] Later on we shall at last attain the golden age of the 'tertiary civilization' of which Fourastié dreams, or the communist paradise of which Marxist materialism dreams. In the meantime, men alienated by the new religion must be patient, bear their sufferings, and actively prepare their own virtual destruction.

In order to help resign the alienated masses to the failure of the golden age, an immediately tangible form of happiness is promised – *that which is acquired by possession of the material goods which technology produces.* The acquisition of a new car, a new gadget, a new object has become the religion, the goal of life of the majority of individuals in the rich nations.

Sustained by advertising, the modern cult of novelty allows the individual to escape, through his desires, from a meaningless present. Once granted that technological man cannot find a means of expressing himself in the abstract, bureaucratic, mechanized and subdivided work of large factories and offices, the attraction of an object to be acquired and the mystical conviction that its acquisition will bring happiness gives a semblance of purpose to his working day. In the words of G. Friedmann, 'the individual, unsatisfied as a producer, tries to find satisfaction as a consumer'.[2]

There is another cult which has also been engendered by the conditions of work in a technological civilization: leisure, which is opposed to work, has become an object of worship. 'The real life of many workers can only be lived in leisure time,' Friedmann writes. But *how can a man who is alienated in his work rediscover himself in his leisure time?* He does not know how to live in the present, to meditate, or to create. For those few who spend their leisure in reading, in educating themselves, in pursuing a hobby, how many are there who are simply bored and kill time in passive distractions which reinforce the alienation created by work? In France – the land of culture – fifty-eight per cent of individuals never open a book, and the majority of

1. Armand, op. cit.
2. Georges Friedmann, *Où va le travail humain?* (Paris: Gallimard).

the rest only read one or two books a year, for the most part detective stories and digests.

When he returns home in the evening, often after a long journey in an overcrowded train, the worker or clerk finds himself confronted with numerous chores, including the form-filling tasks which are multiplied by our bureaucratic society. But when he is finally free of his work and his social obligations, *the individual is supposed to pass* swiftly from a condition of alienation to one of creativity, from passivity to free activity. Many are incapable of this metamorphosis; for them, *alienating leisure follows alienating work.*

If only it were the case that, in this abdication of his individuality, modern man found at least a kind of happiness and relaxation! But it is not so. On the contrary, technological man lives in a state of extreme psychological tension. For many manual workers, work and reward are tied to the clock; production is based upon a competitive system; advertising creates a constant state of desire, and thus of tension, and the rivalry between individuals is carried to the limit of 'competitive display of purchasing power'.[1] The state of tension is accompanied by anxiety and is the cause of many psychosomatic illnesses. Not knowing how to employ his energies except in a life of excitement and tension, modern man no longer knows how to live in a state of relaxation; and so, by way of compensation, he searches passionately in his leisure time for this state of relaxation which he no longer experiences and which he identifies with happiness itself. Relaxation has become one of the absolutes to which modern man aspires most strongly. But genuine relaxation cannot be an object of desire. Genuine relaxation comes from living in a permanent condition of self-control and equilibrium, in working hours, in family life, and in leisure time. When relaxation becomes something *exceptional*, an ideal end, it becomes a new cause of tension. On the occasions when technological man could experience it, especially during leisure time and on his vacation, he is bored and worried. In order to get rid of his boredom and anxiety, he flees from them into new tension-producing activities: he frequents places where life is noisy and hectic, goes to the movies, reads magazines, drives his car or wanders round the shops where his desire to purchase is excited.

1. The phrase is from Georges Friedmann.

In other words, he plunges into useless activities and creates an illusion that his life is full and active.

But the *illusion of activity* is not the only one which sustains technological man. We have seen that technology, confusing adaptation and creation, gives individuals the illusion that they are creative. Only a minority, which G. Friedmann estimates at ten per cent of the personnel of an enterprise, is engaged in work which requires initiative; these are the supervisors and the technicians of the planning office. The rest (ninety per cent) are 'confined to the execution of specialized and subdivided tasks which are totally lacking in interest'.

Those who are aware of the illusions cherished by our technological civilization are harassed by doubt and indecision. What is to be done? Is it better to keep one's individuality, to exercise initiative, to be free and creative, and in consequence to live in relative poverty and without prestige? Or, on the contrary, to keep in step, to amass wealth, to succeed, by adapting oneself to the technological world? To reject social success, alienating work and stupefying distractions is to become an outlaw, to be cut off from one's milieu, to be alone. But every normal human being has a need *to be himself* and at the same time to be *connected with his milieu*. The feeling of isolation is a cause of profound sufferings, and it needs exceptional courage and a solidly based humanist faith to be able to live in opposition to industrial society. That is why so many abdicate and, in order to find security, live like everyone else and become resigned to their alienation.

There can be no doubt that the personality and the equilibrium of the individual are gravely threatened by technological civilization. Must we conclude that the only solution is to return to the life of pre-industrial society? But such a return presupposes that these societies produced a relatively happy and free humanity; and history, with its record of individual misery, of religious, civil and foreign wars, shows us that this is not so. Those who make technology *directly* responsible for the alienation of modern man forget that man has always been more or less alienated, that he has never been the autonomous individual in harmony with the world that he ought to be. *A humanity composed of free men, related creatively to each other and to the world, has still to be achieved*; the development of technology gives a special cast to alienation in the present, but technology is not directly responsible for it. In truth, technological man is not, as is often supposed, a new species, regarded as *superior* by some, and as *inferior* by others. In actuality, man, who conceived this technology, has remained *the same* as he was before. Today as yesterday, man passes the greater part of his life in pursuing illusory absolutes, dreams of paradise, prestige and power; in worshipping idols and leaders; in venerating some men and despising others; in loving only to hate afterwards; in escaping from real freedom and its risks, as Erich Fromm[1] has shown, in order to find the warm security of conforming with the ways of the herd.

Certainly, technology has freed many workers from exhausting tasks and has lightened their sufferings; but their souls have remained enslaved. Technology has not, therefore, 'depersonalized' man; it has only made his alienation more blatant. Technology is neither a beneficent divinity nor a maleficent fiend. It is not an absolute to worship, or an anti-absolute to fight. Such absolutism is the cause of all fanaticism, including technological fanaticism. Actual, existing man has always been ready, through ignorance, to sacrifice himself and to suffer for future man, and to live in the illusion of a celestial or terrestrial paradise. *Technology has become today the new support for this old absolutist and emotional mentality*. Thus, instead of being the means of liberation which it could be, technology has become a new means of enslavement.

Technology would be harmless, or even beneficial, if used by men liberated from their passions; but used by alienated man, it threatens the existence of the individual, of civilization and of the human race itself. The real problem is to know whether the possibilities of liberty, creativity and generosity, which are dormant in everyone, will one day be able to express themselves fully, and whether man can finally become himself. The fundamental problem of man is therefore independent of the problem of technology.

It is necessary, as Jacques Ellul has observed, to demystify

1. See in this connexion the works of Erich Fromm, especially *Escape from Freedom* (New York: Holt, Rinehart & Winston, 1941); *Man for Himself* (New York: Holt, Rinehart & Winston, 1947; London: Routledge & Kegan Paul); *The Sane Society* (New York: Holt, Rinehart & Winston, 1955; London: Routledge & Kegan Paul).

technology and to stop worshipping it as a divinity. But this is not enough. *Man himself must be freed from alienation.* As we saw at the beginning of this study, technology is not *simply* the expression of an alienated consciousness. It is also the expression of a free and creative consciousness which exists in a more or less stifled way alongside the alienated consciousness. The desire to provide a decent material existence for all, to free men from tedious or exhausting jobs, to prolong human life, to create new objects – all these are sensible aspirations. If technology became a *means* instead of an *end*, if it served existing man, it would promote a harmonious synthesis between individuals and their milieu, would become human again and would create a human universe. 'If respect for man is established in the hearts of men,' wrote Saint-Exupéry, 'then men will eventually succeed in constructing a political, social and economic system which consecrates this respect.'

What lesson should humanist socialism draw from the preceding analysis?

In the first place, a genuinely human socialism could not limit its reforms to change in the economic system. It would have to reconsider the uses of technology. In fact, in all economic systems machinery and technology tend to draw men into the path of alienation (the myth of record production, abstract relations of the individual to his work, creation of artificial needs, etc.). A human socialism would strive to remove this alienated character in the use of technology, but, still more, to free man completely from his alienation, through an appropriate ethical code and through psycho-analysis.

Similarly, a humanist socialism could not rely upon history to decide the fate of mankind. *To act in accordance with the trend of history* is to leave the way open for the forces of passion, individual or collective – to arouse new tensions and antagonisms, to accept the enslavement of the individual by technology, to believe that struggle and oppression will give birth, through some mysterious dialectic and by the sacrifice of millions of lives, to free and creative individuals and a healthy society.

But to speak frankly: *machinery and technology have a natural tendency to enslave man, and they are likely to become just as dangerous enemies as the most inhuman type of capitalism.*

The technological milieu is like a new system of cultivation introduced into a region which is suddenly attacked by a parasite which destroys the hopes of the farmers.

Human alienation, like such a parasite (lust for power, egoism, avarice, social climbing, conformism), has found in the technological milieu, in all societies, a new means of sustenance and a particularly favourable field of expansion.

It follows that humanist socialism cannot be limited to changing the property system, but must educate young people to develop freely their personal qualities, and must seek to change the ancient pattern of human relationships. Once these relationships have become fraternal and productive (small and responsible collectivities, work groups, autonomy of the workers), there will be no need to fear the use of technology, for it will be controlled by reason, by friendship, by the rejection of alienation, by the need for a creative life and the love of culture. Technology will then contribute to the prosperity of a fully human socialist system.

Translated by T. B. Bottomore

V. ON PRACTICE

NORMAN THOMAS

⊚ ⊚

Humanistic Socialism and the Future

NORMAN THOMAS is best known for his leadership of the American Socialist Party, which he joined during the First World War because he believed it was the only organization realistically facing the problems of war and the need for economic change. He campaigned for the Presidency of the United States six times on the Socialist ticket and also ran for the Mayor of New York City and the Governor of New York State. Among his books are *The Conscientious Objector in America; War, No Profit, No Glory, No Need; A Socialist's Faith;* and *Great Dissenters*. Chairman of the Post War World Council and the Labor Research Institute and a member of many committees including the National Committee for a Sane Nuclear Policy, and the Workers' Defense League, Mr Thomas was born in 1884 and until the First World War served as a pastor in Harlem. He founded and edited *The World Tomorrow* and was one of the organizers of the Civil Liberties Bureau, which became the American Civil Liberties Union.

If by socialism one understands a highly collective economy with a great deal of government planning and control, sweetened by much welfare legislation, then it is virtually inevitable. It is the logical extension of present developments – always assuming that we do not destroy ourselves in war. If by socialism one understands a fraternal society of free men, managing for their common good the natural resources and the marvellous tools at their command, socialism is far from inevitable.

Not even the election of Senator Barry Goldwater would have seriously checked the present drift towards a vulgar socialism or, more accurately, towards a social order of a garrison state with welfare features. If the cold war should soon subside, as is quite improbable, what we might achieve by drift would be a welfare state capitalism (rather than true socialism) with a tender regard not for the 'free enterprise' it would verbally honour, but for a maximum preservation of private profit, in a managed economy.

All the outstanding developments of this century make a return to anything like a true *laissez-faire* economy impossible. In my own now remote youth when I was taught this economy it was already the victim of the private collectivism of the great corporations which it had bred. Today, it is elementary to say that the population explosion, war and the war economy, automation and the exhaustion of easily obtainable natural resources, including water, require a degree of over-all planning and integration in the economic process inconceivable to Adam Smith. We are on the verge of a possible economy of abundance very different from anything possible in the past history or experience of the human race. Man has made the scientific discoveries and technical inventions necessary for the production of abundance. They have brought him to the threshold of a conquest of space inconceivable as late as the beginning of the Second World War. But in affluent America we still have forty to fifty million persons living below a decent standard of subsistence and in the whole world two-thirds of mankind subsisting within a narrow margin between hunger and starvation. The outlook for a better future is clouded by the alarming increase of population as well as by the follies and gross inadequacies of our political and economic systems. They still point towards war, and, even if it is avoided, we are not assured of the conquest of poverty, illiteracy and disease.

No serious thinker or writer dares to propose that we can use our scientific and technical mastery over natural energy and resources for the solution of these problems except by authoritative planning, requiring, for many years to come, increased governmental control and, probably, ownership. Moreover, a good life for mankind can never be attained or maintained unless in important respects our planning and controls are world-wide, rather than inspired by the now dominant religion of nationalism.

An observer, noting only or chiefly the breathtaking achievements of men in mastery of physical energy and material things, might be astonished at our general and pervasive lack of elation and confidence in our kind. Our literature, arts and daily conversation express at the worst a sort of contempt for ourselves, and a doubt of our rationality. We are passengers on a ship of fools. We pursue happiness, mostly in vain, in the pleasures of the senses. We try to escape by wallowing in sexuality. Utopia has no place in our atlas. For us there is no heavenly vision.

Like all sweeping generalizations, this ignores important exceptions and modifications. But it is true enough to be profoundly disturbing to those of us who remember a higher self-appraisal by our kind. Part of the trouble is the amazing contrast between our mastery of natural forces and our mastery of ourselves and our institutions; part of it is a revulsion from two world wars, while we prepare frantically for a third; part of it is the decline of religious faith and spiritual authority, even as we build more and more churches and temples.

Nevertheless, I do not think that our failure with ourselves and our social institutions is so complete as to compel us to apathy, cynicism and despair. In my lifetime, despite our wars and hates, we have made social progress along many lines, even if it has been so far overbalanced by our progress in command of natural forces. And that progress has been due in large part to the conscious or unconscious power of socialist thinking and organization.

This is not the current faith. As I travel in our beautiful country, addressing many audiences, especially in our colleges and universities, I find from the questions I always encourage after speaking, and from other contacts, singularly little disposition to challenge my criticisms on a moral or humanistic basis or to dispute my warnings concerning our future if we drift. What is alleged is that somehow individual freedom will perish with capitalism – nowadays usually and inaccurately called 'free enterprise'.

This semantic affection for freedom reveals a certain degree of conscience. In my younger days the great argument was that capitalism was the only way to get production, but now capitalism as such is seldom praised, but rather 'freedom', a freedom defined by one college lad as 'my right to try to be as rich as Paul Getty'. Not for him a concern for a society which would give equality of legal right and, so far as possible, opportunity to every man regardless of race, creed or colour; not for him

Milton's passion for the right 'to know, to argue and to utter', above all other rights.

This persistent identification of freedom with the right of strong or lucky men to make great profit out of absentee ownership, or out of management and exploitation of other men's labour, is part of the sickness of our times. It is true that we can have a generally socialist economy under an excessively authoritarian, even a totalitarian, state. From this fact derives my opposition to communism. It is true that nations under socialist governments, e.g. Great Britain and the Scandinavian countries, have not achieved utopia or a perfect balance between the one and the many, but they have released rather than further enslaved the common man.

Rather than allege that socialism would end freedom, my questioners more often profess or imply a profound disbelief that man, the individual, can do anything of importance to avert war or make the whole world a fraternity of free men who will use our marvellous powers for general abundance, for life, not death. The difficulties they raise are real and great, but too largely our generation takes them as a foreordained defeat, not as a challenge. It is the kind and degree of defeat which for more or less fortunate individuals can be indefinitely assuaged by material abundance and sexuality. The one danger they care about arises from a communist devil, not to be analysed and understood, but only to be feared and hated, against which they can be defended only by emulating in some degree his anti-libertarian policies and the endless piling up of weapons of obliteration. It is in this atmosphere that humanistic socialism must live and work. It is to this atmosphere that it must provide an alternative. Its supporters may not proclaim certain victory, but neither can its pessimistic critics prove that forces beyond man's control doom us to suicide.

In the face of this situation, what is required of humanistic socialism? On its positive programme, it must steadily strive to preserve and improve its good record of concern for the individual man, his civil liberties, his place in democracy, his right to adequate educational and health facilities provided by society. It will recognize that, while it must provide and use a strong state, the state must always exist for man, not man for the state; that good government demands more than universal suffrage; that it requires the existence of balancing forces of real strength – labour unions, professional societies, cooperatives, etc. – which are not puppets of the state. And it must be able to deal with the population explosion in terms of regard for the individual in the present context of bitter poverty.

It is much easier to write the foregoing paragraph than to carry out its principles. The machinery of democracy cannot be quite the same in urban and rural societies or in the age of automation, as in earlier stages of the industrial revolution. The American Constitution has served us fairly well; its separation of powers between the Federal and State governments, and among the legislative, executive and judicial powers, has not paralysed action. But the bad record of Congress in recent years begins to challenge that statement. It can do much by reforming its own procedures and by establishing a higher degree of each party's responsibility to its own professed platform. Perhaps some constitutional amendment will be in order. This must be a major concern for socialist consideration.

Socialism ought to be enormously aided in winning men's loyalty because men have reached the threshold of an economy of abundance, as against the economy of scarcity characteristic of the past. This economy, thanks to cybernetics, will make hard, repetitive, assembly-line work, manual and mental, far less necessary. While we should rejoice in these facts, easy satisfaction is impossible, because in our own country we have not found the way to distribute abundance, or to manage the unemployment and the leisure associated with the rapid progress of automation, while the vast majority of the world's people live in nations destitute of the capital goods essential for the production of abundance. In their poverty and ignorance they continue the population explosion which threatens any desirable future. Humanistic socialism must deal with this situation in terms of programmes, going beyond sermons on the beauty of fraternity.

Historically, socialism has been largely based on the doctrine of class conflict and the appeal to the 'working class', but in our present situation that appeal is by no means adequate. Logically, there is a recognizable division between all workers of all types and the owners of the tools and facilities and resources these workers must use in order to live. But various facts make it difficult to organize a humanistic socialist movement almost solely along the lines of this division. Here are some of the reasons:

(a) Historically men have not been united for action only – or even chiefly – by economic class but rather by association in tribes, city-states and nations. Often the outstanding sense of fellowship has been among those who professed the same religion. It is one thing to argue that a dominant economic élite has repeatedly manipulated these loyalties to its own advantage, but this does not prove the primacy of the class struggle.

(b) While the workers of the world may have had nothing to lose but their chains, historically there has been an enormous difference in the weight of these chains in various countries, and between different classes of workers within each nation. In the U.S., thanks quite largely to the trade unions, which have been a class weapon, organized labour has its own organized place in society; many of its members belong to some degree also to an owning class, by reason not merely of ownership of their own homes, but of capitalistic shares of stocks. Collectively the unions have huge resources in stocks and bonds. Despite their well-advertised faults, unions are invaluable to the workers and indeed to any healthy society. But they do not represent the majority of the workers and they can hardly be considered as the surrogate for mankind in the struggle for justice and fraternity. Humanistic socialism needs very urgently to win them to its support, but it cannot be based simply upon that support.

Humanistic socialism therefore cannot escape the ethical appeal to the human family. In some sense it must speak to men's needs as consumers more than producers – especially in the coming age of automation – and its appeal must exalt the great intangibles of peace and fraternity.

Implicit in all this is the recognition of socialism's duty to deal better with such great problems as: control of automation for the general good; democracy in industry – and in the unions – as well as in the political state; the role of management – a factor not to be completely identified with ownership – in the processes of production and distribution; and, above all, the economics and politics of our garrison state. We shall not be able to deal satisfactorily with this last problem while we depend upon peace through balance of terror. And this consideration leads to an affirmation that the supreme business of socialism must be with peace. No longer can we choose between peace or freedom. We must win and preserve freedom in peace. Liberty will not rise from the awful wastes of nuclear war to walk serenely with its miserable survivors among the corpses of the dead and the agonies of the dying.

None of these great problems will be solved simply by a vast extension of public ownership by a mighty state. Yet socialism should still demand extensions of social ownership with the government as agent – which socialist ownership, be it noted, is not synonymous with nationalization. Modern democratic socialists want to extend public ownership, but they by no means believe it necessary or desirable for government – even a socialist government – to own all the means of production and distribution. Controls necessary to the public interest can be established through labour legislation, taxation, etc. There will be a place for the mechanism of price and profit. Cooperatives of both producers and consumers should play a large role under democratic socialism. There should be a place for individual initiative which can be variously encouraged.

Bearing these facts in mind, how far should public ownership be extended in America? Priority in extending it depends in part upon special conditions including the state of public opinion and the particular plans under discussion. Acquisition should be by purchase, because it would be unfair arbitrarily to expropriate some owners without compensation, leaving others to exist as before. Moreover, expropriation invites violence and strife far more costly than compensation. Socialism, however, should be on guard against unloading on the government bankrupt or nearly bankrupt public utilities. It is grimly amusing that the state, the target for the arrows of conservative critics, is accepted by many of them as the essential saviour of ill-run or ill-fated enterprises such as the British coal mines and railroads.

What then should be socially owned? Certainly the natural resources which should be the common possession of mankind. In our country the federal government is in by far the best position to organize socially owned coal, iron or oil industries, but state governments must participate in working out plans, because they own much of the land where minerals exist, and because they depend on land taxation to provide funds for education and other necessary functions.

Large forests and acreages of reforested land should be socially owned and socially used not only for lumber and wood products but for protection against floods.

As for the surface of the earth, man's desire for a piece of land he can call his own is deeply rooted and widespread. Private ownership of land, with exceptions I have mentioned, should therefore be permitted, but on the basis of occupancy and use. It is axiomatic that the rental value of land is a social creation. I may let my lot go to ragweed, but I can get far more for it than my friend who has cultivated his garden if my lot is located near a town or city. I think socialists might well adopt Henry George's principle that the rental value of land, apart from improvements, belongs to society and should be taxed accordingly.

The tax, however, should not be a single tax. Government revenues at all levels should be principally derived from three major sources: a tax on land rather than improvements to it, a very heavy inheritance tax, and income tax. Of course, there can be taxation of a sort that hurts consumers unfairly. I think this is true in general of sales taxes and I suppose there can be taxation of a sort which will unduly inhibit economic initiative by reducing incentive. This might be true of badly devised income taxes but in America I worry less about that than about the escape of excessive wealth from a fair burden of taxes. Very heavy inheritance taxes properly adjusted to the care of widows and minor children would be an expression of social justice that would not unduly paralyse incentive. I doubt many fathers work principally in order that their descendants may not have to.

To public ownership of natural resources I should add public utilities, certainly those which serve us best as monopolies or near-monopolies. The system of ownership should be flexible, allowing for extension both of the T.V.A. type of enterprise, and of the existing rural electrification.

My next candidate for public ownership would be an industry like steel. It is basic to our economy and it is currently in the hands of an oligopoly which manages to administer prices with little or no regard for competition.[1]

Perhaps even more than urging public ownership, socialism

1. These few paragraphs on what should be owned are condensations and partial quotations from my recent book, *Socialism Re-examined* (New York: Norton, 1963).

must challenge the way in which national income is divided among the people. The noblest ideal would be the Marxist theory 'from each according to his capacity, to each according to his needs'. I have been sceptical of the practicality of that ideal, but am now beginning to wonder, along with Robert Theobald, whether automation may not drive us to something very like it, since the provision of jobs in an economy of abundance may become in many ways so difficult.

Let me repeat my conviction that social ownership cannot be a cure-all. It will leave us face-to-face with problems of the role of unions, the relations of management and men, and the effective application of democracy to industry, matters on which socialism has been inclined to mark time. Properly thought-out taxation and the proper control of money and currency also fall into the category of problems requiring further exploration by humanistic socialism.

But let me also repeat that my belief is that socialism's most pressing concern must be with the problem of survival in the nuclear age. Peace by deterrence or balance of terror will someday collapse by accident, passion, miscalculation or design. Meanwhile, the enormous expenditure of the arms race imposes upon us very largely the economy, politics and standards of civil liberty appropriate to a garrison state. It becomes essential to any system seeking the support of thoughtful men to find an alternative to war.

Here socialism ought to be a greater force than it has been, although I think it can be fairly said that statements of the Socialist International and certainly of the American Socialist Party in its 1962 platform have been far the best political utterances on the subject of peace. Democratic socialism wants to win by non-violent methods, and that requires the utilization of machinery of political action in existing states. It is, therefore, not strange that, to quote Paul Henry Spaak, 'the thing socialists have learned to nationalize best is socialism'. It has not, however, forgotten internationalism; it can and should develop not only an opposition to the religion of the absolute sovereign national state, but an alternative to it through a world federation. However, we must relinquish the notion that socialism, victorious in nation after nation, will automatically bring peace. Its principles must consciously be applied on an international rather than a national scale, if it is best to serve humankind. In a world that has seen the rise and the tactics of communism, and the extent of the religion of nationalism, the old easy doctrine that capitalism is the sole cause of war, and socialism its sure and only cure, cannot stand. Socialism must develop a conscious programme for peace.

More than that, it must recover its old dynamic. How that can be done and what political tactics it can most wisely use are questions lying beyond the scope of this article. Humanistic socialism cannot live on its rich heritage. It can only draw wisdom and courage from that heritage to press on.

WOLFGANG ABENDROTH

⊚ ⊚

Planning and the Classless Society

WOLFGANG ABENDROTH, born in Wuppertal-Elberfeld, Germany, in 1906, studied and practised law in the courts of Germany until 1933. In Bern, he completed his studies for the Doctor of Law degree but was imprisoned in 1937 because of illegal activities against the Third Reich. At the end of the Second World War, he entered the Ministry of Justice in Brandenburg and the German Administration of the Soviet Zone of Occupation. He is now professor of law at the University of Marburg-an-der-Lahn and has taught at the Universities of Halle, Leipzig, Jena, and at the College for Social Sciences in Wilhelmshaven. In 1961 he was expelled from the S.P.D. because of his support of the German Socialist Student Union. He is a member of the executive committee of the German Socialist Union and author of *German Trade Unions, Bureaucratic Administration and Social Democracy* and *The Rise and Crisis of German Social Democracy*.

The Problem of Administration and Planning under Organized Capitalism

Organized capitalism grew directly from liberal capitalism, spurred by the *concentration and centralization of capital*[1] as well as by accelerated technological development, which served to expand productivity.[2] *Imbedded* in organized capitalism is the problem of the relationship between planning and economic administration (and also between management and economic

1. [Marx, *Capital*, Kerr edn. The references are to the following sections in Vol. III, Ch. 5, 'Economics in the Employment of Constant Capital'; Part III, 'The Law of the Falling Tendency of the Rate of Profit'; and Ch. 27, 'The Role of Credit in Capitalist Production'. – *Translator*]
2. [Ibid.; the reference is to the note by Engels which appears on pp. 508–9. – *Translator*]

administration). The earliest development of organized capitalism was already distinguished by the rise of limited-liability corporations and of joint stock companies in the place of single
entrepreneurs.

> Capital, which rests on a socialized mode of production and pre-
> supposes a social concentration of means of production and
> labour-powers, is here directly endowed with the form of social
> capital (a capital of directly associated individuals) as distin-
> guished from private capital, and its enterprises assume the form
> of social enterprises as distinguished from individual enterprises.
> Social capital is the abolition of capital as private property within
> the boundaries of capitalist production itself.[1]

Thus the owner of capital becomes 'a mere owner, a mere
money capitalist', and the actual functioning capitalist becomes
'a mere *manager*' (in contemporary terminology, a member of
management), who 'receive[s] . . . a mere wage for a certain kind
of skilled labour, the price of which is regulated in the labour
market like that of any other *labour*'.[2]

Furthermore, 'the wages of superintendence, for both the
commercial and the industrial manager, appear completely
separated from the profits of enterprise in the cooperative factories of the labourers as well as in capitalistic stock companies'.[3]
Since 'a numerous class of industrial and commercial superin-
tendents was formed . . . even the last pretext for the confusion
in matters of profit of enterprise and wages of management was
removed; in theory, mere surplus value, a value for which no
equivalent was paid, realized unpaid labour'.[4] Similarly, 'above
the actual director [is placed] a board of managers or directors,
for whom superintendence and management serve in reality
only as a pretext for plundering stock holders and amassing
wealth'.[5] This system is *prima facie* 'a mere phase of transition to
a new form of production'.[6] Also,

> it establishes a monopoly in certain spheres and thereby chal-
> lenges the interference of the state. It reproduces a new aristo-
> cracy of finance, a new sort of parasite in the shape of promoters,
> speculators and merely nominal directors; a whole system of
> swindling and cheating by means of corporation juggling, stock-

1. Ibid., p. 516.   2. Ibid., pp. 516–17.
3. Ibid., p. 456.   4. Ibid., p. 458.
5. Ibid., p. 458.   6. Ibid., p. 519.

jobbing and stock speculation. It is private production within the control of private property.[1]

This altered system, however, immediately expands the *sphere* of planning, first by enlarging, and then by the automatic combining of enterprises. 'The opposition between the organization of production in the single factory and the anarchy of production in the whole of society'[2] is *eliminated* in the combines, e.g. the trusts; the problem is, as it were, pushed back. 'In the trusts, freedom of competition changes into its very opposite – into monopoly; and the production without any definite plan of capitalistic society capitulates to the production upon a definite plan of the invading socialist society. Certainly this is so far still to the benefit and advantage of the capitalists.'[3] Thus 'the capitalist relationship is *not* abolished'.[4] The scope of planning is expanding but profit remains the goal of planning. The abstractly theoretical hostility to planning, however, has lost all sense and motivation. Where, from the social standpoint of management, it is still asserted, its only function is that of an ideology arising from the objectivity of social consciousness; it assumed the character of cynical manipulation which shows itself in the regular activity of management. This managerial activity shows itself first in the sphere of organizing internal production and distribution of the specific economic combination; secondly, in the differentiation (formally still mediated through the market) from other economic structures which always shows anew that its field is still only 'the market' in the old sense *cum grano salis*, while only a moment before it was based on pure competition. There are numerous *agreements* of suppression of small and middle productive, distributive and credit enterprises which, while retaining formal and juridical independence, lose the possibility of economic self-determination and free development. Alongside of this are *power agreements* with other great combines which, only in the intermediate stages of the power struggle, use simple competition as transitional to the appropriation of the motive forces of the earlier markets.

1. Ibid., p. 519.
2. [Engels, 'Herr Eugen Dühring's Revolution in Science', *Anti-Dühring*, Kerr edn, p. 296. – *Translator*]
3. Ibid., p. 289.
4. Ibid., p. 290.

Third and finally, management is always differentiated from the state, the communes and the necessary organs of political determination to prevent the use of public power and to employ it in its own interest.[1] But all three spheres of public activity have evidently very little in common with 'free enterprise' in the sense of the liberal capitalistic world.

Since the planning of organized capitalism is determined by that organized sector of the economy which is taken as the starting point, its inner contradictions are sharpened. Therefore, in spite of the internationalization of production, national boundaries (or combinations, such as the Common Market) are usually arranged to be able to influence the public struggle. Furthermore, just as many countries find that their many-sided reciprocal economic spheres overlap, so too their respective planning goals are sharply contradictory, and their reciprocal agreements are most *unstable* (e.g. their agreements to limit production artificially, or to divide markets or spheres of capital investments among themselves). At the same time these agreements can break up because of *the law of uneven development*, as Ernest Mandel shows in his detailed examination of many examples of political planning (and their consequences) of a great number of European and American combines and cartels between the world wars and since the Second World War.[2] Therefore, from a long-range international perspective, international planning in no way lessens the inner contradictions of the capitalist mode of production (and thus the danger of crises).

That the struggle for power is determined by economic crises in the form of political crises was first described theoretically by Rudolf Hilferding in 1910.[3] Currently, George W. F. Hallgarten,[4] by a careful study of extensive empirical data, proves that the tendency of governments to pursue an imperialistic foreign policy (and to issue warlike statements) has not changed, particularly when a top-level *mobilization order* can guarantee their

1. Cf. the descriptions, still valid except for details, in Rudolf Hilferding, *Das Finanzkapital* (East Berlin, 1947), p. 238 ff., and Fritz Naphtali, *Wirtschaftsdemokratie* (Berlin, 1928), p. 23 ff.

2. Ernest Mandel, *Traité d'économie marxiste*, Vol. II (Paris, 1962), p. 63 ff.

3. Rudolf Hilferding, op. cit., p. 408 ff. and p. 517.

4. George W. F. Hallgarten, *Der Imperialismus vor 1914*, 2 vols. (Munich, 1951; 2nd edn, 1962).

business and risk-free profit[1] which would otherwise be threatened by the danger of recession or crisis. As a result of the unproductivity of public expenditures brought about by organized capitalism, strong *inflationary* tendencies arise which, in turn, accelerate the tendency to instability. Thus, the modern state, which rests on the foundation of an advanced capitalist society, is increasingly forced to choose between economic crises and permanent direct subsidy of *the value of money*. It thereby repeatedly expropriates the reserve capital of its lower and middle strata.[2] The basis for the budget proposed but not fully revealed by the late President Kennedy was necessitated (despite massive rearmament) by the high rate of unemployment (currently 5.9 per cent).[3]

Under such circumstances, organized capitalism's management inevitably sanctions, in its own interest, a transition from merely occasional state intervention to simultaneous state administration, by the distribution of public funds, of an expanding sector of the social product.[4] In armaments capitalism, the main beneficiary of this public expenditure is the group of great combines of organized capitalism. However, it is precisely this use of public funds to secure the relatively long-lasting stability of the special sector which makes it possible for other groups, depending on their strength, to bring pressure for concessions of a welfare-state type. Thus, workers become involved in political controversy over pay (or other working conditions, e.g. working time), and relatively favourable compromises are secured on questions of social legislation.[5]

This administrative tendency to compromise prevails only with management's influential privileges in government and its control of the economic balance of power, and obviously comes to an end during severe recessions. The tendency then becomes

1. Cf. the extensive materials on the political economy of the advanced capitalist countries after the Second World War and their close connexion with armaments in Ernest Mandel, op. cit., p. 178 ff.
2. Ibid., p. 187; cf. also 'Defense Industry Lacks Plans for Civilian Production', *New York Times* (International Edition), 24 August 1963, p. 5.
3. Mandel, op. cit., p. 192 ff.
4. Ibid., p. 191.
5. Ibid., p. 199 ff.; cf. also Eduard Marz, *Die Marxsche Wirtschaftslehre im Widerspruch der Meinungen* (Vienna, 1959), p. 211 ff. and p. 222 ff.

retrogressive and can suddenly turn from the mere *administration of preparedness* to a drive for open *war planning*.[1] In that event, liberal capitalism's ideological taboo against planning is sloughed off; planning holds no terror for management of organized capitalism because, in its experience, modern war (even when it is not atomic)[2] can be prepared for and conducted only by means of total planning in conjunction with an economy based on scarcity and consumer rationing.

Under the given circumstances, as was proved by the behaviour of German combines during the Second World War,[3] management is prepared to push forward the expansion of centralized production by combining primitive plunder with every additional violation of humanity that suits its purpose. It is typical of the mentality of the great powers influenced by management that, when it became politically opportune to turn from right to 'grace', the situation at the end of the Second World War prevented neither amnesty nor the return of their property to those industrial leaders who were accessories to such acts of horror. The readiness to support immediate war planning means (since the example of the Third Reich) the potential readiness for complicity in a plan whose concrete content is systematized barbarism.[4]

The tendency to 'total' war preparedness gives rise to greater difficulties primarily because the anticipation of immediate profits results in the development of *overcapacity*[5] which cannot be fully utilized. It thus becomes a threat to profits and leads to recession and the consequent breakdown of equilibrium. This strengthens the presupposition that the technical revolution of the twentieth century, predominantly in research and development, could have been (and was) brought about only by the total economic might of the advanced capitalist countries and not by the efficiency of an individual trust. Thus, during the First World War, it was owing to the German government's war

1. Mandel, op. cit., p. 182 ff.
2. Friedrich Lenz, *Wirtschaftsplanung* (Stuttgart, 1948), p. 69 ff.
3. Mandel, op. cit., p. 229 ff.
4. For material on the personnel in the war-planning apparatus of the Third Reich, see: Charles Bettelheim, *L'Économie sous le nazisme* (Paris, 1946), p. 121 ff.; Franz L. Neumann and A. Gartland, *Behemoth* (New York, 1944), p. 235 ff.; and Mandel, op. cit., p. 160 ff.
5. Mandel, op. cit., Vol. I, p. 438 ff. and p. 469 ff.

economy that the *chemical industry* expanded enormously and thereby developed far-reaching production of inorganic fertilizers and synthetic textiles. Thus, during the Second World War, it was due to the war planning of the United States that the prerequisites were developed for the utilization of *atomic energy* and radar technology (as prerequisites to the further development of automation).

This system can concede a relatively high standard of living (not voluntarily but only as a compromise in the class struggle). As a result, even an author like Jürgen Habermas, who eminently recognizes the cultural and socio-philosophical grounds of the system's irrationality,[1] nevertheless seems to postulate first, that the present state of affairs is permanent, stable and unthreatened;[2] and, second, that it has abolished the source of socio-psychological division. It is no accident that such an informed and acute observer of the current scene as Jürgen Habermas could be won over by the continuing economic progress of the German Federal Republic with its full employment and its almost completely contained socialist class consciousness.

Has it been forgotten that the 1929 crisis struck down just such a sense of stability and plunged the workers' standard of living to zero? Wasn't it inherent in that system to beget the Third Reich? Is the permanent structural unemployment in the United States a negligible quantity? Finally, isn't the impulse to alienation in this society, which Habermas[3] sees and whose origins he aptly explains, also determined in his view, by the *economic* structure? Doesn't it characteristically tend to transform economic into political catastrophes? Doesn't its latent power become glaringly obvious in its ever more naked and undisguised elevation of extreme barbarism to power? Isn't the key to the

1. Jürgen Habermas, *Theorie und Praxis* (Neuwied, 1963), p. 334 ff.
2. Ibid., p. 163 ff. Strange to say he doesn't raise the problem of the change in the cost of reproducing labour power as a result of high living standards based on present-day technology. This is replaced by the abstract question of the value-producing function of scientific research (p. 193). This posing of the problem becomes abstract in turn because the immanent-system writer consciously raises the question, not in terms of capitalist society, but of generic industrial society. He thereby overlooks the fact that for Marx the problem of value no longer exists in this sense in a developing socialist society. Cf. Marx, *Grundrisse der Kritik der politischen Oekonomie* (Berlin, 1953), p. 592 ff. and p. 599 ff.
3. Habermas, op. cit., p. 164.

problem of the relationship between the condition of the classes and the workers' class consciousness contained in Karl Marx's opposition to Lassalle's 'Iron Law of Wages'?:

> ... consequently, the system of wage labour is a system of slavery, and indeed of a slavery which becomes more severe in proportion as the social productive forces of labour develop, whether the worker receives better ... or worse payment. ... It is as if, among slaves who have at last got behind the secret of slavery and broken out in rebellion, a slave still in thrall to obsolete notions were to inscribe on the programme of the rebellion: slavery must be abolished because the feeding of slaves in the system of slavery cannot exceed a certain low maximum![1]

And is it true that proletarian class consciousness has disappeared in the *other* highly industrialized countries where, on the social basis of organized capitalism, the workers have at long last obtained a high standard of living – is it true in France, Finland, Belgium, England and North Italy?

The thinking of the ruling class has a different relationship indeed to organized capitalism than it formerly had to liberal capitalism, not only with regard to state intervention but also to managerialism and the formulation of planning. Intervention is no longer regarded as the devil's work. In the most advanced capitalist countries and their alliances (such as Union Minière and the European Common Market), managerialism and planning are recognized as the obvious over-all system, because of the threat of recessions and crises.

In the first place, however, it is conceded that the potential decision-makers of managerialism, with its eventual planning, are only in management, and its allied groups in political leadership, administration and the state apparatus. This is particularly evident in the formation of the European superstructures.[2] It is also evident in the amendments to the supplementary emergency constitution of the German Federal Republic,[3] which, in

1. Karl Marx, *Kritik des Gothaer Programms* (Berlin, 1946), p. 26. [Marx–Engels, *Selected Works*, Vol. II (Moscow: Foreign Languages Publishing House, 1962), *Critique of the Gotha Programme*, pp. 29–39. – *Translator*]

2. Cf. Wolfgang Abendroth, *Europäische Integration und demokratische Legitimation* (Aussenpolitik, 1952), p. 623 ff.

3. Cf. Jürgen Seifert, *Gefahr im Verzuge. Zur Problematik der Notstandsgesetzgebung* (Frankfurt-am-Main, 1963).

the event of internal unrest and the threat or outbreak of war, empowers the government to suspend all democratic rights and to impose total planning (particularly for scarcity and consumer rationing, but also for the militarization of labour).

Secondly, administrative measures of governments continue to be determined by the profit needs of the major economic enterprises and planning aims at the same goal, with all the irrationalities that flow from this. Organized capitalism's form of planning is necessarily irrational because it cannot formulate a rational guiding conception.

It is indeed fitting that even the political structure can be planned in this social system. But since such structural expenditures are viewed as costs that diminish profits, the organization of planning at times even lags behind the immediate needs of the production apparatus, instead of taking the lead in determining the standards for a rise in productivity, so that the participants in the socialized process of production may have meaningful, fulfilled lives.

It is thus necessary for the new productive forces which have been developed by atomic energy and automation to press for a stronger planning tendency at the same time that they threaten to make manual labour increasingly superfluous. (As in the United States today, advanced capitalism inherently produces a structural rise in unemployment and thereby disrupts its own equilibrium.[1] Far from succeeding, however, the attempt to overcome this by traditional means (and thereby to eliminate the rising dangers to the existing system) serves only to sidetrack the content of planning[2] solely to considerations of power and an irrational concentration on the profit motive of large individual enterprises and combinations. Such class privileges are no longer compatible with productive forces, whose constantly rising output of commodities leads to a constantly decreasing amount of socially necessary labour time.

The tendency towards producing the greatest increase in the means for satisfying *each* participant's needs along with the

1. Cf. Friedrich Pollock, *Sozialökonomische Auswirkungen der Automation und der Atomtechnik* (Politische Studien, 1957), p. 4 ff.; and Ludwig Freund, '*Krisen des Atomseitalters*', supplement to *Parlament* (8 March 1963), p. 36 ff.
2. Cf. Mandel, op. cit., Vol. II, p. 276 ff.

greatest increase in the free time available to him for self-development has as its objective not only a developing possibility but a *necessary* realization (otherwise even the use and administration of the equipment threatens to become impossible). The contradiction between the *form of total social planning* and the *limitations* imposed on it by organized capitalism for its own needs must be overcome. Organized capitalism has limited the planners to its own leading strata and has limited the plan to protecting the profit possibilities of its vast economic structures. The immediate necessity of our time is for mankind to eliminate these irrationalities, which give rise to the constant danger of self-annihilation.

The Problem of Planning in a Classless Society

The following well-known passage by Karl Marx comes to mind:

> No social order ever disappears before all the productive forces, for which there is room in it, have been developed; and new higher relations of production never appear before the material conditions of their existence have matured in the womb of the old society. Therefore, mankind always takes up only such problems as it can solve; since, looking at the matter more closely, we will always find that the problem itself arises only when the material conditions necessary for its solution already exist or are at least in the process of formation.[1]

It is clear that the meaning of the socialized labour process can only be its own freedom, *which* is made possible when its movement is determined by its associated cooperative members:

> In fact, the realm of freedom does not commence until the point is passed where labour under the compulsion of necessity and of external utility is required. In the very nature of things it lies beyond the sphere of material production in the strict meaning of the term. Just as the savage must wrestle with nature, in order to satisfy his wants, in order to maintain his life and reproduce it, so civilized man has to do it, and he must do it in all forms of society and under all possible modes of production. With his development the realm of natural necessity expands, because his wants increase; but at the same time the forces of production increase, by which these wants are satisfied. The freedom in this field cannot

1. Karl Marx, *Zur Kritik der politischen Oekonomie*, (Berlin, 1947), p. 14. [*Critique of Political Economy*, Kerr edn, pp. 12–13. – *Translator*]

consist of anything else but of the fact that socialized man, the associated producers, regulate their interchange with nature rationally, bring it under their common control, instead of being ruled by it as by some blind power; that they accomplish their task with the least expenditure of energy and under conditions most adequate to their human nature and most worthy of it. But it always remains a realm of necessity. Beyond it begins that development of human power, which is its own end, the true realm of freedom, which, however, can flourish only upon that realm of necessity as its basis. The shortening of the working day is its fundamental premise.[1]

Thus, the *content of planning* in a classless society is no longer determined by the abstractly rational aim of profits for single economic enterprises or trusts but, on the one hand, by the explicit and always concrete rationality whose goal is the humanization of the labour process as a means of subordinating it to the conscious aims of the associated working people, and, on the other hand, the greatest possible freeing of individuals *from the labour process* in order to secure the greatest possible measure of self-development for every member of society. Both moments of this unity are interdependent. Through the reduction of socially necessary labour time – by immediately shortening the working day, by expanding the scope and duration of education for young people, by increasing vacation time for all able-bodied producers, and by earlier retirement age – the individual's abilities and his impulse to apply them are so greatly expanded that constantly expanding abilities are brought into use in the scientific preparation and administration of the labour process of associated man. Consequently, productivity is so greatly developed and expanded that the universal satisfaction of needs and the further reduction in socially necessary labour time become possible.

Because of this dialectical determination a socially regulated educational system results whose task no longer is to develop 'the detail worker . . . crippled by life-long repetition of one and the same trivial operation' but the 'fully developed individual, fit for a variety of labours, ready to face any change of production, and to whom the different social functions he performs, are but so many modes of giving free scope to his own natural and

1. Karl Marx, *Das Kapital*, Vol. III, p. 954 ff. [Kerr edn. – *Translator*]

343

acquired powers'.[1] With such a broader increase in productivity, a social order arises in which the following principle becomes a reality: 'From each according to his capacity, to each according to his needs.'[2]

The problem of value, both in the old sense of the liberal capitalist market economy and in the modified sense of organized capitalism, is abolished. This can occur by means of all-round planning of the social labour process because the economy is no longer determined independently of, and contrary to, the will of the producers by the alienated law of the market, but rather by means of the rational and conscious decisions of associated mankind.[3] However,

> after the abolition of the capitalist mode of production, but with social production still in vogue, the determination of value continues to prevail in such a way that the regulation of the labour time and the distribution of the social labour among the various groups of production, also the keeping of accounts in connexion with this, become more essential than ever.[4]

Precisely these considerations lead to the consequence that even in a classless society only a *portion* of the *full* output of cooperative labour can be made available for *individual use*, namely, that which remains after a series of deductions:

'*First*, cover for replacement of the means of production used up. *Secondly*, additional portion for expansion of production. *Thirdly*, reserve or insurance funds to provide against accidents, dislocations caused by natural calamities, etc.' From the consumer stock which then remains there has to be deducted again, before it is divided among the producers for their individual use:

> *First, the general costs of administration not belonging to production.* This part will, from the outset, be very considerably restricted in comparison with present-day society and it diminishes in proportion as the new society develops. *Secondly, that which is intended for the common satisfaction of needs*, such as schools, health services, etc. From the outset this part grows considerably in

1. Ibid., Vol. I, p. 534. [Kerr edn. – *Translator*]
2. Karl Marx, *Critique of the Gotha Programme*. [Marx–Engels, *Selected Works*, Vol. II, p. 24. – *Translator*]
3. Cf. Karl Marx, *Das Kapital*, Vol. III. [*Capital*, Kerr edn, Vol. III, p. 773 – *Translator*]; and Friedrich Engels, *Anti-Dühring*. [Kerr edn, p. 295 ff. – *Translator*]
4. *Capital*, Vol. III, p. 992. [Kerr edn. – *Translator*]

comparison with present-day society and it grows in proportion as the new society develops. *Thirdly, funds for those unable to work,* etc.[1]

Thus, planning in an evolving classless society can never become static according to rigid patterns, but must be deliberated by a continuing process of development through the most rational possible relationship between the *increase of productivity* and the *enlargement* of public education, on the one side, and on the other side, by a *rapid reduction in labour time* and an *increase in social production and consumption quotas* no longer dominated by the principle of equivalence. Mistakes will be made again and again – inevitably, because it is human nature to err repeatedly – and such a society will have to count on numerous setbacks in its experimentation. Classless society is a *human* society *neither outside of historical perspective nor a paradise.*[2] But are such repeated gigantic errors in planning a greater source of loss than the sum total of losses caused by liberal capitalist crises, or even by the crises and objectively senseless investments of organized capitalism with its tendency to reconcile its contradictions by the production of armaments?

Planning in and for the Transition to a Classless Society

No heavily industrialized country has yet succeeded, on the basis of its own continuous internal development, in making the transition to a classless society and its rudiments of planning. The first great attempts in this direction took place in countries where the process of industrialization on the basis of capitalist production relations was only in the beginning.

The fact that the fundamentals for planning a classless society were taken over by areas with largely pre-capitalist production forms and social relations, and where there was only an extremely meagre share of capitalistic industrial production was certainly not expected by Karl Marx and Friedrich Engels, or by their

1. Marx, *Critique of the Gotha Programme.* [Marx–Engels, *Selected Works*, Vol. II, p. 22 – *Translator*], and *Capital*, Vol. III. [Kerr edn, p. 1021 ff. – *Translator*]

2. Engels, *Anti-Dühring.* [Kerr edn, p. 295. – *Translator*] According to Engels's thought, history doesn't cease except in the following sense: 'Only from then on, will man make his own history with complete consciousness. . . . It is "the leap of mankind from the kingdom of necessity into the kingdom of freedom".'

intellectual heirs before the First World War. But this transfer neither contradicts nor refutes their thought, because the manner in which industrial capitalism has transformed and unified the world – which was previously predicted by Marx and Engels[1] – has also guaranteed the transference of thought development and problem-posing from the developed industrial nations to those in the first stages of industrialization. The latter could thus take an interest in the solution of the problems that hitherto they had been unable to attempt to solve.

This made it possible, in all cases where these countries were freed from foreign military intervention, for them to initiate attempts resulting from their own social or national conflicts, and on the basis of their own resources. This would not have been possible without reference to Marxist theory. Because this theory arose out of the prior development of liberal capitalism it must be adapted to, and modified by, the specific problems of the new nations.

Because the theory of a transition to classless society was elaborated on the basis of developed industrial production which had already introduced public education and the disciplining of the majority of the population for the modern labour process, such conditions must first be created so that the next stage of development, the overcoming of class society, may be ushered in.

Thus, in Russia for example, it was systematic planning for essential development, instead of residual planning, which accelerated economic growth.[2] In half a century, the population of the U.S.S.R. has been transformed from preponderant illiteracy in 1917 to an average level of education and degree of scientific training that does not lag behind that of the old industrial nations whom Russia is increasingly overtaking. When Western reaction dissolved its hopes of receiving industrial aid, the U.S.S.R. decided upon fully systematized planning for the

1. Karl Marx and Friedrich Engels, *Manifesto of the Communist Party*. [Since there are so many editions, page references serve little purpose, but the reference apparently is to the following passage in the opening pages: 'The bourgeoisie, by the rapid improvement of all instruments of production, by the immensely facilitated means of communication, draws all, even the most barbarian, nations into civilization.' – *Translator*]

2. Cf. Werner Hofmann, *Die Arbeitsverfassung der Sowjet-Union* (West Berlin, 1956), p. 162, n. 3; p. 172 ff.; p. 180 ff.

building up of a highly industrialized society by means of its own resources, whereby it hoped to protect its population from the enormous burdens which early socialist accumulation must entail (as early capitalist accumulation did previously).[1] Such planning fully executed the first Five-Year Plan of 1928,[2] and resulted, as did early capitalist development in the old industrial countries, in the scourge of hunger, mass misery and forced child labour.

By means of open administrative terror the plan was achieved at an astonishingly rapid tempo.[3] Russia thereby narrowed its governmental system from the dictatorship of the Soviets to the dictatorship of the party, then to the dictatorship of a newly arisen bureaucracy, and finally to the brutal and bloody despotism of one man at the top.[4] By barbarous means and frightful errors in planning, Stalin forced industrial advance[5] and made the U.S.S.R. into a world power. Nevertheless, the self-estrangement of the bureaucratic dictatorship at the same time brought forth the conditions that first produced its moderation and, by repeated repercussions, its suspension, as is the case since the Twentieth Party Congress. Despite the estrangement between the ruling bureaucracy and the people, no new class society could develop;[6] the way remained open for planning a classless industrial society and for expanding the spiritual reach of freedom and social democracy.

The Chinese social organization began from deeper strata than the Russian, and forged similar stages of development. But it is still in its first stage. In order to explain this, its leaders still uphold the theory of Stalinism at a time when the industrially developed U.S.S.R. lays it aside.

The Yugoslav social organization, which started on its course under the aegis of Stalinist theory, has developed planning methods *leading to* a classless society which do not contradict planning methods *in* a classless society as is the case in the

1. Ibid., p. 6 ff.
2. Otto Bauer, *Kapitalismus und Sozialismus nach dem Weltkrieg. Rationalisierung–Fehlrationalisierung* (Vienna, 1931), p. 204 ff.
3. Ibid., p. 209 ff.; Hofmann, op. cit., p. 33 ff., p. 90 ff., p. 137 ff., p. 229 ff., p. 259 ff.; and Isaac Deutscher, *Stalin* (Stuttgart, 1962), p. 268 ff.
4. Cf. Deutscher, op. cit., p. 594 ff.
5. Ibid., p. 368 ff.
6. Cf. Hofmann, op. cit., p. 524 ff.

U.S.S.R. or in China.[1] Yugoslavia could do this because the higher degree of education and greater labour discipline of its population – which rested upon greater industrial development before the victory of the people's revolution – enabled it to assign a greater portion of its working population to the decentralized planning and administration of its productive apparatus[2] than was possible in the U.S.S.R.

Planning in the direction of a classless society has not yet succeeded in any fully developed society of organized capitalism. At the end of the world economic crisis of 1919–36, the victory of the fascist counter-revolution in the European countries prevented the development of such planning and by its war-economy method of planning rescued organized capitalism. Nor were the effects of the crisis overcome in the United States by means of the New Deal, but only by the economic consequences of the outbreak of the Second World War. Since 1945, the cold war and the preparedness posture of the two world powers have disrupted the beginnings of planning in a socialistic direction in England, France and Italy. The West European countries have been compelled to comply with the United States demands and return to the prior capitalistic structure of their industrial society.

Therefore, even the theory of planning for the transition of developed industrial nations to the classless society – under the full protection and further development of democratic constitutional structures – is still insufficiently developed. But such writers as A. Angelopoulos,[3] Charles Bettelheim,[4] and recently Ernest Mandel[5] have produced great contributions to it. Certainly since 1956, the Communist Parties have convinced these Western European countries that over-all planning within the framework of a parliamentary democratic constitution can and should result when it becomes possible for the constitutional governments to safeguard themselves against overthrow by authoritarian or fascistic dictatorship.

1. See the informative parliamentary debate on the draft of the Yugoslav Constitution, *Socialist Thought and Practice* (Belgrade, 1962, No. 7/8), p. 7 ff., p. 61 ff., p. 76 ff.
2. Cf. Mandel, op. cit., Vol. II, p. 327 ff.
3. A. Angelopoulos, *Planisme et progrès social* (Paris, 1953).
4. Charles Bettelheim, *Les Problèmes théoriques et pratiques de la planification* (Paris, 1946).
5. Mandel, op. cit., p. 274 ff.

The need for such planning has been made urgent by the development of atomic energy and automation. Because they require aid for rapid industrial construction, the former colonial countries are still neo-colonial dependent nations. *Internationalized* planning towards a no longer antagonistic, and therefore classless, society has become the prerequisite for preserving civilization and for avoiding threatening political catastrophes.

Translated by R. Dunayevskaya

RICHARD M. TITMUSS

⊚ ⊚

Social Welfare and the Art of Giving

RICHARD M. TITMUSS, Professor of Social Administration at the University of London, has served in several cabinet posts in the British government and conducted research projects. Born in 1907, he holds honorary degrees from the University of Wales and the University of Edinburgh. Some of his writings are *Poverty and Population, Problems of Social Policy, The Cost of the National Health Service in England and Wales* and *Income Distribution and Social Change: A Study in Criticism.*

I

The history of social welfare in Western countries as an organized system of 'giving' shows that over the past century it has played a variety of roles in the processes of change. One of the most important but least acknowledged in the historical literature has been its educational role. In Britain and other countries exposed to the early stages of industrialization, it was a major force in sustaining the social conscience. To give aid without regard to economic criteria and to differences in race, colour, religion and class brought it into direct conflict with the values of the market place. To act as an agent of redistributive social justice meant opposing discrimination; the concept of economic man had to be confronted with non-economic criteria; the natural dignity and uniqueness of everyman had continually to be publicly restated, fought for and demonstrated.

While time and circumstances have changed for the mass of the people in the West, the fundamental need for social welfare as an instrument of social justice and community education remains. This is one of the underlying themes of this essay; a second and less explicit one is that only a society which is firmly

350

dedicated to the principle of greater equality and the diffusion of humanistic values will have sufficient moral conviction to make available the resources necessary to help close the gap between the 'have' and the 'have-not' nations of the world. The ideas which move men and which they hold about their own societies must influence them in their attitudes towards the need for change in other societies.

It is of course possible to preach reform for others but not for one's own social group. The history of colonialism and race relations in the East and the West is littered with sad examples of hypocrisy. But, considered in collective terms, such attitudes today require a high degree of calculated cynicism. In effect, they can mean that the rich nations advocate social reform for the poor nations in order to prevent the spread of communism or some other hostile ideology or to further the defence and economic interests of the rich. According to Professor Seymour Martin Lipset (writing of underdeveloped countries): 'only parties which promise to improve the situation of the masses through widespread reform . . . can hope to compete with the Communists.'[1] A philosophy of the *status quo* at home can cynically purvey the notion of social welfare as a reforming agent among the poorer nations of the world simply to protect an already established 'good' society in the West. Fortunately, the development of social welfare values and policies among the poorer nations does not wholly depend on the influence or attitudes of the rich nations.

Nevertheless, however determined and able the 'have-not' nations are to shape their internal policies, there will still remain a major dilemma of 'giving' on an international scale. The income gap between the rich and poor nations is continually widening and, more serious still, there is evidence that this widening is now proceeding at an accelerating rate. Professor Gunnar Myrdal has recently drawn the conclusion that 'without a radical change in policies in both groups of countries, the world is headed for an economic and political cataclysm'.[2] How

1. Seymour Martin Lipset, *Political Man: The Social Bases of Politics* (New York: Doubleday, 1960; London: Heinemann), p. 416.
2. Gunnar Myrdal, *The Urgent Need for Scientific Breakthroughs if Great Misery Shall Not Be the Destiny of Underdeveloped Countries*, paper presented to the Conference on Global Impacts of Applied Microbiology, Stockholm, 2 August 1963.

societies give collectively, and their motives for giving are questions as fundamental to the health of social welfare systems at home and abroad as the question of what they give.

2

We come then to the question of the present and future role of social welfare in the West – particularly in Britain and the United States. If there is any substance in the foregoing view, then this question is of more than national interest: how we conduct our own domestic affairs will influence the quality of our relationships with our poorer neighbours.

'Modern social welfare', it has been said in the United States, 'has really to be thought of as help given to the stranger, not to the person who by reason of personal bond commands it without asking.'[1] It has, therefore, to be formally organized, to be administered by strangers, and to be paid for collectively by strangers.

Social welfare or the social services, operating through agencies, institutions and programmes outside the private market, are becoming more difficult to define in any society with precision. As societies become more complex and specialized, so do systems of social welfare. Functionally, they reflect, and respond to, the larger social structure and its division of labour. This process makes it much harder today to identify the causal agents of change – the microbes of social disorganization and the viruses of impoverishment – and to make them responsible for the costs of 'dis-services'. Who should bear the social costs of the thalidomide babies, of urban blight, of smoke pollution, of the obsolescence of skills, of automation, of the impact of synthetic coffee, which will dispense with the need for coffee beans, on the peasants of Brazil? The private benefits are to some extent measurable and attributable, but the private losses are not. Neoclassical economics and the private market cannot make these allocations; they are not organized to estimate social disruption and are unable to provide adequately for the public needs created by social and economic change.

Our growing inability to identify and connect cause and effect in the world of social and technological change is thus one reason

1. H. L. Wilensky and C. N. Lebeaux, *Industrial Society and Social Welfare* (New York: Russell Sage Foundation, 1958), p. 141.

for the historical emergence of social welfare institutions in the West. Altruism by strangers for strangers was and is an attempt to fill a moral void created by applied science. The services and programmes developed in the West to give aid to the stranger victims of industrialism and change have inevitably and necessarily become more specialized and complex. In this paper we shall only be able to speak of them in general terms.

3

The social services, as they are named in Britain, are largely the product of the twentieth century – a delayed response to the industrialism of the nineteenth century. The term is generally and loosely interpreted today to cover such public (or publicly supported) services as medical care, education, housing, income maintenance in old age and during periods of unemployment, sickness, disability and so forth, child allowances, and a variety of specific services for particular groups of people with special needs, e.g. neglected children, unmarried mothers, the blind, mental defectives, young delinquents, discharged prisoners, and other categories. All these services came apologetically into existence to provide for certain basic needs which the individual, the family and the private market in capitalist societies were unable or unwilling to meet. In the United States and other Western countries, the terms 'social welfare' or 'social policy programmes' are used as alternative generic labels to embrace a similar variety of collectively organized services which may differ widely in scope and structure, methods of administration and finance, and in the fundamental objectives underlying them.

The concept of 'The Welfare State', which entered the arena of political thought in the 1940s, is generally accepted as a wider definition of the role of the state in the field of social and economic policy, embracing more than the provision of social services. Most writers on the subject, whether on the right or left politically, take it to mean a more positive and purposeful commitment by government to concern itself with the general welfare of the whole community and with the social costs of change. In his book *Beyond the Welfare State*, Gunnar Myrdal concluded that

In the last half-century, the State, in all the rich countries in the Western world, has become a democratic 'Welfare State', with

353

fairly explicit commitments to the broad goals of economic development, full employment, equality of opportunity for the young, social security, and protected minimum standards as regards not only income, but nutrition, housing, health and education, for people of all regions and social groups.[1]

In this view, it can be argued that 'Welfare Statism', either as an established fact or as a political objective, is a common phenomenon of large-scale, industrialized societies. The renaissance of private enterprise during the past two decades in North America and Europe, the Keynesian revolution and the adoption of techniques of economic management, rising standards of living and the achievements of political parties and trade unions on behalf of the underprivileged – have led all these culturally different societies along the same road to 'Welfare Statism' – a road unforeseen by Marx. Whether they know it or not, and whether they like it or not, Democrats and Republicans, Conservatives, Socialists, and Liberals in North America and Europe have become 'welfare-statists'. The Germans and the Swedes may have more 'advanced' pension systems, the British a more comprehensive health service, the French more extensive family allowances, and the Americans may spend more on public education but, when all these national differences are acknowledged, the generalized welfare commitment is nevertheless viewed as the dominant political fact of modern Western societies. Governments of the liberal right and the liberal left may come and go; the commitment to welfare, economic growth and full employment will remain with minor rather than major changes in scope and objectives.

4

In historical and comparative terms, these are sweeping conclusions and leave many questions of values and facts unexamined. To what extent are they based on the real facts of income and wealth distribution, property, power and class? Has the 'Welfare State' abolished poverty, social deprivation and exploitation? Has man a greater sense of social control and participation in the work and life of his community? What will be the human consequences of further social and technological changes? Will the future resemble the immediate past, or are

1. Gunnar Myrdal (Yale University Press, 1960), p. 45.

these views a simple projection of a transient phase in the development of large-scale and predominantly competitive societies?

In recent years a growing number of political commentators, economists and sociologists on both sides of the Atlantic, in proclaiming the end of political ideology in the West, have either ignored such questions or have tended to imply that they are no longer of primary importance for our societies. Their reasons for doing so are explicit or implicit in their general thesis. Professor Lipset in his book *Political Man* (1960) spoke for many when he said (in summarizing the discussions of a world congress of intellectuals in 1955) that 'the ideological issues dividing left and right [have] been reduced to a little more or a little less government ownership and economic planning'; and there was general agreement that it really makes little difference 'which political party controls the domestic policies of individual nations'. With minor differences, parties of both the right and the left will attempt to alleviate those social injustices that still remain, and will continue to seek improvements in social welfare, education, medical care, and other sectors of the economy for the general well-being. All will share, rich and poor, in the benefits of growth. By a natural process of market levitation all classes and groups will stand expectantly on the political right as the escalator of growth moves them up. Automatism thus substitutes for the social protest.

To quote Lipset again (though writers in a similar vein in England, France and Germany could equally be cited):

> . . . the fundamental political problems of the industrial revolution have been solved: the workers have achieved industrial and political citizenship, the conservatives have accepted the welfare state, and the democratic left has recognized that an increase in overall state power carries with it more dangers to freedom than solutions for economic problems. This very triumph of the democratic social revolution in the West ends domestic politics for those intellectuals who must have ideologies or utopias to motivate them to political action.[1]

As a generalization, it is conceivable that this statement may

1. Lipset, op. cit., pp. 404–6. For other references to this thesis see Lipset and also Daniel Bell, *The End of Ideology: On the Exhaustion of Political Ideas in the Fifties* (Glencoe, Illinois: Free Press, 1960).

serve as a summing-up for the 1950s in the history books of the next century. But from the perspective of 1960 it is, to say the least, a dubious proposition. However, we would not wish this essay to take the form of a critique of any one particular writer. To do so would carry with it the obligation to discuss in detail an individual interpretation of recent trends and the many qualifications attached to them. We shall, therefore, treat these statements as an expression not of the views of Professor Lipset but of a collective *Weltanschauung*, and one that seems to be growing in influence in the West, to judge by the number of its adherents.

Though we make no attempt to examine the thesis at length, we shall speculate about some of its basic assumptions so far as they relate to the future role of a humanist social policy in Britain and the U.S.A.

First, it is unhistorical. Implicit in the thesis is the assumption that the 'industrial revolution' was a once-and-for-all affair. Thus, it ignores the evidence concerning the trend towards monopolistic concentrations of economic power, the role of the corporation as private government with taxing powers, the problems of social disorganization and cultural deprivation, and the growing impact of automation and new techniques of production and distribution in economically advanced societies. If the first phase of the so-called revolution was to force all men to work, the phase we are now entering may be to force many men not to work. Without a major shift in values, only an impoverishment in social living can result from this new wave of industrialism.

Second, it states that the workers have achieved 'industrial citizenship'. The only comment we feel able to make on this is to say that it is a misuse of language to imply that membership of a trade union is synonymous with 'industrial citizenship'. Conceptions of what constitutes 'citizenship' for the worker must be related to what we now know about man's potential and his basic social and psychological needs; they cannot be compared with conditions of industrial slavery in the nineteenth century.

Third, the thesis implies that the problem of the distribution of income and wealth has either been solved or is now of insignificant proportions in Western society. In any event, such disparities as do exist are justified on grounds of individual differences and the need for economic incentives, and are considered to present no threat to democratic values.

In the 1950s, one per cent of the British population owned forty-two per cent of all personal net capital and five per cent owned 67.5 per cent.[1] Even these proportions are underestimates, for the figures exclude pension funds and trusts (which have grown enormously in recent years), and they do not take account of the increasing tendency for large owners of property to distribute their wealth among their families, to spread it over time, to send it abroad, and to transform it in other ways.

This degree of concentration in the holding of wealth is nearly twice as great as it was in the United States in 1954, and far higher than in the halcyon days of ruthless American capitalism in the early 1920s. Since 1949, wealth inequality has been growing in the United States, the rate of increase being more than twice as fast as the rate of decline between 1922 and 1949. Measured in terms of the increase in the percentage of wealth held by the top one per cent, the growth of inequality during 1949–56 (the latest available data) was more striking than at any time during at least the past forty years. Not unexpectedly, the distribution of income also appears to be becoming more unequal in recent years, affecting in particular the one-fifth to one-quarter of the United States population living below the currently defined 'poverty line'.[2] These are not all Negroes; eighty per cent of the American poor are white, and only one-fifth receive welfare aid. Economic growth in the richest society in the world has not been accompanied by any automatic, built-in equalizer. Crime for the young unemployed acts as a substitute within the prevailing system of values – the modern form of acquisitive social mobility for the lower classes.

There is no evidence to suggest that Britain has not been following in the same path since the end of the 1940s. It is even possible that inequality in the ownership of wealth (particularly in terms of family holdings) has increased more rapidly in Britain

1. See my Introduction to the third edition of R. H. Tawney's *Equality*.
2. R. J. Lampman, *The Share of the Top Wealth-Holders in National Wealth 1922–56* (Princeton: National Bureau of Economic Research, 1962); M. Harrington, *The Other America: Poverty in the United States* (New York: Macmillan, 1962; Harmondsworth: Penguin); Conference on Economic Progress, *Poverty and Deprivation in the United States*, 1961, known as the Keyserling Report.

than in the United States since 1949. The British system of taxation is almost unique in the Western world in its generous treatment of wealth-holders in respect of settlements, trusts, gifts and other arrangements for redistributing and rearranging income and wealth. This is reflected in the remarkable fact that, in the mid 1950s, it was in the young adult age group that the tendency for wealth to be concentrated in a few hands was most marked.

Such evidence as this is ignored by those who proclaim the end of political ideology. Similar trends are probably in operation in De Gaulle's France and Erhard's Germany.[1] Over a quarter of a century of political upheaval, global war, 'welfare statism', managed economies and economic growth have made little impression on the holdings of great fortunes in at least two of the largest industrial nations: the United States and Britain. The institution of concentrated wealth appears to be as tenacious of life as Tawney's intelligent tadpoles. Wealth still bestows political and economic power, more power than income, though it is probably exercised differently and with more respect for public opinion than in the nineteenth century.

Changes in the distribution of incomes appear to be following a similar pattern in Britain as in the United States. Towards the end of the 1940s a wartime movement towards more equality (before and after tax) in both Britain and the United States was reversed. The poorest tenth of the British population were relatively worse off compared with the higher standards of the rest of the nation in 1963 than they were in 1948.[2]

How can these great disparities in the private ownership of wealth and in the exercise of economic power be viewed as consistent with the thesis that we have reached the end of the political dialogue? No political utopia since Plato has ever envisaged such degrees of economic inequality as permanent and desirable states for man. Socialists protest at such disparities not because they want to foster envy; they do so because, as Tawney argued, these disparities are fundamentally immoral. History suggests

1. According to Mr Christopher Johnson, 'The statistics which are available show what is evident to anyone living in France; that the rich are getting richer while the poor are barely maintaining their standard of living.' (*New Society*, 21 February 1963, p. 15.)

2. T. Lynes, 'Poverty in the Welfare State', *Aspect*, No. 7, August 1963.

that human nature is not strong enough to maintain itself in true community where great disparities of income and wealth preside.

Fourth and finally, there is in this thesis an assumption that the establishment of social welfare necessarily and inevitably contributes to the spread of humanism and the resolution of social injustice. The reverse can be true. Welfare, as an institutional means, can serve different masters. A multitude of sins may be committed in its appealing name. Welfare can be used simply as an instrument of economic growth which, by benefiting a minority, indirectly promotes greater inequality. Education is an example. We may educate the young to compete more efficiently as economic men in the private market one with another, or we may educate them because we desire to make them more capable of freedom and more capable of fulfilling their personal differences irrespective of income, class, religion and race.

Welfare may be used to serve military and racial ends – as in Hitler's Germany. More medical care was provided by state and voluntary agencies not because of a belief in everyman's uniqueness, but because of a hatred of men.

Welfare may be used to narrow allegiances and not to diffuse them – as in employers' fringe benefit systems. Individual gain and political quietism, fostered by the new feudalism of the corporation, may substitute for the sense of common humanity nourished by systems of non-discriminatory mutual aid.

What matters then, what indeed is fundamental to the health of welfare, the objective towards which its face is set? To universalize humanistic ethics and the social rights of citizenship, or to divide, discriminate and compete?

5

In reality, of course, the issues are never as clear-cut as this. The historical evolution of social security measures in Britain since the end of the nineteenth century shows how complex and various were the forces at work. Fear of social revolution, the need for a law-abiding labour force, the struggle for power between political parties and pressure groups, a demand to remove some of the social costs of change – for example, industrial accidents – from the back of the worker, and the social conscience of the rich – all played a part.

But the major impulse came from below – from the working-man's ethic of solidarity and mutual aid. It found expression and grew spontaneously from working-class traditions and institutions to counter the adversities of industrialism. By means of a great network of friendly societies, medical clubs, chapel societies, brotherhoods, cooperatives, trade unions and savings clubs, schemes of mutual insurance were developed as a method of prepayment for services the members could claim when they were in need – in sickness, disablement, unemployment, old age, widowhood and death. The 'good' risks and the 'bad' risks, the young and the old, shared one another's lot. They constituted microscopic welfare states, each struggling to demonstrate that man could still exercise some control over the forces of technology. By the end of the century some 24,000 different friendly societies were in existence, with a total membership representing about half the adult male population of the country. Aptly and significantly named, during a century of unbridled competition, they were *the* humanistic institution for the artisan and his family, far outdistancing in active membership all trade unions, political parties and religious bodies.

We can now see this great movement as the amateur's compassionate answer to the challenge of the economic and psychological insecurities of industrialism and individualism. It expressed also the ordinary man's revulsion from a class-conscious, discriminating charity and a ruthless, discriminating poor law. The poor law was hated because it spelled humiliation; it was an assault on the individual's sense of self-respect in an age when 'respectability' – the quality of meriting the respect of others – governed the *mores* of society.

The values and objectives which underlay in the past the search for security in an increasingly insecure world are still relevant to an understanding of the role of social welfare in Britain today. The ways in which they shaped its origins and early development still permeate the principles on which the systems of medical care and social security operate today – comprehensive in scope, universal in membership. That they have not yet solved the problems of poverty and neglect, and still provide little place for citizen participation, is another story, and one that remains as a formidable challenge for socialism. But we cannot retrace our footsteps to the intimate 'friendly societies' of yesterday; we must find imaginative ways and new institutional means of combining humanity in administration with redistributive social justice in the future development of welfare policies.

6

These are two of the central unresolved issues for humanists: the problem of bigness and the problem of inequality. They affect every aspect of social policy: education from the primary school to the university and into adult life; social security in unemployment, sickness and old age; the care of the physically and mentally ill; housing and urban planning; leisure and recreation.

The demand for these services will grow in the future as living standards rise among some sections of the population and fall, relatively or absolutely, among others. The consequences of automation and its technological cousins on the one hand, and more dependent needs in childhood and old age on the other, will call for a much greater investment in people and social service than in consumption goods. Science and technology are today beginning to accomplish as thorough a revolution in social and economic theory as they are in the theory of war and international relations. The conventional doctrine that machines make work is losing its validity; machines are now replacing workers. It is already clear from American experience that these victims of technological displacement are no longer 'resting between engagements' (which is the theory of unemployment insurance): they are *permanently* out of work; permanently liberated from work. By the end of 1962 nearly one-third of all young Negroes between the ages of 16 and 21 who were out of school were also out of work. Relatively speaking, they were also more handicapped educationally than unemployed young Negroes twenty years earlier. Between 1939 and 1958 the disadvantage of not having a college diploma grew in the U.S.A.[1]

In an age of abundance of things, the production of consumption goods will become a subsidiary question for the West. The primary question will be just distribution; in particular, the dis-

1. H. P. Miller, 'Money Value of an Education', *Occupational Outlook Quarterly*, September 1961, p. 4.

tribution of services according to needs in place of the principle of productivity and performance in a market economy which today powerfully influences access to education and other social services.

In the past we have distributed resources on the basis of success and failure in economic competition; in the future we must decide whether it is morally right to do so in an economy of abundance. To distribute services on the basis of needs will help us to discover equality in our neighbours. 'Awareness of equality,' wrote Daniel Jenkins, 'always arises in personal relationships and nearly always confronts us as a challenge, for it means placing a greater value upon our neighbour than we had previously been disposed to do. We are all ready to love ourourselves. The discovery of equality might be defined as the discovery that we have indeed to love our neighbours as ourselves.'[1]

And so we have to ask, 'What are we to do with our wealth?' This is a more relevant social question to ask today than those that seek to find more effective ways of punishing criminals, enforcing the law against deviants, preventing abuse of public assistance, forcing men to search for work, compelling them to save for old age when they cannot feed their children adequately, shifting them out of subsidized housing, inventing cheap technological substitutes for education and charging them more for access to medical care.

Yet these aims reflect the values which are often applied today in the administration of social services. According to one writer, Professor Mencher, 'The present United States welfare [public assistance] programme is in keeping with the philosophy of 1830'[2] – the philosophy of less eligible citizens enshrined in the English Poor Law Act of 1834. Social workers, teachers, doctors and social administrators find their functions imprisoned by the 'virtues' of hard work and profits; virtues that are rooted in the economics of scarcity. Their role is to police these virtues as, in a more ruthless context, medical certification of fitness for work became one of the central directives under the Stalinist régime. They have no relevance to the economics of abundance.

1. D. Jenkins, *Equality and Excellence* (London: S.G.M., 1961), p. 21.
2. S. Mencher, 'Perspectives on Recent Welfare Legislation', *Social Work*, Vol. 8, No. 3, 1963, p. 62.

And, as Gerard Piel has emphasized, any

> hard work that a machine can do is better done today by a machine; 'hard' these days means mostly boring and repetitive work, whether in the factory or the office. But the instinct for workmanship, the need to feel needed, the will to achieve, are deeply felt in every human heart. They are not universally fulfilled by the kind of employment most people find. Full employment in the kind of employment that is commonly available, whether blue-collar or white-collar, has been plainly outmoded by technology. The liberation of people from tasks unworthy of human capacity should free that capacity for a host of activities now neglected in our civilization: teaching and learning, fundamental scientific investigation, the performing arts and the graphic arts, letters, the crafts, politics, and social service. Characteristically these activities involve the interaction of people with people rather than with things. They are admittedly not productive activities; nor are they profitable in the strict sense.[1]

Science and technology in alliance with other structural and demographic changes under way in our societies will call for a major shift in values; for new incentives and new forms of reward unrelated to the productivity principle; for new criteria applied to the distribution of resources which are not tied to individual 'success' as a measure; for new forms of socially approved 'dependencies'. They will make the conventional criteria of capitalism largely irrelevant.

Many years ago Keynes foresaw that the time would come when these changes would be needed:

> . . . we shall be able to rid ourselves of many of the pseudo-moral principles which have hag-ridden us for 200 years, by which we have exalted some of the most distasteful of human qualities into the position of the highest virtues. . . . All kinds of social customs and economic practices affecting the distribution of wealth and of economic rewards and penalties, which we now maintain at all costs, we shall then be freed to discard.

We shall need different rules domestically to live by; more examples of altruism to look up to. Indeed, our societies in Britain and the United States are already in need of them. In no other way in the long run will it be possible for us to prevent the deprived and the unable from becoming more deprived and un-

1. G. Piel, *Consumers of Abundance*, Center for the Study of Democratic Institutions, 1961, p. 9.

able; more cast down in a pool of apathy, frustration, crime, rootlessness and tawdry poverty.

In all this, what we call the social services will have a central role to play. If this role is defined at all it will have to be defined by socialists in the language of equality. Here it is that ethics will have to be reunited to politics. The answers will not come and, indeed, logically cannot come from those who now proclaim 'the end of political ideology'; those who would elevate the principle of pecuniary gain and extend it to social service by equating education and medical care with refrigerators and mink coats; and those who advocate that more and more people should 'contract out' of universal social services and create for themselves new areas of privilege and discrimination. They, today, are the utilitarian doctrinaires; prisoners of the economics of scarcity; oblivious to the social consequences of the march of science and technology; and blind to the need for a sense of moral purpose in their own societies as the motive power in the art of giving to our international neighbours.

T. B. BOTTOMORE

⊕ ⊕

Industry, Work and Socialism

T. B. BOTTOMORE, secretary of the International Socio-
logical Association from 1953 to 1959 and a member of the
British Labour Party, was born in 1920 and educated at
London University, where he obtained a M.Sc. (Econ.) in
Sociology. He is a contributor to sociological journals in
various countries and author of such books as *Classics in
Modern Society, Karl Marx: Selective Writings, Sociology:
A Guide to Problems and Literature* and *Ethics and Society.*

I don't like work – no man does – but I like what is in
the work – the chance to find yourself. Your own reality –
for yourself, not for others – what no other man can ever
know.

JOSEPH CONRAD, *The Heart of Darkness*

The early socialists formulated two related lines of criticism
of capitalist society. One was a criticism of class inequalities, of
the vast and apparently increasing disparities of wealth and enjoyment between property owners and wage earners. The other
was a criticism of the excesses of individualism, of *laissez-faire*
and the competitive struggle, and a counter-assertion of the
value of cooperation and mutual aid. In both there was implied
a new conception of the importance of labour both for society
and for the individual. Saint-Simon, in a famous parable, con-
trasted the idle and useless feudal section of French society with
the productive part composed of scientists, industrialists, crafts-
men and others. His theory of the new social order, the industrial régime, rested upon the idea that useful work was a primary
obligation of the individual, and that the hierarchy of reward
and esteem should correspond with the relative value of men's
contributions to society through productive labour. Saint-

365

Simon's followers developed this theme in their concern with the organization of modern industry, and in their insistence upon useful work as the prime social function upon which social life should be based. The same notion was reflected more faintly in the works of the early economists, in the distinction which they attempted to draw between productive and unproductive labour.

The other aspect of work, as a psychological need of the individual, an element in his education, a means of self-expression, and a bond with other men, was emphasized by Robert Owen, and especially by Fourier. Fourier argued that men are by nature creative and active, and that the work which has to be done in society could be made attractive and pleasant in itself, first by matching occupations more closely with individual tastes and propensities, and secondly by providing variety in work through changes of occupation in the course of the working day.

All these notions are to be found, expressed in a different language, in Marx's critical analysis of capitalist society. The division of society into classes produces at one extreme wealth, leisure, a relative freedom to determine one's own life; and at the other, poverty, excessive and brutalizing work, constraint and lack of freedom. In the process of work itself, the industrial worker is *alienated* (to use the terminology of Marx's early writings):

> he does not fulfil himself in his work, but denies himself, has a feeling of misery rather than well-being, does not develop freely his mental and physical energies but is physically exhausted and mentally debased. . . . His work is not voluntary but imposed, *forced labour*. It is not the satisfaction of a need, but only a *means* for satisfying other needs. (*Economic and Philosophical Manuscripts.*)

The liberation of the individual from such conditions, which Marx saw as the objective of the growing working-class movement, would require changes in the social system as a whole and also within each productive enterprise. The independence and the power over others which the upper class in society enjoyed would be ended by the abolition of private property in the means of production and the consequent disappearance of social classes. But this was only one condition, though fundamental in Marx's theoretical scheme, for the creation of a classless society. It would also be necessary to overcome the division of labour, which enclosed men in narrow spheres of life and condemned large numbers of them to spend their days in dull, mindless, physically exhausting, sometimes harmful activities. The young Marx, like Fourier, saw a solution to the problem in regular changes of occupation; in a notorious passage of *The German Ideology* he observed that in communist society nobody would have 'one exclusive sphere of activity', and the individual would be able to 'hunt in the morning, fish in the afternoon, rear cattle in the evening, criticize after dinner', according to his inclination. Later on, Marx undoubtedly took a more critical view of these possibilities, and in a passage of *Capital* he distinguished between the sphere of production which would always remain a 'realm of necessity', and the sphere of leisure time, 'the true realm of freedom' in which 'the development of human potentiality for its own sake' could take place; but he never abandoned the idea that necessary work could itself become, in some degree, a liberating and educative activity. Again in *Capital* he observes that 'the limited detail worker of today' will be replaced in the future society by 'the fully developed individual', who carries out a number of different social functions, and who has a different relation to his work because he has received a broad general and scientific education. The frequently quoted passage in which Marx criticized Fourier's view of work as an essentially pleasant activity is generally misinterpreted. Marx objected to the idea that work could be regarded simply as an agreeable, spontaneous activity, as a kind of game; he insisted upon the element of painful effort in work, upon the constraints which it imposed, but at the same time he held firmly that it could be rewarding for the individual, in the way that a creative artist's work is rewarding, as a manifestation of human skill and determination, and of the human power to shape and control the natural world. Marx's view is similar to that of Conrad in the passage quoted above, except that Marx also takes account of the social aspects of work; in a classless and humane society, the individual would not only find *himself* in his work, but would also discover and express his cooperative relationship, his friendship, with other men.

In the later development of the labour movement and oı

socialist thought, the problems of the worker in his immediate work situation in an industrial society came to be largely overshadowed by the problems of class relations in society as a whole, of property ownership and political power. They were never entirely neglected, but those movements which paid any serious attention to them – such as the Shop Steward's Movement just before the First World War, Guild Socialism, and the various communitarian experiments – had relatively little influence upon the general ideas and doctrines of the labour movement. It is only in recent years that these problems have moved back into the centre of discussion among socialists; in part because they are seen to be highly significant in the context of the social changes which have occurred in the industrial societies, and in part because a number of practical experiments – the workers' councils in Yugoslavia, the *kibbutzim* in Israel, the community development projects in such countries as India, the communes in China – have furnished actual materials for studying new forms of organization of industrial and agricultural work, which are related directly to the ideas of the early socialists and of Marx.

The most important social changes which need to be considered here in their bearing upon socialist ideas are the extension of public ownership of industry, the changes in the nature of industrial work, and the increase in leisure time. It is plain, at the present day, that the public ownership of industry is not by itself sufficient to establish a socialist society, and that it may in fact produce conditions which are directly inimical to the creation or functioning of such a society. A centrally directed collectivist economy may become the breeding ground of a new élite – comprising the political leaders and the managers of the economy – at least as privileged, remote from the people and authoritarian as the bourgeoisie in capitalist society. The likelihood of such a development is increased if there is a strong emphasis upon the purely economic aspects of socialism – the growth of technology, rapid industrialization and modernization, higher productivity – and especially if, in addition, a single political party assumes control of the society and prevents any organized or effective expression of dissent. In these conditions, and even in those cases where publicly owned industry forms only a part of the economy, so long as industry is regulated from the top through appointed boards of managers, the situation of the worker in industry may be little different, in respect of his self-determination and creative activity, from what it has been in capitalist industry.

These problems are rendered more acute by the nature of modern industry itself. Many of the basic productive activities of society must be carried on by large and complex organizations, the administration of which becomes increasingly impersonal and bureaucratic; while within each enterprise efficient mass production depends upon intensive specialization and the minute subdivision of tasks. The division between the few who plan the productive process and the mass of workers – both clerical and manual – who merely execute the detailed operations, and the standardized, limited, repetitive character of these operations, together reduce almost to zero the active and creative function of the worker. Obviously these conditions may exist whether industry is privately or publicly owned, since they are created largely by the quest for high levels of production based upon modern technology; but it is only recently that socialists and others have begun to pay serious attention to the problem which they present. This reconsideration of industrial work has been one of the important influences leading to a revival of the idea of workers' control, or workers' self-management, and to a lively interest in the Yugoslav experiments in this field. It is clear from the Yugoslav experience that self-management encounters many practical difficulties, among them the initial disinclination of a proportion of the workers to participate actively in management, the emergence of conflicts between the workers' council and the director of the enterprise, and the limitations upon the representative character of the workers' council in very large organizations; but there is little doubt, also, that this is one of the best means in practice for overcoming the fragmentation of work and the tedium associated with industrial mass production. The worker who takes some part in deciding the economic and social policies of his factory obtains a view of the process of production as a whole, enters into new relationships with his fellow workers, has the opportunity to exercise intelligence and initiative, and may be stimulated to pursue his education further in scientific or cultural subjects. Some sociologists have argued that industrial work can be made more interesting and intelligent by the expansion of scientific and technical education, and by regular transfers of workers from one job to another (a vindication of Fourier!), without any fundamental change in the management of the enterprise; but it can hardly be disputed that a régime of workers' councils in publicly owned enterprises would be more likely to effect such improvements, and would add to them the benefits of direct participation in policy-making.

The most recent technological changes in the advanced countries, and especially the spread of automation, are likely to have far-reaching effects upon the work situation not only of industrial workers but also of white-collar workers. In the automated factories which are now being established in some of the major branches of mass production far fewer workers are needed, and these workers must have a much more thorough education in science and technology, must exercise greater intelligence and initiative in their work, and must have a more comprehensive grasp of the productive process as a whole, than was the case with workers on the old-style assembly lines. Thus automation holds out two prospects for the future of work in the industrial societies; first, a new type of work, in which the individual will regain the opportunity to exercise intelligence and judgement in his occupation; and second, a reduction in the hours of labour and an increase in the amount of leisure time.

The progress of automation, besides changing the conditions of work in mass-production factories, and in large clerical organizations such as banks and insurance companies, will also give a new impetus to the transfer of labour from the manufacturing to the service sector of the economy, and thus from the more repetitive and monotonous to the more interesting and responsible kinds of work. Nevertheless, there will remain, in any foreseeable future, a great number of occupations which provide little satisfaction to those engaged in them. It is the recognition of this fact which has led many observers to emphasize the importance of leisure as providing essential compensations for the constraints and dissatisfactions of working life. The effects of the growth of leisure time have not yet, however, been systematically studied, and the prospects for the future are still open to diverse interpretations. There is no doubt that many leisure activities do provide satisfactions which are not to be found in work. Within limits, such activities are freely chosen and freely engaged in; the individual is able to assert his own preferences, to display his skill, to enjoy change and variety, and to make a personal choice of his associates and friends. Moreover, the development of skill in some leisure activity may compensate for low status in the occupational sphere, either through the social esteem which it gains, or at the least through the contribution which it makes to the individual's self-esteem and sense of worth.

It is also clear, however, that much modern leisure is not of an active kind, and that it fails to contribute in any worth-while sense to the development of human faculties. Television and gambling, two of the most common leisure pursuits in modern societies, will illustrate this point. Television programmes may encourage some people to take up a sport or hobby, actively, or to pursue systematically knowledge of an art or science, but for a far greater number they are a substitute for personal activity, a means to live vicariously. Gambling, which provides for many people the excitement lacking in their working lives, is also in a more profound sense an attempt to escape from the tedium of work by means of the wealth which good fortune may suddenly bring, but without any clear conception of an alternative form of life. In earlier societies, in which the leisure time of the mass of the population was extremely limited, the passive use of leisure and indulgence in fantasy were not perhaps of very great social importance, but in an age of mass leisure they come to constitute a major social problem. If the greatly increased leisure available to all members of society is not to lead to boredom and aimlessness (of which there are already numerous signs), but is to become a means for the fuller development of individual faculties, there must be a far more extensive public provision of opportunities for active leisure than has yet been made, or even contemplated, in any industrial society.

Even if that condition were met, however, a number of problems would remain. Work and leisure cannot be isolated from each other, especially in their influence upon the social attitudes of the individual. The man who spends his working hours in a subordinate position, engaged constantly in tedious and meaningless tasks, amid ugly surroundings, is unlikely to be able to express himself fully as an active and creative person in his leisure time. Moreover, to the extent that he succeeds in doing so, he will be all the more frustrated and embittered in his work.

The development of active leisure, if it is to form a harmonious part of a person's whole life, must be accompanied by changes in the organization of work which give the individual greater responsibility, a larger part in the shaping of his environment, and greater variety and interest in his occupation.

A second problematic aspect of leisure is to be found in its predominantly private and individual character. In the past, work, which occupied most of the individual's waking hours, engendered some of the strongest social bonds which united human communities; and the early socialists themselves conceived their ideal society as being based upon cooperative labour. Leisure activities, on the other hand, in the form which they have taken in modern societies, do not necessarily give rise to, or sustain, any enduring social relationships. In some cases they do so, through the formation of voluntary associations, but the greater part of leisure activities tends, on the contrary, to withdraw the individual, or the family, into a purely private life, in which the sense of community with other men and of responsibility for public affairs is altogether lost.

Socialist humanism is in part a response to the new and pressing problems which have arisen from the tremendous advance of science and technology in the developed industrial countries, and from the experience of difficulties and dangers in the socialist forms of society. It is no longer a question, in the industrial countries, of simply transforming the property system, of abolishing the private ownership of large-scale industry and eliminating the social class differences based upon great inequalities of wealth and income. There is also a need to change, in just as radical a fashion, the uses of technology, the organization of work, the division of labour, and the system of authority in business enterprises; to devise new uses of leisure time, which might include the development of arts and crafts as secondary occupations capable of supplementing the mass production of essential goods by the creation of individual objects of beauty; and to encourage far larger numbers of people to take an active part in the management of public affairs, not only in industry, but in voluntary associations of all kinds, and in local and regional communities. In seeking to achieve these ends socialist humanism should be guided by a moral ideal – which was that of the early socialists – namely, the conception of a community of creative, equal and self-governing individuals, on a world scale; and at the same time by a scientific and experimental attitude towards social problems and towards social policies for the reform or replacement of social institutions. In a socialist society there is not a final resolution of all tensions and conflicts, and indeed new forms of conflict may arise. When men begin to shape their individual lives and their social existence deliberately, and in greater freedom from material constraints, there is no guarantee that they will not sometimes act foolishly, or that some of them will not act wickedly; and it is likely always to be the case that particular individuals and social groups will seek to press their own interests beyond reasonable limits. Our hopes must lie in the greater rationality, self-control and sense of responsibility, which equal opportunities to participate in the government of society should bring about; in the ability of an industrially advanced society to satisfy amply the basic material needs of its members; and in the possibility of devising adequate institutions for the control and management of social conflict without stifling dissent and innovation. I can see no overwhelming reason not to entertain such hopes.

SIR STEPHEN KING-HALL

⊚ ⊚

Personal Liberty in an Affluent Society

COMMANDER SIR STEPHEN KING-HALL served in the
Royal Navy from 1906 to 1929 and during the First World
War took part in the Grand Fleet and Submarine defence.
When he retired he joined the staff of the Royal Institute
of International Affairs and began writing and speaking on
the radio and television on current political, economic and
social problems. In 1939, he founded the King-Hall
News-Letter, and from 1939 to 1945 was an Independent
Member of Parliament.

From 1946, he was an active advocate of unilateral
nuclear disarmament for Britain and wrote *Power Politics
in the Nuclear Age, Defence in the Nuclear Age* and *Our
Own Times 1914–1960*. He also wrote books for young
people on modern problems and, in a lighter vein, several
successful comedies. He operated a farm and directed a
large British insurance company. He died in June 1966.

As an independent observer I see no substantial difference of
political principle reflected in the practices, actual and proposed,
of the British political parties as they enter the electoral battle
in 1964.

The British are all planners nowadays, and both socialists and
conservatives are busily competing as to which party can most
expeditiously bury capitalism – or what my father would have
understood by that word.

The Soviets can relax and lean on their spades, and watch the
British bulldozers doing the burial job with the full approval of
ninety per cent of the British electorate. Does the disappearance
of the principle of free enterprise versus socialism and state control mean that there are no principles left?

Not at all, but neither party yet realizes or has the wit to perceive the fact that the great principle now in jeopardy is the freedom of the individual.

How is the personal freedom of the individual, which means the preservation of his personality, to be protected against the activities of the vast bureaucracy which is essential to the technical management of the kind of modern society we demand?

It may be – unless there is a reaction to modern mechanized and planned life – that the economic freedom of the individual has disappeared for ever.

But if Man, the individual, is to be preserved, it is imperative that we do not allow the machine we have created to operate our affluent society, to organize as well our leisure activities. It is essential that, when we emerge from the control of the machine, whether at the end of the working day or when we 'retire' (at an increasingly young age), we should be allowed, and indeed encouraged, to pursue a *private life* and to be as noncomformist as we wish.

It may prove to be technically impossible to combine what we call high standards of living with the personal freedom to choose how we want to enjoy the fruits of our state-directed and controlled labours for wealth production. If this is true, we shall have mistaken means for ends. What shall it profit a man if he gains the whole world and loses his soul?

PAUL MEDOW[1]

◎ ◎

The Humanistic Ideals of the Enlightenment and Mathematical Economics

PAUL MEDOW, born in Prague in 1926, came to the United States in 1939, studied at Cornell University, and received his Ph.D. in economics from Columbia University. Since 1957 he has been assistant professor of economics at Rutgers University, and has contributed articles on the economy of the U.S.S.R. to the McGraw-Hill *Encyclopedia of Russia and the U.S.S.R.*, edited by M. T. Florinsky.

Summary

By separating the concept of an optimal allocation of scarce means from market processes and also from a broader concept of macroeconomic rationality, the use of mathematical methods in economic science has freed the humanistic ideals of the Enlightenment from their long association with the market and has returned them to the political sphere.

Aside from an emphasis on the primacy of inner values, the humanization of a society must allow the life-situation within which individuals are placed by prevailing institutions to permit choices that differ significantly from each other with regard to one's way of life. In an industrial society, the freedom of the individual is limited by the functional requirements of the economy itself. Both he and his fellow citizens derive their vital means from a nation-wide structure of technologically determined relationships whose manipulation lies beyond the range of individual decisions. Above all, in the absence of special arrangements, the individual possesses no information concerning the extent to which it is actually possible to adjust the

1. I wish to express my gratitude to Professor Karl Polanyi for valuable advice during the preparation of this article.

economy to different ways of life. In such circumstances it is natural for him to assume that he must simply accept whatever the further development of industrial economies will bring, both to his personal fate and to the historical fate of his nation; accordingly, he assumes that, in the industrial era, an active concern with humanistic norms is utopian.

The relevance of economic science to the humanization of industrial societies is defined by this very problem. Its function must be not only to ensure an effective production and distribution of material means, but also to assist the political sphere in selecting the particular ends that the economy is to serve and in identifying the limitations that may safely be imposed upon its influence.

Although its prolonged association with the study of self-regulating market systems has long caused economic science to support policy norms that are directly opposed to such a function, its recent re-examination of basic processes in the light of mathematical analysis, together with the availability of electronic computers and of a variety of new calculation techniques, has led some of the most prominent international economists to take an altogether new position in this regard, and to view the subordination of industrial economies to an increasing humanization of social life as the primary function of a new conception of central planning.

1. *The humanistic ideals of the Enlightenment and the problem of scarce means in neo-classical economics*

Paradoxically, it was precisely a concern with the humanistic values of the Enlightenment that served to restrain the founders of economic science from exploring the different types of societies that economies might serve. The rationalist reinterpretation of the medieval concept of the Law of Nature stated that since the use of reason was sufficient to gain a knowledge of the Law of Nature, that is, of the criteria needed for making judgements with regard to the problems of life, only a society based on the individual judgements of persons, and hence one in which the contractual principle of mutual consent tended to govern the formulation of social obligations, could be regarded as a 'natural' one. It is the additional belief that man's pursuit of personal gain also represented a 'natural' type of behaviour, in the sense that made it possible for Adam Smith to regard the market as an institutional embodiment of the Law of Nature itself.

Subsequently, both industrial production and international trade, instituted through self-regulating systems of markets, stimulated the concern of economic science with markets and hence with the pursuit of personal gain, even though the earlier optimism concerning the social merits of the personal-gain ethic quickly vanished. The attention of economics was directed to the remarkable capacity of a self-regulating structure of monetary flows, created solely by transactions of the market type, to regulate automatically the production as well as the distribution of goods in society. At first, there was little awareness of the historical uniqueness of such an arrangement for organizing an economy, and of the fact that an abandonment of the fictitious commodities called 'labour', 'land' and 'money' to the laws of the market had become a permanent and far-reaching source of social disorganization and tensions, as well as of technological change.[1]

Since the end of the nineteenth century, however, the association of market economics with the formal analysis of efficiency has created a belief that the institutional structure of a self-regulating market system possesses a specifically economic as well as a social claim to universality, derived from its embodiment of the principle of scarcity in nature.[2] But it is the further belief that industrial production itself requires the presence of prices that correctly reflect the relative scarcity of individual means in a society that has since identified neo-classical economics with a strong opposition to the very thought of eliminating competitive social behaviour or of making industrial production responsive to broader social aims.

What has been the basis in logic for such a position? And what are the elements of this basis that have now been affected by the application of mathematical methods to the analysis of economic processes?

1. Cf. Karl Polanyi, *The Great Transformation*, in which it is emphasized that the abandonment of industrial economies to this kind of self-regulation brought about a 'disembedding of the economy from society'. Also Karl Polanyi, 'Our Obsolete Market Mentality.'
2. Cf. Karl Polanyi, 'The Economy as Instituted Process'.

Briefly, it had been noted that if one attempts to identify the optimal form of allocating resources, a knowledge of the relative scarcities of resources in various uses is required. Such knowledge makes it possible partly to reallocate each resource from uses in which it is initially relatively abundant (in the sense that the significance of a withdrawal of a few units is not very great) to uses in which it is initially relatively 'scarce' (in the sense that the significance of 'productivity' of adding a few units is greater). Obviously, if one repeats this process until no further improvement is possible (until in formal terms, the 'productivity' of adding a few more units of the resource has been equalized in all uses), that pattern of allocation which is 'optimal', or preferable to all others, will have been identified.

Precisely such a process appears to result from the very functioning of a self-regulating market system. Under such a system the capacity of an enterprise to divert a greater share of resources to its own use generally derives from its greater capacity to satisfy the wishes of consumers. If one agrees to regard the latter, accordingly, as the ultimate objective of the economic process as a whole, and if the prices that enterprises must pay for additional resources do correctly reflect their significance in other uses (as should be the case when all resources are sold to the highest bidders), then both the firm that maximizes its own profits and the owner of a resource who withholds it from the economy until the highest possible price is paid appear to be performing a vital economy-wide function as well.

It then follows logically that an unhampered manifestation of a 'natural' striving for maximum gain on the part of consumers, enterprises and persons supplying the basic inputs into the system must be regarded as a functional necessity if one wishes to bring about a state of 'general equilibrium' with regard to the allocation of resources which thus represents the best possible integration of the economy as a whole. In an industrial economy, however, the freedom not to choose its best possible integration is clearly limited by the threat of a disorganization of production itself. In the absence of more precise knowledge concerning such a possibility, therefore, it has not been difficult to view an opposition to the use of markets for organizing economies not only as a rejection of the humanistic norms of the Enlightenment, but as a threat to industrial production as well.

PAUL MEDOW

The discovery that the orienting of decisions on scarcity is a functional as well as possibly a 'natural' phenomenon was followed by the adoption of a new definition of the very subject of economic science. The view that it concerns those processes in a society that bring about the production and distribution of material means was replaced by the view that it concerns the economizing of all scarce means in society, and the name 'Political Economy' was changed to 'Economics'. However, the new interest in the capacity of simple acts of reallocation to be 'productive', in the sense of creating an additional measure of utility, resulted in a neglect of production in the technological sense. Similarly, the association of allocation with the norms of a particular definition of optimality resulted in a neglect of the social aspects of the relevant decisions. Aside from creating a considerable amount of confusion within economic science itself, this has made it particularly difficult to identify the relation of economic science to other social disciplines.

2. The non-deterministic policy framework of mathematical economics

A first challenge to the central position of the concept of a 'competitive' or 'general' equilibrium was contained in Joseph Schumpeter's *Theory of Economic Development* (1911), which stressed the role of technological and other innovations, rather than of better allocation patterns, in increasing the abundance of an economy's output.

Subsequently, its position was weakened in the course of a prolonged debate concerning the relevance of 'competitive' prices to a centrally planned economy; and also through empirical studies of pre-industrial economies, in which both the absence of a self-regulating market system and the active role of a wide variety of non-market institutions in organizing the economy are apparent.[1,2] A continued lack of clarity concerning the

1. The debate concerning central planning established that it is possible, in principle, to identify the 'scarcity prices' of industrial resources without the help of either competitive markets or mathematical calculations. (O. Lange, *On the Economic Theory of Marxism*); that in a centrally planned economy the meaning of economic rationality ceases to depend on the preferences of consumers, and must be inferred from broader features of the type of society that is sought (K. Polanyi, '*Sozialistische Rechnungslegung*'; J. A. Schumpeter, *Capitalism, Socialism, and Democracy*); and

actual relation of production decisions to monetary indices of various types, both in pre-industrial economies and in centrally planned industrial economies, together with the obvious soundness of the logical analysis of efficiency contained in the concept of 'general equilibrium' have cast further doubt on the claim to universality of Schumpeter's theory.

More recently, the debate concerning the relevance of 'equilibrium' prices to central planning has been shifted to new grounds by the rapid development of applied mathematics. Briefly, the use of mathematics in the analysis of economic processes has made clear not only the extent to which industrial economies are actually flexible, but also the existence of a distinction between the concept of an optimal allocation of scarce means and a wider concept of macroeconomic rationality. This has become possible, however, only in connexion with a shift from the study of market processes to the study of technologically determined relationships.

(a) *The analysis of technologically determined relationships*

In a general way it is self-evident that if a comprehensive knowledge were available of all the technological processes employed in a particular economy, together with adequate mathematical methods for representing the technologically determined interdependence among individual industries, and also electronic computers capable of exploring systematically the different ways in which existing industries might be combined, then a new basis would exist for adjusting industrial economies to selected social objectives. It would then be possible to provide comprehensive information to the political sphere not only on what kind of production patterns are technically feasible at a given time, but also on the exact nature of the alternative possibilities that are sacrificed whenever a particular set of objectives is selected for implementation. The subsequent selection of one particular production pattern rather than another could then be made to reflect a wide variety of social as well as of purely economic considerations, within which the role of personal

---

that political decisions to give priority to non-economic objectives can be made sounder by calculations of their economic costs (Polanyi, op. cit.).

2. Cf. K. Polanyi, C. Arensberg, H. W. Pearson, eds., *Trade and Market in the Early Empires*.

consumption need no longer play a determining part. In such a context the question whether its implementation would or would not require a subsequent transformation of physical targets into a set of calculated 'scarcity prices' for the corresponding inputs appears as a subordinate point.

In spite of important limitations, however, all three of these elements have in fact become available in recent years, and their existence has already led the government of one major industrial nation – France – to declare its intention to employ them systematically for adjusting the economy to social objectives.

A comprehensive representation of all technological processes in an industrial economy has been achieved indirectly, by dividing the economy into a varying number of 'productive sectors' or 'industries', and then considering what transfers from other industries are required by the production of a unit of output in a given industry.

More specifically, the values of such 'technical coefficients' have been calculated for many of the industrially developed economies by first recording the actual deliveries of individual industries to others within an economy-wide 'input–output table', and then comparing the recorded level of production in each with the levels of each type of input that it receives.

A knowledge of all such 'technical coefficients' then makes it possible to infer the required levels of production of individual industries under a wide variety of circumstances, without referring to institutional arrangements or to actual selection criteria. It makes it possible, for instance, to calculate the extent by which the production of petroleum and of rubber must be increased in order to support a twenty-five-per-cent increase in the production of automobiles; and in a similar way, the required levels of production of all industries corresponding to a given combination of final goods. But since the corresponding calculations centre on first setting aside that share of the production of each industry required for the support of postulated levels of activity in the receiving industries, and then considering the residual available for consumption or for exports, these calculations themselves identify the precise conditions under which a disruption of industrial production will not take place.

While this alone has freed the analysis of resource allocation from its traditional dependence on market processes, the availability of 'technical coefficients' for an entire economy has also brought about a fundamental reappraisal of the actual relevance of optimal prices to the aims of the economic process. It has made it possible to apply a purely mathematical procedure for allocating scarce resources in an optimal way.

(b) *The distinction between the concept of macroeconomic rationality and that of an optimal allocation of scarce means*

In its simplest form the mathematical formulation of the analysis of optimal resource allocation has become known as 'linear programming', due to the 'linear' character of the mathematical equations employed to represent means–ends relationships. It may be applied to any type of means–ends structure in which the ends can be achieved with more than one set of means, and in which the possibility of substituting one set of means for another is therefore present.

Essentially, the calculations described as 'programming' refer to an elimination by trial and error of all 'feasible' sets of means except one – which thus emerges as best from the point of view of some formally specified criterion.

Among the unexpected features of such an 'optimal' solution is the fact that it can be described in either of two fully equivalent forms: either in the form of an optimal structure of ends or activities, specified in physical terms; or of a corresponding set of optimal 'shadow prices' attaching to individual means, which reflect their relative importance for maximizing the dominant objective.

While the discovery of this method and its wide application to a variety of industrial and military problems in the last ten years have served to confirm to neo-classical economists the soundness of the logical principles on which they had relied, its additional implications have undermined the very postulates on which the claim to universality of neo-classical economics had been founded.

In particular, it has now become fully evident that there is nothing specifically economic about the analysis of 'scarcity prices'. 'It has been made apparent,' as Professor J. R. Hicks has observed, 'not only that a price system is inherent in the problem of maximizing against restraints.[1] . . . The logic of choice,' he

---

1. J. R. Hicks, 'Linear Theory'. This general point has also been discussed in K. Polanyi *et al.*, eds., *Trade and Market in the Early Empires*; and O. Lange, *Political Economy*.

adds, 'now that it has been fully mathematized, appears as nothing else but pure technics – the distilled essence of a general technology.'[1]

In addition, since it has now become possible to identify optimal scarcity prices through the use of electronic computers, a need for competitive institutions can no longer be inferred from the relevance of such prices to the general problem of allocating scarce means.

The most important implication of linear programming for neo-classical economics, however, concerns the long-held conviction that an optimal allocation of scarce means is by its very nature the most rational one. The formal aspects of mathematical programming have made it fully clear that an optimal allocation of means can be identified only *after* there is full agreement concerning the basic ends that the economy is to serve, the particular set of policy objectives that are to be regarded as dominant, and the nature of the additional non-technological constraints that should be included in the basic system of equations. It follows, accordingly, that within the possibilities determined by technology, there exist, in fact, as many optimal ways of allocating resources as there are political opinions concerning the best choice of these more basic elements; that, should they be needed, calculated 'shadow prices' for inputs can be made to reflect any one of these choices; and that a more fundamental definition of macroeconomic rationality must therefore be sought in political processes and in the broader social ends that political processes can serve.

3. *The separation of the humanistic ideals of the Enlightenment from the market and their return to the political sphere*

In spite of remaining problems concerning the collection and presentation of data, concerning the relative place of mathematical processes, in which the various feasible adjustments of the less desirable possibilities, and also concerning the nature of the institutional arrangements through which the implementation of a selected set of objectives will best be carried out, the technical possibility of an adjustment of industrial production systems to non-economic criteria had thus been established through a clarification of the very grounds on which it had earlier been

1. Ibid.

denied. At the same time, the emphasis 'not only on pecuniary measures of output, national income, etc., but even more on *social goals*'[1] that this suggests has been associated with a new image of political processes, in which the various feasible adjustments of the production system calculated by the experts are made to reflect a variety of political objectives, as well as the requirements of non-economic organizations; in which the selection of a particular alternative is preceded by a public debate; and in which the political power of central authorities has been checked through decentralization.[2, 3]

The new optimism that this makes possible with regard to the ideals of humanism has been expressed by a leading mathematical economist, Ragnar Frisch, who notes that the advent of electronic computers and of econometric methods has removed what was previously a technical obstacle to 'safeguarding the freedom and ethical and moral dignity of the individual in the true spirit of the age of Enlightenment'.[4]

Similarly the official adoption of the principle of balancing a variety of social objectives against economic objectives in determining the aims of central planning in France has led a prominent French economist to state that the broad, society-oriented type of growth that this implies defines a function for the economic process that is 'neither the increasing of consumption, nor the increasing of leisure, but the creation *for all*, and in the first place for those who are in the least favoured circumstances, of the material conditions in which their freedom will blossom out'.[5]

That a capacity to adjust economic processes to different courses of social and historical development does not in itself guarantee precisely such an outcome is made evident by the fact that at present the new methods of central planning have

1. R. Frisch, 'A Preface to the Oslo Channel Model', p. 258.
2. Ibid., p. 256.
3. It has also been noted that an application of the new methods of planning to the foreign trade of individual nations, and, beyond this, to a coordination of the trade of many nations on the basis of preferences that they themselves express, could reduce the present vulnerability of national economies to developments occurring in distant parts of the world. Cf. R. Frisch, 'A Multilateral Trade Clearing Agency'.
4. Frisch, 'A Preface to the Oslo Channel Model', p. 258.
5. F. Perroux, *Le IVᵉ Plan français (1962–65)*, p. 17.

found their widest application in the planning of military systems.[1] In addition, the nature of the real limitations on the flexibility of complex production systems has yet to be explored. The new optimism appears to be more than justified, nevertheless, not only because it is no longer possible to employ the authority of economic science in advocating a continued subordination of society to a spontaneously developing economic sphere, but also because the liberation of the ideals of humanism from their association with contractual relationships and with markets makes it possible to conceive a type of social development based on a deeper and more realistic understanding of these ideals than was available in the eighteenth century.[2]

BIBLIOGRAPHY

E. Cassirer, *Essay on Man* (New York: Doubleday, 1944, 1953).

H. B. Chenery and P. B. Clark, *Interindustry Economics* (New York: John Wiley, 1959).

R. Frisch, 'A Preface to the Oslo Channel Model', *Europe's Future in Figures*, ed. R. C. Geary (Amsterdam: North Holland Publishing Co., 1962); 'A Multilateral Trade Clearing Agency', *Statsokonomisk Tidsskrift* (Norway, No. 1, 1963).

E. Fromm, *Man for Himself* (New York: Holt, Rinehart & Co., 1947; London: Routledge & Kegan Paul); *Psychoanalysis and Religion* (New Haven: Yale University Press, 1950).

J. R. Hicks, 'Linear Theory', in *Economic Journal* (December 1960), pp. 671–709.

C. J. Hitch, 'The New Approach to Management in the U.S. Defense Department', *Management Science* (October 1962), pp. 1–8; and with R. N. McKean, *The Economics of Defense in the Nuclear Age* (Cambridge, Mass.: Harvard University Press, 1960; Oxford: O.U.P.).

1. C. J. Hitch, 'The New Approach to Management in the U.S. Defense Department', pp. 1–8. Also, C. J. Hitch and R. M. McKean, *The Economics of Defense in the Nuclear Age.*

2. The two major events in this regard have been the confrontation of these ideals with the reality of means–ends relationships in society (since Hegel and Marx); and more recently their association with the cultural symbol structure of a society (Cf. E. Cassirer, *Essay on Man*) with unconscious processes (Cf. E. Fromm, *Psychoanalysis and Religion*, and *Man for Himself*) and with the existential problems of man.

O. Lange, *On the Economic Theory of Socialism* (Minneapolis: University of Minnesota Press, 1938; Oxford: O.U.P.); *Introduction to Econometrics* (New York and Oxford: Pergamon Press, 1959, 1963); *Political Economy* (New York: Macmillan, 1963; Oxford: Pergamon Press).

Karl Polanyi, '*Sozialistische Rechnungslegung*', *Archiv für Sozialwissenschaft und Sozialpolitik* (Band 49, Heft 2, 1922), pp. 377–402; *The Great Transformation* (New York: Holt, Rinehart & Co., 1944); 'Our Obsolete Market Mentality', *Commentary* (New York, February 1947), pp. 109–17; 'The Economy as Instituted Process', in K. Polanyi, C. Arensberg and H. W. Pearson, eds., *Trade and Market in the Early Empires* (Glencoe, Illinois: Free Press, 1957).

F. Perroux, *Le IVe Plan français (1962–65)* (Paris: Presses Universitaires, 1962).

J. A. Schumpeter, *The Theory of Economic Development* (New York: O.U.P., 1911, 1961); *Capitalism, Socialism and Democracy* (New York: Harper & Row, 1942, 1950, 1962).

DANILO DOLCI

⊚ ⊚

Reflections on Planning and Groups, Decentralization and Planning

DANILO DOLCI, born in Trieste in 1924, left his study of architecture at the Universities of Rome and Milan to join Don Zeno Saltini in the Nomadelfia community. He founded and directed the Centro Studi e Iniziative per la Piena Occupazione in Partinico, a centre for study and action for the development of Western Sicily, and was awarded the Lenin Peace Prize in 1959. Some of his writings deal with his work in Sicily, *Bandits at Partinico, Inquest at Palermo, Sicilian Tales, Conversations* and *Waste.*

If we reflect, it is evident that there must be a unified planning that is both fulfilling and corrective, dedicated to realizing simultaneously the maximum personality and the maximum fluidity of the group and of the individual. Since a problem must be considered in all its aspects, the problem of life – life for everyone – demands the interest and involvement of each one of us. Hence an educational work dedicated to the goal of having each person recognize his own true interests, the interests of all the groups to which he belongs and, by extension, the interests of all is of fundamental importance. In other words, the most fruitful and the most complete opportunity for being educated and educating lies in social planning.

I believe that we are already, more or less consciously, on this path; we can easily see the signs if we look around us. If I look out of my window, I see the clouds above Partinico; their movements are being observed by meteorological stations which are coordinated, like so many other scientific stations, throughout the world. There are some books on my table; it is somewhat like having around me the keen, merry smile of Bertrand Russell, the blue-eyed, slightly fixed glance of Aldous Huxley, and

Gandhi, Lenin and Einstein. In the sky above my house the jet stream of an aeroplane is dissolving. Not long ago I spent a week-end of work in New Delhi, and a little before that I flew to New York in less time than it takes me to go by car across Western Sicily. Already today one nation cannot draw up a plan without taking into account what is happening in the rest of the world. I who am not yet forty have heard mass declamations about the heroism of the fatherland fighting the enemy across the border, while today thousands of young people whom I encounter have ideas suffused with a belief in human unity (it is true that this is also because the vision of youth is limited in its perception of the difficulties). If I wander about the countryside in certain nations, the dogs, instead of barking at me with hostility as their Sicilian counterparts still do, readily come to be patted; and the birds, even though still wary, do not flee hurriedly at my advance; they already possess another 'nature'. In a few decades, every inhabitant of one continent will be able to visit the other continents. In a few centuries, mankind will be able to communicate via a common language. Eyvind is thirty-four years old, Marco twenty-five – we are collaborators. In working with people they accept setback and defeat smilingly, as if they were in their fifties. I thought that my son Amico, when he was roaring around the tables and chairs with a pot-lid in his hands, was driving a car; no, he was driving a rocket through the stars.

What are some of the general conditions that would permit us to hypothesize a united mankind? I will list a few necessary conditions:

(a) *The instruments of production and of sound economic management should be concentrated according to those who show themselves capable of the responsibility,* taking into consideration that the prevention of exploitation is not only a structural problem, but also a problem of participation and control in ever new and more adequate forms. We must dedicate ourselves directly as well as indirectly to the raising of the technical, cultural and moral level of all mankind, for the employment of the most efficient techniques of production tends to increase the potential of man, not to extinguish it. The rigidifying processes working against the new world will be attenuated as the level of mankind rises (the role of production, and whether the passage will be gradual or in leaps and bounds, depending on the resistance offered by self-interest and privilege, were emphasized especially in the nineteenth century);

(*b*) *The groups, the structures, and the intermediary organisms between individual and centre must be formed,* inviting everyone to participate in the formation, the realization, and the control of decisions. The more the necessary intermediary organisms are lacking, the more possibility there will be of regimentation or of chaos, of inhumane pressures or of privation and disintegration. The discussion of method during the last four centuries has concentrated on the physical world; it is urgent that we turn now, with prudence and patience but also with haste, to the theory and method, so to speak, of a better relationship between men. (Particular attention must be devoted to the problem of intermediaries. The greatest temptation, at least in our primitive world, is to tend towards the summit, to assimilate oneself to the centre: we must avoid the danger of the centre becoming the superlative, of administration becoming discipline and the individual becoming a source of renunciation. Each representative, each holder of responsibility must continue to grow in a fruitful relationship with his group, that he may continue to express authentically the decisions of the base that he represents, and not fragment and fossilize the intermediation.)

Each person must be a dedicated centre in himself, but correlated to the centres for data collection and to the centres of coordination; we must be ever more precise as to what must be the contribution of the individual from the base and what must be the contribution from the intermediates and from the centre. (I have used the term 'base' for years, solely to make myself understood, adding immediately that I would consider absurdly utopian a planning solely from the base or one solely from the summit: what is necessary is a planning which fosters the maximum participation from the base and the most intimate rapport between the base and the centre.)

(*c*) *The continuous process of give and take, that is, the dynamics of the development process between individual and centre via the necessary intermediate groups, must be better formulated, and function better:*

↓	individual ↑
	group/groups
↓	all ↑

or, in territorial terms:

| the individual ↑
| his locality
| his zone
| his region
| . . . .
↓ the world.

The spiral process through which we arrive at fundamental decisions must be ever more alive:

the collection and verification of data from which to depart –
elaboration according to the possibilities and the necessities –
formulation of plans –
realization and verification of the plans –

with a spiralling dynamic of velocity sensitive and faithful in its transmission:

principles
hypotheses
methods of procedure
action.

It is not so much a question of finding the perfect forms, or of projecting a utopia – the forms change, after all, according to different conditions – as of knowing how to arrive at the necessary living forms, knowing how to put into operation clearly and exactly the various positions, and guaranteeing their intercommunication.

To realize the hypotheses, we must press forward from every point of view, on all possible fronts, contemporaneously and continually, conscious of the enormous effort necessary, by trying to perceive and form in the present world the directions of the new world, by constructing, struggling, never passing up an occasion to make a step or a leap forward, and by having clear certain fundamental premises.

Conventions, it is understood, must be founded according to the original sense of the word, and then respected. Civil life cannot exist without conventions, but they must be treated as conventions.

The old world speaks in these terms: 'One must obey the ruling law and its representatives; he prospers who complies with his duties and enjoys his rights.' To make appeal only to their rights and duties when treating people is not to communicate with the intelligence and the joyful creativity that exists in people, but to treat them like the inmates of a barracks. Perhaps it would not be pointless to include here a comparison between typical expressions of the 'old' world and their counterparts in the 'new' world (I am obviously not referring to old and new in a strictly chronological sense):

command	→ coordinate
power	→ responsibility
exploitation	→ valorization
obey	→ agree
merit	→ capacity
sin	→ insufficiency
punishment	→ cure
duty	→ necessity
right	→ effective possibility
privilege	—
revenge	—
slave	—
death penalty	—

In the world of good sense, in which authority is entrusted to knowledge and love, certain words change their sense (authority, discipline, dignity, honour, faith, creed, *law* are some examples). Naturally if the transformation is more in the linguistics than in the substance, the result is hypocritical formalism ('human relations office', for example).

All the affirmations of good sense concerning man that could be added here are part of the sense of non-violence; and they find not only their integration but also their possibility of resolution and of life in that creative capacity that men have sometimes called love.

To return to earth, lest I become lost in the clouds:

(*a*) In order to transform, there are two extremes:

1. to destroy for the sake of destroying, or to destroy in order to reconstruct (an inadequate, primitive position);
2. to discover the most true, most just nature of a situation in order to modify it most rapidly in the best manner possible.

(*b*) It is necessary to know ever more clearly what violence or what non-violence we desire, to know how to weigh complexities in the balance; and we must distinguish between the soft, passive, ingenuous non-violence and the revolutionary, strong, intelligent, and even holy non-violence.

(*c*) He who is underdeveloped must realize that the causes of his backwardness and of the impediments to his life are to be found first of all in his own lack of clearness, in his lack of organization, in his lack of coherence, and in his lack of creative force, rather than in the wickedness of others; he must obligate himself to not permitting others, as well as himself, to be inorganic, monstrous.

(*d*) To the measure in which one does not succeed in moving a population from within according to its exigencies, there is the risk that the unhealthy violence will perpetuate itself or impose itself in a thousand ways: in the various types of exploitive tyrannies, in diverse fascist doctrines, and so forth. It is clear at the same time that the most advanced, most aware forces must intervene in an attempt to eliminate the resistance 'from the outside'.

(*e*) It is true that what has in itself universal values will sooner or later affirm itself. But areas that have had very different experiences and histories (western Sicily and northern Italy; Africa and Europe; at one time Russia and America) naturally have cultures and moralities that are diverse, and cannot communicate easily with each other. Every act of a determined culture or morality, when it does not have sufficient presuppositions in common with another, will not be accepted, and will only succeed in being efficacious with regard to the other culture. From this arises the necessity of strengthening the living relationships between diverse cultures.

The presence of a hero is in a certain sense a symptom of insufficiency, of a group that, lacking the normal instruments of organization, the normal technical and cultural tools, must, in order to survive and to advance, subject some of its members, even if indirectly, to a superhuman tension. But as it has been shown that we mature better in a group or in groups (take, for example, the human maturation in certain northern European peoples through various collective forms, in comparison to the fresh but often infantile behaviour of people who proceed in isolation, as is frequently the case in southern Europe), so also has the risk of leaning too heavily on the group been demonstrated, as the group increases in size and diminishes individual stature and creativity. To me it therefore appears necessary to safeguard both the maturation, the guarantee of quantity and quality that is attainable through communal action, and the equally necessary individual tension, which is as exact, disciplined, and sensitive to planning as it is fresh, vivacious, spontaneous and true to itself. In short, the new hero, the new saint, or rather the new heroes, the new saints, are those who know that things are true and real in the measure to which they become so and to which we make them become so.

GALVANO DELLA VOLPE

⊙ ⊙

The Legal Philosophy of Socialism

> GALVANO DELLA VOLPE, born in Bologna in 1895, is pro-
> fessor of the history of philosophy at Messina University.
> His main publications include *Rousseau e Marx, Umane-
> simo positivo e emancipazione marxista, La libertà comunista,
> Logica come scienza positiva, Critica del gusto,* and studies of
> David Hume.

Karl Marx, in one of his most important works, writes:

> Only the French Revolution completed the transformation of
> political classes into social classes; or, rather, it transformed the
> differences of social class in civil society into purely social differ-
> ences – differences in the sphere of private life which had no
> significance in political life. In this way was brought about the
> separation of political life from civil society [a separation which
> had not existed in feudal society]. . . . And, in that same society,
> such differences no longer constituted permanent barriers; they
> became, instead, crossable boundaries, and the principle by
> virtue of which they were crossed was that of free will. Its main
> criteria are *money* and *culture*.[1]

With regard to those criteria, Marx outlined the following related concept of a 'political', or bourgeois, revolution (which, he
says, was already a 'Utopian dream' in the semi-feudal Germany of the 1840s):

> What is required for a partial, or *merely political*, revolution?
> Simply this, that *one part of civil society emancipate itself* and
> attain hegemony; and that a certain class undertake, *starting
> from its own situation*, the general emancipation of society. This
> certain class emancipates the whole of society – but only on condi-
> tion that *the whole of this society find itself in the same situation as*

1. Karl Marx, *Kritik des Hegelschen Staatsrechts, Die Frühschriften,* ed.
S. Landshut (Stuttgart, 1953).

that class; that is, that it possess wealth and culture, or that it be able to procure them.[1]

In other words, according to Marx, that 'certain class' does *not*, in fact, emancipate the *whole* of society. Later on, we see Marx's conclusion on the 'role of the liberator': it belongs essentially to the proletariat as a class, which, 'by organizing all the conditions of human existence on the basis of *social liberty*' – and not merely of 'political' liberty – transforms partial, or bourgeois, emancipation into a 'general and human' emancipation of man.[2]

Now, is it wholly true, and is it the whole truth, that the 'political' or bourgeois revolution (that which established the equality of all citizens before the law) liberates only those who belong to the bourgeois class? That it does not liberate, from the standpoint of constitutional guarantees, the whole society as a *state*? In other words, is it the entire truth to say that solely the 'social' revolution – i.e. that which realizes the 'social' liberty or the free expansion of society at all levels – attains a 'general and human' emancipation of man?

This is the great question from which scientific socialism cannot hide, as traditional Marxism has hidden. Marx himself always remained faithful, in substance, to that youthful, drastic and unilateral critique of the bourgeois revolution. But, although he had such an acute awareness of the historical necessity for a bourgeois juridic infrastructure as to show the extension of it in the socialist state itself,[3] Marx was never overly concerned with emphasizing as well the necessity for extending, in that same socialist state, the juridic and constitutional guarantees of every person – citizen. Certainly he was too fully absorbed by the problem of 'social' revolution to be able to embrace the substantial and undeniable inheritance from the 'political' revolution (i.e. the measure of duration of certain bourgeois values) for the future, as he had embraced the whole concept of it with respect to the medieval past. The true secret of the Commune of '71, Marx says in *Civil War in France*, 'is that it will be, essentially,

---

1. Introduction, *Critique of the Hegelian Philosophy of Law*, 1844.
2. See *On the Jewish Question* (1844).
3. That is, under the aspect of 'equal' measure in the distribution of goods produced by common labour – a residual right of bourgeois economy, as Marx stated in *Critique of the Gotha Programme*, his last important theoretical work.

a government of the working class, the result of a struggle between producer and exploiter; it will be the political form, eventually to be discovered, under which it will be possible to realize the economic emancipation of the worker'. In this Lenin followed Marx with his theory of the 'dictatorship of the proletariat'.[1] For Lenin, it should be noted, 'democracy means equality', but equality only of a social nature, because, as he explains it,[2] 'One can understand what a great deal of importance is attached to the struggle of the proletariat for equality, and to the word equality itself, if it is understood precisely in the sense of the *suppression of class.*'

In dealing with this problem of the relationship of Marxism to the substantial juridic heritage received from the bourgeois revolution – that problem which has come of age, historically, in the last forty years, but to which a solution (and not merely a historical one) is found in the Soviet socialist philosophy of law – it is expedient to consider first the extremely complex question of what is meant by 'modern democracy', given that the difficulty in question, when reduced to essentials, is identical with that of the relationship of social democracy (and revolution) to political democracy (and revolution). Let us begin, therefore, by examining, in that context, two aspects of the modern concepts of liberty and democracy. Rather than 'aspects', in fact, modern liberty and democracy have two faces, and two souls: there is *civil*, or *political*, liberty, founded by parliamentary or political democracy and theorized by Locke, Montesquieu, Kant, Humboldt, Constant; and there is *egalitarian*, or *social*, liberty, founded by social democracy and theorized primarily by Rousseau and, later, more or less explicitly, by Marx, Engels and Lenin.

Civil liberty – the so-called 'bourgeois' liberty – is, in its historical and technical sense, the liberty, or the complex of liberties, of the members of a 'civil society' of classes composed of individual producers. It is the whole of the liberties or of the rights of individual economic initiative, of security of private ownership of means of production, of *habeas corpus*, of worship,

---

1. See *State and Revolution*, III, 5, where is found – in the slightly dated context of the 'destruction of the parasitic state' – the text of Marx cited above.
2. Ibid., V, 4.

of conscience, of the Press, etc. (The question implicit in our point of departure is precisely whether or not any of these rights transcend the bourgeois state and affect the *universal* man who constitutes any political body.) The principal juridico-political expressions of civil liberty are basically the separation of the various powers of the state, and the organization of legislative power as representative of the national sovereignty, viz. the parliamentarianism of the liberal bourgeois state.

Social or egalitarian liberty, on the other hand, expresses an application which is universal and unconditional because it is apolitical. It signifies the right of *any human being* to a *social* recognition of his *personal abilities and potential*; it is, in short, the genuinely and absolutely democratic application to labour of the criterion of merit (and therefore of justice); in other words, it is the recognition of the social potential of the human individual *in genere*, as a person. Social liberty, therefore, is more than mere liberty, for it is also social justice; it is, in fact, a kind of *libertas major*, inasmuch as it is the liberty of the masses. 'I thought that to be endowed with talent would be the greatest protection against misery.' Such was the typical protest, still valid today, of Jean-Jacques Rousseau; it was adopted by Engels, who added that the greatest possible expression of such protection would be 'a [social] system which assures to every man the possibility of developing all of his physical and moral capacities'.

This contrast between the *two souls* of democracy, of the two modern interpretations of democracy, signifies, in political terms, the contrast between *liberalism*, which is a political system of liberty without equality or social justice, and *socialism*, which is a political system of liberty with social justice (i.e. justice for all) and which is, therefore, egalitarian liberty in its development.

We cannot deny, however, the obvious historical extension of that liberalism of Locke and of Kant into the first phase of the communization of society as actually attained by the socialistic Russian state, and particularly into the present legal philosophy of that state. To this aspect is related, at least indirectly, the question raised by Norberto Bobbio[1] concerning the workability of the 'technical juridic norms' (of bourgeois guarantees) in a proletarian state. Bobbio seeks simply to demonstrate the legitimacy of 'the necessity for inviting the advocates of the dictatorship

1. *Politica e cultura* (Turin, 1955).

of the proletariat to consider the forms of *liberal*–democratic régimes with respect to their more refined and more progressive juridic techniques'. For Bobbio, in effect, 'the important thing is that one begin to think of law not only as a bourgeois phenomenon, but as a complex of technical norms which may be made use of as much by the proletariat as by the bourgeoisie, so as to attain certain ends which are common to both parties inasmuch as they are both social beings'. Now, how valid is this 'necessity' described by Bobbio?

We know that the post-Stalin Constitution of the Soviet Union (reprinted in 1960, but almost identical to that of 1936) reiterates Articles 123–8, concerning the equal rights of individual citizens regardless of their nationality or race – liberty of conscience, of speech, of the Press, of assembly, of organizing labour unions, and the right of *habeas corpus* or of the 'inviolability of the person', by virtue of which 'no one may be arrested unless by judgment of a court of law or with the authorization of a magistrate'. The specific and basic reasons for these liberties, however, cannot be the same as those which obtain in a liberal or democratic bourgeois state, if for no other reason than that those liberties and subjective rights, those technical constitutional norms, are incorporated into the social and political philosophy of the first socialist state – and that state has foundations which are original and proper to itself. In order to establish the validity of the necessity formulated by Bobbio, therefore, it is not sufficient merely to adduce those *facts* which comprise the Soviet constitution in question; it is necessary, rather, to examine the *how* and *why* of the abolition, in that constitution, of the 'rationing of (civil) liberty, in favour of (egalitarian) liberty',[1] and to investigate, similarly, the *how* and *why* of the relative restitution of bourgeois juridic norms, i.e. of the norms of the 'legitimate state'.

The *how* of that abolition and that restitution is found in the *selective re-establishment* of resuscitated rights or civil liberties.

1. The abolition of such 'rationing' to the advantage of egalitarian liberty is, according to a dictum of Lenin, the dictatorship of the proletariat in the strict sense. It does not, then – unless one wishes to 'absolutize' historical events – exclude the alternative of a peaceful take-over of power by the proletariat by virtue of popular consent; it does not, therefore, necessarily characterize the socialist revolution, the main purpose of which is to socialize the means of production.

Such re-establishment or restitution is *selective*, or discriminating, because it *excludes the right of private ownership of the means of production* – a 'right' which history has proved to be anti-economic, anti-social and inhuman; one, moreover, which becomes transformed eventually into a privilege. Accordingly, we have Articles 9 and 10 of the Soviet constitution, where 'alongside the socialist economic system' are considered 'the small private holdings of peasants and artisans who are not organized' (into communes or cooperatives, in which 'every family of the commune, in addition to the basic proceeds of the collective economy of the commune, has for its own enjoyment and use the small parcel of land belonging to the house, and has as personal property such produce of the land, the house, the cattle, etc., as is based on personal labour, but excluding any exploitation of the work of another'). Such citizens have 'the right of *personal property* of citizens over the proceeds of their labour and their savings, over their house . . . their *consumer goods* and items of *personal convenience*, as well as the *right of inheriting the personal property of citizens*'. To this may be added the consideration that, in the restored freedom of worship, religion has lost its traditional character of 'the opium of the people' and been freed from regulation by public law; it has become strictly a private matter. It should be apparent, then, to what extent the norms of the 'legitimate state are at once *preserved* and *transformed, transvaluated* and *renewed*, in the progressive politico-socio-economic philosophy of a socialist state as a 'state of *all* the people' (Khrushchev). And it should be noted that these facts, in their precise historical substance, rectify what remains abstract and dogmatic in the liberal optimism of Bobbio's generous 'necessity'.

As to the *why* of this socialist restitution of the norms of the 'legitimate state', suffice it to say that so long as a state exists – even an enlightened state such as the socialist state – the fundamental principle of the 'legitimate state', viz. the principle of a limit to the power of the state over the persons of the citizens, remains supreme; indeed, it may be disregarded only at an incalculable price of unrest and of human suffering. (For an example of these consequences, one has only to think of an important corollary of this principle, the right of *habeas corpus*, and of the violations of that right during the Stalinist era.) As

Bobbio says, therefore, it is unquestionably true that

> it is very easy to disengage oneself from liberalism if one identi-
> fies it with the theory and practice of liberty as the power of the
> bourgeoisie; but it is much more difficult to do so when one con-
> siders liberalism as the theory and practice of limiting the power
> of the state . . . because liberty, as the power to *do* something,
> affects only those who are the fortunate possessors of it, while
> liberty as a *non-impediment* to action affects *all* men[1] [italics
> added].

The basis for such limitation is stated in the Kantian ethical
principle, that 'man is always an end, and never a means'. And,
paradoxically enough, that principle has its full and universal
application only in the Soviet socialist legal system, by reason of
the socialist *renovation* of subjective rights or civil liberties *inspired by that principle*; and this application consists in the extir-
pation of the right, among others, of private ownership of the
means of production, with all the abuses implied by such
ownership. Thus the profound and original liberal spirit of recent socialist history is destined to surprise the most critical
liberal philosopher.

In order to reach a conclusion, therefore, regarding the bourgeois juridic heritage at work in the socialist state, one must remember: (1) that in socialist constitutional guarantees there is a
renovation of civil liberties as well as of the popular-council style
of parliamentarianism (the soviets), and of the economico-bour-
geois right expressed in the dictum, 'for one part of work, an
equal part of goods' (and, regarding this last right, it should be
noted that the socialist *renovation* is evident in the acknowledged
social character of labour and of its product); (2) that the cataly-
tic agent which renovates the substance of the liberal state and
transforms it into the reality of the socialist state is an equality
based on materialism; (3) that, finally, the state is destined, according to the classic Marxist–Leninist theory, to be 'extin-
guished' in that 'society of free and equal men' which is the true
and proper communist society – i.e. a classless society in which
'public functions will lose their political character and become
simply administrative functions for assisting the members of
society'.[1]

1. Bobbio, op. cit.
2. Engels, quoted by Lenin in *State and Revolution*.

In the communist society of today can be recognized the Programme of Action presented at the Twenty-Second Congress of the Communist Party of the Soviet Union, in which were outlined 'the methods of development for a transition to a communist society in the next twenty years'. For example:

> The working class is the only class in history which does not propose to perpetuate its own power. . . . The transition to communist means the maximum growth of personal liberty and of the rights of Soviet citizens. . . . The increase of material well-being, of the cultural level, and of the consciousness of the workers holds out the promise of arriving finally at the complete substitution of corrective education for the misery of penal justice. . . . The evolution of the socialist organization of the state will lead, gradually, to its transformation into a communistic self-governing republic in which the soviets, the unions, the co-operatives, and other associations of workers will be united. This process will involve a further development of (social) democracy. . . . The organs of planning and of execution, of economic management and of cultural growth, which today are contained in the apparatus of the state, will lose their political character and become organs of social self-government. The communist society will be a highly organized community of working-men. . . . The course of history leads inevitably to the extinction of the state. And because the state finally is to be extinguished, it is necessary that there be realized both the internal conditions for it (the building up of a developed communist society) and the external conditions (a definitive solution in the international area of the contradictions between capitalism and communism – in favour of communism).

The legal concerns of socialism seem to resolve themselves into a complex of those economic and social problems, essentially political in nature, which have accumulated since the advent of the 'legitimate state'. Under Marxist influence, they are further resolved into a historical synthesis of Rousseau and Kant – viz. liberty as a function of equality, and the converse – wherein Rousseau's 'general sovereign will' is no longer *reduced* to a popular, national bourgeois sovereignty, but rather is *realized* as a sovereignty of the working class. Further, it is able to accept and reconcile, in its democratic working-class centralism, those bourgeois civil liberties, which are not opposed to the liberty of the masses. On the other hand, Kant's juridic arrangement, renovated by that working-class centralism (and only by virtue of that renovation), acquires the universal validity to which, in its original bourgeois rigidity, it aspired in vain. In this respect, it should be noted that (1) continuance in the path of historic growth (i.e. the class struggle culminating in the socialist state), or continuance in the path of Kantian non-*a priori* liberalism, is clear confirmation of the classical foundations of Kant's thought no less than of Locke's (the opinion of the late Mr Solari notwithstanding); furthermore, the historic vitality of Kant's thought may be explained by the fact that, in its rational formulation, it is superior to that of Locke; (2) it is not conceivable, in this Kantian liberalism so paradoxically universalized in socialist law, that man will be able to rest content 'eternally' (as thought Solari, with respect to the original Kantian liberalism), because it is obvious that such liberalism will not endure longer than the socialist state – and the latter is destined to final extinction in the social self-government of the classless communist society.

How, then, is it possible to accuse the Soviet socialist state – a state of *all* the people – of 'totalitarianism'? This accusation, however persistent, may be explained only by a blind self-interest, founded on class. In any case, the truth is slowly becoming known, as may be seen from recent legal literature. Michel Mouskhély and Zygmunt Jedryka,[1] among others, have recently given a fairly exact idea of Soviet socialist legal philosophy. Here, for instance, is the Rousseauean element:

In establishing the control of the electors over the elected, and its sanction (the *recall* [dismissal of elected representatives]), the Constitution of 1936 [Article 142, which is also Article 142 of the 1960 Constitution] seems to be inspired by the ideas of Rousseau. . . . Since the precedent of 1936, participation by the people in legislation requires that, before major reforms be adopted by competent agencies, they be the object of a public inquiry. . . . The workers' conferences, regularly scheduled by the Central Committee of the Party and by the government, furnish another example of that *participation by the people in the direction of public affairs*. When there is a concrete question to be discussed, a certain legal project to consider, a decision to be enforced, *those concerned are appealed to*. . . . Thus, we can speak, to that extent, of an indirect participation by the masses in the legislative work of the state. . . . For the professional unions, this collaboration almost takes the form of a sharing of public power. In matters

1. *Le Gouvernement de l'U.R.S.S.* (Paris: Presses Universitaires, 1961).

regarding work and wages, the state associates them to the exercise of its legislative and executive powers. Thus, acts in this area emanate jointly from the Central Committee of the Party, from the Council of Ministers, and from the Central Council of Unions. . . . *For the unions, then, participation in legislation and in administration is direct*[1] (italics supplied).

And here is the Kantian element:

Those presently in power do everything possible to *guarantee and safeguard the essential rights of man and of the citizen before the organs of judicial instruction.* (1) *The court, the sole administrator of justice.* . . . Henceforth, no one can be judged and condemned except by the ordinary organs of justice. In losing its omnipotence in the state, the Security Police, too, lose their character of political police . . . consequently, many actions which were handled, until now, by the 'police courts', or which were treated with extreme rigor as counter-revolutionary crimes or as violations of socialist work discipline, henceforth are regarded with more leniency by the ordinary tribunals. (2) *The participation of popular assessors in the conduct of affairs of all courts* – the principle of the collegiality of courts. . . . The popular assessors take an active part not only in the proceedings themselves but also in all phases of the procedure and of judicial instruction. The voice of each one of them carries as much weight as that of the judge. . . . (3) *The eligibility of judges and of popular assessors* – they are subject to recall by their electors or by a decision of the court. From this principle flows, logically, the duty for soviet magistrates of presenting reports to their electors and, for the electors, that of requiring regular reports. . . . (4) *The independence of judges and their subjection only to the laws.* The constitutional principle of the independence of the courts has, as an indispensable corollary, the independence of judges. . . .[2]

To summarize the substantial juridic contrast between the Soviet present and the Soviet past (years of the dictatorship of the proletariat), it is worth while quoting the following conclusive judgement of Rudolf Schlesinger on Pasukanis and his school of penal law so famous in the twenties and thirties:

It was logically implied in the general theory of law of Pasukanis that, so long as there existed antagonistic classes and a penal law was still necessary, it was inevitable that that law be dominated by

1. Mouskhély and Jedryka, op. cit., p. 176 ff.; cf. also p. 175.
2. Ibid., p. 234 ff. Cf. also T. Napolitano, *Il nuovo codice penale sovietico* (Milan, 1963).

the principle of 'equivalence', or, to use a current term, the principle of an eye for an eye. Otherwise, penal law, in an attempt to apply justice in the case of a culpable individual, would have lost its *foreseeability*, and thus its general preventive efficacy[1] (italics supplied).

Having arrived at the end of this investigation, we should pause to consider the dialectic of those two modern expressions of liberty, the civil and the egalitarian. It is a dialectic of which the Soviet legal system offers the most advanced historical instance, even though that system has not yet realized the full scope of egalitarian liberty; for that system is working towards a universal *social* equality for all persons and, as such, is conditioning the historical significance of civil liberty so that the latter eventually will be absorbed into a complex of essential civil liberties – that is, reduced to its human essentials by abolishing the liberty-privilege of private ownership of means of production.[2] This means that egalitarian liberty, in its full realization,

1. *La teoria del diritto nell'Unione Sovietica* (Turin: Einaudi, 1952), p. 266.
2. In this respect, there are some particularly relevant texts which resulted from a confrontation, typically Rousseauean, between eighteenth-century absolutist France and parliamentary England: (1) 'In England', writes Saint-Preux to Julie in *Nouvelle Héloïse*, II, 19, 'it is quite different. . . . Since the people have a share in the government, one's public standing is the greatest means of credit.' (2) 'For which reason, he [Saint-Preux] prefers England to France as a place to exercise his talents.' (J.-J. Rousseau, *Œuvres Complètes*, Paris, 1961, Vol. II, pp. 263, 783.) It should be noted that: (*a*) Rousseau's interest in a democratic–bourgeois government in the English style hinges on the social recognition of personal merit (of the middle-class '*parvenus*': 'Will Julie [noble Julie, the lady of quality] decide to become the wife of a *parvenu*?') 'In England . . . , even though custom has less force than in France, still, there are more honourable ways of doing things. Since the people have a share in the government, one's public standing is the greatest means of credit.' (*b*) Only in the middle-class egalitarianism which gives birth to the *parvenus* do political democracy and social democracy have a meeting point, in that the first is conditioned by the second. And in this Rousseau had a share of the glorious responsibility for the French Revolution. But this does not exhaust the historical influence of Rousseau – of his social–democratic *élan* – directed against the limited bourgeois equality which was overcome by the universal egalitarianism of merit (and of work) which is the essence of social democracy. ('I *honour merit* in the very *lowest ranks*.' [*Letter to Bordes*, 1740.]) And this explains Rousseau's criticism of the general subjection of the poor to the rich – a criticism used for his own ends by Marx in *Das Kapital* (I, 3, c. 30). (*c*) Thus may be understood the corresponding differences between the two political methods – bourgeois–democratic

will transcend mere civil liberty and, with it, the state in general (including the socialist state) with its classes. That is actually being accomplished in the communist society which is classless and metapolitical, and which has economic bases adequate to its task. Such is the paradoxical destiny, or perhaps simply the historical destiny, of that liberty conceived originally on the basis of Rousseau's humanitarian, and therefore interclass, moralism!

On the other hand, it should be remembered that these two forms of liberty, as disparate as they may seem from the standpoint of usable formulae,[1] are in harmony solely in the legal system of the socialist state, and most properly in the renovation of, or reduction to, the human essentials of civil liberty within the expansion of egalitarian liberty of the centralism of the workers' democracy; and so this antinomy which has affected the whole of the history of liberty and of modern democracy is resolved. In the socialist (Soviet) legal system, therefore, there co-exist liberty-as-a-function-of-egalitarianism (Rousseau's major liberty) and egalitarianism-as-a-function-of-liberty (Kant's minor liberty), in such a way that the Soviet proletariat is becoming the liberator of the human race by securing, in cooperation with its government, the effectiveness of civil liberties by conferring on them an adequate egalitarian exponent. Every civil liberty, then, or at least every one worthy of the name, is

and social–democratic: the first consists in parliamentarianism and constitutionalism as a function of a popular national sovereignty; the second is a democracy acting as a function of a popular radical sovereignty. The two methods are in harmony solely, as we have seen, in that original socio-political synthesis represented by the Soviet socialist legal system, which itself is but a prelude to that communist society which will see the final triumph of egalitarian liberty (as described by Marx in *Critique of the Gotha Programme* (1875), and by Lenin in *State and Revolution* (1917)). See above the triumphal return of Rousseau's criterion of the social recognition of the merits or talents or abilities of every man as expressed in the Marxist formula, 'from each according to his capacity, to each according to his needs'; and see my *Rousseau e Marx* (Rome, 1962), pp. 43–58 and 75–88, for a dialectical analysis of the following fundamental and conclusive passage (among others) from *Discourse on the Origins and Foundations of Inequality Among Men:* 'The *ranks* of citizens should be regulated . . . according to the real *services* [i.e. proportionate to their talents and strength] rendered by them to the state.'

1. For example, that of social liberty for the human potential of every individual, or that of liberty as a guarantee of the non-impediment of the person by the state.

comparable to a quantity which has an exponent not inferior to itself; and that is the egalitarian exponent which confers on any civil right or liberty the grade of value which prevents its decay into privilege. Thus, the major liberty guarantees the minor.

If the right of the citizen to vote (a typical civil or constitutional liberty) had not had as its purpose the affirmation of its egalitarian scope, inasmuch as it is the effect of social recognition accorded to the personal merits of every member of the 'third estate' (and therefore is the means of entry into, and elevation in, the social life of a new class), what value in civil progress would it have signified? On the other hand, did it not come about that the original bourgeois discrimination between 'active' and 'passive' citizens – or, in Kant's words, between 'citizens' and 'associates' – caused, by its anti-egalitarian character, the decline of that 'right' to vote to the status of a privilege? What must be introduced, sooner or later, by the bourgeois, is that typical egalitarian institution called *universal suffrage*, with all the devices of modern electoral techniques.[1]

In similar fashion, the right of private ownership of means of production has degenerated into privilege in that it excludes adequate social recognition of the personal merits of members of the fourth estate (of the wage-earning masses), and therefore excludes also the development of the individual person. Hence, the inferior, insufficient egalitarian exponent of that right today degrades bourgeois proprietorship to that point of privilege at which a revolutionary action for egalitarian liberty always intervenes. It intervenes today in the form of socialist democracy; it intervened yesterday as parliamentary democracy against the propertied nobility and ecclesiastics, etc. The historic process of equating an egalitarian exponent to its corresponding civil liberty culminates in the legal system which is proper to a true socialist state: a system in which civil liberties with an inferior egalitarian exponent are eradicated (such as economic free enterprise and relative private ownership of means of production), and those with adequate egalitarian exponents are preserved (among which, other than the *habeas corpus*, is property for personal use as contemplated by present-day Soviet codes). In this way the tension ceases between political democracy and social democracy, between civil liberty and egalitarian liberty; a tension

1. Cf. the Italian Fraud Law of 31 March 1953.

which has no place in a communist society which presupposes the wasting away of the (socialist) state and, with it, the disappearance of classes, and which therefore implies the triumph of egalitarian liberty. Such a situation is in accord with the definition of a 'society of free and equal members', viz. a society whose motto is 'from each according to his capacity, to each according to his needs'.[1] This classic character persists in the 'people's state' which is the present-day U.S.S.R., with its socialist legal system, and is evident in the direct participation in legislation and administration by the workers' syndicates. This signifies that the institution of the syndicate belongs to the sphere of public power before it belongs to the sphere of citizens' liberties or civil liberties.

In the foregoing, we have replied *implicitly* to the questions raised by those classic texts of Marxism cited at the beginning. Now, let us say *explicitly* that it is not properly true, that it is not all the truth, that the political or bourgeois revolution emancipated only the bourgeoisie, even though it laid the foundations – built upon, paradoxically, by the socialist legal system of the present Soviet state – for the politico-juridic emancipation of the *whole of society qua society*, i.e. of society built on the relationship of the governing to the governed. Thus, so long as there is a state, even a proletarian state, that admonition of Montesquieu – provoked by the absolute monarchy of his time, but applicable to all political, even workers', power – remains true: 'It is of the utmost importance not to revile or degrade human nature.'[2] Thus, the human emancipation of man – so far as it is possible prior to the advent of the communist society – requires and implies both political liberty and social liberty; or, better, the first in harmony with the second.

Translated by Jack F. Bernard

1. Marx, *Critique of the Gotha Programme*.
2. *Esprit des lois*, XV, 1.

●●●●●●●●●●●●●●●●●●●●●●●●●●●●●●●●●●●●●●

The Triple Revolution

A Letter

The following letter was sent on 22 March 1964, by the *Ad Hoc* Committee on the Triple Revolution to President Lyndon B. Johnson. The White House reply from Mr Lee White, Assistant Special Counsel to the President, was received shortly. The letter to the President, together with the Report, was also sent to the Majority and Minority leaders of the Senate and the House of Representatives and to the Secretary of Labour. Texts follow:

22 March 1964

Dear Mr President:

We enclose a memorandum, The Triple Revolution, for your consideration. This memorandum was prepared out of a feeling of foreboding about the nation's future. The men and women whose names are signed to it think that neither Americans nor their leaders are aware of the magnitude and acceleration of the changes going on around them. These changes, economic, military and social, comprise The Triple Revolution. We believe that these changes will compel, in the very near future and whether we like it or not, public measures that move radically beyond any steps now proposed or contemplated.

409

We commend the spirit prompting the War on Poverty recently announced, and the new commissions on economic dislocation and automation. With deference, this memorandum sets forth the historical and technological reasons why such tactics seem bound to fall short. Radically new circumstances demand radically new strategies.

If policies such as those suggested in The Triple Revolution are not adopted we believe that the nation will be thrown into unprecedented economic and social disorder. Our statement is aimed at showing why drastic changes in our economic organization are occurring, their relation to the growing movement for full rights for Negroes, and the minimal public and private measures that appear to us to be required.

Sincerely,

Donald G. Agger	Gunnar Myrdal
Dr Donald B. Armstrong	Gerard Piel
James Boggs	Michael D. Reagan
W. H. Ferry	Ben B. Seligman
Todd Gitlin	Robert Theobald
Roger Hagan	William Worthy
Michael Harrington	Alice Mary Hilton
Tom Hayden	David T. Bazelon
Ralph L. Helstein	Maxwell Geismar
Dr Frances W. Herring	Philip Green
Brigadier General Hugh B. Hester	H. Stuart Hughes
Gerald W. Johnson	Linus Pauling
Irving F. Laucks	John William Ward

THE WHITE HOUSE
WASHINGTON

6 April 1964

Dear Mr Ferry:

The President has asked me to thank you for your letter of 19 March, in which you enclose the memorandum, The Triple Revolution, drawn up by your Committee.

In recent months the President has taken a number of steps addressed to the problems discussed in your memorandum – poverty, unemployment, and technological change. He has committed this Administration to an unrelenting war on poverty and, as you are of course aware, has submitted to the Congress major new legislation requesting the necessary weapons for the prosecution of this war. On 21 December he established the Committee on Economic Impact on Defense and Disarmament. The

Committee will provide central review and coordination of activities in the Executive branch designed to improve our understanding of the economic impact of changes in defense expenditures. The President has also asked the Congress to establish a Presidential commission to study the impact of technological change on the economy and to recommend measures for assuring the full benefits of technology while minimizing any adverse effects.

Rapid advances in technology and sharp changes in the direction and location of economic activity pose both challenges and problems for the Nation. Your Committee has clearly been willing to take a completely fresh look at these matters. You may be sure that the Committee's analysis and recommendations will be given thoughtful consideration by all of those in the Executive branch who are concerned with these problems.

Sincerely,
s/Lee C. White
Assistant Special Counsel
to the President

Mr W. H. Ferry
The *Ad Hoc* Committee on the
Triple Revolution

The Triple Revolution

This statement is written in the recognition that mankind is at a historic conjuncture which demands a fundamental re-examination of existing values and institutions. At this time three separate and mutually reinforcing revolutions are taking place:

The Cybernation Revolution

A new era of production has begun. Its principles of organization are as different from those of the industrial era as those of the industrial era were different from the agricultural. The cybernation revolution has been brought about by the combination of the computer and the automated self-regulating machine. This results in a system of almost unlimited productive capacity which requires progressively less human labour. Cybernation is already reorganizing the economic and social system to meet its own needs.

The Weaponry Revolution

New forms of weaponry have been developed which cannot win wars but which can obliterate civilization. We are recognizing only now that the great weapons have eliminated war as a

411

method for resolving international conflicts. The ever-present threat of total destruction is tempered by the knowledge of the final futility of war. The need of a 'warless world' is generally recognized, though achieving it will be a long and frustrating process.

The Human Rights Revolution

A universal demand for full human rights is now clearly evident. It continues to be demonstrated in the civil rights movement within the United States. But this is only the local manifestation of a world-wide movement toward the establishment of social and political régimes in which every individual will feel valued and none will feel rejected on account of his race.

We are particularly concerned in this statement with the first of these revolutionary phenomena. This is not because we underestimate the significance of the other two. On the contrary, we affirm that it is the simultaneous occurrence and interaction of all three developments which make evident the necessity for radical alterations in attitude and policy. The adoption of just policies for coping with cybernation and for extending rights to all Americans is indispensable to the creation of an atmosphere in the U.S. in which the supreme issue, peace, can be reasonably debated and resolved.

The Negro claims, as a matter of simple justice, his full share in America's economic and social life. He sees adequate employment opportunities as a chief means of attaining this goal: the March on Washington demanded freedom *and* jobs. The Negro's claim to a job is not being met. Negroes are the hardest-hit of the many groups being exiled from the economy by cybernation. Negro unemployment rates cannot be expected to drop substantially. Promises of jobs are a cruel and dangerous hoax on hundreds of thousands of Negroes and whites alike who are especially vulnerable to cybernation because of age or inadequate education.

The demand of the civil rights movement cannot be fulfilled within the present context of society. The Negro is trying to enter a social community and a tradition of work-and-income which are in the process of vanishing even for the hitherto privileged white workers. Jobs are disappearing under the impact of highly efficient, progressively less costly machines.

412

The U.S. operates on the thesis, set out in the Employment Act of 1964, that every person will be able to obtain a job if he wishes to do so and that this job will provide him with resources adequate to live and maintain a family decently. Thus job-holding is the general mechanism through which economic resources are distributed. Those without work have access only to a minimal income, hardly sufficient to provide the necessities of life, and enabling those receiving it to function as only 'minimum consumers'. As a result, the goods and services which are needed by these crippled consumers, and which they would buy if they could, are not produced. This in turn deprives other workers of jobs, thus reducing their incomes and consumption.

Present excessive levels of unemployment would be multiplied several times if military and space expenditures did not continue to absorb ten per cent of the gross national product (i.e. the total goods and services produced). Some six to eight million people are employed as a direct result of purchases for space and military activities. At least an equal number hold their jobs as an indirect result of military or space expenditures. In recent years, the military and space budgets have absorbed a rising proportion of national production and formed a strong support for the economy.

However, these expenditures are coming in for more and more criticism, at least partially in recognition of the fact that nuclear weapons have eliminated war as an acceptable method for resolving international conflicts. Early in 1964 President Johnson ordered a curtailment of certain military expenditures. Defence Secretary McNamara is closing shipyards, airfields and Army bases, and Congress is pressing the National Space Administration to economize. The future of these strong props to the economy is not as clear today as it was even a year ago.

How the Cybernation Revolution Shapes Up

Cybernation is manifesting the characteristics of a revolution in production. These include the development of radically different techniques and the subsequent appearance of novel principles of the organization of production; a basic reordering of man's relationship to his environment; and a dramatic increase in total available and potential energy.

The major difference between the agricultural, and industrial

413

cybernation revolutions is the speed at which they developed. The agricultural revolution began several thousand years ago in the Middle East. Centuries passed in the shift from a subsistence base of hunting and food-gathering to settled agriculture.

In contrast, it has been less than two hundred years since the emergence of the industrial revolution, and direct and accurate knowledge of the new productive techniques has reached most of mankind. This swift dissemination of information is generally held to be the main factor leading to widespread industrialization.

While the major aspects of the cybernation revolution are for the moment restricted to the U.S., its effects are observable almost at once throughout the industrial world and large parts of the non-industrial world. Observation is rapidly followed by analysis and criticism. The problems posed by the cybernation revolution are part of a new era in the history of all mankind but they are first being faced by the people of the U.S. The way Americans cope with cybernation will influence the course of this phenomenon everywhere. This country is the stage on which the machines-and-man drama will first be played for the world to witness.

The fundamental problem posed by the cybernation revolution in the U.S. is that it invalidates the general mechanism so far employed to undergird people's rights as consumers. Up to this time economic resources have been distributed on the basis of contributions to production, with machines and men competing for employment on somewhat equal terms. In the developing cybernated system, potentially unlimited output can be achieved by systems of machines which will require little cooperation from human beings. As machines take over production from men, they absorb an increasing proportion of resources while the men who are displaced become dependent on minimal and unrelated government measures – unemployment insurance, social security, welfare payments.

These measures are less and less able to disguise a historic paradox: that a substantial proportion of the population is subsisting on minimal incomes, often below the poverty line, at a time when sufficient productive potential is available to supply the needs of everyone in the U.S.

Industrial System Fails to Provide for Abolition of Poverty

The existence of this paradox is denied or ignored by conventional economic analysis. The general economic approach argues that potential demand, which if filled would raise the number of jobs and provide incomes to those holding them, is underestimated. Most contemporary economic analysis states that all of the available labour force and industrial capacity is required to meet the needs of consumers and industry and to provide adequate public services: schools, parks, roads, homes, decent cities and clean water and air. It is further argued that demand could be increased, by a variety of standard techniques, to any desired extent by providing money and machines to improve the conditions of the billions of impoverished people elsewhere in the world, who need food and shelter, clothes and machinery, and everything else the industrial nations take for granted.

There is no question that cybernation does increase the potential for the provision of funds to neglected public sectors. Nor is there any question that cybernation would make possible the abolition of poverty at home and abroad. But the industrial system does not possess any adequate mechanisms to permit these potentials to become realities. The industrial system was designed to produce an ever-increasing quantity of goods as efficiently as possible, and it was assumed that the distribution of the power to purchase these goods would occur almost automatically. The continuance of the income-through-jobs link as the only major mechanism for distributing effective demand – for granting the right to consume – now acts as the main brake on the almost unlimited capacity of a cybernated productive system.

Recent administrations have proposed measures aimed at achieving a better distribution of resources, and at reducing unemployment and underemployment. A few of these proposals have been enacted. More often they have failed to secure congressional support. In every case, many members of Congress have criticized the proposed measures as departing from traditional principles for the allocation of resources and the encouragement of production. Abetted by budget-balancing economists and interest groups they have argued for the maintenance of an economic machine based on ideas of scarcity to deal with the facts of abundance produced by cybernation. This time-consuming criticism has slowed the workings of Congress and has thrown out of focus for that body the interrelated effects of the triple revolution.

An adequate distribution of the potential abundance of goods and services will be achieved only when it is understood that the major economic problem is not how to increase production but how to distribute the abundance that is the great potential of cybernation. There is an urgent need for a fundamental change in the mechanisms employed to insure consumer rights.

Facts and Figures of the Cybernation Revolution

No responsible observer would attempt to describe the exact pace or the full sweep of a phenomenon that is developing with the speed of cybernation. Some aspects of this revolution, however, are already clear:

The rate of productivity increase has risen with the onset of cybernation.

An industrial economic system postulated on scarcity has been unable to distribute the abundant goods and services produced by a cybernated system or potential in it.

Surplus capacity and unemployment have thus coexisted at excessive levels over the last six years.

The underlying cause of excessive unemployment is the fact that the capability of machines is rising more rapidly than the capacity of many human beings to keep pace.

A permanent impoverished and jobless class is established in the midst of potential abundance.

Evidence for these statements follows:

(*a*) The increased efficiency of machine systems is shown in the more rapid increase in productivity per man-hour since 1960, a year that marks the first visible upsurge of the cybernation revolution. In 1961, 1962 and 1963, productivity per man-hour rose at an average pace above 3·5 per cent – a rate well above both the historical average and the post-war rate.

Companies are finding cybernation more and more attractive. Even at the present early stage of cybernation, costs have already been lowered to a point where the price of a durable machine may be as little as one-third of the current annual wage-cost of the worker it replaces. A more rapid rise in the rate of productivity increase per man-hour can be expected from now on.

(*b*) In recent years it has proved to increase demand fast enough to bring about the full use of either men or plant capacities. The task of developing sufficient additional demand promises to become more difficult each year. A $30 billion annual increase in gross national product is now required to prevent unemployment rates from rising. An additional $40 to $60 billion increase would be required to bring unemployment rates down to an acceptable level.

(*c*) The official rate of unemployment has remained at or above 5·5 per cent during the sixties. The unemployment rate for teenagers has been rising steadily and now stands around fifteen per cent. The unemployment rate for Negro teenagers stands about thirty per cent. The unemployment rate for teenagers in minority ghettoes sometimes exceeds fifty per cent. Unemployment rates for Negroes are regularly more than twice those for whites, whatever their occupation, educational level, age or sex. The unemployment position for other racial minorities is similarly unfavourable. Unemployment rates in depressed areas often exceed fifty per cent.

Unemployment is Far Worse than Figures Indicate

These official figures seriously underestimate the true extent of unemployment. The statistics take no notice of underemployment or featherbedding. Besides the 5·5 per cent of the labour force who are officially designated as unemployed, nearly four per cent of the labour force sought full-time work in 1962 but could find only part-time jobs. In addition, methods of calculating unemployment rates – a person is counted as unemployed only if he has actively sought a job recently – ignore the fact that many men and women who would like to find jobs have not looked for them because they know there are no employment opportunities.

Underestimates for this reason are pervasive among groups whose unemployment rates are high – the young, the old and racial minorities. Many people in the depressed agricultural, mining and industrial areas, who by official definition hold jobs but who are actually grossly underemployed, would move if there were prospects of finding work elsewhere. It is reasonable

417

to estimate that over eight million people are not working who would like to have jobs today as compared with the four million shown in the official statistics.

Even more serious is the fact that the number of people who have voluntarily removed themselves from the labour force is not constant but increases continuously. These people have decided to stop looking for employment and seem to have accepted the fact that they will never hold jobs again. This decision is largely irreversible, in economic and also in social and psychological terms. The older worker calls himself 'retired'; he cannot accept work without affecting his social security status. The worker in his prime years is forced on to relief: in most States the requirements for becoming a relief recipient bring about such fundamental alterations in an individual's situation that a reversal of the process is always difficult and often totally infeasible. Teenagers, especially 'drop-outs' and Negroes, are coming to realize that there is no place for them in the labour force but at the same time they are given no realistic alternative. These people and their dependants make up a large part of the 'poverty' sector of the American population.

Statistical evidence of these trends appears in the decline in the proportion of people claiming to be in the labour force – the so-called labour force participation rate. The recent apparent stabilization of the unemployment rate around 5·5 per cent is therefore misleading: it is a reflection of the discouragement and defeat of people who cannot find employment and have withdrawn from the market rather than a measure of the economy's success in creating jobs for those who want to work.

(d) An efficiently functioning industrial system is assumed to provide the great majority of new jobs through the expansion of the private enterprise sector. But well over half of the new jobs created during 1957–62 were in the public sector – predominantly in teaching. Job creation in the private sector has now almost entirely ceased except in services; of the 4,300,000 jobs created in this period, only about 200,000 were provided by private industry through its own efforts. Many authorities anticipate that the application of cybernation to certain service industries, which is only just beginning, will be particularly effective. If this is the case, no significant job creation will take place in the private sector in coming years.

(e) Cybernation raises the level of the skills of the machine. Secretary of Labor Wirtz has recently stated that the machines being produced today have, on the average, skills equivalent to a high-school diploma. If a human being is to compete with such machines, therefore, he must at least possess a high-school diploma. The Department of Labor estimates, however, that, on the basis of present trends, as many as thirty per cent of all students will be high-school drop-outs in this decade.

(f) A permanently depressed class is developing in the U.S. Some thirty-eight million Americans, almost one-fifth of the nation, still live in poverty. The percentage of total income received by the poorest twenty per cent of the population was 4·9 per cent in 1944 and 4·7 per cent in 1963.

Secretary Wirtz recently summarized these trends:

> The confluence of surging population and driving technology is splitting the American labor force into tens of millions of 'haves' and millions of 'have-nots'. In our economy of sixty-nine million jobs, those with wanted skills enjoy opportunity and earning power. But the others face a new and stark problem – exclusion on a permanent basis, both as producers and consumers, from economic life. This division of people threatens to create a human slag heap. We cannot tolerate the development of a separate nation of the poor, the unskilled, the jobless, living within another nation of the well-off, the trained and the employed.

New Consensus Needed

The stubbornness and novelty of the situation that is conveyed by these statistics is now generally accepted. Ironically, it continues to be assumed that it is possible to devise measures which will reduce unemployment to a minimum and thus preserve the overall viability of the present productive system. Some authorities have gone so far as to suggest that the pace of technological change should be slowed down 'so as to allow the industrial productive system time to adapt'.

We believe, on the contrary, that the industrial productive system is no longer viable. We assert that the only way to turn technological change to the benefit of the individual and the service of the general welfare is to accept the process and to utilize it rationally and humanely. The new science of political economy will be built on the encouragement and planned expansion of cybernation. The issues raised by cybernation are particularly amenable to intelligent policy-making: cybernation itself provides the resources and tools that are needed to ensure minimum hardship during the transition process.

But major changes must be made in our attitudes and institutions in the foreseeable future. Today Americans are being swept along by three simultaneous revolutions while assuming they have them under control. In the absence of real understanding of any of these phenomena, especially of technology, we may be allowing an efficient and dehumanized community to emerge by default. Gaining control of our future requires the conscious formation of the society we wish to have. Cybernation at last forces us to answer the historic questions: What is man's role when he is not dependent upon his own activities for the material basis of his life? What should be the basis for distributing individual access to national resources? Are there other proper claims on goods and services besides a job?

Because of cybernation, society no longer needs to impose repetitive and meaningless (because unnecessary) toil upon the individual. Society can now set the citizen free to make his own choice of occupation and vocation from a wide range of activities not now fostered by our value system and our accepted modes of 'work'. But in the absence of such a new consensus about cybernation, the nation cannot begin to take advantage of all that it promises for human betterment.

Proposal for Action

As a first step to a new consensus it is essential to recognize that the traditional link between jobs and incomes is being broken. The economy of abundance can sustain all citizens in comfort and economic security whether or not they engage in what is commonly reckoned as work. Wealth produced by machines rather than by men is still wealth. We urge, therefore, that society, through its appropriate legal and governmental institutions, undertake an unqualified commitment to provide every individual and every family with an adequate income as a matter of right.

This undertaking we consider to be essential to the emerging economic, social and political order in this country. We regard it as the only policy by which the quarter of the nation now dispossessed and soon to be dispossessed by lack of employment can be brought within the abundant society. The unqualified right to an income would take the place of the patchwork of welfare measures – from unemployment insurance to relief – designed to ensure that no citizen or resident of the U.S. actually starves.

We do not pretend to visualize all of the consequences of this change in our values. It is clear, however, that the distribution of abundance in a cybernated society must be based on criteria strikingly different from those of an economic system based on scarcity. In retrospect, the establishment of the right to an income will prove to have been only the first step in the reconstruction of the value system of our society brought on by the triple revolution.

The present system encourages activities which can lead to private profit and neglects those activities which can enhance the wealth and the quality of life of our society. Consequently, national policy has hitherto been aimed far more at the welfare of the productive process than at the welfare of people. The era of cybernation can reverse this emphasis. With public policy and research concentrated on people rather than processes we believe that many creative activities and interests commonly thought of as non-economic will absorb the time and the commitment of many of those no longer needed to produce goods and services.

Society as a whole must encourage new modes of constructive, rewarding and ennobling activity. Principal among these are activities such as teaching and learning that relate people to people rather than people to things. Education has never been primarily conducted for profit in our society; it represents the first and most obvious activity inviting the expansion of the public sector to meet the needs of this period of transition.

We are not able to predict the long-run patterns of human activity and commitment in a nation when fewer and fewer people are involved in production of goods and services, nor are we able to forecast the overall patterns of income distribution that will replace those of the past full employment system. However, these are not speculative and fanciful matters to be contemplated at leisure for a society that may come into existence in three or four generations. The outlines of the future press sharply into the present. The problems of joblessness, inadequate incomes, and frustrated lives confront us now; the

American Negro, in his rebellion, asserts the demands – and the rights – of all the disadvantaged. The Negro's is the most insistent voice today, but behind him stand the millions of impoverished who are beginning to understand that cybernation, properly understood and used, is the road out of want and toward a decent life.

The Transition*

We recognize that the drastic alterations in circumstances and in our way of life ushered in by cybernation and the economy of abundance will not be completed overnight. Left to the ordinary forces of the market such change, however, will involve physical and psychological misery and perhaps political chaos. Such misery is already clearly evident among the unemployed, among relief clients into the third generation and more and more among the young and the old for whom society appears to hold no promise of dignified or even stable lives. We must develop programmes for this transition designed to give hope to the dispossessed and those cast out by the economic system, and to provide a basis for the rallying of people to bring about those changes in political and social institutions which are essential to the age of technology.

The programme here suggested is not intended to be inclusive but rather to indicate its necessary scope. We propose:

(*a*) A massive programme to build up our educational system, designed especially with the needs of the chronically undereducated in mind. We estimate that tens of thousands of employment opportunities in such areas as teaching and research and development, particularly for younger people, may be thus created. Federal programmes looking to the training of an additional 100,000 teachers annually are needed.

(*b*) Massive public works. The need is to develop and put into effect programmes of public works to construct dams, reservoirs,

---

* This view of the transitional period is not shared by all the signers. Robert Theobald and James Boggs hold that the two major principles of the transitional period will be (1) that machines rather than men will take up new conventional work openings and (2) that the activity of men will be directed to new forms of 'work' and 'leisure'. Therefore, in their opinion, the specific proposals outlined in this section are more suitable for meeting the problems of the scarcity-economic system than for advancing through the period of transition into the period of abundance.

ports, water and air pollution facilities, community recreation facilities. We estimate that for each $1 billion per year spent on public works 150,000 to 200,000 jobs would be created. $2 billion or more a year should be spent in this way, preferably as matching funds aimed at the relief of economically distressed or dislocated areas.

(c) A massive programme of low-cost housing, to be built both publicly and privately, and aimed at a rate of 700,000–1,000,000 units a year.

(d) Development and financing of rapid transit systems, urban and inter-urban; and other programmes to cope with the spreading problems of the great metropolitan centres.

(e) A public power system built on the abundance of coal in distressed areas, designed for low-cost power to heavy industrial and residential sections.

(f) Rehabilitation of obsolete military bases for community or educational use.

(g) A major revision of our tax structure aimed at redistributing income as well as apportioning the costs of the transition period equitably. To this end an expansion of the use of excess profits tax would be important. Subsidies and tax credit plans are required to ease the human suffering involved in the transition of many industries from manpower to machine power.

(h) The trade unions can play an important and significant role in this period in a number of ways:

1. Use of collective bargaining to negotiate not only for people at work but also for those thrown out of work by technological change.
2. Bargaining for perquisites such as housing, recreational facilities and similar programmes as they have negotiated health and welfare programmes.
3. Obtaining a voice in the investment of the unions' huge pension and welfare funds, and insisting on investment policies which have as their major criteria the social use and function of the enterprise in which the investment is made.
4. Organization of the unemployed so that these voiceless people may once more be given a voice in their own economic destinies, and strengthening of the campaigns to organize white-collar and professional workers.

(i) The use of the licensing power of government to regulate

423

the speed and direction of cybernation to minimize hardship; and the use of minimum wage power as well as taxing powers to provide the incentives for moving as rapidly as possible toward the goals indicated by this paper.

These suggestions are in no way intended to be complete or definitely formulated. They contemplate expenditures of several billions more each year than are now being spent for socially rewarding enterprises, and a larger role for the government in the economy than it has now or has been given except in times of crisis. In our opinion, this is a time of crisis, the crisis of a triple revolution. Public philosophy for the transition must rest on the conviction that our economic, social and political institutions exist for the use of man and that man does not exist to maintain a particular economic system. This philosophy centres on an understanding that governments are instituted among men for the purpose of making possible life, liberty and the pursuit of happiness and that government should be a creative and positive instrument towards these ends.

Change Must be Managed

The historic discovery of the post Second World War years is that the economic destiny of the nation can be managed. Since the debate over the Employment Act of 1946 it has been increasingly understood that the federal government bears primary responsibility for the economic and social well-being of the country. The essence of management is planning. The democratic requirement is planning by public bodies for the general welfare. Planning by private bodies such as corporations for their own welfare does not automatically result in additions to the general welfare, as the impact of cybernation on jobs has already made clear.

The hardships imposed by sudden changes in technology have been acknowledged by Congress in proposals for dealing with the long- and short-run 'dislocations', in legislation for depressed and 'impacted' areas, retraining of workers replaced by machines, and the like. The measures so far proposed have not been 'transitional' in conception. Perhaps for this reason they have had little effect on the situation they were designed to alleviate. But the primary weakness of this legislation is not ineffectiveness but incoherence. In no way can these disconnected measures be seen as a plan for remedying deep ailments but only, so to speak, as the superficial treatment of surface wounds.

Planning agencies should constitute the network through which pass the stated needs of the people at every level of society, gradually building into a national inventory of human requirements, arrived at by democratic debate of elected representatives.

The primary tasks of the appropriate planning institutions should be:

To collect the data necessary to appraise the effects, social and economic, of cybernation at different rates of innovation.

To recommend ways, by public and private initiative, of encouraging and stimulating cybernation.

To work towards optimal allocations of human and natural resources in meeting the requirements of society.

To develop ways to smooth the transition from a society in which the norm is full employment within an economic system based on scarcity, to one in which the norm will be either non-employment, in the traditional sense of productive work, or employment on the great variety of socially valuable but 'non-productive' tasks made possible by an economy of abundance; to bring about the conditions in which men and women no longer needed to produce goods and services may find their way to a variety of self-fulfilling and socially useful occupations.

To work out alternatives to defence and related spending that will commend themselves to citizens, entrepreneurs and workers as a more reasonable use of common resources.

To integrate domestic and international planning. The technological revolution has related virtually every major domestic problem to a world problem. The vast inequalities between the industrialized and the underdeveloped countries cannot long be sustained.

The aim throughout will be the conscious and rational direction of economic life by planning institutions under democratic control.

In this changed framework the new planning institutions will operate at every level of government – local, regional and federal – and will be organized to elicit democratic participation in all their proceedings. These bodies will be the means for giving direction and content to the growing demand for improvement in all departments of public life. The planning institutions will show the way to turn the growing protest against ugly cities, polluted air and water, an inadequate educational system, disappearing recreational and material resources, low levels of medical care, and the haphazard economic development into an integrated effort to raise the level of general welfare.

We are encouraged by the record of the planning institutions both of the Common Market and of several European nations and believe that this country can benefit from studying their weaknesses and strengths.

A principal result of planning will be to step up investment in the public sector. Greater investment in this area is advocated because it is overdue, because the needs in this sector comprise a substantial part of the content of the general welfare, and because they can be readily afforded by an abundant society. Given the knowledge that we are now in a period of transition it would be deceptive, in our opinion, to present such activities as likely to produce full employment. The efficiencies of cybernation should be as much sought in the public as in the private sector, and a chief focus of planning would be one means of bringing this about. A central assumption of planning institutions would be the central assumption of this statement, that the nation is moving into a society in which production of goods and services is not the only or perhaps the chief means of distributing income.

The Democratization of Change

The revolution in weaponry gives some dim promise that mankind may finally eliminate institutionalized force as the method of settling international conflict and find for it political and moral equivalents leading to a better world. The Negro revolution signals the ultimate admission of this group to the American community on equal social, political and economic terms. The cybernation revolution proffers an existence qualitatively richer in democratic as well as material values. A social order in which men make the decisions that shape their lives becomes more possible now than ever before; the unshackling of men from the bonds of unfulfilling labour frees them to become citizens, to make themselves and to make their own history.

But these enhanced promises by no means constitute a guarantee. Illuminating and making more possible the 'democratic vistas' is one thing; reaching them is quite another, for a vision of democratic life is made real not by technological change but by men consciously moving towards that ideal and creating institutions that will realize and nourish the vision in living form.

Democracy, as we use the term, means a community of men and women who are able to understand, express and determine their lives as dignified human beings. Democracy can only be rooted in a political and economic order in which wealth is distributed by and for people, and used for the widest social benefit. With the emergence of the era of abundance we have the economic base for a true democracy of participation, in which men no longer need to feel themselves prisoners of social forces and decisions beyond their control or comprehension.